From
Modern Yoga
To
Ancient Yog

Shattering the Myths and Misconceptions

Tushar Prajapati

2nd edition 2024
e-mail: tusharprajapati.books@gmail.com
website: linktr.ee/tushar.prajapati

Disclaimer

To my beloved mother,

For your endless love, unwavering support, and the inspiration you provide every day.

"आपको देखा तो ये ख्याल आया, ज़िन्दगी धूप, आप घना साया…"

"When I saw you, this thought came to my mind: life is scorching sunlight, and you are the comforting shade…"

This book is for you.

Contents

Preface

Yoga, in its essence, is a profound science of self-realization, guiding us on the path toward ultimate freedom—Moksha. Yet, in the modern world, its true meaning has often been obscured by commercialization and superficial understanding. What once was a sacred spiritual practice, deeply rooted in ancient wisdom, has now largely become synonymous with mere physical postures and fitness routines.

This book aims to cut through the myths and misconceptions surrounding yoga today. It is a journey back to the heart of this ancient discipline, an exploration of its real purpose, and an invitation to rediscover the paths of realization that lead us beyond the physical into the depths of our consciousness.

As a lifelong seeker and practitioner of yoga, I have delved into the sacred texts of the Upanishads, the Gitas, the Sutras, etc, seeking to comprehend the truths that transcend time and culture. Through these pages, I wish to share insights from the rich traditions of Jnana (Gyana) Yoga, Bhakti Yoga, Karma Yoga, and Raja Yoga, among others, shedding light on how these paths intertwine and lead to the same ultimate goal: union with the Self.

Throughout this book, you will find discussions on key concepts such as the nature of the Self (Atman), the interplay of the three Gunas, the five Koshas that veil human consciousness, and the intricate system of Chakras and Nadis that form our subtle body. By understanding these fundamental principles, we can transcend the illusions of Maya and move toward the realization of our true nature.

I have also sought to address the common obstacles and challenges that arise on the spiritual journey, known as the Kleshas, and the ways in which yoga provides practical tools to overcome them. It also integrates Ayurveda, the sister science of yoga, and offers reflections on mantras, the power of OM, and the significance of the guru in one's spiritual journey. In addition to spiritual guidance, the book touches on broader topics such as non-violence, the caste system, and overcoming social divisions based on race, religion, gender, and disability.

The later chapters delve into advanced yogic concepts such as kundalini, samadhi, and the sacred hour of Brahma Muhurta. Inspirational stories are shared to motivate readers, and the book concludes with a call to awaken to the true potential of yoga as a path to ultimate realization.

The holistic nature of yoga is explored as a complete system for physical, mental, and spiritual well-being.

This book is not just a guide for practitioners of yoga but for anyone who seeks to understand the deeper aspects of life and existence. Whether you are a beginner or an advanced yogi, my hope is that these pages inspire you to look beyond the surface and embark on a journey of self-discovery.

I would like to express my gratitude to the sages and masters whose teachings continue to illuminate the path for seekers across generations. Their timeless wisdom is the foundation upon which this book stands.

May this work serve as a bridge between ancient knowledge and modern understanding, helping us to reconnect with the essence of yoga and realize the infinite potential within us all.

In peace and light,

Tushar Prajapati

Introduction

Yoga Beyond the Mat and Poses

Yoga, often reduced to a set of physical postures and breathing techniques, is much more than just a fitness regimen. The term "yoga" is derived from the Sanskrit root "yuj," meaning union or connection. The physical asanas (postures) are just one component of a holistic system designed to bring harmony to the body, mind, and spirit. When practiced in its entirety, yoga is a way of life that goes far beyond the mat.

The commercialization of yoga, especially in the West, has narrowed its perception to primarily physical aspects. This focus often obscures its spiritual and philosophical depth. According to a study by *Yoga Journal* in 2022, while 36 million Americans practice yoga, the majority see it mainly as a means to enhance flexibility and physical fitness. The deeper aspects, like mindfulness, ethics, and spiritual growth, often get overlooked in mainstream culture.

Yoga is not just about physical well-being but about self-realization and connection with the Divine. Yoga is a complete path to spiritual awakening, not just an exercise routine.

Is it Yog or Yoga?

The evolution of the term "yog" to "yoga" is a fascinating reflection of linguistic changes and cultural shifts as this ancient practice spread from its origins in India to the rest of the world.

Sanskrit Origins and Linguistic Adaptation

The term "yog" comes from the Sanskrit (योग), which means "union" or "yoking." In classical Sanskrit, the term was pronounced closer to "yog," with the final "a" being less emphasized or sometimes silent, depending on the dialect and context.

As yoga spread to regions outside India, particularly through texts and oral traditions, the word was transcribed into different languages. When Western scholars and practitioners encountered the word, it was often transcribed phonetically into "yoga," with the final "a" being pronounced more distinctly. This became the standard form in English and many other languages.

Cultural Shifts and Globalization

During British colonial rule in India, many Sanskrit and other Indian terms were transliterated into English. The pronunciation "yoga" became more standardized in English literature and scholarship during this period.

The 19th and 20th centuries saw a significant spread of Indian spiritual and philosophical traditions to the West. Pioneers like Swami Vivekananda and others who taught yoga abroad often used the term "yoga" to make it more accessible and consistent with Western phonetic systems.

As yoga became popular worldwide, "yoga" became the universally accepted term. This version of the word helped to create a unified brand that could be easily recognized and marketed globally. The pronunciation and spelling "yoga" thus became ingrained in global consciousness, often detached from its original linguistic roots.

Cultural Adaptation and Popularization

The practice of yoga also adapted to fit the cultural contexts of the regions it spread to, leading to variations in its interpretation and practice. The word "yoga" became associated not just with spiritual practice but also with physical fitness, wellness, and lifestyle, particularly in the West.

In the modern era, "yoga" is often marketed and understood as a holistic wellness practice, sometimes detached from its spiritual and philosophical origins.

In this book, I'll be using the modern word "yoga" for my modern readers.

The Evolution of Yoga in the Modern World

Yoga has undergone a remarkable transformation over centuries. Originally practiced by ancient Indian sages, yoga was a deeply spiritual discipline aimed at achieving liberation (moksha) from the cycle of birth and death. The teachings were transmitted orally, with a focus on meditation, self-discipline, and ethical living.

As said before, the 19th and 20th centuries saw yoga's global expansion, largely due to the efforts of figures like Swami Vivekananda and Sri Aurobindo. Vivekananda introduced yoga to the West at the

World's Parliament of Religions in Chicago in 1893, where he emphasized the meditative and philosophical aspects of the practice. Later, teachers like B.K.S. Iyengar and Pattabhi Jois brought Hatha Yoga into the global spotlight, with a focus on physical postures and breath control.

Today, yoga is a multi-billion-dollar industry, practiced by millions worldwide. However, the spiritual and philosophical teachings are often diluted, with many practitioners unaware of yoga's deeper roots.

What is Yoga?

Yoga is much more than the physical postures (asanas) that are commonly associated with it. At its essence, yoga is the profound union of the individual soul, or *Atman*, with the infinite universal consciousness, or *Brahman*. This union transcends the boundaries of the ego and leads to a realization of one's true nature—a state of complete self-awareness and liberation. The ancient Katha Upanishad captures this beautifully:

"The self-existent Brahman pierced the openings outward; hence one looks outward, not within oneself. A wise man, however, seeking immortality, turns his eyes inward and sees the inner self."

This inward journey, which yoga facilitates, helps us transcend the distractions of the external world, allowing us to explore our inner self. It's natural to feel perplexed by concepts such as *Atman*, *Brahman*, the ego, and their distinctions. These profound ideas will be explored in more depth as we proceed through this book, so I invite you to journey alongside me with patience and curiosity.

Patanjali's Definition of Yoga

One of the most authoritative and influential definitions of yoga comes from the sage Patanjali, who is credited with compiling the *Yoga Sutras*, a key text for yoga philosophy. In Sanskrit, the word *sutra* means "thread," symbolizing a concise and profound thread of knowledge. The *Yoga Sutras* weave together essential teachings on the mind, body, and spirit. Patanjali defines yoga in *Sutra 1.2* as:

"Yogas citta vritti nirodhah" which translates to, Yoga is the cessation of the fluctuations of the mind.

This definition brings into focus the heart of yoga: controlling and calming the restless nature of the mind. The fluctuations (*vrittis*) of the mind—thoughts, emotions, desires—are like ripples on the surface of water. Yoga teaches us to still these ripples so that the mind becomes clear and tranquil, leading to self-realization and inner peace. Through sustained practice, one begins to transcend mental disturbances and access a deeper, more serene state of consciousness.

The Bhagavad Gita's Perspective on Yoga

The *Bhagavad Gita*, a revered text within the Indian epic *Mahabharata*, offers another illuminating perspective on yoga. In Chapter 2, Verse 48, Lord Krishna defines yoga as:

"Be steadfast in the performance of your duty, O Arjuna, abandoning attachment to success and failure. Such evenness of mind is called yoga."

This verse emphasizes *equanimity*—the ability to remain centered and undisturbed in both success and failure. Yoga, in this sense, is the practice of mental stability, where the practitioner is not swayed by the dualities of life (pleasure and pain, gain and loss, praise and blame). It is through this evenness of mind that we cultivate spiritual growth.

Other Ancient Texts on Yoga

The *Yoga-Vasishtha*, an expansive philosophical dialogue between sage Vasishtha and Prince Rama, provides yet another powerful definition:

"Yoga is the means to calm the mind."

The simplicity of this statement underscores the profound truth that yoga is about mastering the mind. When the mind is tranquil, wisdom shines forth, and the soul aligns with the higher self.

Similarly, in the *Katha Upanishad* (2.6.11), we find a poetic depiction of yoga:

"When the five senses and the mind are still, and reason itself rests in silence, then begins the highest path. This is yoga."

Here, yoga is portrayed as a process of inner stillness, where mastery over the senses and the mind is achieved. It points to a state where the body, mind, and intellect cease their constant activity, allowing one to enter a space of deep inner reflection and self-awareness.

The Four Major Paths of Yoga

Yoga offers multiple paths to suit different personalities, inclinations, and temperaments. While all paths lead to the same goal—self-realization—they take different routes. Here are four of the most well-known paths:

1. **Jnana (Gyana) Yoga** – The path of wisdom and knowledge. This path involves deep inquiry and reflection, aiming to realize the ultimate truth by discriminating between the real and the unreal.

2. **Bhakti Yoga** – The path of devotion and love. Practitioners surrender to the Divine, expressing love and devotion to a personal deity or universal principle.

3. **Karma Yoga** – The path of selfless action. It teaches the importance of performing one's duties without attachment to the outcomes, cultivating detachment and humility.

4. **Raja Yoga** – The path of meditation and mental discipline. This path emphasizes techniques such as meditation, breath control, and ethical discipline to bring the mind into stillness.

These paths are not mutually exclusive; in fact, many practitioners blend elements of each path to align with their unique spiritual journey.

Yoga as a Journey

As the *Bhagavad Gita* (6.20) says, "Yoga is the journey of the self, through the self, to the self."

Yoga is ultimately a personal path to self-discovery, where each individual charts their own course. No path is superior or inferior; each is merely a different means to the same end—self-realization. What matters most is sincerity, dedication, and an open heart.

Therefore, as you continue your exploration of yoga, remain detached from the idea of following a particular path or being attached to one method. Remember that yoga is about harmonizing with your own inner truth, and that inner truth is unique to you. Allow yourself to grow through your practice, and let it unfold naturally as a path to discovering the deepest aspects of your being.

Rediscovering the True Essence of Yoga

To rediscover the true essence of yoga, one must look beyond the surface-level practices and delve into its philosophical depths. Yoga is a system that integrates ethical living, self-discipline, devotion, and mindfulness into daily life. It teaches that the ultimate goal is to recognize our true nature – that we are not the body or the mind, or the ego, but the eternal self (Atman).

This realization transforms our perception of the world. Every action, thought, and intention becomes a step toward spiritual growth. As Swami Sivananda eloquently puts it, "Put your heart, mind, and soul into even your smallest acts. This is the secret of success."

Yoga is not about renouncing the world but about living in it with awareness and purpose. It is about seeing the divine in every moment, every interaction, and every breath.

Swami Vivekananda's practice of Karma Yoga exemplifies this philosophy. He believed in selfless action and devoted his life to spreading the teachings of Vedanta and serving humanity without attachment to the results.

Rediscovering the true essence of yoga involves shifting our understanding from a physical exercise to a comprehensive spiritual discipline. It is about integrating yoga into every aspect of life, cultivating awareness, compassion, and connection to the universal consciousness. This journey transforms not just the individual but also their relationships with the world around them. Through yoga, we realize that every moment holds the potential for spiritual growth, both on and off the mat.

1

Common Misconceptions About Yoga

Yoga, one of the most profound and ancient traditions of India, has captured global attention in recent decades. Unfortunately, with its widespread popularity, numerous misconceptions have emerged, clouding its true essence. Yoga is often misunderstood as merely a physical exercise or a trendy lifestyle choice. In this chapter, we will address and clarify common misconceptions about yoga, bringing forth a more holistic and accurate understanding of this spiritual practice.

1. Yoga is Just a Physical Exercise

One of the most pervasive misconceptions is that yoga is synonymous with physical postures (asanas). While *asanas* are an integral part of yoga, they represent only one of the eight limbs (Ashtanga Yoga) mentioned in Patanjali's *Yoga Sutras*. The primary goal of yoga is not physical fitness but spiritual liberation (moksha) through the union of the individual self (*Atman*) with the universal consciousness (*Brahman*).

Patanjali's *Yoga Sutras* (2.29) lists the eight limbs of yoga:

1. **Yama** (ethical restraints)
2. **Niyama** (observances)
3. **Asana** (postures)
4. **Pranayama** (breath control)
5. **Pratyahara** (withdrawal of senses)
6. **Dharana** (concentration)
7. **Dhyana** (meditation)
8. **Samadhi** (absorption)

Asana is just one aspect of this comprehensive system.

A modern study conducted by the *National Center for Complementary and Integrative Health* (NCCIH) in 2017 found that while yoga is widely practiced for stress reduction and physical health, few practitioners in the West delve into its meditative and spiritual dimensions.

Many people may benefit physically from yoga but miss out on its deeper purpose. For instance, Sri Aurobindo emphasized yoga as a tool for self-transformation and integral development of body, mind, and soul, rather than a mere workout routine.

2. Yoga is a Religion

Another widespread misconception is that yoga is a religious practice tied exclusively to Hinduism. While yoga originated in ancient India and has deep connections with Hindu philosophy, it transcends religious boundaries. Yoga is a spiritual discipline that offers tools for self-realization, which can be practiced by individuals of any faith or belief system.

Swami Vivekananda stated, "Yoga is a science. It is not a creed. Yoga does not interfere with any religion or belief. It teaches the way to live a healthy and peaceful life."

The global spread of yoga has seen its adoption by people of various religions, including Christians, Buddhists, and Muslims. The integration of yoga into secular settings like schools, hospitals, and workplaces further demonstrates its universal appeal.

A 2021 survey conducted by the *Yoga Alliance* found that yoga practitioners in the United States come from diverse religious backgrounds, with many identifying as Christian, atheist, or spiritual but not religious.

Many prominent yoga teachers have emphasized that yoga is not about religion but about self-realization. Father Joe Pereira, a Catholic priest in India, is a well-known yoga practitioner who integrates yoga into his Christian faith. His foundation, Kripa, helps individuals recover from addiction using yoga and spirituality.

3. Yoga is Only for the Flexible

Many people believe that one must be flexible to practice yoga, deterring beginners from even attempting it. However, yoga is for everyone, regardless of physical ability. The purpose of yoga is not to achieve perfect poses but to develop self-awareness, balance, and inner peace.

T. Krishnamacharya, often referred to as the father of modern yoga, said, "If you can breathe, you can do yoga." This highlights that yoga is accessible to all, irrespective of body type or flexibility.

Adaptive yoga programs, such as those for individuals with disabilities, demonstrate that yoga can be modified to suit any body type. The popularity of chair yoga, yoga for seniors, and therapeutic yoga underscores this inclusivity.

A study published in the *Journal of Bodywork and Movement Therapies* (2018) showed that yoga could significantly improve quality of life in individuals with limited mobility, emphasizing its adaptability and focus on mental well-being over physical prowess.

4. Yoga is a Quick Fix for Health Problems

In recent years, yoga has been marketed as a cure-all for various ailments, leading to the misconception that it can provide quick fixes. While yoga offers significant health benefits, it is not a substitute for medical treatment. The practice of yoga should be seen as a long-term commitment to overall well-being rather than a quick solution to specific health issues.

Although yoga can help manage conditions such as anxiety, hypertension, and chronic pain, it should be practiced in conjunction with medical advice. For instance, the *American Heart Association* acknowledges that while yoga can be a complementary therapy for heart health, it should not replace conventional treatments.

Dr. Dean Ornish, a pioneer in integrative medicine, emphasized that yoga is part of a holistic lifestyle approach that includes diet, exercise, and stress management. He remarked, "Yoga is not a magic bullet; it's part of an overall way of living healthfully."

According to a report by the *Harvard Medical School* (2019), while yoga can reduce the symptoms of conditions like anxiety and depression, it typically requires consistent practice over several months to produce measurable changes.

5. Yoga is Only About Meditation

Another common misconception is that yoga is solely about meditation and achieving a calm mind. While meditation (Dhyana) is one aspect of yoga, it is part of a broader system aimed at self-realization. Yoga also includes ethical living, physical postures, breath control, and other practices that lead to holistic development.

The Ashtanga Yoga system emphasizes the importance of the first two limbs—Yama and Niyama, which focus on moral conduct and personal discipline. Without a foundation in these ethical principles, meditation alone cannot lead to spiritual growth.

The Bhagavad Gita (6.6) highlights the integration of different aspects of yoga, stating, "A person who has conquered the mind, senses, and body is one who has conquered the self." This verse underscores that yoga is about mastery of the self, not just meditation.

6. Yoga is Only for Women

A pervasive stereotype in the modern world is that yoga is primarily for women. Media representations often showcase women practicing yoga, leading to the belief that it is a feminine pursuit. However, yoga has its roots in ancient India, where it was predominantly practiced by men, including sages and warriors.

Historically, the primary teachers and practitioners of yoga were male, such as Patanjali, the sage who compiled the *Yoga Sutras*, and various rishis (sages) mentioned in the Vedic texts. Lord Shiva, regarded as the Adiyogi, is traditionally considered the first yogi and teacher of yoga.

Renowned male yogis like Swami Vivekananda, B.K.S. Iyengar, and Paramahansa Yogananda played pivotal roles in spreading yoga across the globe, demonstrating that yoga transcends gender.

B.K.S. Iyengar emphasized that "yoga is for everyone," regardless of gender, age, or background. His work inspired countless men to embrace the practice as a means to physical and spiritual health.

A 2020 report by the Yoga Alliance revealed that while the majority of yoga practitioners in the West are women (approximately 72%), the number of male practitioners has been steadily rising, indicating a shift in perceptions.

7. Yoga is Just About Relaxation

Many people associate yoga solely with relaxation and stress relief. While these benefits are certainly aspects of yoga, the practice is much more comprehensive. Yoga is designed to lead practitioners toward self-realization and liberation from the cycle of birth and death (samsara). The relaxation aspect of yoga is simply a byproduct of a deeper, transformative process.

The Katha Upanishad (2.12) states, "When all the senses are stilled, when the mind is at rest, when the intellect wavers not, then, say the wise, is the highest state attained." This verse indicates that relaxation is only a stepping stone toward achieving higher states of consciousness.

Advanced practices like Kundalini yoga, which aim to awaken the dormant spiritual energy within, are not necessarily relaxing but can be deeply challenging and transformative.

Swami Sivananda once said, "Yoga is a discipline of the mind, senses, and physical body. It helps one to see the reality, separating the chaff from the grain, the unreal from the real."

8. Yoga is a Hindu Ritual

Many people mistakenly believe that practicing yoga means engaging in Hindu rituals or worshiping Hindu deities. While yoga has its origins in ancient India and shares concepts with Hinduism, it is not tied to any specific religious rituals. Instead, yoga is a spiritual science designed to unite the individual consciousness with the universal consciousness.

Yoga's techniques can be adapted and practiced by people of all religions or none at all. It is a universal system of self-development. Swami Vivekananda popularized this idea when he introduced yoga to the West in the 1890s, emphasizing its scientific and non-religious aspects.

There are countless practitioners of yoga from various religious backgrounds, including Jews, Christians, Muslims, and Buddhists, who use yoga as a tool for personal growth without adopting any particular religious rituals.

Sri Aurobindo emphasized, "All life is yoga." His teachings reflect that yoga is about the union of the individual soul with the divine, and it transcends religious boundaries.

9. Yoga is Incompatible with Modern Life

Some believe that yoga, with its ancient roots, is incompatible with the fast-paced, modern lifestyle. This misconception arises from the idea that yoga requires retreating from society, living in isolation, or renouncing material life. However, yoga is designed to be adaptable to any era and circumstance.

In modern times, householders (grihasthas) can practice yoga while managing careers, families, and social obligations. The teachings of Swami Sivananda and Paramahansa Yogananda, among others, show that yoga can be practiced in daily life, integrating spirituality with modern responsibilities.

Swami Sivananda wrote, "Yoga is not separate from life. It is the science of right living, and as such, is intended to be incorporated in daily life. It works on all aspects of the person: the physical, vital, mental, emotional, psychic, and spiritual."

A 2019 survey by the *Yoga Journal* showed that more than 80% of yoga practitioners in the U.S. incorporated yoga into their daily routine, whether it was through meditation, breathing exercises, or short asana practices, illustrating that yoga can easily integrate into modern life.

10. Yoga Conflicts with Science

Some people believe that yoga is incompatible with modern science and that it is a mystical practice without scientific backing. This misconception stems from a misunderstanding of yoga's methods and outcomes.

Yoga is increasingly being studied and validated by scientific research, particularly in fields such as psychology, neuroscience, and medicine. The effects of meditation, pranayama (breathing exercises), and asanas have been shown to benefit mental health, improve physical well-being, and enhance cognitive function.

Numerous studies have shown that meditation and yoga can reduce stress, improve focus, and even change the structure of the brain. Harvard Medical School has conducted research that shows yoga can reduce stress levels and improve mental clarity.

Dr. Herbert Benson, a pioneer in mind-body medicine, noted, "The relaxation response [elicited by yoga] is the opposite of the stress response. Through yoga, meditation, and prayer, people can influence their autonomic nervous systems, quieting their minds and improving their health."

A study published in *The Journal of Alternative and Complementary Medicine* in 2017 found that regular yoga practice led to a significant reduction in levels of cortisol, the body's stress hormone, demonstrating the tangible physiological benefits of yoga.

11. Yoga is Incompatible with an Active Lifestyle

Some individuals, especially athletes or those engaged in high-intensity physical activities, may believe that yoga is too slow or incompatible with their active lifestyle. They may view yoga as a practice for relaxation or flexibility rather than strength and endurance.

Yoga can complement an active lifestyle by improving balance, flexibility, and mental focus, all of which are crucial for athletes and active individuals. Practices like Power Yoga, Vinyasa Flow, and Ashtanga Yoga are dynamic and physically challenging, offering a full-body workout that builds strength and stamina.

Athletes like LeBron James and Novak Djokovic have integrated yoga into their training routines, using it to enhance flexibility, mental focus, and injury prevention. Yoga's emphasis on mindfulness and breath control can also improve performance in sports and other physical activities.

12. Yoga is a Fad

Due to its recent surge in popularity, some may believe that yoga is just another fitness trend that will eventually fade. This misconception overlooks yoga's deep historical roots and enduring relevance.

Yoga has been practiced for thousands of years, evolving and adapting to different cultures and contexts. Its longevity is a testament to its profound impact on the human mind, body, and spirit. Far from being a passing fad, yoga is a timeless practice that continues to be relevant in modern society.

The enduring influence of ancient yogic texts such as the Bhagavad Gita and Patanjali's Yoga Sutras speaks to the depth and resilience of yoga's teachings. These texts have inspired generations of practitioners and continue to be studied around the world today.

T.K.V. Desikachar, a renowned yoga teacher, wrote, "Yoga is not a fad, it is the essence of life itself. Yoga is for everyone, regardless of age, religion, or lifestyle."

13. Yoga is About Controlling the Mind

A prevalent misconception is that yoga is about controlling the mind, suppressing thoughts, or forcing mental stillness. Many beginners believe that in order to practice yoga effectively, they must achieve immediate mental control or silence.

Yoga is not about suppressing thoughts or controlling the mind forcefully. Instead, it is about cultivating awareness and developing a balanced relationship with the mind. In the Bhagavad Gita (6.6), Krishna teaches Arjuna that the mind can be a friend or an enemy, depending on how it is trained. Yoga provides the tools to discipline the mind gently, not through force but through practice and detachment (abhyasa and vairagya).

Meditation, one of the key practices of yoga, is often misunderstood as a way to stop thinking. In reality, it is about observing the mind and developing the ability to remain centered despite the fluctuations of thoughts. Over time, the mind becomes more peaceful naturally, without coercion.

As the famous Zen saying goes, "You cannot stop the waves, but you can learn to surf." This captures the essence of yogic practice—learning to ride the waves of the mind without getting overwhelmed by them.

14. Yoga is an Instant Solution

There is a misconception that yoga provides instant results, whether in terms of physical fitness, mental peace, or spiritual enlightenment. This misunderstanding can lead to disappointment when immediate transformations are not experienced.

Yoga is a lifelong practice. The benefits of yoga—whether physical, mental, or spiritual—accrue over time with consistent practice. Like any profound discipline, yoga requires patience, dedication, and perseverance. The results are cumulative, not instantaneous.

The concept of *sadhana* in yoga refers to disciplined and dedicated practice. As with any discipline, whether learning a musical instrument or mastering a sport, results take time and sustained effort. The gradual unfolding of benefits is part of the yogic journey.

B.K.S. Iyengar said, "Yoga teaches us to cure what need not be endured and endure what cannot be cured." This quote highlights the transformative power of yoga, but it also reminds us that true transformation takes time and persistence.

15. Yoga is Only About Personal Well-Being

Many people approach yoga solely as a means to enhance their personal well-being, whether it is through physical health, relaxation, or mental peace. This narrow view of yoga as a self-centered practice misses the larger, more altruistic dimensions of yoga.

Yoga is not just about personal well-being; it is about connecting with the larger world and serving others. The practice of yoga leads to a deep sense of unity with all beings (sarvatmabhava), fostering compassion and selfless service. In the Bhagavad Gita (6.32), Krishna explains that a true yogi sees the self in all beings and all beings in the self.

Many yogis, both ancient and modern, have dedicated their lives to serving others, inspired by their spiritual practice. For instance, Swami Sivananda founded the Divine Life Society, which provides free education, healthcare, and spiritual guidance to countless individuals. His life exemplifies the principle of *seva* (selfless service), which is a key aspect of yoga.

Swami Vivekananda stated, "The greatest religion is to be true to your own nature. Have faith in yourselves!" However, this faith is not meant to isolate the individual but to empower them to serve others and the greater good.

16. Yoga and Pranayama Are Dangerous Without Guidance

Another misconception is that practices like yoga and pranayama (breathing exercises) are dangerous if practiced without a teacher's guidance. While it's true that advanced practices should be done with care, this misconception discourages people from exploring these vital aspects of yoga on their own.

Pranayama and asana practice can be safe and beneficial when approached with mindfulness and respect for the body's limits. Basic breathing exercises and postures can be practiced independently without danger. However, advanced techniques, such as *kumbhaka* (breath retention) or inversions, should be approached with caution and ideally under the guidance of an experienced teacher.

Basic pranayama practices, such as *nadi shodhana* (alternate nostril breathing) or simple asanas like *sukhasana* (easy pose), are accessible to almost anyone and can be practiced safely at home. However, complex practices, like *kriyas* or intense breath retention, require deeper study and supervision.

B.K.S. Iyengar stated, "The body is your temple. Keep it pure and clean for the soul to reside in." This underscores the importance of approaching yoga with awareness and care, treating the body with respect and not forcing it beyond its natural limits.

17. Yoga Requires Renunciation of Worldly Life

There is a misconception that to practice yoga seriously, one must renounce worldly life, material possessions, and relationships. This idea often stems from the image of ascetics and monks who have devoted their lives to spiritual practice.

Yoga can be practiced by anyone, regardless of their lifestyle. It does not require renunciation of the world, but rather a balanced approach to life. The Bhagavad Gita (6.1) teaches that the true yogi is one who performs their duties with detachment, without attachment to the fruits of their actions. This is known as *karma yoga*, the yoga of action.

Many householders and working professionals practice yoga and lead spiritual lives without renouncing their careers or families. Swami Vivekananda himself advocated for a form of yoga that could be integrated into daily life, combining spiritual practice with active engagement in the world.

Sri Ramakrishna, the great Bengali saint, said, "Remain in the world, but be not of the world." This highlights the essence of *karma yoga*—engaging fully in life while maintaining a sense of inner detachment and spiritual focus.

18. Yoga is Only About Posture Perfection

A common misconception is that yoga is all about achieving perfect postures and that the ultimate goal is to perform asanas with flawless precision. This misunderstanding can lead to a focus on external appearance rather than internal experience.

While alignment and precision are important, the true essence of yoga lies in the inner experience. The purpose of asanas is to prepare the body and mind for deeper practices such as meditation. As the Yoga Sutras (2.46) state, "Sthira sukham asanam"—asana should be steady and comfortable. The emphasis is on creating a stable and comfortable seat for the mind, not on achieving aesthetic perfection.

The practice of *Savasana* (corpse pose), though seemingly simple, is one of the most profound asanas, as it teaches complete relaxation and surrender. This pose is not about physical mastery but about letting go of all tension and becoming deeply aware of the body and mind.

T.K.V. Desikachar emphasized, "The success of yoga does not lie in the ability to perform postures but in how it positively changes the way we live our life and our relationships."

19. Yoga is Only for Calm and Peaceful Individuals

There's a misconception that one must already be calm, peaceful, or emotionally balanced to start practicing yoga. This notion discourages people who feel stressed, anxious, or mentally unsettled from pursuing yoga.

Yoga is not just for those who are already peaceful; it is designed to help cultivate that inner peace. Yoga provides tools to manage stress, anxiety, and emotional turbulence. The practices of Pranayama (breathing exercises), Asanas (postures), and Dhyana (meditation) are aimed at helping individuals achieve balance, regardless of where they start. Yoga meets you where you are, emotionally and mentally, and gradually helps transform your inner state.

20. The Ultimate Goal of Yoga is Attaining Superhuman Powers

Some individuals are drawn to yoga with the belief that advanced practice can grant them superhuman abilities, such as levitation, telepathy, or immortality.

While ancient yogic texts like the Yoga Sutras of Patanjali describe "siddhis" or extraordinary powers that can arise from deep meditation and discipline, these are seen as distractions on the path to enlightenment, not the goal of yoga. The true purpose of yoga is self-realization and liberation (moksha), not the attainment of supernatural abilities. The emphasis in authentic yoga practice is on spiritual growth, not magical powers.

The Yoga Sutras of Patanjali mention siddhis, but they are seen as obstacles on the path to enlightenment rather than goals. Patanjali advises focusing on the practice of yoga itself rather than seeking these powers.

"The yogi who is distracted by supernatural powers will lose sight of the ultimate goal of yoga." — Patanjali, Yoga Sutras

21. Yoga is Always Gentle and Safe

Some practitioners believe that yoga is inherently gentle and cannot cause harm, leading them to ignore the importance of proper alignment, guidance, and self-awareness during practice.

Although yoga can be gentle, it is not without risks if practiced improperly. Incorrect alignment in poses, pushing the body beyond its limits, or neglecting to modify postures based on individual needs can lead to injuries. It's essential to practice under the guidance of a knowledgeable teacher, especially for beginners, and to listen to one's own body. The safety of yoga comes from mindful practice, not from the assumption that all postures are universally harmless.

The *American College of Sports Medicine* acknowledges that while yoga is generally safe, injuries can occur if poses are performed incorrectly or without proper guidance.

22. Yoga Requires a Perfect Lifestyle

A misconception exists that in order to practice yoga, one must adopt a perfect lifestyle, including a strict diet, regular meditation, and a disciplined routine. This belief can deter those who feel they cannot live up to these standards from even starting yoga.

Yoga encourages discipline, but it is a process of gradual transformation, not an all-or-nothing endeavour. You don't need to be perfect to begin your yoga journey. The practice itself helps cultivate healthier habits over time. Yoga is about progress, not perfection. Small, consistent steps toward a balanced lifestyle are more valuable than unrealistic expectations of overnight transformation.

The concept of *ahimsa* (non-violence) in yoga philosophy promotes compassion towards oneself and others, acknowledging that perfection is not required. It encourages practitioners to focus on progress rather than perfection.

"Yoga is not about being perfect. It's about being yourself and making small improvements along the way." — T.K.V. Desikachar

23. Yoga Alone Can Solve All Health Issues

While yoga has many health benefits, it is not a substitute for medical treatment. Yoga can complement traditional medical care but should not replace it. For chronic conditions or serious health issues, yoga should be used as part of a broader treatment plan.

Research published in *The New England Journal of Medicine* (2014) found that while yoga can help with conditions like lower back pain and hypertension, it should be part of a comprehensive approach including medical advice.

24. Yoga is Incompatible with Athletic Training

Some athletes or physically active individuals believe that yoga is incompatible with their rigorous training, seeing it as too passive or gentle.

Yoga can enhance athletic performance, improving flexibility, balance, strength, and mental clarity. For example, NBA star LeBron James incorporates yoga into his training regimen. He credits yoga with enhancing his flexibility and helping him recover from the physical demands of professional basketball. Yoga's ability to improve body awareness and injury prevention makes it a valuable tool for athletes.

"Yoga helps me calm down off the court and helps me balance everything out," LeBron James has said, highlighting the mental and physical benefits of integrating yoga into athletic training.

25. Yoga Must Be Practiced Indoors

A common misconception is that yoga should only be practiced indoors, in a studio or a controlled environment, often due to its portrayal in media.

Yoga can be practiced anywhere—outdoors in nature, on the beach, in the mountains, or even in the quiet of a personal space. In ancient times, rishis and sages practiced yoga in forests and caves, in close connection with nature. Modern practitioners also find that outdoor yoga can enhance their experience by connecting them with the natural world.

The International Day of Yoga, initiated by the United Nations, is often celebrated with mass outdoor yoga events, where thousands of people practice together in parks, stadiums, or open fields, embracing the global community aspect of yoga.

As Maharishi Patanjali said in the Yoga Sutras, "Yogas chitta vritti nirodhah"—yoga is the cessation of the fluctuations of the mind. This practice transcends the physical space and can be achieved in any environment, as long as the mind is focused.

26. Yoga is Only for the Young and Fit

There is a misconception that yoga is only suitable for the young and physically fit, excluding older adults or those with physical limitations.

Yoga is accessible to people of all ages and physical abilities. There are various styles of yoga that cater to different needs, including chair yoga for seniors or those with mobility issues, and restorative yoga for gentle, supportive practice. The true essence of yoga lies in self-awareness and inner peace, which can be cultivated at any stage of life.

Tao Porchon-Lynch, a yoga teacher who taught well into her nineties, is a prime example of how yoga is ageless. She started practicing yoga in the 1920s and continued to teach and inspire others until her passing at the age of 101.

"Age is just a number. You can do anything you want to do," Tao Porchon-Lynch often said, reflecting her belief that yoga can be embraced at any stage of life.

27. You Need Expensive Equipment or Clothing for Yoga

There is a misconception that practicing yoga requires special equipment or expensive attire, which can be a barrier for some individuals.

Yoga can be practiced with minimal equipment. A mat or even a towel can suffice for most practices. Clothing should be comfortable but does not need to be costly. Yoga's essence lies in the practice itself, not in the material aspects.

Many traditional yogis practiced in simple clothing or even in their daily attire, emphasizing the practice's focus rather than external appearances.

"The true essence of yoga is not in the props or the clothes you wear but in the depth of your practice and the sincerity of your intent." – T.K.V. Desikachar

28. Yoga Requires a Specific Body Type

There is a belief that yoga is only for people with a certain body type or those who are naturally flexible and fit.

Yoga is for every body type and ability level. The practice is designed to adapt to individual needs, promoting flexibility, strength, and balance regardless of one's starting point. Yoga is inclusive and can be modified to fit different physical conditions.

Adaptive yoga and chair yoga are specialized practices designed to accommodate individuals with varying physical abilities and body types, demonstrating that yoga is for everyone.

"Yoga is not about achieving a perfect pose; it is about finding harmony within yourself, no matter your body type or physical condition." – Rodney Yee

29. Yoga is a Replacement for Spiritual or Religious Beliefs

Some people assume that practicing yoga is a way to replace or negate their existing spiritual or religious beliefs.

Yoga is a practice that can complement, rather than replace, existing spiritual or religious beliefs. It is a tool for personal growth and self-awareness that can be integrated with one's own faith or spirituality.

Many practitioners integrate yoga with their own religious practices, such as using yoga as a means to enhance their prayer life or spiritual discipline.

"Yoga does not conflict with any religion or spiritual belief; rather, it enhances one's own faith and understanding." – Swami Satchidananda

30. Yoga Makes You Unambitious

This misconception arises when people equate ambition solely with material pursuits and competitive achievements. Yoga encourages non-attachment (Vairagya) to outcomes, but this does not mean giving up on ambition. Instead, yoga teaches individuals to pursue their goals with focused effort (Abhyasa) while remaining detached from the fruits of their actions.

A yogi can be ambitious, but their ambition is often directed towards self-realization, personal growth, and contributing to the welfare of society. Many yogis throughout history, including Swami Vivekananda and Sri Aurobindo, were driven by a higher purpose and had a strong vision for their lives.

The Bhagavad Gita highlights this philosophy in Chapter 2, Verse 47, "You have a right to perform your duty, but not to the fruits of your actions."

Conclusion

By clarifying these misunderstandings, I hope you are empowered to engage with yoga more fully, recognizing it as a journey toward self-realization and unity with the divine. I'll clarify more misconceptions and provide a deeper understanding of yoga in the chapters to come.

2

The Six Schools of Indian Philosophy

Indian philosophy, also known as Darshana, offers one of the richest intellectual traditions in human history. Its depth of inquiry into the nature of reality, the self, and the cosmos has produced a vast array of schools of thought, each with its unique perspectives. The six orthodox schools of Indian philosophy, collectively called the shaddarshanas, represent the foundation of classical Indian intellectual tradition. These schools are:

1. **Nyaya** (Logic and Epistemology)
2. **Vaisheshika** (Atomism and Metaphysics)
3. **Samkhya** (Dualism of Purusha and Prakriti)
4. **Yoga** (Discipline and Meditation)
5. **Purva Mimamsa** (Rituals and Dharma)
6. **Vedanta** (Philosophy of the Upanishads)

This chapter delves into each school of thought, its founder, key teachings, and contributions, while also exploring the historical significance, etc that make these philosophies foundational pillars of Indian thought.

1. Nyaya

- **Founder**: Sage Gautama (also known as Akshapada Gautama)
- **Foundational Text**: Nyaya Sutras

Nyaya is renowned for its emphasis on logic, epistemology, and the pursuit of valid knowledge, or *pramana*. Rooted in the intellectual traditions of ancient India, Nyaya meticulously explores how knowledge is acquired and validated, offering a rigorous framework for reasoning and debate.

At the heart of the Nyaya system is its theory of *pramanas*, or the means of acquiring true knowledge. These are fourfold:

- **Perception (pratyaksha)**: Direct sensory experience, considered the most immediate and fundamental form of knowledge.

- **Inference (anumana)**: Knowledge derived from reasoning, particularly when direct perception is unavailable. This method plays a critical role in forming conclusions based on observation and logic.

- **Comparison (upamana)**: Knowledge gained through analogy or comparison, often used to identify unfamiliar objects by relating them to known ones.

- **Testimony (shabda)**: Knowledge derived from authoritative or trustworthy verbal statements, such as sacred texts or reliable sources.

Key Concepts:

- **Pramanas**: The foundation of Nyaya's epistemology, these methods serve as tools for discerning valid knowledge from falsehoods.

- **Tarka**: Logical reasoning and debate. Nyaya prioritizes the methodical use of argumentation to resolve doubts and establish truth. *Tarka* is essential in philosophical discussions and has influenced the development of formal logic in Indian thought.

- **Hetvabhasa**: Fallacies or defects in reasoning. Nyaya identifies five major types of fallacies that can lead to incorrect conclusions, thus providing a robust method for identifying flaws in arguments.

Nyaya's impact extends beyond the confines of its own school. Its methods of logical reasoning became a foundation for philosophical discourse across multiple traditions in India. The tradition of *vada* (debate) in Indian metaphysics, ethics, and theology owes much to Nyaya's rigorous dialectical approach. This framework allowed thinkers to defend or refute complex philosophical positions systematically.

In particular, Nyaya's logical methods were instrumental in debates between orthodox (*astika*) schools, such as Vedanta, and heterodox (*nastika*) schools, like Buddhism and Jainism. The medieval period saw a flourishing of these debates, with scholars like Udayana—a towering figure in the Nyaya tradition—applying its logic to defend theism against Buddhist arguments. Udayana's work in particular was pivotal in maintaining the intellectual vibrancy of the Nyaya school, and his contributions marked a high point in the defense of Hindu theistic thought.

The Nyaya Sutras, the foundational text of this school, encapsulate its epistemological framework: "Perception, inference, comparison, and verbal testimony are the four means of valid knowledge." (Nyaya Sutras 1.1.3)

This concise yet profound statement highlights the depth of Nyaya's inquiry into the nature of knowledge and its relentless pursuit of truth.

2. Vaisheshika

- **Founder**: Sage Kanada (also known as Uluka)
- **Foundational Text**: Vaisheshika Sutras

Vaisheshika is the school of atomism, concerned with categorizing the nature of reality. Founded by the sage Kanada, Vaisheshika explores the nature of existence through a detailed classification of substances, qualities, and actions, laying the groundwork for an intricate metaphysical and physical framework. This school is primarily concerned with understanding the material world, and it teaches that everything is composed of eternal, indivisible atoms (*paramanu*), which combine to create the physical universe.

Key Concepts:

- **Dravya (Substances)**: Vaisheshika classifies reality into nine fundamental types of substances: **Earth** (*prithvi*), **Water** (*apah*), **Fire** (*tejas*), **Air** (*vayu*), **Ether** (*akasha*), **Time** (*kala*), **Space** (*dik*), **Soul** (*atman*), **Mind** (*manas*). These substances form the building blocks of reality, and everything in the universe arises from their interactions. The first four—earth, water, fire, and air—are composed of atoms, while ether, time, space, soul, and mind are considered non-material but essential for the existence and functioning of the cosmos.

- **Guna (Qualities)**: Every substance possesses inherent qualities, or *gunas*, which define its nature. These qualities include attributes like colour, taste, and motion, and they vary depending on the substance they inhere in. Vaisheshika's analysis of *gunas* provides a sophisticated system for understanding the physical and metaphysical properties of all entities.

- **Anu (Atomic Theory)**: The most notable feature of Vaisheshika is its theory of atomism. According to this view, all matter is composed of indivisible particles called atoms (*anu*). These atoms are eternal, indestructible, and combine in various ways to create the material forms we observe. Vaisheshika postulates that atoms of earth, water, fire, and air combine to form complex objects, governed by laws of motion and interaction.

Vaisheshika's atomic theory is often lauded for its striking similarity to modern scientific understandings of atomic structure, making it a remarkable early formulation of materialist philosophy. The concept that everything is reducible to atomic particles was revolutionary for its time, and it predates many Western ideas of atomism by centuries. While Vaisheshika's atomism differs from modern atomic theory in certain aspects, such as the absence of the modern understanding of subatomic particles, it still represents a sophisticated attempt to explain the physical world.

Vaisheshika's contributions extend beyond metaphysics to the fields of physics and material sciences in ancient India. Its focus on the nature of matter, motion, and the composition of the universe significantly influenced later philosophical systems and scientific thought. The school's meticulous categorization of substances and qualities also laid the foundation for a broader metaphysical discourse in Indian philosophy, where the material and immaterial aspects of existence were rigorously analyzed.

In later centuries, Vaisheshika's theories were integrated with Nyaya, creating a combined Nyaya-Vaisheshika tradition. This synthesis blended Vaisheshika's metaphysical and physical insights with Nyaya's logical and epistemological framework, leading to a more comprehensive philosophical system.

The foundational text of the school, the *Vaisheshika Sutras*, succinctly captures its atomic theory: "The ultimate substances are eternal and indivisible atoms, which combine to form the material world."

This statement emphasizes the core belief of Vaisheshika that the entire physical universe arises from the interaction of these eternal atoms, guided by natural laws, a vision that foreshadowed many later developments in both Indian and Western scientific thought.

3. Samkhya

- **Founder**: Sage Kapila
- **Foundational Text**: Samkhya Karika by Ishvara Krishna

Samkhya is one of the most ancient and influential schools of Indian philosophy, offering a dualistic framework that clearly separates *Purusha* (pure consciousness) from *Prakriti* (the material universe). It presents a comprehensive cosmology that explains the origin and functioning of the universe as the interaction of these two eternal, independent principles. This philosophical system not only explores the metaphysical nature of reality but also provides a pathway to liberation (*moksha*) through the realization of the true self.

Key Concepts:

- **Purusha (Consciousness)**: *Purusha* is the eternal, unchanging, and passive witness, representing pure consciousness or the true self. It is beyond time, space, and causality, and it remains untouched by the material world. According to Samkhya, there are innumerable *Purushas*, each representing a distinct individual self. The realization of one's identity as *Purusha* is central to achieving liberation.

- **Prakriti (Material Nature)**: *Prakriti* is the fundamental principle of matter, the source from which the entire cosmos evolves. Unlike *Purusha*, *Prakriti* is active, dynamic, and composed of various elements that give rise to the physical and mental aspects of the universe. Everything we experience—intellect, mind, senses, and even the body—is an expression of *Prakriti*. While it is unconscious, it evolves through its interaction with *Purusha*, setting in motion the process of cosmic manifestation.

- **Gunas (Qualities of Nature)**: *Prakriti* is governed by the interplay of three fundamental qualities, or *gunas*, that are responsible for the diversity and complexity of the universe:

1. **Sattva**: The quality of purity, clarity, and harmony. It is associated with light, balance, and knowledge.

2. **Rajas**: The quality of activity, energy, and passion. It drives movement, change, and desire.

3. **Tamas**: The quality of inertia, darkness, and ignorance. It is responsible for stagnation, confusion, and destruction.

The entire process of evolution within *Prakriti* is driven by the constant interaction of these three *gunas*, resulting in the diversity of life forms, emotions, and experiences.

Samkhya posits that the universe is a product of the evolution of *Prakriti*, beginning with the most subtle elements and moving toward the gross physical world. The first manifestation from *Prakriti* is *mahat* (cosmic intellect), followed by *ahamkara* (ego), and then the mind, senses, and the elements. This evolution is non-conscious, and it happens without the direct intervention of *Purusha*. However, the mere presence of *Purusha* as a witness enables the activation of *Prakriti*.

The core goal of Samkhya philosophy is liberation (*moksha*) from the cycle of birth, death, and suffering. This liberation is achieved by recognizing the true nature of the self as *Purusha*, which is distinct from *Prakriti*. Due to ignorance (*avidya*), individuals identify with the body, mind, and ego—forms of *Prakriti*—and are trapped in the cycle of suffering. Enlightenment occurs when one realizes that the self (*Purusha*) is separate from the material world (*Prakriti*) and is beyond all forms of physical and mental phenomena.

Once this realization is attained, the individual ceases to be affected by the activities of *Prakriti*, experiencing liberation and detachment from worldly entanglements. *Purusha* remains the passive observer, completely free from the binding influence of the material world.

Samkhya's dualism between *Purusha* and *Prakriti* has deeply influenced several other philosophical systems, most notably the Yoga school, which adopts Samkhya's metaphysical framework. In Yoga, the same distinction between consciousness and material nature is essential for the practice of meditation and spiritual discipline. Additionally, Samkhya's insights have influenced Vedanta, especially in its discussions about the nature of the self and the ultimate reality, as well as Buddhism and Jainism, particularly in their explorations of consciousness and materiality.

Samkhya's cosmology, with its detailed analysis of *gunas* and the evolution of the universe, provided a comprehensive system for understanding the material and spiritual dimensions of existence. This made it an essential foundation for later metaphysical and ethical debates in Indian philosophical thought.

The essential teachings of Samkhya are encapsulated in the *Samkhya Karika*, one of the foundational texts of the school. One of its key verses emphasizes the distinction between *Purusha* and *Prakriti*: "The entire creation, from intellect to physical matter, is an evolution of Prakriti, while Purusha remains eternally pure and untouched." (Samkhya Karika 11)

This passage highlights the central tenet of Samkhya: the dynamic, evolving nature of the material universe stands in stark contrast to the immutable, eternal nature of the conscious self.

4. Yoga

- **Founder**: Sage Patanjali
- **Foundational Text**: Yoga Sutras

Yoga, as a school of philosophy, is closely associated with Samkhya but focuses on the practical aspects of achieving liberation through disciplined practices. The Yoga system outlines an eightfold path (Ashtanga Yoga) that leads to self-realization and union with the Supreme Consciousness. The practice of Yoga involves ethical disciplines, physical postures, breath control, meditation, and the withdrawal of the senses.

Key Concepts:

- **Ashtanga Yoga**: The eight limbs of Yoga—Yama (ethical restraints), Niyama (observances), Asana (posture), Pranayama (breath control), Pratyahara (withdrawal of the senses), Dharana (concentration), Dhyana (meditation), and Samadhi (absorption).

- **Chitta Vritti Nirodha**: The cessation of mental modifications, which is the ultimate goal of Yoga.

Yoga has become one of the most recognized and practiced philosophies worldwide. Modern interpretations often focus on the physical postures (Asanas), but traditional Yoga emphasizes the complete integration of body, mind, and spirit.

"Yoga is the cessation of the fluctuations of the mind." (Yoga Sutras 1.2)

Some readers might think of the phrase, "An idle mind is the devil's workshop," and may confuse it with the meaning of Patanjali's sutra. Let me clarify this:

Idle Mind vs. Controlled Mind

The saying "An idle mind is the devil's workshop" suggests that a mind left unoccupied and without purpose is vulnerable to negative or harmful thoughts. This "emptiness" is dangerous because it lacks focus and direction, creating space for unwanted influences.

In contrast, Patanjali's teachings emphasize not an "empty" mind in the negative sense, but a mind that is controlled, disciplined, and free from distractions. Patanjali speaks of quieting the mind, but this does not mean leaving it idle. Instead, the mind becomes focused, peaceful, and attuned to a higher state of awareness.

The Concept of Emptiness

In the proverb, "emptiness" represents a lack of meaningful activity, making the mind susceptible to negativity. However, in Patanjali's sutra, the cessation of mental activity refers to the stilling of restless or chaotic thoughts, which leads to a meditative state of clarity and calmness. This state is not a void or vacuum but a place of heightened consciousness and inner peace.

Purpose and Practice

The proverb warns against inactivity, suggesting that a mind should be engaged in positive, productive endeavours to avoid negative consequences. Patanjali, on the other hand, teaches that through disciplined practice (abhyasa) and detachment (vairagya), one can quiet the mind, not to render it idle, but to achieve deep inner calm and self-realization. Yoga is about cultivating mindfulness and awareness, ensuring the mind does not wander aimlessly but remains anchored in presence and purpose.

By understanding these distinctions, we see that Patanjali's sutra advocates a controlled, focused, and aware mind, while the proverb warns of the dangers of aimlessness and inactivity.

Imagine a shallow lake, its surface disturbed by ripples and small waves. As long as the water is in motion, it obscures the depths beneath, making it difficult to see the clarity and beauty of what lies below. However, when the wind ceases and the surface becomes still, the water turns mirror-like, revealing the stones, plants, and life beneath. Similarly, when the mind is restless, filled with thoughts and distractions, it hides the true Self. But when the mind becomes still, like the calm surface of the lake, the essence of our being—the Self—reveals itself with crystal clarity. In that stillness, the illusion fades, and we recognize our true nature.

5. Purva Mimamsa

- **Founder**: Sage Jaimini
- **Foundational Text**: Mimamsa Sutras

Mimamsa, also referred to as *Purva Mimamsa*, is primarily concerned with the ritualistic and ethical teachings of the Vedas, particularly the earlier sections dealing with rituals and duties. The school aims to provide a systematic interpretation of Vedic texts, especially focusing on the performance of *karma* (ritual actions) as a means to fulfill one's duties and uphold *dharma* (righteousness). Mimamsa is not a speculative or metaphysical system but a practical one, focusing on the right conduct of life and the proper performance of rituals as prescribed in the Vedas.

Key Concepts:

- **Dharma (Righteous Duty)**: In Mimamsa, *dharma* is considered the highest guiding principle, referring to the ethical and ritualistic duties enjoined by the Vedic scriptures. These duties, whether daily rituals or special sacrificial ceremonies, are seen as crucial for maintaining cosmic order and ensuring personal and societal well-being. Unlike other schools that may emphasize knowledge or devotion as the means to liberation, Mimamsa insists that the performance of duties, as specified in the Vedas, is the key to prosperity and spiritual merit.

- **Karma (Vedic Rituals)**: Central to Mimamsa is the concept of *karma*, which here refers specifically to the Vedic rituals that are meticulously prescribed for different stages of life. Mimamsa teaches that the proper performance of these rituals brings about tangible and spiritual benefits, influencing the future outcomes of the performer. The emphasis is on action—ritual action—rather than belief or devotion. By following the Vedic injunctions, individuals contribute to the cosmic order and ensure their own prosperity, health, and spiritual progress.

- **Apurva (Unseen Force)**: Mimamsa introduces the concept of *apurva*, which is the unseen potency or force generated by the performance of Vedic rituals. According to Mimamsa, the benefits of a ritual may not be immediately apparent, but they are guaranteed to manifest in the future due to the *apurva* created by the ritual. This unseen force links the ritual action with its eventual outcome, whether in this life or in future births. It operates as the unseen causal mechanism that ensures the fulfillment of the results promised by the Vedas.

Mimamsa is primarily concerned with the orthopraxy of Vedic rituals and duties. It emphasizes that the proper understanding and execution of Vedic injunctions is essential for the well-being of both the individual and society. These Vedic rites are not performed for liberation (*moksha*), but rather to fulfill *dharma*, ensuring prosperity in this life and the next. Mimamsa holds that every detail of the ritual—whether it is the specific mantra to be chanted or the precise offering to be made—has a vital role in producing the intended results.

One of Mimamsa's critical contributions to Indian thought is its rigorous method of interpreting the Vedic texts. It developed a detailed exegesis of the Vedas, using hermeneutical principles to resolve ambiguities in the scriptures and ensure that the ritual prescriptions were followed accurately. This attention to detail in interpreting the sacred texts also helped preserve the Vedic tradition through centuries.

Mimamsa's focus on rituals significantly influenced Hindu temple practices and religious ceremonies that continue to this day. The elaborate systems of Vedic rituals, sacrificial rites, and ethical duties it outlines have shaped not only individual religious observance but also communal and temple-based worship. The school's emphasis on the efficacy of *karma* (ritual action) as a means to secure worldly benefits and spiritual merit continues to resonate in various Hindu practices.

Mimamsa's views on *dharma* also played a role in the development of Hindu law and ethics. By asserting that *dharma* is derived from the Vedic injunctions, Mimamsa linked moral and ethical behavior directly to religious duty, establishing a foundational principle for both personal conduct and societal order.

While Mimamsa does not directly concern itself with metaphysical questions like the nature of the self or the ultimate reality (*Brahman*), which are central to other schools like Vedanta, it plays a crucial role in preserving the ritualistic and ethical aspects of the Vedas. In later developments, Mimamsa's emphasis on *karma* was integrated into the broader philosophical discussions, influencing schools like Vedanta, which addressed the tension between ritual action and knowledge in their quest for liberation.

Mimamsa also engaged in philosophical debates with the Buddhist and Jain traditions, defending the authority of the Vedas and the importance of rituals against the non-Vedic philosophies, which either rejected or minimized the role of rituals.

The *Mimamsa Sutras*, composed by Jaimini, is the foundational text of this school and outlines its key teachings on rituals, duties, and interpretation of the Vedas. A pivotal verse from this text succinctly captures the essence of Mimamsa's focus: "Dharma is that which is enjoined by the Vedas, and which leads to the attainment of the highest good." (Mimamsa Sutras 1.1.2)

This verse underscores the belief that the Vedas are the ultimate authority on what constitutes righteous action and that adhering to these scriptural instructions ensures both material and spiritual welfare. Through this, Mimamsa emphasizes that the Vedic ritual system is not merely symbolic but a powerful means to achieve desired results and uphold cosmic and social order.

6. Vedanta

- **Founder**: Sage Badarayana
- **Foundational Text**: Brahma Sutras

Vedanta, which literally means "the end of the Vedas," is a profound and expansive school of Indian philosophy that focuses on the nature of the ultimate reality (*Brahman*) and the individual soul (*Atman*), as well as the relationship between the two. As one of the most influential schools of thought in Indian tradition, Vedanta forms the philosophical basis for much of Hindu spiritual and religious life. It seeks to interpret and elaborate upon the teachings found in the *Upanishads*, which represent the final sections of the Vedas, and are considered the essence of Vedic wisdom.

Key Concepts:

- **Brahman (Ultimate Reality)**: In Vedanta, *Brahman* is the supreme, formless, all-pervading reality that is the source and substance of everything in existence. It is beyond all attributes and limitations, and it transcends time, space, and causality. *Brahman* is described as infinite, eternal, and unchanging, and is considered the fundamental essence of the universe. It is both immanent (present in all things) and transcendent (beyond all things).

- **Atman (Individual Soul)**: *Atman* refers to the individual soul or the inner self. In Advaita Vedanta (non-dualism), *Atman* is ultimately identical to *Brahman*, meaning that the essence of each individual is the same as the essence of the entire cosmos. However, due to ignorance (*avidya*), individuals fail to realize this oneness and perceive themselves as separate beings. Liberation (*moksha*) is attained when one recognizes that the *Atman* is not distinct from *Brahman*.

- **Maya (Illusion)**: The concept of *maya* plays a crucial role in Vedanta, particularly in Advaita. *Maya* refers to the cosmic illusion that veils the true nature of reality. It is responsible for the appearance of the material world as separate and distinct from *Brahman*. *Maya* creates the illusion of duality, leading individuals to perceive multiplicity, change, and individuality in what is actually a singular, unchanging reality. Overcoming this illusion is essential for realizing the truth of non-dualism.

Sub-Schools of Vedanta

There are several major sub-schools of Vedanta, each offering distinct interpretations of the relationship between *Brahman* and *Atman*:

- **Advaita Vedanta (Non-Dualism)**: Advaita Vedanta, expounded by the philosopher Adi Shankaracharya, teaches that *Brahman* alone is real, and the apparent diversity of the world is an illusion caused by *maya*. According to Advaita, there is no fundamental distinction between *Brahman* and *Atman*; they are one and the same. Liberation is achieved when one realizes this non-duality and transcends the illusory world of *maya*. Adi Shankaracharya encapsulates this teaching in his famous statement: "Brahman is real, the world is illusory, and the individual self is none other than Brahman."

- **Vishishtadvaita (Qualified Non-Dualism)**: Vishishtadvaita, formulated by the philosopher Ramanuja, teaches that while *Brahman* is the ultimate reality, it is not formless or impersonal. Instead, *Brahman* possesses qualities (*vishishta*) and is identified with a personal God, often Vishnu. In this view, the individual soul (*Atman*) is distinct from *Brahman* but inseparably connected to it, much like a part of a whole. Liberation in Vishishtadvaita is attained through loving devotion (*bhakti*) to God, culminating in union with *Brahman* without losing one's individuality.

- **Dvaita Vedanta (Dualism)**: Dvaita Vedanta, founded by the philosopher Madhvacharya, asserts a strict dualism between *Brahman* (God) and *Atman* (individual souls). According to Dvaita, *Brahman* is a personal deity, separate and distinct from individual souls and the material world. Liberation is achieved through devotion to God, but the individual soul remains eternally distinct from *Brahman* even after liberation. This view contrasts with Advaita's non-dualism and highlights the eternal difference between the creator and the created.

In all schools of Vedanta, the ultimate goal is *moksha*, or liberation, but the understanding of liberation differs based on the school. In Advaita, liberation is the realization of the oneness of *Atman* and *Brahman*, leading to the dissolution of the false ego and the end of the cycle of rebirths (*samsara*). In Vishishtadvaita and Dvaita, *moksha* is union with or proximity to God, attained through devotion, and involves an eternal relationship with the divine, where individuality is either preserved or remains distinct.

Vedanta, particularly Advaita, has had an enduring impact on Indian philosophy, spirituality, and religious practice. The non-dualistic interpretation offered by Adi Shankaracharya reshaped the landscape of Indian philosophical thought, emphasizing the oneness of existence and the illusory nature of the world. Vedanta's teachings also influenced a wide range of spiritual movements, including the Bhakti traditions, the modern interpretations of Hinduism, and even non-Hindu philosophies like Buddhism and Jainism in their discussions of self and reality.

Vedanta's integration of metaphysics, ethics, and spirituality has made it one of the most adaptable and comprehensive philosophical systems. Its teachings continue to resonate with spiritual seekers both in India and worldwide.

Conclusion: The Unified Pursuit of Truth

The six schools of Indian philosophy, while distinct in their approaches, share a common goal: the pursuit of truth and liberation from the cycle of suffering. Whether through logical inquiry, metaphysical exploration, ritual practice, or meditation, each school offers valuable insights into the nature of reality and the path to spiritual realization.

These philosophies, deeply rooted in the Vedic tradition, continue to influence modern spiritual practices, both in India and globally. By understanding the unique contributions of each school, one gains a deeper appreciation for the diversity and unity of Indian thought, and the profound wisdom it offers for those seeking liberation and self-realization.

3

The Essence of Yoga and Paths of Realization

Yoga, is a profound spiritual discipline with roots stretching back thousands of years. Understanding the journey of yoga requires exploring its roots and the various paths of realization that have been passed down through generations. In this chapter, we will delve into the essence of yoga from ancient to modern times, highlighting the traditions and texts that have shaped its evolution.

Ancient Period (Pre-600 CE)

Foundational Texts and Practices

The ancient period of yoga is where we find the foundational texts and teachings that laid the groundwork for all subsequent developments. The origins of yoga can be traced back to the Indus Valley Civilization (c. 3000 BCE), where early depictions of meditative postures have been found on seals in Mohenjo-Daro. However, the most significant early references to yoga are found in the *Vedas*, particularly the *Rigveda*, and later, the *Upanishads*.

The **Rigveda** (c. 1500 BCE), where the term is used to describe the disciplined path to union with the divine. The period saw the rise of **Vedic** rituals, hymns, and meditation practices designed to lead practitioners towards realization.

The **Upanishads** (c. 800–200 BCE), often referred to as the end of the Vedas, deepened this understanding. They emphasized *Brahman* (universal consciousness) and *Atman* (individual soul) as one and the same. For example, the *Mandukya Upanishad* declares, "Aum, the word, is all this, the past, the present, and the future. All that is, is Aum." (Mandukya Upanishad 1).

The *Katha Upanishad* introduces the concept of the self (Atman) as separate from the material body and speaks of yoga as a path to realizing this self. One famous verse is, "When the five senses are stilled, when the mind is stilled, when the intellect is stilled, that is called the highest state by the wise." (Katha Upanishad, 2.3.10)

The **Bhagavad Gita** (c. 500 BCE) presents a more systematic and diverse understanding of yoga, categorizing it into three main paths: Karma Yoga (the path of selfless action), Bhakti Yoga (the path of devotion), and Jnana (Gyana) Yoga (the path of knowledge). The Gita emphasizes that these paths are not mutually exclusive but can be practiced together, "Whosoever offers to Me with devotion a leaf, a flower, a fruit, or water, I accept that offering of love from the pure of heart." (Bhagavad Gita, 9.26)

Paths of Realization

Jnana (Gyana) Yoga: The path of knowledge, as exemplified in both the Bhagavad Gita (c. 500 BCE) and the Ashtavakra Gita, highlights the pursuit of knowledge as a path to self-realization. In the Bhagavad Gita, Lord Krishna instructs Arjuna on the importance of transcending individuality: "He who sees the Self in all beings, and all beings in the Self, is free from fear" (Bhagavad Gita 6.29). Similarly, the Ashtavakra Gita presents profound teachings on the nature of the Self, going beyond the mind and body. It emphasizes pure awareness, where Ashtavakra declares, "You are not the body, nor is the body yours. You are not the doer, nor the enjoyer. You are pure Awareness, the witness of all things."

Both texts guide seekers toward the realization of their eternal essence, stripping away layers of illusion and attachment.

Karma Yoga: The Gita also stresses the importance of selfless action, stating, "Your right is to perform your duty only, but never to its fruits." (*Bhagavad Gita* 2.47). This encapsulates Karma Yoga, the path of action without attachment to the results.

The teachings of the *Bhagavad Gita* and the *Upanishads* continue to influence millions globally. According to a 2017 study by *Yoga Alliance and Yoga Journal*, 36 million Americans practiced yoga, and many have been introduced to its spiritual aspects through texts like the *Gita*. The influence of these ancient texts can be seen in the practices of great sages like Swami Vivekananda, who popularized Jnana Yoga in the West through his teachings and writings.

Early Medieval Period (600–1200 CE)

Patanjali and the Systematization of Yoga

The early medieval period is marked by the formalization of yoga practices through the **Yoga Sutras of Patanjali** (c. 400 CE). Maharishi Patanjali is known as the founder of yoga philosophy, and is often referred to as "The Father of Yoga." He is credited with codifying yoga practices, meaning, and related knowledge in his Yoga Sutras, a collection of 195 aphorisms. Patanjali's systematization of yoga into the eightfold path forms the cornerstone of classical yoga:

Patanjali's **Eightfold Path**, or **Ashtanga Yoga**, is a comprehensive spiritual framework that guides practitioners toward self-realization and liberation (Moksha). This path is often referred to as **Raja Yoga**, the **"Royal Path,"** because it emphasizes mental discipline, ethical conduct, and spiritual insight. Below is an overview of each of the eight limbs:

1. **Yama** (moral discipline)
2. **Niyama** (observances)
3. **Asana** (posture)
4. **Pranayama** (breath control)
5. **Pratyahara** (withdrawal of the senses)
6. **Dharana** (concentration)
7. **Dhyana** (meditation)
8. **Samadhi** (absorption or liberation)

1. Yama (Moral Discipline)

Yama focuses on ethical principles and how we interact with others and the world. It encourages the cultivation of virtues and the elimination of harmful behaviours. The five Yamas are:

- **Ahimsa (Non-violence)**: Ahimsa is the practice of non-violence in thought, word, and deed. It extends beyond physical harm to include mental and emotional actions, promoting compassion, kindness, and empathy towards all living beings, including oneself. Ahimsa invites us to act with love and awareness, refraining from actions that cause harm or suffering, and fostering peace in all aspects of life.

- **Satya (Truthfulness)**: Satya is the commitment to truth in speech, thought, and action. It involves being honest with ourselves and others, ensuring that our words and actions are aligned with integrity and authenticity. Truthfulness also requires discernment, as sometimes the full truth may cause harm, and the higher principle of Ahimsa must guide us in how we express the truth.

- **Asteya (Non-stealing)**: Asteya goes beyond the literal sense of theft, encompassing all forms of taking that do not belong to us. This includes material possessions, ideas, time, or energy from others. Practicing Asteya cultivates a sense of contentment and gratitude for what we have, helping us avoid envy and greed. It encourages us to contribute to the world rather than take from it unfairly.

- **Brahmacharya (Moderation or Self-control)**: Traditionally, Brahmacharya referred to celibacy, especially in the context of monastic life. However, in a broader sense, it represents the wise use of energy, especially sexual energy, directing it toward spiritual growth rather than indulgence in sensual pleasures. Brahmacharya promotes balance and moderation in all aspects of life—whether in eating, consumption, or behaviour—enabling us to focus on higher spiritual goals without being distracted by excessive desires.

- **Aparigraha (Non-possessiveness or Non-greed)**: Aparigraha teaches us to let go of attachment to material possessions, people, and outcomes. It encourages simplicity, contentment, and freedom from the need to hoard or accumulate more than necessary. By releasing greed and possessiveness, we create space for generosity, inner peace, and an understanding that true happiness lies not in material wealth but in spiritual abundance.

2. Niyama (Personal Observances)

The **five Niyamas** are personal disciplines that guide the practitioner toward self-purification and spiritual growth. While the Yamas focus on ethical conduct in our external interactions, the Niyamas emphasize internal development, cultivating a harmonious inner life that supports the path to self-realization:

- **Saucha (Purity)**: Saucha refers to cleanliness and purity on both physical and mental levels. Physically, it means maintaining hygiene, cleanliness of the body, and purity of one's environment. Mentally, it involves purifying the mind from negative emotions like anger, greed, jealousy, and pride. Saucha helps to clear the inner clutter, creating space for higher awareness and a calm, focused mind, essential for spiritual practice.

- **Santosha (Contentment)**: Santosha is the practice of cultivating inner contentment and peace, regardless of external circumstances. It encourages us to embrace gratitude for what we have and to accept life's challenges with equanimity. By avoiding excessive desires and the pursuit of material gains, Santosha teaches us to find joy in the present moment and to understand that true happiness comes from within, not from external sources.

- **Tapas (Discipline or Austerity)**: Tapas refers to the burning desire for self-discipline, persistence, and effort toward personal and spiritual growth. It involves the willingness to endure discomfort and hardship for a higher purpose, developing resilience and inner strength. Tapas is about maintaining consistent effort in spiritual practices like meditation, asana, or ethical conduct, even when it is difficult, leading to the purification of body and mind.

- **Svadhyaya (Self-study or Study of Scriptures)**: Svadhyaya involves the practice of introspection and the study of spiritual texts to gain deeper self-awareness and wisdom. It is the exploration of one's inner self through meditation, reflection, and the study of sacred scriptures such as the Vedas, Upanishads, the Ashtavakra Gita, or the Bhagavad Gita. This practice leads to greater self-understanding and the realization of the divine essence within oneself, bridging the gap between the individual self and universal consciousness.

- **Ishvara Pranidhana (Surrender to a Higher Power)**: Ishvara Pranidhana is the practice of surrendering the ego and dedicating one's actions and life to a higher power, whether conceived as God, the universe, or universal consciousness. It involves trusting in the divine will, letting go of the need for control, and accepting that there is a higher intelligence guiding the course of life. Through surrender, one attains peace, humility, and the dissolution of the ego, facilitating the experience of union with the divine.

3. Asana (Posture)

Asana refers to the physical postures practiced in yoga, designed to prepare the body for meditation. In Patanjali's Yoga Sutras, the emphasis is not on complex physical feats but on finding a **stable and comfortable seat** (Sthira Sukham Asanam) that allows the practitioner to sit in meditation for extended periods without discomfort. The aim is to cultivate steadiness and ease in the body, creating a foundation for deeper inner work.

4. Pranayama (Breath Control)

Pranayama involves controlling and expanding the breath, which is intimately connected to prana, or life force energy. Through conscious breath regulation, one can influence the flow of energy within the body and mind, leading to greater clarity and focus. The three stages of pranayama include:

- **Inhalation (Puraka)**

- **Exhalation (Rechaka)**

- **Retention (Kumbhaka)**, which can be either after inhalation or exhalation

Pranayama helps in balancing the mind, calming the nervous system, and preparing for meditation.

5. Pratyahara (Withdrawal of the Senses)

Pratyahara is the practice of withdrawing the senses from external stimuli, turning the attention inward. It is a crucial step in shifting the focus from the outer world to the inner landscape. This withdrawal allows the mind to become less reactive and more centered, laying the groundwork for concentration and meditation. It marks the beginning of internalizing the spiritual practice.

6. Dharana (Concentration)

Dharana is the practice of focused concentration, where the mind is trained to remain steady on a single point, whether it be a mantra, a candle flame, or the breath. This stage involves the discipline of attention, strengthening mental focus and reducing distractions. By practicing Dharana, one builds the capacity to quiet the mind, which leads naturally to deeper states of meditation.

7. Dhyana (Meditation)

Dhyana is an uninterrupted flow of concentration, a deep and sustained meditation where the meditator and the object of meditation merge. It is a state of profound stillness where the fluctuations of the mind are completely stilled, allowing one to experience a state of pure awareness. Dhyana transcends ordinary thought, opening the door to spiritual insight and self-realization.

8. Samadhi (Absorption or Liberation)

Samadhi is the ultimate goal of the Eightfold Path, a state of deep spiritual absorption where the practitioner merges with the object of meditation, transcending the ego and experiencing oneness with the universe. It is the state of **self-liberation** (Moksha), where the boundaries between the individual self and cosmic consciousness dissolve. In Samadhi, the practitioner attains the highest state of bliss and enlightenment, realizing their true nature as pure consciousness beyond time, space, and form.

Patanjali's Eightfold Path is not merely a step-by-step process but an integrated approach to spiritual evolution. Each limb builds upon the others, creating a harmonious balance between ethical living, physical well-being, mental discipline, and spiritual realization. Through sincere and consistent practice of these principles, one can progress toward the **ultimate goal** of self-realization and liberation from the cycle of suffering.

Tantra and Esoteric Yoga

Around the 7th century, **Tantric Yoga** emerged, focusing on the awakening of spiritual energy through elaborate rituals, mantra recitation, and meditation. The *Vijnana Bhairava Tantra*, a key text in this tradition, presents 112 methods of meditation, all designed to transcend duality and realize the oneness of existence.

The Vijnana Bhairava Tantra teaches, "The mind should be absorbed in the space that is neither inside nor outside; then one will experience the vast, boundless reality." (Vijnana Bhairava Tantra Verse 51).

The intricate carvings at temples like **Ellora** and **Khajuraho** reflect the intertwining of spiritual and physical disciplines during this period, showing how yoga permeated every aspect of life.

Medieval Period (1200–1700 CE)

The Rise of Hatha Yoga

The medieval period saw the rise of **Hatha Yoga**, which focused on mastering the body to achieve spiritual liberation. The three classical texts of Hatha Yoga are *Gheranda Samhita*, *Hatha Yoga Pradipika* and the *Shiva Samhita*. The **Hatha Yoga Pradipika** (15th century) by Swatmarama is one of the seminal texts of this tradition, elaborating on physical postures (asanas), breath control (pranayama), and the use of energy locks (bandhas) to control the flow of vital energy (prana).

The *Hatha Yoga Pradipika* states, "Asanas give steadiness, health, and lightness of body." (Hatha Yoga Pradipika 1.17). The text emphasizes the role of discipline and purity in preparing the body and mind for higher states of consciousness.

"When the breath wanders, the mind is unsteady, but when the breath is still, so is the mind still." (Hatha Yoga Pradipika, 2.2)

On the other hand, unlike other classical texts that primarily focus on physical postures and pranayama (breath control), the *Gheranda Samhita* presents a more holistic and systematic approach to yoga, emphasizing both the physical and mental purification processes. It describes yoga as a form of "Ghatastha yoga" which is defined as the "yoga of the pot" (ghata), referring to the human body as a vessel that needs to be purified and strengthened to achieve spiritual liberation.

The Seven Limbs of Yoga in Gheranda Samhita:

1. **Shatkarma** (Six Cleansing Techniques)

   There are six purification practices aimed at cleansing the body. The techniques include:

   - **Dhauti** (Cleansing the stomach and intestines)
   - **Basti** (Cleansing the colon)
   - **Neti** (Cleansing the nasal passages)
   - **Trataka** (Concentration on a point or object to cleanse the eyes and mind)
   - **Nauli** (Massaging the abdominal organs)
   - **Kapalabhati** (Cleansing the lungs and respiratory system)

2. **Asana** (Postures)
3. **Mudra** (Gestures and Seals)
4. **Pratyahara** (Withdrawal of the Senses)
5. **Pranayama** (Breath Control)
6. **Dhyana** (Meditation)
7. **Samadhi** (Absorption or Union)

Bhakti Yoga and Devotion

Alongside the development of Hatha Yoga, there was a significant rise in Bhakti Yoga, a path of devotion that became deeply embedded in the spiritual practices of the time. Bhakti Yoga focuses on cultivating deep love, surrender, and personal devotion to the Divine, seeing such devotion as the most direct route to spiritual realization. Saints like **Ramanuja**, **Kabir**, **Mirabai**, and **Tulsidas** were instrumental in spreading this practice, creating a movement that appealed to people from all walks of life, transcending the rigid caste systems that had long dominated Indian society.

Ramanuja (1017–1137 CE), one of the most prominent proponents of Bhakti Yoga, deeply influenced the Vaishnavism tradition with his teachings on devotion. His seminal work, the **Sri Bhasya**, a commentary on the Brahma Sutras, advocates for **Vishishtadvaita** (qualified non-dualism), a philosophy that emphasizes a personal relationship with the Divine, particularly with **Vishnu**. In this school of thought, liberation (**moksha**) is not merely the dissolution of the individual self into the universal Brahman but rather a union with the Divine through love and devotion. Ramanuja's teachings highlighted that true devotion (bhakti) is the highest form of worship, wherein the seeker surrenders completely to God, realizing the Divine within the framework of the personal and the universal.

The influence of **Kabir** further deepened the significance of Bhakti Yoga. Kabir, a 15th-century poet and mystic, transcended religious boundaries, drawing from both Hindu and Islamic traditions to spread his message of divine love. His famous couplets (**Dohas**) captured the essence of Bhakti Yoga with simplicity and profound wisdom. One of his most quoted lines, "The river that flows in you also flows in me. There is but one life, one reality," reflects the deep non-dualistic understanding central to Bhakti. Kabir's teachings emphasized that true devotion comes from recognizing the Divine as the common essence of all beings, rejecting outward rituals in favour of inner purity and love.

The **Bhakti movement** of this era witnessed a flowering of devotional literature and the creation of sacred spaces. Saints like **Mirabai** and **Tulsidas** gave voice to their intense love for the Divine through poetry and song. **Mirabai**, a princess turned mystic in the 16th century, became a symbol of unwavering devotion to **Krishna**, often expressing her longing and union with the Divine through her bhajans (devotional songs). Her life and works embody the principle that Bhakti transcends all societal barriers—she defied norms of caste, gender, and status in her single-minded devotion to her chosen deity.

Tulsidas, a contemporary of Mirabai, authored the **Ramcharitmanas**, an epic retelling of the Ramayana, composed in the vernacular Awadhi language rather than Sanskrit, making it accessible to the common people. His work emphasized the virtues of devotion, righteousness, and love for **Rama** and became a spiritual cornerstone for millions of devotees. Through his writings, Tulsidas brought the sacred into the lives of ordinary people, allowing them to connect with the Divine through the simple act of love and faith.

The Bhakti movement during this period led to the construction of hundreds of temples across India and the establishment of devotional communities that celebrated the Divine through song, dance, and prayer. Pilgrimage sites dedicated to deities like Krishna, Vishnu, and Rama flourished, as did the practice of communal worship. These sacred spaces and festivals became powerful centers of spiritual expression and social unity, offering people from all castes and social backgrounds the opportunity to connect with the Divine on an equal footing.

The profound influence of Bhakti Yoga reshaped the spiritual and cultural landscape of India. The movement democratized spirituality, making it accessible to the masses, regardless of social status, gender, or caste. The legacy of Bhakti can still be seen today in the devotional music, poetry, and rituals that continue to inspire spiritual seekers across the globe. Devotional practices such as **kirtans** (devotional songs), **bhajans**, and pilgrimage remain vibrant, embodying the timeless message of Bhakti Yoga—that through love and surrender to the Divine, one can experience the ultimate truth and attain liberation.

Modern Period (1700 CE–Present)

Global Expansion of Yoga

The modern period is marked by the global expansion of yoga, spurred by figures like **Swami Vivekananda**, who introduced yoga to the West at the **Parliament of the World's Religions** in Chicago in 1893. Vivekananda's teachings emphasized the universality of yoga and its application in daily life.

In his work **Raja Yoga**, Vivekananda writes, "Each soul is potentially divine. The goal is to manifest this Divinity within by controlling nature, external and internal." This encapsulates the modern interpretation of yoga as a path to realizing one's full potential.

Hatha Yoga Revival

The revival of Hatha Yoga in the 20th century can largely be attributed to **T. Krishnamacharya**, who taught influential figures like **B.K.S.**

Iyengar and **Pattabhi Jois**. Their systems of **Iyengar Yoga** and **Ashtanga Yoga** have become globally recognized styles, focusing on precise alignment and dynamic movement, respectively.

The widespread popularity of yoga in the West is evident in the exponential growth of yoga studios, retreats, and teacher training programs. According to a 2016 *Yoga Journal* report, over 36 million Americans practiced yoga, a figure that has steadily risen.

The modern yoga movement has led to exponential growth in the practice of yoga worldwide. According to a 2020 report, the global yoga market is expected to reach $66.2 billion by 2027, driven by increased awareness of the health benefits of yoga.

The International Day of Yoga, celebrated annually on June 21st, is a testament to the global recognition of yoga's importance. Initiated by India and endorsed by the United Nations in 2014, this day is observed by millions across the world.

Additional Notable Traditions

In addition to the major schools mentioned, several other traditions have contributed to the diversity and depth of yoga practice:

Swara Yoga: An esoteric form of breath control aimed at balancing the body's energy systems, detailed in the *Shiva Swarodaya*. This tradition explores the cyclical nature of breath and its influence on consciousness.

Kriya Yoga: Paramahansa Yogananda, through his work *Autobiography of a Yogi* (1946), introduced the world to **Kriya Yoga**, a meditative practice aimed at accelerating spiritual evolution. His *Self-Realization Fellowship* continues to teach these methods globally. "The true basis of religion is not belief, but intuitive experience. Intuition is the soul's power of knowing God." (Autobiography of a Yogi). Yogananda's teachings emphasize the experiential aspect of yoga, making spirituality accessible to all.

The increasing number of yoga retreats worldwide that focus on Swara Yoga, Kriya Yoga, and other traditions underscores the enduring appeal of diverse yogic practices.

Conclusion

The essence of yoga lies in its transformative power—uniting the individual with the universal, transcending the limitations of the body and mind, and leading to self-realization. As this chapter illustrates, yoga has continuously evolved, adapting to the needs of different eras while preserving its core principles. From the ancient sages of India to modern spiritual teachers, yoga remains a timeless guide on the path to realization.

4

Which Path of Realization is for You?

Choosing the right path of realization is a deeply personal journey. In the vast tradition of yoga, multiple paths have emerged, each offering unique methods for spiritual growth. Understanding these paths can help individuals align with a practice that resonates with their personality, life circumstances, and spiritual goals. In this chapter, we will explore different paths of yoga and provide guidance on how to choose the one that suits you best.

The Four Main Paths of Yoga

There are four primary paths of yoga that are widely recognized:

1. **Karma Yoga** (the path of action)
2. **Bhakti Yoga** (the path of devotion)
3. **Jnana (Gyana) Yoga** (the path of knowledge)
4. **Raja Yoga** (the path of meditation)

Each path offers a different approach to self-realization, catering to various temperaments and inclinations.

1. Karma Yoga: The Path of Selfless Action

Karma Yoga is the path of selfless action, where individuals engage in work without attachment to the results. It is ideal for those who find fulfillment in serving others and wish to spiritualize their daily actions.

The *Bhagavad Gita* extensively discusses Karma Yoga, emphasizing the importance of performing one's duties without attachment. One famous verse encapsulates this philosophy, "You have a right to perform your prescribed duties, but you are not entitled to the fruits of your actions." (Bhagavad Gita, 2.47)

Karma Yoga is best suited for individuals who are active and engaged in the world, whether through work, family, or community service. If you find meaning in helping others and believe in contributing to society, this path may resonate with you.

Lord Hanuman is seen as the ideal Karma Yogi. He performed all his duties with complete devotion to Lord Rama, never seeking rewards for his service. His dedication, strength, and tireless efforts in serving a higher cause are key traits of Karma Yoga.

A British social reformer and a prominent Theosophist, Annie Besant's work in India advocating for social justice, women's rights, and Indian self-rule is an example of Karma Yoga in action. Her devotion to causes larger than herself, without personal gain, aligns with the principles of selfless service.

In the practice of Karma Yoga, the focus is on performing your duties with complete dedication, without attachment to the outcomes. It's about engaging in work with a sense of purpose, knowing that your efforts are an offering to the greater good rather than a means to personal gain. By letting go of the need for recognition or reward, you transform even the simplest tasks into opportunities for spiritual growth. This path teaches that true fulfillment comes not from the results of your actions but from the purity of your intentions and the joy of serving others. Karma Yoga allows you to live fully in the present moment, doing your best in every situation while trusting that the universe will take care of the rest.

2. Bhakti Yoga: The Path of Devotion

Bhakti Yoga is the path of devotion and love for the Divine. It involves surrendering to a higher power and cultivating a deep emotional connection with God through prayer, chanting, and rituals.

The *Narada Bhakti Sutra* and the *Bhagavad Gita* are central texts for Bhakti Yoga.

The Bhagavad Gita emphasizes devotion as a means to attain liberation, "Whoever offers Me with devotion a leaf, a flower, a fruit, or water, I accept that loving offering from the pure of heart." (Bhagavad Gita, 9.26)

Bhakti Yoga appeals to those who are emotionally inclined and naturally devotional. If you are someone who feels a strong connection to a personal deity or find joy in rituals, chanting, and communal worship, this path may be the right choice for you.

Saints like Mirabai and Ramakrishna exemplify Bhakti Yoga. Mirabai's unwavering devotion to Lord Krishna is legendary, while Ramakrishna's intense love for the Divine Mother influenced countless seekers on the path of devotion.

In my experience, to become a true devotee, cultivate unconditional love for your chosen God, deity, angel, or any form of the divine that resonates with you. Follow the path that your divine guides you to follow. When your devotion is genuine and your heart is filled with purity, any mantra you chant, any ritual you perform, or any prayer you offer will carry immense power. True devotion is when merely hearing the name of your chosen divine melts your heart, and singing their praises brings tears to your eyes. In time, this unwavering devotion will lead to divine grace, whether it manifests as a direct experience of your chosen deity or by clearing obstacles from your path. You will be blessed with what is truly meant for you, whether it be material or spiritual fulfillment.

Avoid rushing or hurrying through your prayers or songs. Engage in them with deep love, and let their meaning resonate clearly within you. Don't impose goals like praying or singing or chanting a certain number of times. Reflect on how, in the past, when we received a letter from a beloved, we would naturally read it multiple times, imagining the person and cherishing their words throughout the day. We didn't schedule specific times to remember them or count how often we read the letter—it was a spontaneous expression of our love. Approach your devotion to the divine in the same way, with a pure heart and sincere intention, and not in a superficial manner.

3. Jnana (Gyana) Yoga: The Path of Knowledge

Jnana Yoga is the path of knowledge and wisdom, focusing on self-inquiry and the realization of the true nature of the self (Atman). It is a path of intellectual discrimination and meditation on the formless Absolute (Brahman).

The *Upanishads* and the *Ashtavakra Gita* are foundational texts for Jnana Yoga.

The Mandukya Upanishad famously declares, "The Self is beyond thought, beyond mind, beyond intellect, beyond the senses. It is pure consciousness, the eternal witness." (Mandukya Upanishad, 7)

Jnana Yoga is best suited for those who are intellectually inclined and seek to understand the nature of existence through study and contemplation. If you are drawn to philosophy, logic, and meditation, this path may be the most appropriate for you.

Adi Shankaracharya, the great proponent of Advaita Vedanta, is a shining example of a Jnana Yogi. His teachings on non-duality and his commentaries on the *Upanishads* and *Brahma Sutras* continue to inspire seekers on the path of knowledge.

In my experience, on the path of Jnana Yoga, one of the important aspects, is to become a witness, cultivating the ability to observe your thoughts, emotions, and actions without attachment or judgment. Instead of identifying with the mind and its fluctuations, step back and watch everything unfold as a silent observer. This practice allows you to see that you are not the body, mind, or ego, but the pure consciousness that witnesses it all. By consistently witnessing your inner and outer experiences with detachment, you gradually transcend the illusions of the world (maya) and realize your true Self (Atman). This witnessing awareness is one of the keys to liberation on the path of knowledge. The self is always pure, free from duality, bondage, and liberation, as well as from enlightenment. You simply need to realize this to understand it.

4. Raja Yoga: The Path of Meditation

Raja Yoga, often referred to as the **"royal path,"** is a comprehensive system that emphasizes meditation and mental discipline. It is based on Patanjali's Eightfold Path (Ashtanga Yoga) and aims at achieving self-mastery and union with the Divine through deep meditation.

The Yoga Sutras of Patanjali is the seminal text for Raja Yoga. Patanjali outlines the stages of mental control and meditation that lead to samadhi (liberation).

Raja Yoga is ideal for those who seek to control their minds and are drawn to meditation and introspection. If you are naturally contemplative and enjoy practices like mindfulness, breath control, and meditation, this path may be the best fit for you.

Swami Vivekananda was a key advocate of Raja Yoga. His lectures and writings introduced this path to a global audience, emphasizing the importance of mental discipline and meditation for spiritual growth.

In a practical sense, Raja Yoga encourages you to cultivate mental clarity, focus, and inner calm by establishing a daily routine of meditation and mindfulness. By controlling the mind and its tendencies, you gradually gain mastery over your thoughts, emotions, and behaviours. Raja Yoga is about creating balance and harmony within yourself, enabling you to respond to life's challenges with equanimity and wisdom. Through this practice, you align your mind and body, opening the door to deeper spiritual realization.

How to Choose Your Path

Choosing the right path of spiritual realization is an important and deeply personal journey of self-discovery. The four main paths of yoga—**Jnana Yoga**, **Bhakti Yoga**, **Karma Yoga**, and **Raja Yoga**—offer distinct yet complementary approaches to spiritual growth. Each path aligns with different personality types, temperaments, and life circumstances, allowing individuals to find a practice that resonates with their unique nature. Below are some guiding questions to help you discover which path may be best suited for your journey:

What Are Your Natural Inclinations?

One of the most effective ways to choose a spiritual path is to align it with your natural tendencies and personality traits. Understanding your core inclinations can provide insight into which path will feel most authentic and sustainable for you.

- **Are you intellectually curious and love to study philosophy?**

If you are driven by a desire to understand the nature of reality, the universe, and the self, then **Jnana Yoga** (the path of wisdom) may appeal to you. This path focuses on self-inquiry, philosophical study, and the pursuit of knowledge to achieve spiritual liberation.

- **Are you emotionally inclined and drawn to devotion?**

If your heart resonates with love, surrender, and devotion, then **Bhakti Yoga** (the path of devotion) might be your ideal path. Through worship, prayer, and acts of devotion, Bhakti Yoga seeks union with the Divine by channelling emotions into love for a higher power.

- **Are you action-oriented and motivated by service?**

If you feel called to actively contribute to the world, serve others, and engage in selfless acts, then **Karma Yoga** (the path of action) may resonate with you. Karma Yoga emphasizes service without attachment to results, transforming work into a form of spiritual practice.

- **Are you introspective and drawn to meditation?**

If you enjoy mindfulness, self-reflection, and stillness, **Raja Yoga** (the path of meditation) could be the best fit for you. Raja Yoga focuses on mental discipline, meditation, and the control of the mind to reach higher states of consciousness and inner peace.

What Is Your Life Situation?

Your current life circumstances and responsibilities can also help guide your choice of practice. While spiritual growth is achievable through any path, some may be more practical given your lifestyle.

- **Are you deeply involved in work or family?**

If your daily life is filled with responsibilities at work or home, **Karma Yoga** may be more accessible. This path allows you to transform your day-to-day activities into a spiritual practice by focusing on selfless service and mindfulness in action.

- **Do you have time for regular meditation or introspection?**

If you have more time and space in your life for regular spiritual practices like meditation, **Raja Yoga** may be more suitable. This path requires a disciplined approach to meditation and mental training to cultivate inner peace and spiritual awakening.

What Are Your Spiritual Goals?

Clarity about your spiritual aspirations is key to choosing a path that aligns with your goals. Reflect on what you hope to achieve through your spiritual practice.

- **Do you seek to understand the nature of reality and the self?**

If your primary goal is intellectual clarity and self-realization, **Jnana Yoga** may be the most appropriate path. This path emphasizes the direct experience of truth through knowledge and insight into the nature of existence.

- **Do you seek union with the Divine?**

If your goal is to feel connected to a higher power or experience divine love, then **Bhakti Yoga** could be the answer. This path offers a deep emotional connection to the Divine through prayer, chanting, and devotion.

The Modern Spiritual Seeker

In today's world, spiritual seekers are often exploring their paths outside of traditional religious frameworks. A 2016 survey conducted by the *Pew Research Center* revealed that **37% of Americans consider themselves spiritual but not religious**. This indicates a growing interest in personal spiritual practices like yoga, meditation, and mindfulness, as individuals search for meaning and fulfillment outside conventional religious settings. By understanding which path of yoga aligns with your natural inclinations, life situation, and spiritual goals, you can embark on a practice that brings greater fulfillment, clarity, and connection.

Ultimately, the choice of path is a dynamic process that evolves with your personal growth. You may find yourself blending elements from multiple paths as your journey progresses, creating a unique, holistic approach to your spiritual practice.

Combining Paths: A Holistic Approach

While the four paths of yoga—Karma Yoga, Bhakti Yoga, Jnana Yoga, and Raja Yoga—are often presented as distinct, they are not mutually exclusive. In fact, many spiritual traditions encourage a balanced approach that integrates elements of all four, acknowledging that different individuals may resonate with various paths at different stages of their spiritual journey. By combining these paths, practitioners can achieve a more comprehensive and harmonious spiritual evolution.

A prime example of this integrative approach is found in Sri Aurobindo's **Integral Yoga**, which advocates for the synthesis of all four paths. Rather than isolating each path, Integral Yoga seeks to harmonize them, creating a dynamic and holistic framework for spiritual growth. Sri Aurobindo's teachings emphasize that no single path alone can lead to the complete transformation of the individual. Instead, true transformation occurs when the active engagement of **Karma Yoga**, the devotion and surrender of **Bhakti Yoga**, the wisdom of **Jnana Yoga**, and the mental discipline of **Raja Yoga** work in concert to elevate the practitioner's entire being.

Sri Aurobindo's famous declaration, **"All life is yoga,"** underscores his expansive view of spirituality. For him, yoga was not confined to practices on the mat or in meditation but extended to every moment and action in life. Every thought, emotion, and deed becomes an opportunity for inner growth, a way to align with the Divine and integrate higher consciousness into daily existence.

This approach challenges the idea of compartmentalizing spiritual life from everyday responsibilities. Instead, it invites us to see each action—whether in the workplace, at home, or in relationships—as part of our spiritual practice. The synthesis of the four paths, in this sense, becomes a blueprint for living a life where the boundaries between spiritual practice and worldly activity dissolve. Each moment becomes infused with purpose, dedication, and divine presence, leading to not just personal transformation, but the potential upliftment of humanity as a whole.

Thus, the holistic approach not only respects the uniqueness of each path but also highlights the profound synergy that arises when they are practiced together. When we combine action, devotion, knowledge, and meditation, we become more aligned with the divine flow of life, engaging with the world from a place of greater balance and spiritual awareness.

Conclusion

The path to realization is unique for every individual. Whether you are drawn to the intellectual rigor of Jnana Yoga, the devotional love of Bhakti Yoga, the selfless service of Karma Yoga, or the meditative discipline of Raja Yoga, the key is to follow your heart and remain dedicated to your practice. Remember, the ultimate goal of all these paths is the same: the realization of your true self.

5

The Spectrum of Seekers: Navigating Diverse Spiritual Paths

The spiritual path is a deeply personal and varied experience. Spiritual traditions recognize that different individuals approach spirituality in different ways, depending on their temperament, disposition, and goals. The ancient texts, such as the *Yoga Vasistha* and the *Bhagavad Gita*, have categorized seekers to help them understand their spiritual journey better.

The Mundaka Upanishad beautifully captures the essence of this diversity, "The knower of Brahman attains the Supreme. In the path to the Supreme, some are far away, some are on the way, and some are on the threshold of realization."

To fully appreciate the variety of spiritual seekers, let's first explore some foundational categories of seekers based on their readiness and motivation for spiritual growth.

Foundational Categories of Spiritual Seekers

Spiritual traditions like Vedanta and Yoga further categorize seekers based on their spiritual maturity and clarity of purpose. Two such important categories are:

1. **Mudha** (The Deluded or Ignorant Seeker)
2. **Mumukshu** (The One Desirous of Liberation)

1. The Mudha: The Ignorant One

The **Mudha** represents the state of deep spiritual ignorance, where an individual is entirely bound by the illusions of the material world. This person is so engrossed in the pursuit of sensory pleasures, desires, and attachments that they remain unaware of their true essence— the soul, the Atman. Their life is dictated by the fluctuations of the external world, leading to suffering and dissatisfaction.

The term *Mudha* is often used in sacred spiritual texts to describe someone who is blinded by *Maya* (illusion). Maya represents the veil of ignorance that covers reality, making the transient seem permanent and the unreal appear real. The *Mudha* is far from the path of enlightenment, stuck in the cycle of birth and death, or *Samsara*, and fails to recognize the fleeting nature of material pursuits.

The Tale of Nachiketa's Father

A poignant illustration of a *Mudha* can be found in the **Katha Upanishad**, where the story of Nachiketa and his father, Vajashrava, serves as a symbolic narrative. Vajashrava was a man deeply rooted in materialistic rituals, wealth, and external achievements, believing that his actions would secure divine rewards. He performed a great ritual in which he gave away cattle, but they were old and of no use, highlighting his superficial understanding of spiritual generosity.

Nachiketa, his son, saw through this facade and questioned his father's intentions, realizing that his father was trapped in the illusion of materialism. Vajashrava, like a typical *Mudha*, was too attached to appearances and did not see the futility of his actions. This story represents the state of spiritual ignorance where one is preoccupied with outer achievements and fails to comprehend the deeper truths of existence.

It was only through Nachiketa's bold questioning and eventual encounter with **Yama**, the Lord of Death, that the contrast between ignorance and true wisdom became evident. Yama imparted the teachings of immortality and the nature of the soul, guiding Nachiketa toward higher knowledge and spiritual liberation. Nachiketa's journey stands as a reminder that even in a world dominated by *Mudha* consciousness, one can transcend ignorance through wisdom, discernment, and the pursuit of truth.

The Transformation of Ajamil

Ajamil's story, from the *Bhagavata Purana*, is a timeless example of how even the most wayward soul can find redemption through grace. Born into a virtuous family, Ajamil was once a devout and righteous man, well-versed in the sacred scriptures. However, as he grew older, his path took a dark turn. He became entangled in a life of indulgence, drawn into the snares of sensual pleasures, and succumbed to immoral acts. His once-pure heart became clouded with ignorance, and he strayed far from the righteous path.

For many years, Ajamil lived a life steeped in desire and sinful behaviour, oblivious to the spiritual truth he once knew. He fathered children through questionable relationships, and his mind remained absorbed in worldly pleasures. He was what the scriptures refer to as a *Mudha*—a deluded soul, lost in ignorance.

However, fate intervened in a most unexpected way. In his final moments, as death approached and his sinful deeds threatened to drag him into the depths of suffering, Ajamil experienced a moment of divine grace. Lying on his deathbed, surrounded by fear of the unknown, he called out to his youngest son, Narayana, a name of the Divine. Though he was merely thinking of his child, the sacred name had a transformative power.

Hearing the holy name "Narayana," celestial beings—the Vishnudutas—appeared before him, countering the messengers of Yama, the god of death, who had come to claim his soul. The Vishnudutas argued that since Ajamil had uttered the name of Narayana, he was now under divine protection, despite his past misdeeds.

In that moment, Ajamil's consciousness awakened. He realized the enormity of his wasted life and the divine grace that had saved him. The mere utterance of the Lord's name, even unintentionally, had purified him. Filled with repentance and newfound understanding, Ajamil dedicated the remainder of his life to sincere spiritual practice, finally attaining liberation.

Ajamil's story is a powerful reminder that no matter how lost we may seem, the door to spiritual awakening is never fully closed. Even in the darkest moments, the light of divine grace can illuminate the path back to truth.

"Ignorance is the greatest obstacle to spiritual growth. The ignorant one wanders in the dark, unaware of the light that surrounds them." (Yoga Vasistha)

The Parable of the Deer

A famous story in Hindu tradition compares the *Mudha* to a deer that is captivated by the scent of musk. Unaware that the musk is coming from within itself, the deer runs around endlessly searching for the source, much like the deluded seeker who looks for happiness outside rather than within.

"The ignorant pursue the senses like a deer chasing after a mirage in the desert." (Katha Upanishad)

This illustrates how the *Mudha* is lost in the illusions of the world, unaware of their inner divinity.

The Wheel of Samsara and the Mudha's Ignorance

The *Katha Upanishad* states: "Caught in the wheel of samsara, the Mudha knows not the truth, but only the fleeting pleasures of the world." This line captures the essence of the Mudha's existence. The Mudha is trapped in the endless cycle of Samsara, which is marked by birth, death, and rebirth, all driven by karma. Unaware of the true self, they chase impermanent pleasures and worldly gains, mistaking them for fulfillment. This relentless chase keeps them bound to the material plane, further deepening their ignorance and delusion.

Only by breaking free from this cycle, which requires self-realization and the cultivation of wisdom, can one move from the state of a *Mudha* to a seeker of truth. This liberation is not achieved through external rituals or material wealth but through inner transformation and a deep understanding of one's true nature as the eternal, unchanging soul.

Thus, the *Mudha* is a symbol of the unawakened state of consciousness, but their story also serves as a reminder that there is always the possibility for awakening and liberation.

A study by the *World Happiness Report* in 2020 found that individuals who prioritize material gains over inner well-being report lower life satisfaction, highlighting the challenge faced by *Mudhas* in finding lasting happiness.

A 2021 survey by *Gallup* found that 76% of people in developed countries primarily seek happiness through material success, suggesting that the majority of the population still operates from a *Mudha* state, unaware of deeper spiritual possibilities.

2. The Mumukshu: The Seeker of Liberation

The **Mumukshu** is a spiritual aspirant who has come to a profound realization: the material world and its fleeting pleasures are not the ultimate aim of life. Unlike the *Mudha*, who remains mired in ignorance, the *Mumukshu* recognizes that the pursuit of sensory enjoyment and worldly attachments leads only to temporary satisfaction, not lasting peace. This individual feels a deep, burning desire for **Moksha** (liberation)—freedom from the cycle of birth, death, and rebirth—and actively seeks a path toward self-realization and enlightenment.

At this stage, the Mumukshu is at a pivotal point in their spiritual journey. No longer distracted by external pleasures, they turn their attention inward, cultivating wisdom, detachment, and an intense yearning for the ultimate truth. The Mumukshu moves from the fog of ignorance toward the light of knowledge, understanding that liberation is the highest goal of life.

The Transformation of King Janaka

The story of **King Janaka** illustrates the transformative journey of a Mumukshu. Although Janaka was a king, deeply involved in ruling his kingdom and managing worldly affairs, he realized the impermanence and insignificance of material wealth and power. This insight sparked a deep yearning for liberation within him. Despite his royal duties, Janaka was drawn to the teachings of **Sage Ashtavakra**, a wise master who guided him toward self-realization.

King Janaka achieved enlightenment while continuing to fulfill his responsibilities as a ruler. His state of inner detachment allowed him to remain unaffected by the turbulence of the external world, making him an exemplary figure of one who pursues liberation without renouncing their worldly duties.

As the **Ashtavakra Gita** says: "The desire for liberation burns like a fire in the heart of the Mumukshu, leading them to the feet of the Guru and the path of wisdom." Janaka's quest shows that true freedom lies in mastering the mind and detaching oneself from desires, even while living within society.

Nachiketa's Quest for Liberation

Another archetypal Mumukshu is **Nachiketa** from the **Katha Upanishad**. As a young boy, Nachiketa was disillusioned with the hollow materialism of his father, who was obsessed with superficial rituals. Nachiketa's desire to understand the deeper truths of existence led him to seek out **Yama**, the god of death, and question him about the mysteries of the soul and the nature of liberation.

Nachiketa's relentless pursuit of knowledge and his intense desire to break free from the cycle of birth and death represent the quintessential qualities of a Mumukshu. His courage to question death itself and his unwavering focus on spiritual wisdom make him a prime example of an aspirant seeking liberation.

Adi Shankaracharya highlights this in the **Vivekachudamani**: "He alone who seeks liberation with an intense thirst can cross this ocean of worldly existence." Nachiketa's journey embodies this principle, where the intensity of his desire for liberation propelled him beyond the ordinary concerns of life.

Sage Vasistha's Teachings to Lord Rama

In the **Yoga Vasistha**, **Sage Vasistha** imparts teachings to **Lord Rama** that emphasize the qualities of a Mumukshu. Though born a prince and heir to a powerful kingdom, Rama experiences deep disillusionment with the transient nature of worldly life. He questions the purpose of existence and the means to attain freedom from the suffering inherent in the material world.

Sage Vasistha, recognizing Rama's intense desire for liberation, advises him that the path of a Mumukshu requires one to abandon all desires for material things and strive solely for **Self-realization**. This dispassion toward the world is a hallmark of the Mumukshu's mindset, for they have recognized that nothing in the material world can offer lasting peace.

As the **Yoga Vasistha** states: "He who desires liberation must abandon all desires for worldly things and constantly strive for Self-realization." This teaching encapsulates the core essence of the Mumukshu's quest: the renunciation of worldly attachments and the single-pointed focus on attaining the highest truth.

Modern Reflections on the Mumukshu's Journey

Recent studies and spiritual research also shed light on the path of the Mumukshu. According to a 2018 study by the *Spiritual Science Research Foundation*, around 12% of practitioners engaged in advanced spiritual practices identify themselves as Mumukshus. These individuals are driven not by material gain or social recognition but by an intense desire for liberation and spiritual growth. Their lives are oriented around seeking wisdom, practicing meditation, and cultivating detachment from worldly concerns.

Furthermore, the 2019 *World Happiness Report* reveals that individuals who actively engage in spiritual practices with the intent of self-discovery report significantly higher levels of life satisfaction. This suggests that the inner fulfillment sought by the Mumukshu can lead to a more meaningful and contented existence. The desire for liberation aligns with the natural human quest for lasting happiness, which is not found in the external world but through the realization of one's true nature.

Classifications from the Bhagavad Gita

The spiritual path is as unique as the individuals who walk it. Different people are drawn to various spiritual practices based on their temperament, goals, and innate tendencies. In the Bhagavad Gita, Lord Krishna states:

"Four kinds of virtuous people worship me: the distressed, the seeker of knowledge, the seeker of wealth, and the wise." (Bhagavad Gita, 7.16)

This verse highlights that people approach spirituality for different reasons—some are driven by personal suffering, some seek knowledge, some desire material gains, and others pursue wisdom for its own sake. These different motivations shape the path each individual follows.

The Four Types of Spiritual Seekers

Spiritual traditions across the world often classify individuals on their spiritual journeys according to their dispositions and goals. The four broad types are:

1. **The Arta** (The Distressed Seeker)
2. **The Jijnasu (Jigyasu)** (The Seeker of Knowledge)
3. **The Artharthi** (The Seeker of Wealth)
4. **The Jnani (Gyani)** (The Wise Seeker)

Each of these types reflects different stages of spiritual maturity and understanding.

1. The Arta: The Distressed Seeker

The *Arta* is someone who turns to spirituality out of suffering or distress. Life's challenges—such as personal loss, illness, or existential crises—push these individuals to seek solace and refuge in spirituality. Historically, many saints and sages began their spiritual journeys as distressed seekers. For example, the transformation of Valmiki from a dacoit to a sage is a tale of redemption through spiritual guidance.

The Life of Saint Valmiki

Valmiki, one of the greatest sages in Indian tradition and the revered author of the *Ramayana*, was not always the enlightened soul he is remembered as today. His early life was a far cry from the saintly figure we know. Born as Ratnakara, Valmiki started his life as a common man, but circumstances led him down a dark path. He became a thief, living off the spoils of travellers he would rob in the forests. His moral compass was skewed, and he justified his actions by believing that the survival of his family depended on them.

One fateful day, while lying in wait for his next victim, he encountered the great sage, Narada. Narada, seeing beyond the surface of Ratnakara's sinful life, engaged him in a conversation that would forever change his destiny. When Ratnakara tried to rob him, Narada calmly asked him why he lived this life of crime. Ratnakara explained that he did it to support his family. Narada then posed a simple but profound question: "Will your family share the consequences of your sins as willingly as they share the fruits of your labour?"

This question struck Ratnakara deeply, unsettling his beliefs. Determined to find the truth, he tied Narada to a tree and hurried back to his family to ask if they would share the burden of his sins. To his shock, they refused. They loved him for the provisions he brought, but the weight of his wrongdoings was his alone to bear.

Disillusioned, Ratnakara returned to Narada, seeking guidance. Narada, seeing the remorse and potential in him, instructed him to meditate on the name of *Rama*, the divine Lord. Ratnakara took to this practice with intense dedication, sitting motionless in deep meditation for years. So deep was his penance that an anthill grew around his body, giving him the name "Valmiki," meaning "one born of an anthill."

Through his unwavering devotion and meditation, Valmiki achieved spiritual enlightenment. No longer a thief, he transformed into a sage of immense wisdom and compassion. His spiritual awakening culminated in the divine inspiration to compose the *Ramayana*, the epic story of Lord Rama, which has since become one of the most revered and cherished scriptures in Hindu tradition.

The transformation of Valmiki is a powerful testament to the fact that no matter how far one has strayed from the path of righteousness, the light of wisdom and divine grace can lead to redemption and greatness.

"Desperation makes a person seek refuge in the divine, and in that seeking, they often find more than just relief—they find transformation." (Upanishads)

This illustrates the power of spirituality to turn suffering into a catalyst for spiritual growth.

A 2022 study by the *American Psychological Association* found that 58% of individuals who sought spiritual practices in times of distress reported significant improvements in mental well-being, showcasing the impact of spirituality on coping with challenges.

2. The Jijnasu: The Seeker of Knowledge

The *Jijnasu* is driven by a thirst for knowledge and understanding. This seeker is intellectually curious and seeks answers to profound existential questions like "Who am I?" and "What is the nature of reality?" Many philosophers and scientists, such as Albert Einstein and Swami Vivekananda, fall into this category.

Swami Vivekananda's Quest for Truth

Swami Vivekananda was a *Jijnasu* who sought to understand the mysteries of life and the nature of existence. His quest led him to Ramakrishna Paramahamsa, under whom he studied and realized the ultimate truth. Vivekananda's journey was fueled by a relentless pursuit of knowledge, which eventually made him a beacon of wisdom for others.

"Arise, awake, and stop not until the goal is reached." (Swami Vivekananda)

This quote encapsulates the relentless pursuit of knowledge that defines the *Jijnasu.*

According to a study by the *Pew Research Center* in 2021, 35% of people who consider themselves spiritual but not religious report that their primary motivation for spiritual practice is the pursuit of knowledge and self-discovery.

3. The Artharthi: The Seeker of Wealth

The *Artharthi* is motivated by material desires, whether they seek wealth, success, or personal fulfillment. While this may appear to be a worldly pursuit, many spiritual traditions acknowledge that seeking material benefits can be an entry point into deeper spiritual practice. The *Artharthi* often starts with external goals but may evolve towards a more profound understanding of life.

Kubera, the Lord of Wealth

In Hindu mythology, Kubera stands as the divine embodiment of wealth and prosperity, revered as the guardian of treasures and the protector of the north. Unlike many deities associated with wealth, Kubera's story is unique, as it illustrates the balance between material success and spiritual wisdom. His life symbolizes the *Artharthi*—a seeker of wealth—who has not only achieved material abundance but also transcended it to attain higher spiritual growth.

Kubera was born as the son of Sage Vishrava, making him the half-brother of Ravana, the demon king of Lanka. However, while Ravana chose the path of power and ego, Kubera was drawn toward a life of righteousness and devotion. He performed severe penance to please Lord Brahma, seeking blessings that would help him achieve his rightful place in the cosmic order. Pleased with Kubera's devotion and steadfastness, Brahma granted him the position of the Lord of Wealth, entrusting him with the divine task of distributing wealth and guarding the treasures of the world.

Kubera was given the city of Alakapuri, nestled in the Himalayas, as his divine abode, and he was provided with the *Pushpaka Vimana*, a flying chariot of unparalleled beauty. His wealth and prosperity were unmatched, but unlike many who are consumed by greed and attachment, Kubera used his fortune to uplift others. His story demonstrates that material wealth, when pursued with the right intention and used for the welfare of others, becomes a tool for spiritual elevation rather than bondage.

Kubera's role in the cosmic order goes beyond the mere accumulation of wealth. He symbolizes the understanding that prosperity, when aligned with righteousness (dharma), leads not to attachment, but to a higher state of being. His association with the divine, especially his friendship with Lord Shiva, further underscores his spiritual wisdom. Kubera is often depicted as a humble devotee of Shiva, reinforcing the idea that wealth and spirituality are not mutually exclusive.

Through Kubera's example, we learn that material success can coexist with spiritual growth when it is guided by higher principles. His life teaches that wealth, when sought with pure intentions and used responsibly, becomes a pathway to both worldly success and spiritual fulfillment, offering a balanced approach to living.

"Wealth is not evil, but the attachment to it can bind the soul." (Mahabharata)

This reflects the balance between material pursuits and spiritual understanding.

A 2020 report from the *University of Chicago* found that 45% of individuals who engage in spiritual practices initially do so to improve their financial or personal situations, with many later transitioning to a deeper spiritual inquiry.

4. The Jnani: The Wise Seeker

The *Jnani* is the highest type of seeker, who pursues spirituality for the sake of wisdom and liberation (moksha). This individual has transcended worldly desires and suffering, focusing instead on the realization of the Self. *Jnani* seekers are often spiritual teachers themselves, sharing their wisdom with others.

Ramana Maharshi

Ramana Maharshi is a quintessential *Jnani* who, through the practice of *Atma Vichara* (self-inquiry), realized the truth of non-duality and became a beacon of wisdom for thousands of seekers. His teachings focused on the direct realization of the Self, bypassing ritualistic or external practices.

"The Self is not somewhere far away to be reached. You are always That." (Ramana Maharshi)

This succinctly captures the essence of *Jnana Yoga*—the path of wisdom.

A survey conducted by the *Ramana Maharshi Foundation* in 2019 found that 70% of participants who studied the teachings of *Jnana Yoga* reported a significant reduction in stress and anxiety, attributing it to the deeper understanding of the Self and the nature of reality.

Other Classifications of Spiritual Seekers

While the Bhagavad Gita provides a broad categorization, spiritual traditions often have more nuanced classifications based on individual temperaments and inclinations. Below are some additional ways of categorizing spiritual seekers:

Bhakti-Oriented Seekers (Devotional Path): These seekers are driven by love and devotion to a personal deity or divine principle. The teachings of saints like Mirabai and Sri Chaitanya Mahaprabhu inspire this category. Their spiritual journey is fueled by emotion, devotion, and surrender.

Karma-Oriented Seekers (Action-Oriented Path): These individuals seek spiritual growth through selfless action and service to others.

Tantric Seekers: Tantric seekers focus on harnessing and transcending energies within the body to achieve spiritual enlightenment. The left-hand and right-hand paths of Tantra offer two distinct approaches, often misunderstood but deeply transformative.

Vairagya-Oriented Seekers (Renunciants): These seekers, like the ancient sannyasis, renounce the material world in pursuit of liberation. They are driven by the desire to transcend worldly attachments and experience the ultimate truth.

The Buddha's Middle Path

The life of the Buddha, Siddhartha Gautama, serves as a profound illustration of the value of balance and moderation. Born into royalty, he experienced the comforts and luxuries of a prince, living in indulgence without understanding the suffering beyond palace walls. Yet, in his quest for spiritual awakening, he later turned to the extreme opposite—adopting the life of a wandering ascetic, denying himself basic necessities and practicing severe self-discipline. However, neither extreme—sensual indulgence nor harsh asceticism—brought him closer to the truth.

It was through these contrasting experiences that Siddhartha realized the futility of both extremes. This realization led him to discover the **Middle Path**—a way of living that avoids both excessive self-indulgence and extreme self-denial. This path, which balances the body and mind, became the foundation of his teachings and the route to enlightenment. It emphasizes moderation, wisdom, and mindfulness, guiding individuals to a life of harmony and inner peace.

The Middle Path is not just a practice of balance in material life, but a profound spiritual principle. It underscores the importance of avoiding rigid attachments to any single way of living, thought, or belief. Instead, it encourages adaptability, openness, and a thoughtful approach to life's challenges. Siddhartha's journey through indulgence and austerity illustrates that extremes often limit our growth, while balance enables the discovery of deeper truths.

In modern times, this notion of balance is echoed in the evolving spiritual goals of practitioners across various traditions. A 2018 study by the *World Values Survey* revealed that 67% of spiritual practitioners reported a significant evolution in their spiritual aspirations. Initially driven by personal desires—such as seeking success, happiness, or health—many of these individuals shifted toward broader existential inquiries, like the meaning of life, the nature of existence, and interconnectedness. This shift mirrors the Buddha's own journey, demonstrating the fluid and dynamic nature of spiritual evolution. Just as Siddhartha evolved from a seeker of worldly pleasures to a spiritual guide, modern practitioners find that their spiritual goals change as they grow and deepen their understanding of themselves and the universe.

The Middle Path offers a timeless message: spiritual growth is not a rigid, one-size-fits-all approach. It is a journey that requires balance, reflection, and, above all, a deep understanding of one's own nature.

Conclusion: Embracing the Diversity of Spiritual Seekers

The spiritual journey is deeply personal, and there is no one-size-fits-all approach. Whether one begins their path through distress, a desire for knowledge, material pursuits, or an innate wisdom, every seeker is valuable in the tapestry of spiritual evolution. The diversity of spiritual seekers enriches the collective experience, reminding us that the path to truth is as varied as the seekers who walk it.

As Swami Sivananda beautifully puts it, "There are many ways to the peak of the mountain, but the view from the summit is the same."

The journey to self-realization may take different forms, but the destination remains universal—union with the Divine.

6

Why Yoga?

In today's fast-paced world, where stress and distractions are rampant, many seek solace in various practices that promise peace and well-being. Yoga, a time-tested tradition, is more than a practice; it is a way of life that touches every aspect of our existence. Yet, in the modern world, yoga is often misunderstood as merely a physical exercise or a means to relaxation. To truly understand yoga, we must delve deeper into its purpose, which is to transcend the illusions of life (Maya) and realize the ultimate truth. This chapter explores the profound reasons for practicing yoga and how it addresses the most fundamental aspects of human life: Dharma, Artha, Kama, and Moksha.

Understanding Maya: The Illusion of the World

In Vedantic philosophy, Maya refers to the cosmic illusion that distorts our perception of reality. It is the force that obscures our vision of the eternal truth and compels us to see the material, transient world as the ultimate reality. Due to Maya, we become attached to the physical world, mistaking it for something permanent and real. This illusion keeps us bound to the endless cycle of birth, death, and rebirth (Samsara), trapping us in a web of desires, fears, and suffering.

Maya operates at a level so subtle that it clouds the mind and senses, preventing individuals from recognizing their true essence. The Upanishads, the ancient wisdom texts of India, describe Maya as the force that creates duality—causing us to perceive separation where there is none. This duality blinds us to the unity of all existence and hinders our understanding of Brahman (the ultimate, unchanging reality). As long as we remain deluded by Maya, we see ourselves as distinct beings, separate from others and the world, when in fact, we are one with Brahman.

Consider the example of a rope mistaken for a snake in dim light. This is a common analogy used in Vedanta to illustrate Maya. Just as we may see a snake where there is only a rope, we perceive the world through distorted senses, believing in the reality of things that are not truly real. The snake causes fear, anxiety, and confusion, just as Maya creates suffering by making us believe in a reality that is, in essence, illusory.

The Bhagavad Gita offers another example in the form of Arjuna's internal struggle on the battlefield. Arjuna is overwhelmed with grief and confusion about fighting in the war because he sees only the immediate reality—the possibility of killing his loved ones. However, Krishna, representing divine wisdom, reminds him that the soul is eternal and not bound by the physical body. Arjuna's perception of death and loss is distorted by Maya, which clouds his understanding of the eternal truth of the soul (Atman).

The Ashtavakra Gita echoes this teaching when it states: "You are not the body nor the mind. You are the pure consciousness, the witness of all existence" (Ashtavakra Gita 1.3). This verse emphasizes that our true nature is not tied to the physical or mental dimensions but exists as the pure, untainted consciousness that observes the world without attachment. When we identify ourselves with our body and mind, we become trapped in the illusion of Maya, forgetting our true nature as consciousness.

"Look at friends, land, money, wife and other properties as a dream in Maya to be destroyed in three to five days" (Ashtavakra Gita 10.2). Ashtavakra's teaching here is a call for **detachment**. Life feels so real—our bonds with loved ones, the comforts of home, the security of wealth—yet beneath it all, there's a quiet, unsettling truth. Like a dream, everything we cherish in this world is fleeting. One moment, we're surrounded by friends, family, and possessions that seem to define us, and the next, it can all vanish, as if erased by time's swift hand. In just days, we may face the loss of what we thought was permanent. This realization stirs the heart, bringing both sorrow and clarity. It's as if the verse from the Ashtavakra Gita is a gentle, bittersweet reminder: life is fragile, and clinging to its illusions brings suffering. Yet, in this fragility lies the key to freedom—when we see through the mirage, we awaken to a peace beyond the fleeting moments, one rooted in the eternal. Letting go is hard, but in that release, there's a quiet, profound liberation.

The **Mundaka Upanishad** offers a powerful metaphor to describe the illusory nature of the universe: "As the web issues out of the spider and is withdrawn, as herbs and trees spring from the earth, as the hair grows from the body, so springs the universe from the Imperishable" (Mundaka Upanishad 1.1.7). Just as the spider creates its web and can retract it, the universe arises from the eternal reality of Brahman and will eventually return to it. The material world, although it appears real, is as ephemeral as the web spun by the spider. It is only through wisdom and spiritual practice that we can see beyond this illusion.

Another practical example is the pursuit of wealth and material possessions. Many people spend their lives chasing money, power, or status, believing these things will bring lasting happiness. However, when these goals are achieved, the satisfaction is often temporary, and new desires quickly take their place. This endless cycle of desire and dissatisfaction is a clear manifestation of Maya. It distracts us from the deeper reality that true happiness comes from within, from recognizing our oneness with the eternal.

The **illusion of time** is another aspect of Maya. We often become anxious about the past or fearful of the future, failing to live in the present moment. Yet time itself, as experienced by the mind, is an illusion. The Bhagavad Gita (2.16) reminds us, "That which is real never ceases to be; that which is unreal never comes into existence." Our worries about time stem from Maya, which creates the illusion that we are bound by the clock, when in fact, our true self is timeless.

Maya's influence is pervasive, yet it can be transcended through self-awareness and spiritual growth. By understanding and recognizing the limitations of the physical world, we can begin to see beyond the illusion, unveiling the eternal truth hidden behind the veil of Maya.

Yoga: A Path to Transcend Maya

Yoga offers a profound means of breaking through the veil of Maya. By practicing self-discipline, meditation, and self-inquiry, we can begin to pierce the illusion that ties us to the body and mind. Through *yoga*, we gradually detach from the impermanent aspects of life and experience our true, unchanging nature.

The *Bhagavad Gita* teaches that the essence of yoga is *equanimity*—a state of balance where we are no longer swayed by the ups and downs of the material world. By cultivating this inner balance, we can rise above

Maya and its delusions. The goal of yoga is not simply physical flexibility or strength but the liberation of the soul from the limitations of worldly existence. When we fully realize that we are not our body or our mind, but the pure consciousness that underlies all existence, we experience true freedom, known as *moksha* or *nirvana*.

The life of the Buddha offers a powerful example of breaking free from the constraints of Maya. Born into a royal family, Siddhartha Gautama was shielded from the harsh realities of life. However, his encounters with suffering, sickness, and death led him to renounce his princely comforts and embark on a quest for truth. Through deep meditation and self-inquiry, the Buddha realized the impermanence of the material world and attained Nirvana, or liberation from the cycle of Samsara. The Buddha's enlightenment represents the ultimate triumph over Maya—the realization that the world of appearances is fleeting, and true freedom comes from recognizing the imperishable nature of reality.

Maya, though it can seem all-encompassing, is not invincible. The teachings of Vedanta, along with the spiritual disciplines of yoga and meditation, provide us with the tools to see through the illusions that bind us. Whether through the teachings of the Upanishads, the example of enlightened masters, or our own practice of self-awareness, we are given the opportunity to transcend Maya and awaken to the truth of our eternal, boundless nature. By realizing that we are the pure witness, untouched by the fluctuations of the world, we can find lasting peace and liberation.

The Four Purusharthas: The Goals of Human Life

According to Hindu philosophy, life is guided by four primary goals, known as the Purusharthas:

1. **Dharma** (righteousness)
2. **Artha** (prosperity)
3. **Kama** (desire)
4. **Moksha** (liberation)

Yoga plays a crucial role in harmonizing these goals and leading one toward spiritual fulfillment.

1. Dharma: The Path of Righteousness

Dharma is often regarded as one of the most essential principles guiding human life, representing not just individual responsibility but a universal cosmic law that sustains order and harmony in the world. Derived from the Sanskrit root "dhr," meaning "to hold" or "to sustain," Dharma is the force that upholds the moral fabric of society and the natural world.

At its core, Dharma refers to the duties and responsibilities specific to one's role in life—whether as a parent, teacher, leader, or student—based on one's age, nature (Svabhava), and circumstances. However, Dharma goes beyond mere duty; it is about living in accordance with truth, virtue, and the eternal principles that govern existence.

In the **Bhagavad Gita**, Dharma is emphasized as the path toward selfless service and inner balance. Lord Krishna explains to Arjuna that the greatest virtue lies in following one's **Swadharma** (individual Dharma) even if imperfectly:

"Better to do one's own Dharma imperfectly than to do another's Dharma perfectly." (Bhagavad Gita 3.35)

This idea suggests that staying true to one's nature and responsibilities—no matter how challenging—is preferable to excelling in something that is not aligned with one's inner calling. Following Dharma is not just about action, but about authenticity and integrity. It emphasizes inner alignment with one's purpose, even in the face of external pressures or comparisons.

A famous teaching from the **Mahabharata** further encapsulates the protective and reciprocal nature of Dharma:

"Dharma protects those who protect it."

This underscores the understanding that when individuals live righteously, according to their Dharma, they contribute to the greater order of the universe, and in return, they are safeguarded by the very principles they uphold. Dharma, thus, serves as a shield, offering both inner peace and societal harmony.

In the context of **Yoga**, Dharma becomes a lived practice, not just an abstract idea. Yoga, particularly in its spiritual dimensions, fosters mindfulness, self-awareness, and discipline, helping individuals recognize and fulfill their Dharma. One of the key branches of Yoga, **Karma Yoga**, teaches us the art of **selfless action**—to perform our duties with full commitment but without attachment to the fruits of our labour. In Karma Yoga, actions are undertaken in the spirit of service and surrender to the Divine, fostering inner harmony and reducing ego-driven desires.

Through Yogic practices, such as **meditation** and **mindful living**, one becomes attuned to the subtleties of Dharma. Yoga enables us to strip away distractions, delusions, and ego-based motives, allowing us to connect with our true purpose. By harmonizing the mind and body, Yoga aligns us with the rhythm of Dharma, making it easier to navigate life's challenges with grace and balance.

Thus, living in accordance with Dharma through the practice of Yoga leads to an existence rooted in **balance, compassion, and authenticity**. Whether it is through daily duties or spiritual pursuits, when our actions are aligned with cosmic law, we contribute to both our personal growth and the collective well-being of the world.

2. Artha: The Pursuit of Prosperity

Artha refers to the pursuit of material wealth, security, and overall well-being. While often associated with financial prosperity, Artha encompasses all resources necessary to sustain life, from food and shelter to education and social stability. In this sense, it is indispensable for maintaining a stable, functional existence in the world.

However, the pursuit of Artha must be carefully balanced with *Dharma* (moral and ethical principles). When pursued in alignment with Dharma, material wealth becomes a tool for promoting the well-being of individuals, families, and societies. Conversely, when sought without the guidance of Dharma, it can lead to greed, corruption, and societal decay. This delicate balance is essential for a harmonious life, both individually and collectively.

The classic Indian treatise *Arthashastra*, written by the renowned strategist and philosopher **Chanakya** (Kautilya), is a key text that discusses the ethical acquisition, management, and utilization of wealth. Chanakya's philosophy underscores that material prosperity should never be an end in itself but rather a means to support a just and righteous society.

In *Arthashastra*, Chanakya highlights that wealth is necessary for both personal happiness and the effective governance of a kingdom. He emphasizes the importance of leadership that is committed to the welfare of the people, including the ethical taxation and use of resources for public infrastructure and security. The ethical pursuit of Artha, therefore, involves recognizing the role of wealth in sustaining not only the individual but the entire community.

Chanakya also warns against the dangers of unchecked desire and greed. He notes that a wise ruler, or any individual in a position of power, should be vigilant about the corrupting influence of wealth, striving to use it for the benefit of all and not just for personal gain.

Yoga, as a practice of inner discipline and self-realization, offers invaluable tools for managing desires and attachments, particularly in relation to wealth. Through the practices of meditation, mindfulness, and self-control, yoga teaches individuals to distinguish between needs and wants, enabling them to pursue Artha without falling prey to materialism or greed.

By cultivating a clear and focused mind, yoga helps in making wise decisions regarding the acquisition, use, and distribution of wealth. A yogic mindset fosters *vairagya* (non-attachment), where one understands the impermanent nature of material possessions and recognizes that true fulfillment lies beyond the accumulation of riches. This does not mean rejecting wealth but managing it with awareness and responsibility. When practiced sincerely, yoga allows an individual to navigate worldly success without being overwhelmed by it.

The Indian historical and spiritual tradition is replete with examples of rulers who harmonized the pursuit of Artha with Dharma, thus establishing prosperous and ethical reigns. One such figure is Emperor **Ashoka**, who initially sought wealth and power through conquest but later embraced Dharma after the transformative experience of the Kalinga War. Ashoka redirected his empire's resources toward the welfare of his people, building hospitals, schools, and roads, and spreading the teachings of non-violence and compassion throughout his kingdom. His rule exemplified how material prosperity can be aligned with ethical governance and spiritual values.

Similarly, the legendary King Janaka of Videha, revered in both Vedic and yogic traditions, demonstrated that material wealth and spiritual wisdom are not mutually exclusive. Janaka, though a wealthy and powerful king, was known for his deep detachment and spiritual insight. His life serves as a model for how one can be fully engaged in worldly duties while remaining anchored in higher consciousness.

In today's globalized society, the pursuit of Artha is more relevant than ever. We live in a world where material success is often equated with happiness, and the relentless drive for wealth can lead to stress, anxiety, and an erosion of moral values. Balancing Artha with Dharma is a timeless lesson that modern society can greatly benefit from.

Ethical entrepreneurship, corporate social responsibility, and sustainable development are modern manifestations of this ancient principle. When individuals, companies, and nations prioritize Dharma alongside Artha, they contribute to a more equitable, compassionate, and harmonious world.

In conclusion, the pursuit of Artha is essential for survival and flourishing, but it must be guided by ethical principles and spiritual awareness. By integrating the wisdom of texts like *Arthashastra* with the mindfulness practices of yoga, individuals can achieve prosperity in a manner that is balanced, responsible, and aligned with the deeper purposes of life.

3. Kama: The Fulfillment of Desires

Kama represents the pursuit of pleasure, enjoyment, and emotional fulfillment. Kama encompasses not only physical pleasure but also the appreciation of beauty, art, music, love, and all experiences that bring joy and contentment to life. It is about embracing the fullness of life's pleasures, but like Artha, it must be pursued within the ethical framework of *Dharma* (righteousness).

In this sense, Kama is not inherently about indulgence but about finding pleasure in harmony with higher moral principles. When pursued without Dharma, Kama can lead to attachment, greed, or hedonism, which distracts from one's true purpose. But when balanced with responsibility and ethical considerations, Kama becomes an integral part of living a well-rounded, fulfilling life.

The *Kama Sutra*, attributed to the sage Vatsyayana, is often misunderstood as merely a text about sexual pleasure. However, it is far more expansive in its scope, exploring the art of living, relationships, and the ethical pursuit of sensual enjoyment. Vatsyayana emphasizes that Kama should be enjoyed with mindfulness and balance, and it should not dominate one's life. He offers guidance on how to cultivate meaningful relationships, respect boundaries, and maintain harmony in both romantic and social interactions.

The *Kama Sutra* also outlines how individuals can fulfill their desires without causing harm to themselves or others. It acknowledges that human beings are emotional and physical creatures, and that these aspects of life deserve attention and care, but not at the cost of personal integrity or social duty. The pursuit of Kama, in this light, becomes an art—a balanced and ethical way to enjoy life's pleasures while maintaining one's Dharma.

Yoga provides a unique perspective on desires by helping practitioners understand their true nature. According to yogic philosophy, desires themselves are neither good nor bad, but it is our relationship to them that determines whether they lead to fulfillment or suffering. Yoga cultivates awareness, helping individuals recognize which desires are healthy and conducive to growth and which are harmful or excessive.

Through practices like meditation, *Pranayama* (breath control), and mindfulness, yoga enables us to manage and regulate our desires. This prevents the mind from becoming overly attached or enslaved to fleeting pleasures. Yoga encourages us to appreciate life's joys without being consumed by them. This balance is central to living a spiritually aligned and emotionally fulfilling life.

Additionally, certain forms of yoga, like *Bhakti Yoga* (the path of devotion), offer a transformative approach to Kama. Instead of suppressing desires, Bhakti Yoga channels them toward love and devotion to the Divine. By focusing one's emotions and love on the Divine, the practitioner sublimates worldly desires into a higher form of fulfillment, leading to spiritual bliss rather than just temporary gratification.

A powerful historical example of this transformation is the life of the poet-saint **Mirabai,** whose devotion to Lord Krishna transcended the worldly realm of Kama. Born into a royal family, Mirabai rejected the conventional expectations of pleasure and wealth that her status afforded her. Instead, she directed her intense longing, love, and emotional desire toward Krishna, whom she considered her eternal lover and companion.

Mirabai's life and poetry demonstrate how Kama, when directed toward a higher spiritual ideal, can lead to profound inner fulfillment. Her songs are filled with passionate longing, yet this longing is not for worldly pleasures but for union with the Divine. In her devotion to Krishna, Mirabai found a fulfillment far deeper and more enduring than anything material could offer.

Through her life, she showed that desire itself is not the problem; it is how that desire is channelled that matters. When directed toward fleeting material pleasures, Kama leads to impermanence and dissatisfaction. But when it is transformed into spiritual love, it can lead to liberation and union with the Divine.

In the modern world, where desires and pleasures are often marketed as the ultimate goals of life, it is easy to become trapped in a cycle of consumption and attachment. The constant pursuit of sensory pleasures, from entertainment to material possessions, can lead to temporary satisfaction but often results in deeper emotional emptiness. Here, the teachings of Kama within the broader framework of the *Purusharthas* offer a vital reminder: it is not pleasure itself that is the problem, but our attachment to it.

Modern life offers countless opportunities to enjoy the world's beauty and pleasures—whether through relationships, the arts, or nature. These experiences can enrich our lives when pursued mindfully and ethically. But if we lose sight of Dharma in the process, we risk falling into patterns of excess and dissatisfaction.

By integrating practices like yoga, meditation, and self-reflection, individuals can cultivate a healthier relationship with their desires. Rather than rejecting pleasure or becoming a slave to it, we can learn to appreciate life's joys while remaining anchored in a higher purpose. In this way, Kama becomes a path to deeper fulfillment, not through constant indulgence, but through mindful enjoyment and spiritual alignment.

In conclusion, Kama represents an essential aspect of human experience—the pursuit of pleasure, love, and emotional fulfillment. When aligned with Dharma, Kama enriches life and provides joy without causing harm or imbalance. Through the wisdom of texts like the *Kama Sutra* and the transformative practices of yoga, we learn how to fulfill desires in a way that is both ethical and deeply satisfying, ultimately leading to a higher, more spiritual form of fulfillment.

4. Moksha: The Ultimate Liberation

Moksha is the highest and ultimate goal of human life in the philosophy of *Purusharthas*. It represents liberation from the cycle of *samsara*—the endless cycle of birth, death, and rebirth—and the realization of one's oneness with the Divine or the Supreme Reality (*Brahman*). Achieving Moksha is the culmination of spiritual evolution, where the individual soul (*Atman*) merges with the infinite consciousness, experiencing eternal bliss and freedom from all worldly attachments and limitations.

In this state, the individual transcends the ego, desires, and ignorance that bind them to the material world, and they awaken to their true, divine nature. Moksha is not just a future state to be attained after death; it is also a living experience of freedom, where one moves beyond suffering and illusion while still in the physical body.

The essence of Moksha is beautifully described in the *Mundaka Upanishad*, which declares that ultimate liberation comes through the direct knowledge and realization of the Supreme Brahman. In verse 3.2.9, it is stated:

"He who knows the Supreme Brahman becomes Brahman." (*Mundaka Upanishad*, 3.2.9)

This verse emphasizes the profound idea that Moksha is not about reaching an external state or place but about realizing our true nature. The knower of Brahman realizes their inherent divinity and understands that there is no separation between the individual self (*Atman*) and the Supreme Reality (*Brahman*). Once this truth is realized, the illusions of the material world dissolve, leading to ultimate freedom.

Yoga, in all its forms, provides the pathway to attaining Moksha. Through various disciplines, individuals are given tools to transcend the limitations of the mind and body, moving toward the ultimate goal of spiritual liberation. The different forms of yoga address the diversity of seekers, allowing each individual to choose a path most suited to their nature and temperament. Whether through meditation (Raja Yoga), selfless service (Karma Yoga), devotion (Bhakti Yoga), or knowledge (Jnana Yoga), liberation can be achieved.

The great philosopher and saint **Adi Shankaracharya** (8th century CE) played a pivotal role in systematizing the philosophy of **Advaita Vedanta**, which teaches that the individual soul (*Atman*) and the Supreme Reality (*Brahman*) are one and the same. According to Advaita Vedanta, the perception of duality—of separation between the self and the universe—is due to *Avidya* (ignorance). Once this ignorance is dispelled through self-realization, Moksha is attained.

Adi Shankaracharya's teachings emphasize that Moksha is not something to be achieved in the future but is the recognition of one's true, eternal nature. In his commentaries on the *Upanishads* and *Brahmasutras*, Shankaracharya explains that the world we experience is *Maya* (illusion), and only the knowledge of the Self can free us from the delusion of separateness.

Shankaracharya's famous statement, "Brahma Satyam, Jagat Mithya, Jivo Brahmaiva Na Aparah" (Brahman alone is real, the world is illusory, and the individual self is none other than Brahman), encapsulates the core of Advaita Vedanta and the path to Moksha. His teachings continue to inspire countless seekers in their quest for liberation.

The life of **King Janaka**, a philosopher-king and a revered figure in Hindu mythology, is a prime example of how Moksha can be attained while fulfilling worldly duties. Janaka was a wise and just ruler of the kingdom of Videha, yet he was also a highly realized soul who attained enlightenment while still engaged in the responsibilities of governance.

King Janaka practiced **Karma Yoga** by performing his royal duties without attachment to the fruits of his actions. He ruled with justice and compassion, adhering to Dharma while pursuing Artha (material wealth) and Kama (pleasure) in a righteous manner. Despite his active engagement in worldly life, Janaka remained detached and spiritually centered, embodying the harmonious integration of all four Purusharthas.

Janaka's life illustrates that Moksha is not limited to renunciates or those who abandon the world. It can be realized by anyone who remains inwardly free from attachment while outwardly fulfilling their responsibilities. His life serves as a reminder that liberation is possible in any circumstance, as long as one's actions are aligned with spiritual wisdom.

In today's fast-paced, material-driven world, the pursuit of Moksha may seem distant or unattainable. However, the timeless teachings of the Upanishads, the Bhagavad Gita, and the great sages remind us that the ultimate goal of life remains the same, even in modern times. Liberation is not about escaping the world but about freeing oneself from the inner limitations of ego, desire, and ignorance.

For modern spiritual seekers, the path to Moksha may involve balancing material and spiritual pursuits, much like King Janaka. Through yoga, meditation, selfless service, devotion, and the study of sacred texts, individuals can transcend the distractions of the material world and move toward a deeper understanding of their true nature.

Moksha is not a distant, abstract concept but a living reality that can be experienced by anyone who sincerely seeks the truth. It is the ultimate freedom—a liberation not only from the cycle of rebirth but from the illusions and suffering that bind us to a limited existence.

In conclusion, Moksha represents the pinnacle of spiritual achievement and the fulfillment of life's deepest purpose. Whether through the paths of yoga, the teachings of Advaita Vedanta, or the inspiring examples of enlightened figures like King Janaka, Moksha offers the promise of eternal peace, freedom, and union with the Divine. It is the realization that, at our core, we are already one with Brahman—immortal, infinite, and free.

The Three Bodies: Understanding Our Existence

Yoga also provides insight into the nature of our existence through the concept of the three bodies:

1. **Sthula** Sharira (the physical body)
2. **Sukshma** Sharira (the subtle body)
3. **Karana** Sharira (the causal body)

Understanding these layers helps us comprehend the comprehensive scope of yoga practice.

1. Sthula Sharira: The Physical Body

The **Sthula Sharira**, or the physical body, is the most tangible and gross form of existence. Comprised of the five great elements—**earth (Prithvi), water (Apas), fire (Agni), air (Vayu), and ether (Akasha)**—this body represents our interface with the external world through the senses and actions. It is the vessel through which we experience physical sensations, engage in activities, and navigate the material world.

In **yoga**, the **asana** (postures) practice is dedicated to the care and maintenance of the physical body. The purpose of asanas is not just for physical fitness but to prepare the body as a stable and healthy container for spiritual evolution. By cultivating **strength, flexibility, and balance,** we refine the body's capabilities and clear the pathways for energy (prana) to flow without obstruction. This becomes essential in deepening spiritual practices. As the physical body aligns with nature's harmony, it becomes less of an obstacle and more of a conduit for higher states of awareness.

In this state of alignment, the **Sthula Sharira** is no longer an inert mass but a vibrant vehicle for self-realization. Yoga teaches that by caring for the body through proper exercise, diet, and rest, we prepare it to endure the rigors of spiritual practice, making the journey inward smoother and more profound.

2. Sukshma Sharira: The Subtle Body

Beneath the physical sheath lies the **Sukshma Sharira**, or the subtle body, composed of the **mind (manas), intellect (buddhi), and ego (ahamkara)**. This body governs our thoughts, emotions, and perceptions, acting as the bridge between the physical and spiritual realms. It is within the subtle body that we experience emotions, desires, and the inner dialogue that shapes our understanding of the world.

In the yogic tradition, **pranayama** (breath control) and **dhyana** (meditation) play vital roles in purifying and stabilizing the subtle body. **Prana**, the life force energy, flows through the **nadis** (subtle channels) and **chakras** (energy centers), energizing and supporting the mind and emotional states. By mastering the breath through pranayama, we can regulate the flow of prana, calming the fluctuations of the mind (chitta vrittis) and cultivating a state of inner tranquillity.

Meditation, when practiced with intention and focus, acts as a cleansing process for the mind and ego. It helps dissolve attachments and identifies less with fleeting thoughts and emotions, leading to **inner clarity and emotional balance**. As the **Sukshma Sharira** is harmonized, one becomes less reactive to external stimuli and more attuned to the deeper layers of existence. The purification of the subtle body allows for the expansion of consciousness, where intuition sharpens, and the sense of **"I"** begins to transcend beyond the limitations of individual ego.

3. Karana Sharira: The Causal Body

The **Karana Sharira**, or the causal body, represents the seed of our existence, the innermost core where **karma** is stored and where our deep subconscious tendencies (vasanas) reside. It is beyond the grasp of the intellect and the senses, for it is the layer of pure potential, the cause behind all manifested experiences. Often called the **bliss sheath (Anandamaya Kosha)**, this body connects us to the highest dimension of our being, where **Atman** (the true self) resides in its purest form.

In the pursuit of self-realization, the causal body is accessed through **Jnana Yoga**, the path of wisdom and knowledge. By inquiring deeply into the nature of reality—asking "Who am I?" and engaging in **self-reflection**—one begins to peel away the layers of ignorance (avidya) that obscure the understanding of the true self. Practices of deep meditation, where the mind becomes absorbed in the contemplation of **Brahman** (the Absolute), help dissolve the illusion of separateness.

When one is fully established in the **Karana Sharira**, the sense of individual identity (ego) dissolves, and there is a direct experience of **oneness** with the divine. This is the realization of the **Atman**, our true nature, which is eternal, infinite, and beyond the constraints of time, space, and causality.

Transcending the Three Bodies: The Path to Liberation

In his teachings, **Swami Vivekananda** often emphasized the importance of understanding the **three bodies** as key to the spiritual journey. He stressed that through the practice of yoga—whether it be the physical disciplines of **Hatha Yoga**, the mental purification through **Raja Yoga**, or the wisdom teachings of **Jnana Yoga**—one can transcend these layers of existence and experience the highest truth.

The ultimate goal of yoga is not just to balance and purify these bodies but to transcend them altogether. By understanding that the **Sthula Sharira** is impermanent, the **Sukshma Sharira** is a reflection of the mind's conditioning, and the **Karana Sharira** is the storehouse of karma, we move beyond identification with any of these layers and recognize that we are the eternal **Atman**, free from all limitations.

When these layers are transcended, we realize the **oneness of all existence**, experiencing liberation or **moksha**—the freedom from the cycle of birth and death (samsara) and the awakening to our **true essence** as divine consciousness.

The Three Gunas: The Qualities of Nature

In the ancient philosophy of yoga and Sankhya, the concept of the three **gunas**—**Sattva** (purity), **Rajas** (activity), and **Tamas** (inertia)—explains the inherent qualities that govern all of nature, including human behaviour, thoughts, and actions. These three gunas are ever-present and fluctuate, influencing our mental states, choices, and reactions. The practice of yoga aims to cultivate **Sattva**, the quality of purity and harmony, while managing and balancing the influences of **Rajas** and **Tamas** to achieve clarity, peace, and spiritual progress.

1. Sattva (Purity)

Sattva is the quality of light, purity, and balance. It represents harmony and wisdom, and is associated with virtues like truth, peace, and righteousness. When **Sattva** dominates, it elevates our consciousness, fostering spiritual insight, compassion, and inner tranquillity.

Dominant Qualities: Purity, harmony, goodness, light, wisdom, peace, and balance.

Mindset: A **Sattvic** mindset is calm, content, compassionate, and focused on spiritual growth. Such individuals radiate positive energy and engage in activities that benefit themselves and others.

Activities that Cultivate Sattva

- **Service to Others:** Selfless service, or seva, is a hallmark of Sattvic living, especially when directed towards those who are in genuine need of help—whether individuals, communities, or institutions. Through acts of charity, assisting the less fortunate, and uplifting society, one transcends the ego and fosters a deeper sense of unity and compassion for all. True seva arises from recognizing where help is most needed and offering it with sincerity and humility.

- **Spiritual Practices:** Daily spiritual practices like meditation, yoga, prayer, and studying sacred texts are essential to developing **Sattva**. These practices calm the mind, elevate awareness, and open the heart to divine wisdom.

- **Healthy Lifestyle:** A **Sattvic** lifestyle involves eating pure, vegetarian food, maintaining a clean and serene environment, and exercising regularly. This balanced approach nourishes both the body and mind, supporting physical health and mental clarity.

- **Mindful Actions:** Individuals dominated by **Sattva** approach life with calmness, clarity, and deliberate intention. Every action is carried out with mindfulness, ensuring that it aligns with higher ethical values. Decisions are made thoughtfully, avoiding impulsive reactions.

- **Pursuit of Knowledge:** The thirst for knowledge and wisdom is central to **Sattva**. Sattvic individuals engage in study, introspection, and self-reflection, seeking deeper understanding of life's mysteries. Intellectual and spiritual growth are intertwined in this pursuit.

- **Compassion and Non-Violence:** Rooted in **ahimsa** (non-violence), **Sattva** fosters love, empathy, and respect for all living beings. Actions stem from compassion, recognizing the interconnectedness of all life, and working toward the well-being of others.

- **Detachment:** A hallmark of **Sattvic** action is performing duties without attachment to outcomes. Whether in success or failure, the individual remains centered and balanced, accepting results with equanimity. This detachment from the fruits of actions is a pathway to inner freedom.

- **Simplicity:** A **Sattvic** person lives a life of simplicity, free from excessive material desires. The focus is on cultivating inner peace and self-realization rather than acquiring external wealth or fame.

Increasing Sattva Through Yoga

The practice of yoga, particularly meditation and ethical living, enhances **Sattva** by purifying the mind and body. The ethical principles of **Yama** and **Niyama** (moral disciplines from Patanjali's Yoga Sutras) guide one toward righteous living, while regular meditation helps quiet the mind and connect with the higher Self. As **Sattva** increases, inner peace and spiritual wisdom naturally arise, leading to the ultimate goal of self-realization.

In essence, **Sattva** represents the highest quality of nature, leading one toward liberation (moksha). Through cultivating **Sattva**, one aligns with truth, harmony, and the divine, progressing on the path of spiritual awakening.

2. Rajas (Activity)

Rajas is the quality of movement, action, and passion. It is responsible for creating dynamism and drive in life, leading to growth and progress. However, when imbalanced, it can also result in restlessness, anxiety, and attachment to material outcomes. In individuals where **Rajas** dominates, there is a strong inclination toward worldly desires, goals, and achievements. While **Rajas** propels progress and activity, it can also be a source of suffering if not balanced with **Sattva**.

Dominant Qualities: Passion, activity, dynamism, restlessness, ambition, and desire.

Mindset: Those with a **Rajasic** mindset are driven by desires, goals, and ambitions. They often find themselves restless, anxious, and constantly seeking validation from external achievements. There is a strong urge to act and achieve, but this can sometimes lead to stress and dissatisfaction.

Activities Associated with Rajas

- **Goal-Oriented Work:** A **Rajasic** individual is focused on personal success, often striving for fame, recognition, and material prosperity. They work hard to achieve their ambitions but may be driven by ego and desire for external rewards.

- **Competitive Spirit:** Competition and comparison are key features of **Rajas**. These individuals are always striving to outdo others, whether in professional settings, sports, or personal achievements, seeking validation and approval from society.

- **Desire for Power and Influence:** Many **Rajasic** individuals pursue leadership positions, wealth, or influence. Whether in business, politics, or social organizations, they aim to control and dominate their environments to fulfill their personal desires for success.

- **Restlessness and Lack of Peace:** There is a constant need for activity, and **Rajasic** individuals often find themselves overwhelmed by multitasking and a packed schedule. They may struggle with stillness and have little time for rest or reflection, leading to burnout or anxiety.

- **Indulgence in Sensory Pleasures: Rajas** also drives indulgence in sensory pleasures such as rich food, entertainment, luxury, and other forms of gratification. These desires can become overwhelming, causing individuals to chase pleasure over inner fulfillment.

- **Emotional Reactivity: Rajasic** individuals are prone to strong emotional reactions, such as anger, frustration, excitement, or disappointment. Their actions are often impulsive, driven by temporary emotions rather than reflective thought.

- **Attachment to Outcomes:** An important characteristic of **Rajas** is attachment to the fruits of one's labour. **Rajasic** individuals derive happiness from success and are easily discouraged by failure, leading to a cycle of pleasure and pain that binds them to worldly pursuits.

- **Leadership and Social Influence:** Driven by ambition, those with a **Rajasic** temperament are often involved in leadership roles, organizing movements, or managing large-scale efforts. While they can have positive impacts, their actions are frequently influenced by personal gain rather than selfless service.

Balancing Rajas through Yoga

Rajas can be a positive force if channelled correctly. Yoga helps regulate **Rajas** by guiding this energy into constructive, purposeful action while reducing attachment to outcomes. Practices like **Karma Yoga** (selfless action) teach the individual to work diligently without desire for reward. Meditation and mindfulness help reduce restlessness, bringing calm and focus. The balance of **Rajas** leads to efficient, dynamic action without the emotional turbulence often associated with it.

3. Tamas (Inertia)

Tamas is the guna of inertia, darkness, and ignorance. It manifests as lethargy, confusion, and attachment to material objects and delusions.

While **Tamas** is essential in certain aspects of life, such as rest and regeneration, when it becomes dominant, it leads to stagnation, laziness, and a disconnection from reality. Overcoming **Tamas** is crucial for personal and spiritual growth, as it binds the individual to ignorance and illusion.

Dominant Qualities: Inertia, laziness, confusion, ignorance, negativity, and darkness.

Mindset: A **Tamasic** mindset is marked by lethargy, confusion, and a tendency to avoid challenges. Individuals dominated by **Tamas** may experience apathy, delusion, and a sense of hopelessness, often leading to destructive behaviours or avoidance of personal responsibility.

Activities Associated with Tamas

- **Laziness and Procrastination:** Those under the influence of **Tamas** avoid activities that require effort or responsibility. They tend to postpone tasks, preferring idleness over productivity. This procrastination reinforces the cycle of inertia and stagnation.

- **Indulgence in Negative Habits: Tamas** fosters indulgence in unhealthy habits like overeating, addiction to substances (drugs, alcohol), and excessive sleep. These behaviours provide temporary comfort but contribute to long-term harm, further entrenching inertia.

- **Violence and Aggression:** In extreme cases, **Tamas** can lead to violence and destructive behaviours, often devoid of moral or ethical consideration. This aggression may arise from frustration, confusion, or ignorance and can harm both the individual and those around them.

- **Ignorance and Rejection of Wisdom:** A **Tamasic** person may reject knowledge, wisdom, or self-reflection, preferring to remain in a state of ignorance. There is little desire for learning or self-improvement, which keeps them disconnected from their higher potential.

- **Depression and Negativity:** Feelings of hopelessness, pessimism, and withdrawal from life often accompany **Tamas**. The individual may feel trapped in a cycle of negativity, which manifests as depression and disconnection from the joys of life.

- **Unethical Actions:** Under the sway of **Tamas**, individuals may engage in dishonest or corrupt behaviour without considering the consequences for others. Their actions are often driven by self-interest and delusion, rather than ethical principles.

- **Attachment to Illusion: Tamas** keeps one trapped in a world of delusion, often leading to poor decision-making and confusion. The individual may live disconnected from reality, caught up in fantasies or false perceptions.

- **Destructive Habits: Tamasic** individuals may engage in wasteful or irresponsible behaviours, often leading to harm for themselves or others. This can include activities that destroy personal health, relationships, or the environment.

Reducing Tamas through Yoga

The practice of yoga helps transform **Tamas** into energy and purpose by cultivating awareness, discipline, and knowledge. **Pranayama** (breath control), meditation, and physical yoga practices energize the body and mind, helping to break free from lethargy. The adoption of a **Sattvic** diet, clean living, and daily discipline replaces the inertia of

Tamas with clarity and purposeful action. Through self-awareness and conscious effort, one can gradually overcome the downward pull of **Tamas** and awaken to higher states of being.

Balancing the Gunas

The three gunas—**Sattva**, **Rajas**, and **Tamas**—are not static; they exist in varying proportions within each person. Our dominant guna can change over time depending on our lifestyle, actions, and spiritual practices. The teachings of the **Bhagavad Gita** emphasize the importance of cultivating **Sattva** through yoga and self-awareness, while managing the influences of **Rajas** and overcoming **Tamas**. The goal is to live a balanced life where **Sattva** predominates, leading to clarity, wisdom, and spiritual growth.

As *Bhagavad Gita* (14.11) states: "When Sattva is predominant, the light of wisdom shines through every gate of the body."

In addition to yoga, mindful eating also plays a role in balancing the gunas. A **Sattvic** diet—pure, natural, and fresh foods—supports mental clarity, physical health, and spiritual elevation. By aligning our lifestyle, diet, and actions with the principles of **Sattva**, we move toward a life of harmony, balance, and inner peace.

Scientific Evidence and Modern Relevance

In the modern era, yoga has gained widespread recognition not only as a spiritual practice but also as a scientifically supported method for enhancing physical, mental, and emotional well-being. Numerous studies have confirmed its effectiveness in managing various health conditions, such as stress, anxiety, depression, and chronic illnesses, highlighting the relevance of yoga in today's fast-paced, often stressful lifestyle.

Mental and Emotional Health

One of the most significant areas where yoga has shown profound benefits is in mental health.

A study published in *The Lancet* found that regular yoga practice led to a **50% reduction in symptoms of depression** in participants over a 12-week period. This study highlights the powerful potential of yoga in treating mood disorders, offering a natural, holistic alternative to medication.

Research from the *National Institutes of Health* **(NIH)** has further supported these findings, showing that yoga improves **mental focus**, reduces symptoms of **anxiety**, and enhances **emotional resilience**. By promoting mindfulness, breath control, and body awareness, yoga helps individuals develop tools to manage stress, calm the mind, and improve overall mental health.

Physical Health

In addition to mental and emotional benefits, yoga significantly improves physical health. Modern studies have explored the physiological changes that occur through regular practice, affirming its potential in managing chronic health conditions.

According to the **NIH**, yoga has been shown to **improve heart health** by reducing blood pressure, cholesterol, and improving circulation. Regular practice helps strengthen the cardiovascular system, making it an excellent complement to traditional medical treatments for heart disease.

Yoga is also known to **increase flexibility** and **improve muscle strength**, both essential for maintaining physical mobility and preventing injuries, particularly as people age. This is especially relevant in modern lifestyles, where sedentary work and prolonged periods of sitting lead to stiffness and back pain.

Additional research has shown that yoga can enhance **immune function**, reduce **inflammation**, and improve overall **metabolic health**, helping to combat diseases such as diabetes and obesity.

Conclusion

Yoga is not just about physical fitness; it is a holistic system that addresses every aspect of human life—body, mind, and spirit. By practicing yoga, we can break free from the illusions of Maya, harmonize the Purusharthas, and transcend the limitations of the three bodies and the gunas. Yoga is the key to living a life of balance, fulfillment, and ultimately, liberation.

7

The Five Koshas: The Layers of Human Consciousness

In yogic philosophy, the human experience is understood through the concept of the *koshas*, or sheaths, which are layers of consciousness that envelop the true self (Atman). These five koshas represent different dimensions of our existence, from the physical body to the subtlest level of consciousness. Understanding the koshas helps us recognize the various aspects of our being and how yoga can guide us toward the realization of our true nature.

The five koshas are:

1. **Annamaya Kosha** (The Physical Sheath)
2. **Pranamaya Kosha** (The Vital Energy Sheath)
3. **Manomaya Kosha** (The Mental Sheath)
4. **Vijnanamaya Kosha** (The Wisdom Sheath)
5. **Anandamaya Kosha** (The Bliss Sheath)

Each of these sheaths is interconnected, and as we progress through them, we move closer to the experience of the true self.

1. Annamaya Kosha (The Physical Sheath)

Annamaya Kosha is the outermost layer of human existence, often referred to as the "food sheath" because it is sustained and nourished by food. This kosha represents the physical body, composed of the five elements—earth, water, fire, air, and space. It includes all bodily functions, organs, and sensory experiences, making it the most visible and tangible aspect of our existence. Our daily identification with this sheath often leads to the belief that our physical body is our true self, though this is only the surface level of our being.

The **Taittiriya Upanishad** provides profound insight into the nature of the physical body, emphasizing that while it is integral to life, it is not the essence of who we are. The body undergoes cycles of birth, growth, aging, and death. According to the Upanishad, "From food, indeed, are produced all creatures—whatsoever dwell on earth. By food alone, they live and to food, they return" (Taittiriya Upanishad, 2.2.1). This highlights the transient and impermanent nature of the physical body, which is intricately linked to the food we consume. It reminds us that the body is sustained by the same earth from which all beings originate and eventually return.

Yoga's Role: Yoga emphasizes the cultivation of balance and health within the Annamaya Kosha to support spiritual progress. Through the practice of **asanas** (physical postures), the body is kept strong, flexible, and vital. These postures are designed not only to improve physical well-being but also to create a sense of awareness and mindfulness about the body.

Proper diet, or **Ahara**, is another crucial component of maintaining the health of the Annamaya Kosha. In yogic philosophy, food is seen as more than just physical nourishment—it affects both the mind and body. A sattvic (pure) diet, rich in fresh fruits, vegetables, and whole grains, is recommended to promote vitality, clarity, and balance within the body.

As practitioners advance in their yoga journey, they begin to understand that while the physical body is essential, it is merely the outer shell of a much more complex and profound system of koshas. Yoga teaches us to detach from excessive identification with the physical form, viewing it instead as a vehicle for higher spiritual experiences. By honouring and caring for the Annamaya Kosha, we create a stable foundation from which we can explore the subtler layers of our existence.

2. Pranamaya Kosha (The Vital Energy Sheath)

The Pranamaya Kosha is the sheath of **vital energy** or **prana**, the life force that animates and sustains the physical body. While the Annamaya Kosha governs our physical form, the Pranamaya Kosha encompasses the vital energy that keeps the body alive and functioning. This prana flows through a network of **nadis** (subtle energy channels), which are similar to the circulatory or nervous system but exist on a more subtle level. This sheath regulates essential functions such as breathing, heartbeat, digestion, and the overall circulation of life energy.

The **Prashna Upanishad** emphasizes the fundamental role of prana as the sustaining force of all beings: "Prana is the life breath of all beings, for it is the universal energy that flows through all things" (Prashna Upanishad, 2.1). Prana is not merely the breath we take in through our lungs but an all-pervading, universal force. It permeates every living entity and connects us to the broader cosmos, linking the physical body with the subtler layers of our being.

Yoga's Role: The health and balance of the Pranamaya Kosha are essential for vitality and well-being. **Pranayama** (breath control) practices are the key methods in yoga for regulating the flow of prana. These techniques are designed to clear blockages in the nadis and ensure the free flow of energy throughout the body, supporting both physical health and mental clarity.

One such practice is **Nadi Shodhana** (alternate nostril breathing), which balances the flow of prana between the two main energy channels, the **Ida** (left) and **Pingala** (right) nadis. By harmonizing these channels, Nadi Shodhana promotes balance between the mind and body, leading to calmness and focus.

Kapalabhati (skull-shining breath) is another pranayama technique, characterized by rapid, forceful exhalations and passive inhalations. It invigorates the Pranamaya Kosha, increases lung capacity, and stimulates digestion and circulation by awakening prana at a deeper level. This practice is said to "shine" the energy centers, bringing clarity to the mind and vitality to the body.

Through pranayama, we begin to understand that prana is more than just breath; it is the vital link between the physical body and the mind. As we gain mastery over the Pranamaya Kosha, we prepare ourselves to explore deeper layers of consciousness, establishing a foundation for spiritual growth and inner peace.

3. Manomaya Kosha (The Mental Sheath)

The Manomaya Kosha is the sheath governing the mind and emotions. It includes our thoughts, feelings, perceptions, and mental patterns, shaping the way we perceive the world and react to it. This kosha is responsible for our sense of individuality and ego, forming the basis of how we identify with our experiences. The mind's constant activity—its endless stream of thoughts, memories, judgments, and desires—often traps us in a cycle of attachments and distractions, veiling our true nature and keeping us from experiencing deeper layers of consciousness.

The **Bhagavad Gita** sheds light on the power of the mind, illustrating its dual potential to either liberate or bind us. "For him who has conquered the mind, the mind is the best of friends; but for one who has failed to do so, his mind will remain the greatest enemy" (Bhagavad Gita, 6.6). This profound teaching reveals that mastering the mind leads to peace and self-realization, while an undisciplined mind creates suffering and confusion. The Manomaya Kosha can therefore either be a tool for self-awareness or an obstacle to inner peace, depending on how we manage it.

Yoga's Role: To overcome the limitations of the Manomaya Kosha and free ourselves from mental agitation, yoga offers various practices aimed at calming and purifying the mind. **Meditation** is one of the primary techniques used to still the mind. By focusing attention on a single point—such as the breath, a mantra, or an image—meditation helps to quiet the mental chatter, reducing the influence of thoughts and emotions on our consciousness. As the mind becomes quieter, the veil of the Manomaya Kosha begins to lift, allowing us to access deeper states of awareness.

Mantra chanting is another powerful tool for calming the mind. Repeating sacred sounds or phrases, such as "Om" or specific **Bija mantras**, helps to align the mind with higher vibrations, reducing the fluctuations of thought and emotion. Mantras have a purifying effect on the mind, dissolving negative patterns and clearing mental blockages.

Mindfulness practices—such as being fully present in the moment, observing thoughts without judgment, and focusing on sensations—can also reduce the distractions of the Manomaya Kosha. These techniques help us recognize the mind's tendencies and begin to detach from them, creating space for inner stillness and awareness.

Through consistent practice, we learn to observe the mind rather than being controlled by it. This shift in perspective weakens the hold of the Manomaya Kosha, allowing us to experience the deeper layers of the self. As the mind becomes a tool rather than a master, we move closer to our true essence, which lies beyond the limitations of thought and emotion.

4. Vijnanamaya Kosha (The Wisdom Sheath)

The Vijnanamaya Kosha is the sheath of **wisdom, discernment,** and **higher knowledge**. This kosha transcends the mental and emotional patterns of the **Manomaya Kosha**, guiding us towards a deeper understanding of life, self, and spiritual truth. It encompasses our intuition, insight, and moral discernment, helping us differentiate between right and wrong, real and unreal, and leading us toward our higher purpose. The Vijnanamaya Kosha enables us to see beyond the superficial layers of existence and perceive the deeper realities of life.

In the **Yoga Sutras of Patanjali**, the cultivation of discernment (Viveka) is emphasized as essential for spiritual liberation. "When the mind is clear of the obstacles, the light of wisdom shines forth" (Yoga Sutras, 2.28). This sutra reminds us that wisdom emerges when the mind is purified of distractions, attachments, and misconceptions. The clarity of the Vijnanamaya Kosha is what illuminates the path to self-realization, revealing the truth of our existence and guiding us away from ignorance.

Yoga's Role: To purify and activate the Vijnanamaya Kosha, yoga offers paths like **Jnana Yoga** (the path of knowledge) and **self-inquiry**. These practices encourage us to question the nature of reality, our identity, and the purpose of life, leading to profound insights that arise from within. Jnana Yoga involves deep contemplation of philosophical teachings, such as the Upanishads and the Bhagavad Gita, combined with critical thinking and inner reflection. By engaging in self-inquiry, we challenge the illusions created by the mind and move toward an experiential understanding of our true self.

Contemplative practices, such as silent reflection, journaling, or meditative visualization, also activate the Vijnanamaya Kosha. These practices allow us to connect with our inner wisdom, opening the mind to higher truths and intuitive guidance. As we refine our discernment, we begin to recognize the transient nature of worldly experiences and attachments, shifting our focus toward more meaningful and enduring spiritual pursuits.

As the Vijnanamaya Kosha becomes more active and purified, we start to see beyond the illusions of the mind and emotions. We gain the ability to make choices aligned with our higher purpose and live with a greater sense of moral clarity and spiritual insight. This evolution of wisdom is key in moving beyond the limitations of the ego and preparing us for the final layer of existence, the **Anandamaya Kosha**, where bliss and unity with the true Self are experienced.

The more we cultivate wisdom and insight through yoga, the closer we come to our true nature, allowing us to live in alignment with the deeper truths of existence and to experience the inherent wisdom that resides within.

5. Anandamaya Kosha (The Bliss Sheath)

The Anandamaya Kosha is the innermost koshas, representing the sheath of **bliss, joy, and spiritual fulfillment**. It is closest to the true Self, experienced as an expansive sense of happiness and contentment that arises when we are in harmony with our deeper spiritual nature. The Anandamaya Kosha is the subtle layer through which we experience moments of deep inner peace, joy, and bliss, often encountered in meditation or moments of profound spiritual insight. While this sheath brings us closer to the ultimate reality, it is still a layer of experience—an indirect encounter with the true Self, and thus not the final realization.

The **Taittiriya Upanishad** beautifully expresses the nature of this sheath: "He who dwells in the bliss sheath is enveloped in pure joy, for he has realized his true Self" (Taittiriya Upanishad, 2.5.1). This quote reflects the Anandamaya Kosha as the sheath of pure joy, where the individual begins to experience the vastness of the true Self. However, it is important to note that the bliss encountered here, while profound, can still be transient. It is a reflection of the absolute, not the absolute itself.

Yoga's Role: Accessing the Anandamaya Kosha requires deep meditative practices that transcend the more superficial layers of the mind and body. **Meditation** and **Samadhi** (a state of intense concentration and union) are the primary tools in yoga for experiencing this sheath. In meditation, as the mind becomes completely still and thoughts dissolve, practitioners can experience moments of pure bliss, untainted by external circumstances. This bliss arises naturally from within, reflecting the soul's true nature.

Samadhi, the highest state of meditative absorption described in the **Yoga Sutras of Patanjali**, allows for a deeper immersion in the Anandamaya Kosha. In this state, the fluctuations of the mind cease, and one experiences a profound connection with the underlying unity of existence. The Anandamaya Kosha is experienced directly as bliss, joy, and spiritual fulfillment, offering a glimpse into the true nature of the Self.

However, while the Anandamaya Kosha brings us closer to the ultimate realization, it remains a sheath—a subtle layer of experience. The bliss we encounter here, although extraordinary, is still not the absolute truth. To go beyond this, yoga teaches us to continue our inward journey, ultimately transcending all the koshas to realize the **Atman**, or true Self, which is beyond all layers of experience. This is the state of **Moksha**, or liberation, where the individual self merges completely with the universal consciousness, free from all layers of illusion and separation.

Thus, yoga's ultimate goal is not merely to experience the bliss of the Anandamaya Kosha but to transcend even this sheath and discover the timeless, unchanging reality of the true Self.

Relationship Between the Three Bodies and the Five Koshas

In yogic philosophy, the human being is often described in terms of both the *three bodies* (Shariras) and the *five koshas* (sheaths). These two models are interconnected and provide a comprehensive framework for understanding the multidimensional nature of existence. While the three bodies give a broad categorization of the human being's physical, subtle, and causal aspects, the five koshas offer a more detailed exploration of the layers that make up these bodies.

Interconnection: How the Three Bodies (Shariras) and Five Koshas Relate

Gross Body (Sthula Sharira) and Annamaya Kosha: The gross body is aligned with the Annamaya Kosha, as both are concerned with the physical, material aspects of existence. This is the layer that is most obvious and is nourished by food and sensory experiences.

Subtle Body (Sukshma Sharira) and Pranamaya, Manomaya, Vijnanamaya Koshas: The subtle body spans three koshas—Pranamaya, Manomaya, and Vijnanamaya. This reflects the complexity of the subtle body, which involves both energy (prana) and the mind's cognitive functions. The Pranamaya Kosha governs the flow of energy, while the Manomaya Kosha manages mental activities, and the Vijnanamaya Kosha oversees intellectual discernment and wisdom.

Causal Body (Karana Sharira) and Anandamaya Kosha: The causal body corresponds to the Anandamaya Kosha, which represents the blissful core of our being. The causal body is the subtlest of the three bodies, and its connection with the Anandamaya Kosha emphasizes the deep peace and happiness that come from realizing the true Self.

Summary of the Relationship

- **Gross Body = Annamaya Kosha:** The physical body, sustained by food.

- **Subtle Body = Pranamaya, Manomaya, and Vijnanamaya Koshas:** The energy body, mental body, and wisdom body represent different layers of the subtle body.

- **Causal Body = Anandamaya Kosha:** The causal body, or the seed of existence, aligns with the bliss sheath, representing pure joy and the closest connection to the Self.

Understanding the relationship between the three bodies and the five koshas provides a deeper insight into how the human experience is structured. Yoga, in its various forms, seeks to purify each layer, helping the practitioner transcend the limitations of the bodies and koshas to realize their true nature, the Atman.

Conclusion: Moving Through the Koshas

The journey through the five koshas is a journey inward, from the outermost layer of the physical body to the innermost experience of bliss. Yoga helps us peel away these layers, moving closer to the realization of the self (Atman), which lies beyond all the koshas. By integrating yoga practices into our lives, we can harmonize each sheath, leading to a holistic sense of well-being and spiritual growth. Ultimately, the koshas remind us that while we experience life through these layers, our true essence is the eternal self that transcends them all.

8

The Four Antahkarana

In yogic philosophy, the term *Antahkarana* refers to the "inner instrument" or the subtle mental framework through which we experience, perceive, and interact with both the external world and our inner self. It is the foundation of cognition, awareness, and individuality, and plays a central role in shaping our reality.

The *Antahkarana* is divided into four distinct faculties, each contributing to different aspects of thought and consciousness:

1. **Manas** (the mind)
2. **Buddhi** (the intellect)
3. **Chitta** (the memory or subconscious)
4. **Ahamkara** (the ego or sense of "I")

Together, these four components of the *Antahkarana* form the mental apparatus through which we experience life. They shape our inner reality and influence how we interact with the external world.

Understanding and mastering the *Antahkarana* is essential for spiritual seekers on the path to self-realization, as it is the means by which one transcends the mind's limitations and dissolves the ego. When the *Antahkarana* is purified and harmonized through practices such as meditation, self-inquiry, and ethical living, it becomes a conduit for higher knowledge and spiritual awakening.

In this chapter, we will explore the intricate nature of the *Antahkarana*, examining how each of its four faculties functions, influences our daily lives, and plays a crucial role in spiritual progress. By understanding and refining these inner mechanisms, we can embark on the journey to inner freedom, ultimately transcending the constraints of the mind and ego to realize our true, eternal self.

1. Manas: The Mind (Perception and Thought Processing)

The *Manas* is the aspect of the mind responsible for receiving sensory inputs and processing them into thoughts, emotions, and desires. It acts as the interface between the external world and our internal experience, constantly interpreting stimuli from the senses and generating reactive responses. The *Manas* operates in the realm of perception, often reacting impulsively to the environment, making it a dynamic but also restless part of the mind.

Due to its reactive nature, the *Manas* is prone to distraction, restlessness, and attachment. It is continuously generating thoughts based on sensory experiences, which can create an endless loop of desires, fears, and emotions. This makes it a powerful yet often unruly aspect of the mind, one that requires discipline and control to avoid being overwhelmed by external influences.

In the *Katha Upanishad*, the *Manas* is metaphorically compared to the reins of a chariot in the analogy of the soul's journey. The self (*Atman*) is the rider, the body is the chariot, and the intellect (*Buddhi*) is the charioteer. The *Manas*, as the reins, plays a crucial role in controlling the senses, which are likened to the horses. This symbolism illustrates how the *Manas* guides sensory inputs, shaping our perceptions and reactions: "Know the self as the rider in a chariot, and the body as the chariot. Know the intellect as the charioteer, and the mind as the reins." (*Katha Upanishad*, 1.3.3-4)

The restless and reactive nature of the *Manas* can often lead to distractions, anxiety, and attachment to external objects. When left unchecked, it pulls the mind toward fleeting desires and momentary pleasures, creating a turbulent inner life. However, this same *Manas* can be tamed through focused practices, allowing for a more serene and balanced state of being.

Yogic practices like meditation, *Japa* (repetition of a mantra), and mindfulness are effective tools for calming the *Manas*. These practices work by focusing the mind, reducing its reactive nature, and cultivating inner stillness. For example, *Japa* allows the mind to anchor itself in the repetition of a sound or phrase, reducing its tendency to wander and react to sensory inputs. Similarly, mindfulness brings attention to the present moment, helping the *Manas* disengage from habitual thought patterns and emotional reactivity.

Interestingly, modern psychological approaches such as cognitive-behavioural therapy (CBT) echo the ancient yogic understanding of the *Manas*. CBT emphasizes the importance of recognizing and altering thought patterns to influence emotions and behaviours, aligning with the yogic principle that the mind's reactivity directly impacts one's inner and outer experiences. By becoming aware of the *Manas'* habitual responses and learning to manage them, individuals can develop greater control over their thoughts and emotions, fostering a more peaceful and centered state of being.

Through spiritual discipline and psychological insight, the reactive *Manas* can be transformed from a source of distraction and attachment into a tool for deeper awareness and self-mastery. Mastering the *Manas* is the first step toward understanding the deeper layers of the mind and progressing on the path to spiritual realization.

2. Buddhi: The Intellect (Discernment and Decision Making)

Buddhi is the higher faculty of the mind responsible for reasoning, discernment, and decision-making. It operates beyond the reactive nature of the *Manas* and serves as the mind's guiding light, enabling one to make choices based on wisdom, reflection, and understanding, rather than impulse or desire. It is through *Buddhi* that we are able to discriminate between right and wrong, truth and falsehood, and make decisions that are aligned with deeper truths and moral values.

The *Buddhi* is closely linked to wisdom and intelligence, but it goes beyond intellectual knowledge. It is the seat of discernment (*Viveka*), helping us see beyond surface-level appearances and guiding us toward truth and righteousness. The *Buddhi* has the unique power to pause, reflect, and choose actions that promote inner growth, spiritual progress, and harmony with the world.

In the *Bhagavad Gita*, the importance of the *Buddhi* in maintaining a balanced and righteous life is emphasized. A person who is guided by their *Buddhi* is able to maintain equanimity even in the face of life's challenges: "He whose mind is not shaken by adversity, who does not hanker after pleasures, who is free from attachment, fear, and anger, is called a sage of steady intellect (Buddhi)." (*Bhagavad Gita*, 2.56)

This verse highlights how a steady *Buddhi* allows a person to transcend emotional turmoil and stay focused on higher ideals, unaffected by external fluctuations of pleasure and pain.

A strong and clear *Buddhi* is essential not only for spiritual seekers but also for everyday decision-making. When the *Buddhi* is sharp and active, it helps individuals navigate complex situations, making decisions that are aligned with long-term well-being and ethical considerations. It is the *Buddhi* that stops us from being carried away by the fleeting desires and emotions generated by the *Manas*, instead offering a deeper, more thoughtful perspective.

However, when the *Buddhi* is weak or clouded by confusion, attachment, or ignorance, it can lead to poor decision-making and inner conflict. In such cases, one may find themselves making choices based on short-term gratification or emotional impulses rather than wisdom and clarity. Strengthening the *Buddhi* is therefore crucial for achieving mental clarity and making sound decisions that lead to inner peace and progress.

The path of *Jnana Yoga* (the yoga of knowledge) offers a method for strengthening the *Buddhi* through self-inquiry, study, and contemplation. By engaging in reflective practices, studying sacred texts, and questioning the nature of reality, one develops the ability to discern the eternal truth from the transient. The practice of *Jnana Yoga* trains the *Buddhi* to go beyond superficial understanding and grasp the deeper truths of existence.

Swami Vivekananda placed great emphasis on the development of the *Buddhi* through education, self-discipline, and reason. He believed that intellectual development was key to understanding the deeper truths of life and attaining spiritual growth. Vivekananda encouraged individuals to question everything, to engage in self-study and inquiry, and to use their *Buddhi* to rise above ignorance and delusion.

He also highlighted the need for a well-rounded education, one that trains both the intellect and the heart. According to Vivekananda, the goal of education is not just to acquire knowledge but to develop the capacity to think clearly, to discern truth from falsehood, and to cultivate wisdom.

By harnessing the power of the *Buddhi*, one can navigate the challenges of life with greater clarity, make decisions that are aligned with one's highest values, and ultimately progress toward self-realization.

In summary, *Buddhi* is the discerning faculty of the mind that leads us toward right action, wisdom, and truth. Strengthening it through reflection, self-discipline, and knowledge is essential for both spiritual and practical growth, enabling us to live with greater wisdom, clarity, and peace.

3. Chitta: The Memory and Subconscious Mind

Chitta is the part of the mind that functions as the storehouse of impressions (*Samskaras*) and memories from past experiences. It holds both conscious memories and unconscious tendencies that shape our thoughts, emotions, and actions, even when we are unaware of their influence. Like a vast ocean, the *Chitta* contains innumerable impressions that can surface as waves at any moment, influencing our present state of mind and behavior.

The *Yoga Sutras of Patanjali* describe the *Chitta* as the field where mental fluctuations (*Vrittis*) arise. These fluctuations are shaped by the impressions stored in the *Chitta*, affecting how we perceive and react to the world around us. Patanjali identifies the stilling of these fluctuations (*Chitta Vritti Nirodha*) as the central goal of yoga, recognizing that when the *Chitta* is calm and purified, we can experience our true self.

Unresolved impressions and deep-seated *Samskaras* in the *Chitta* often lead to recurring patterns of thought, behavior, and emotional reaction. These latent impressions can manifest as habits, fears, desires, or even unconscious biases that colour our perception and influence our choices. Therefore, understanding and cleansing the *Chitta* is crucial for spiritual growth and mental clarity.

The *Chitta* also plays a significant role in the concept of *Karma*. The impressions stored in the *Chitta* are the results of past actions, thoughts, and experiences. These *Samskaras* can create unconscious tendencies (*Vasanas*) that drive behavior, leading to the repetition of certain actions and emotional reactions over time. This cycle of action, reaction, and impression keeps individuals bound in patterns of *Karma*.

Breaking free from these patterns requires cleansing the *Chitta* and resolving the unresolved impressions that cloud our perception. When the *Chitta* is purified, the subconscious tendencies are weakened, allowing for greater clarity, self-awareness, and the ability to act with conscious intent rather than being driven by past conditioning.

Yogic practices such as meditation, *Yoga Nidra*, and *Vipassana* offer powerful methods for accessing and purifying the *Chitta*. These techniques allow practitioners to penetrate deeper layers of consciousness, bringing hidden impressions and patterns to the surface for resolution.

- **Yoga Nidra** (yogic sleep) is a guided meditation practice that helps individuals enter a deep state of relaxation and heightened awareness. In this state, practitioners can access the subconscious mind and release stored tension, impressions, and unresolved emotions. Through regular practice, *Yoga Nidra* can help cleanse the *Chitta* of deeply rooted *Samskaras*.

- **Vipassana** (insight meditation) involves observing the mind and body with detached awareness, allowing unconscious patterns and memories to rise to the surface. By witnessing these impressions without judgment or attachment, practitioners can dissolve the mental and emotional residues that bind them. This practice leads to a profound purification of the *Chitta* and the release of past *Karmas*.

The concept of the *Chitta* parallels modern psychology's understanding of the subconscious mind. Many psychotherapeutic techniques, such as psychoanalysis and Jungian therapy, aim to bring hidden patterns and repressed memories from the subconscious mind into conscious awareness for healing. By examining and addressing these subconscious patterns, individuals can resolve internal conflicts and experience greater psychological freedom.

Similarly, the yogic approach to the *Chitta* involves clearing the subconscious mind through meditative practices. Both traditions—psychological and yogic—recognize that our thoughts, emotions, and behaviours are deeply influenced by past experiences stored in the subconscious. The process of healing and transformation involves accessing these hidden layers, understanding their impact, and releasing the unresolved impressions that keep us trapped in repetitive cycles.

Ultimately, purifying the *Chitta* is essential for achieving inner freedom and spiritual clarity. When the *Chitta* is cleansed of accumulated impressions, the mind becomes calm, focused, and clear. The emotional reactivity and unconscious patterns that once dictated behavior lose their hold, allowing the individual to act from a place of conscious awareness.

This purification of the *Chitta* not only liberates one from the limitations of past conditioning but also opens the doorway to deeper states of meditation and higher consciousness. In this state of purity, the practitioner can connect with their true self (*Atman*), experience profound inner peace, and transcend the cycle of *Karma*.

In summary, the *Chitta* serves as the reservoir of subconscious memories and impressions, influencing our mental and emotional patterns. Through meditation and self-inquiry, we can access and purify the *Chitta*, freeing ourselves from past conditioning and moving toward inner clarity and spiritual freedom.

4. Ahamkara: The Ego (Sense of 'I')

Ahamkara refers to the ego or the sense of individuality—the part of the mind that identifies with the body, mind, and emotions as the self. It is the faculty responsible for creating the "I" identity, forming a sense of ownership over one's thoughts, actions, and experiences. While *Ahamkara* is essential for functioning in the world, enabling us to navigate social interactions, take responsibility, and protect ourselves, it can become a significant obstacle to spiritual growth when it becomes overly dominant.

The function of *Ahamkara* is to create a sense of separateness, distinguishing "me" from "you" and establishing personal boundaries. This identification with the individual self, however, can lead to attachments, pride, and feelings of superiority or inferiority. When left unchecked, *Ahamkara* causes us to become deeply entangled in material concerns, desires, and the illusion of separateness from others and the Divine.

The *Bhagavad Gita* warns about the dangers of an overactive *Ahamkara*, which deludes individuals into believing they are the sole agents of their actions. This false sense of doership—thinking "I am the one performing the actions"—creates attachment to the fruits of one's actions and deepens the illusion of separateness. In reality, as explained in the *Gita*, it is the *gunas* (qualities) of *Prakriti* (nature) that drive all activity: "Deluded by egoism, a person thinks, 'I am the doer.' But it is the gunas of Prakriti that do all the work." (*Bhagavad Gita*, 3.27)

This verse underscores how the ego takes credit for actions that are, in truth, governed by the forces of nature. The sense of "I" as the doer leads to attachment, pride, and the perpetuation of suffering, as individuals become trapped in the cycle of action and reaction. Overcoming the delusion of ego-driven doership is a critical step on the path to liberation.

When *Ahamkara* dominates, it creates a false sense of separation from the Divine and from others. This identification with the individual self reinforces the illusion of duality—"I" versus "you," "me" versus "the world." This sense of separateness leads to fear, insecurity, competition, and ultimately suffering. The ego, by creating attachments to the body, possessions, and social identity, obstructs the realization of our true, divine nature, which is infinite and unbounded.

In spiritual practice, the goal is not to destroy the ego entirely, as *Ahamkara* serves a functional role in navigating the material world. Instead, the aim is to transcend the ego's dominance, to see through its illusory nature, and to shift from a limited sense of "I" to a broader understanding of oneself as connected with the whole.

Two yogic paths—*Karma Yoga* (the yoga of selfless service) and *Bhakti Yoga* (the yoga of devotion)—are particularly effective in dissolving the grip of the *Ahamkara* by cultivating humility and surrender to a higher power.

Karma Yoga teaches the art of selfless action, where one performs duties without attachment to the results. In *Karma Yoga*, the practitioner acts as a channel for divine will, understanding that they are not the ultimate doer of their actions. This helps to weaken the sense of individual ego and foster a deeper connection with the universal flow of life. By surrendering the fruits of actions to the Divine, the ego is humbled, and the practitioner moves closer to experiencing the true self beyond the limited "I."

Bhakti Yoga, the path of devotion, focuses on surrendering the ego to a higher power, such as God or the Divine. In *Bhakti Yoga*, the ego is dissolved through love, devotion, and complete trust in the Divine. By directing all thoughts, actions, and emotions toward the object of devotion, the practitioner transcends the self-centered tendencies of the *Ahamkara*. This devotional surrender weakens the ego's hold and fosters a sense of unity with the Divine.

Both of these practices work to loosen the grip of the *Ahamkara* by shifting the focus away from the individual self and toward a higher purpose or divine reality. By gradually dissolving the ego's dominance, one can experience the interconnectedness of all life and the presence of the divine within and around us.

The *Ahamkara* is the root cause of much suffering, as it binds individuals to their limited identities, desires, and attachments. When the ego becomes too attached to material success, relationships, or societal roles, it creates expectations and fears that lead to dissatisfaction and anxiety. The sense of separation perpetuated by the *Ahamkara* also fosters feelings of isolation, insecurity, and competition, leading to further emotional turmoil.

Recognizing the limitations of the ego and learning to transcend its influence is key to achieving spiritual freedom. As one becomes less identified with the *Ahamkara* and more aligned with the higher self (*Atman*), the sense of separateness begins to dissolve, leading to greater inner peace, compassion for others, and a direct experience of unity with all of creation.

The *Ahamkara* plays a necessary role in creating the sense of individuality that allows us to function in the world. However, when it becomes overly dominant, it fosters attachment, pride, and the illusion of separateness, which obstructs spiritual growth. By transcending the limitations of the *Ahamkara*, we can move beyond suffering and experience the boundless freedom of the higher self.

Saints like Ramakrishna Paramahamsa and Ramana Maharshi exemplified the dissolution of the ego through devotion and self-inquiry. Their teachings highlight that true liberation comes when the sense of individuality is transcended, and one realizes their oneness with the universal consciousness.

Relationship Between the Four Antahkarana and the Five Koshas

The relationship between the Four Antahkarana (*Manas, Buddhi, Chitta,* and *Ahamkara*) and the Five Koshas (*Annamaya, Pranamaya, Manomaya, Vijnanamaya,* and *Anandamaya*) is a profound aspect of yogic philosophy. This connection illustrates how our inner mental faculties are interwoven with the layers of our existence, influencing both our external experiences and internal consciousness.

Manas (Mind) and the Manomaya Kosha (Mental Body)

Manas: The *Manas* is the faculty responsible for processing sensory input and generating thoughts. It is the reactive and perceptive aspect of the mind, constantly receiving information from the external world and shaping our mental landscape.

Manomaya Kosha: The *Manomaya Kosha* is the sheath of the mind, encompassing our thoughts, emotions, and sensory perceptions. It is directly influenced by the *Manas*, as the thoughts generated by the *Manas* contribute to the overall state of the *Manomaya Kosha*.

Relationship: The *Manas* operates within the *Manomaya Kosha*, shaping our mental and emotional responses to the world. For example, a restless *Manas* can lead to a disturbed *Manomaya Kosha*, resulting in anxiety and mental agitation. Meditation and mindfulness practices help calm the *Manas*, leading to a more harmonious *Manomaya Kosha*.

Buddhi (Intellect) and the Vijnanamaya Kosha (Wisdom Body)

Buddhi: The *Buddhi* is the intellect, responsible for discernment, decision-making, and wisdom. It allows us to analyze, reason, and understand the deeper truths of existence.

Vijnanamaya Kosha: The *Vijnanamaya Kosha* is the sheath of wisdom and higher knowledge. It is the layer where intellectual and intuitive insights reside, enabling us to make wise decisions and discern truth from falsehood.

Relationship: The *Buddhi* functions within the *Vijnanamaya Kosha*, guiding our intellectual and intuitive faculties. A well-developed *Buddhi* enhances the *Vijnanamaya Kosha*, leading to clarity of thought, wisdom, and the ability to discern the real from the unreal. Conversely, a clouded *Buddhi* can obscure the *Vijnanamaya Kosha*, leading to confusion and poor decision-making.

Chitta (Memory/Subconscious) and the Manomaya Kosha (Mental Body)

Chitta: The *Chitta* is the repository of memories, subconscious impressions, and samskaras (mental imprints). It stores past experiences and influences our present thoughts, emotions, and behaviours.

Manomaya Kosha: As the mental sheath, the *Manomaya Kosha* is also influenced by the *Chitta*. The impressions stored in the *Chitta* can surface in the *Manomaya Kosha* as thoughts, desires, and emotions.

Relationship: The *Chitta* affects the *Manomaya Kosha* by bringing up past memories and samskaras that shape our mental and emotional responses. For instance, unresolved traumas stored in the *Chitta* can cause disturbances in the *Manomaya Kosha*, leading to stress or anxiety. Practices like *Yoga Nidra* and deep meditation help in purifying the *Chitta*, thereby harmonizing the *Manomaya Kosha*.

Ahamkara (Ego) and the Manomaya and Vijnanamaya Koshas

Ahamkara: The *Ahamkara* is the sense of ego or individuality, creating the feeling of "I" and "mine." It is responsible for the identification with the body, mind, and emotions, often leading to attachment and suffering.

Manomaya Kosha: The *Ahamkara* interacts with the *Manomaya Kosha* by reinforcing the thoughts and emotions that revolve around the ego. It shapes our mental landscape by creating a strong sense of personal identity and attachment to mental patterns.

Vijnanamaya Kosha: The *Ahamkara* also influences the *Vijnanamaya Kosha*, as the ego can cloud our wisdom and discernment, leading to misjudgements and ignorance.

Relationship: The *Ahamkara* has a dual influence on both the *Manomaya* and *Vijnanamaya Koshas*. In the *Manomaya Kosha*, it strengthens the sense of individuality, contributing to ego-based thoughts and emotions. In the *Vijnanamaya Kosha*, it can obscure true wisdom by creating false identifications and attachments. Through practices like *Jnana Yoga* (the path of knowledge) and *Bhakti Yoga* (the path of devotion), the *Ahamkara* can be transcended, allowing the *Vijnanamaya Kosha* to shine with true wisdom and the *Manomaya Kosha* to be free from egoic disturbances.

Summary of the Relationship

- **Manas and Manomaya Kosha:** The mind's thought processes influence and are influenced by the mental sheath.

- **Buddhi and Vijnanamaya Kosha:** The intellect's discernment enhances the wisdom sheath, leading to clarity and insight.

- **Chitta and Manomaya Kosha:** The subconscious memories stored in the *Chitta* affect the mental sheath, shaping thoughts and emotions.

- **Ahamkara and Manomaya/Vijnanamaya Koshas:** The ego influences both the mental and wisdom sheaths, impacting thoughts, emotions, and discernment.

Understanding the interplay between the Four Antahkarana and the Five Koshas provides a holistic view of how our mental faculties interact with the layers of our existence. This knowledge is vital for spiritual practitioners, as it offers insights into how to purify and master these layers, ultimately leading to self-realization and liberation from the cycle of birth and death (Samsara).

Conclusion

The Four Antahkarana—*Manas, Buddhi, Chitta,* and *Ahamkara*—form the framework of the inner mind and are essential in shaping our perception, decisions, memories, and sense of self. Yoga provides tools to purify and master these faculties, enabling us to transcend the limitations of the mind and ego and realize our true nature. By understanding and refining the Antahkarana, we can lead a life of greater clarity, wisdom, and spiritual fulfillment.

9

The Four States of Consciousness

Consciousness has been a central theme in spiritual and philosophical discussions for millennia, weaving through the fabric of various traditions and cultures. In the Vedic and Upanishadic traditions, the exploration of consciousness goes beyond mere intellectual inquiry—it is seen as the essence of existence itself. These ancient texts describe four fundamental states of consciousness, each representing a unique level of awareness and connection to the universe:

1. **Jagrat** (waking)
2. **Svapna** (dreaming)
3. **Sushupti** (deep sleep)
4. **Turiya** (the transcendental state)

These four states are not merely psychological phenomena but are deeply interconnected with the individual's relationship to the cosmos. They represent a journey inward, from the external engagement of waking life to the transcendental realization of one's true nature. Understanding and experiencing these states are central to Vedic philosophy and spiritual practice, offering a roadmap to enlightenment and liberation.

1. Jagrat: The Waking State

The Jagrat state, or waking state, is the most familiar to us as it is the realm in which we interact with the physical world through our senses. In this state, consciousness is outwardly directed, focused on material experiences and external reality. The mind engages with the world around us, processing sensory input, managing daily tasks, and making decisions. It is in this state that the ego strongly identifies with the body, perceiving itself as a separate entity navigating the external environment.

In Jagrat, the individual is absorbed in worldly concerns—work, social interactions, eating, and various other physical activities. The mind and body collaborate to respond to stimuli, perform tasks, and create experiences rooted in the tangible world. It is a state governed by practicality, where the mind is active, and thought processes are in constant motion.

From a **neuroscientific** perspective, this state corresponds to the **beta brainwave frequency**, typically associated with heightened alertness, concentration, and cognitive function. Beta waves indicate an active and engaged mind, allowing us to focus, reason, and problem-solve, all essential functions for navigating daily life.

In the **Mandukya Upanishad**, the Jagrat state is described as **Vaishvanara**, a term that conveys the idea of universal consciousness turned outward to engage with the external world. The Upanishad explains, "The first quarter (Pada) is Vaishvanara. Its sphere of activity is the waking state; it is conscious of the external world." Here, Vaishvanara represents the individual as connected to the larger universal force, though still primarily aware of the gross, physical aspects of existence.

This state, while crucial for daily life, is seen in Vedic thought as limited because it is outwardly focused. The deeper essence of the Self remains obscured by the distractions of material reality. The waking state, therefore, is only the surface of consciousness—an initial layer of experience in the broader spiritual journey toward self-realization.

2. Svapna: The Dreaming State

Svapna, or the dreaming state, represents a shift from external awareness to an internal journey. In this state, consciousness turns inward, no longer bound by the physical world or the senses. The mind creates its own reality, weaving together experiences, emotions, and symbols from both the waking state and the deeper subconscious. Unlike the waking state, where reality is shaped by external stimuli, the Svapna state is a realm where imagination, memories, and latent impressions come alive, often providing insight into the inner workings of the mind.

Dreams have long fascinated both spiritual traditions and modern psychology. In the Vedic tradition, dreams are seen as windows into the subconscious, allowing for the expression of unresolved emotions, past experiences, and karmic influences. Dreams in Svapna serve as a bridge between the outer world of Jagrat and the deeper, subtler layers of the psyche.

In **modern psychology**, particularly through the work of **Carl Jung** and **Sigmund Freud**, dreams are analyzed as reflections of the unconscious mind. Freud believed that dreams reveal repressed desires and unresolved conflicts, while Jung saw them as expressions of the collective unconscious, filled with archetypal symbols that carry universal meaning. Both approaches emphasize that the dream state offers profound insight into hidden aspects of our psyche, often revealing truths that elude us in waking life.

On a physiological level, **REM (Rapid Eye Movement) sleep** is strongly associated with the dreaming state. During REM, the brain becomes highly active, with neural activity resembling that of the waking state. The brain "lights up" in regions responsible for processing emotions, memories, and sensory input, suggesting that during Svapna, the mind is sorting through and organizing information gathered during waking hours. REM sleep is crucial for cognitive functions such as memory consolidation and emotional regulation.

In the **Mandukya Upanishad**, Svapna is described as **Taijasa**, which means "the luminous one," highlighting the illuminated, subtle nature of the dream state. The Upanishad explains, "The second quarter is Taijasa. Its sphere of activity is the dream state; it is conscious of the internal world." Here, consciousness is directed inward, and instead of interacting with gross objects, as in Jagrat, it perceives subtle objects—the impressions and experiences imprinted on the subconscious mind.

Taijasa represents a higher level of awareness than Jagrat because it accesses the inner world, yet it is still limited by the duality of subject and object. Though this state allows for profound exploration of the mind, it remains one step away from the ultimate realization of the Self. Svapna offers a unique space where the conscious and unconscious minds intersect, making it a valuable state for both spiritual inquiry and psychological insight.

3. Sushupti: The Deep Sleep State

Sushupti, or the state of deep, dreamless sleep, is a state where consciousness is undifferentiated and devoid of both external and internal awareness. In this state, the mind, senses, and ego are completely withdrawn, and there is no perception of the physical world or the subconscious realm of dreams. It is a state of profound rest, where the individual is temporarily free from the dualities and distractions that characterize waking and dreaming.

In **deep sleep**, the mind ceases its active functioning, and the body undergoes a period of deep restoration. While there is no awareness of self or surroundings, the consciousness remains present, albeit in an unmanifested form. This state is considered vital not only for physical rejuvenation but also for mental and emotional well-being.

Scientific studies on deep sleep, specifically during the **delta wave stage**, reveal that this phase is crucial for the most restorative forms of sleep. Delta brainwaves, which are the slowest of all brainwave patterns, signal a time when the body and brain engage in healing, growth, and memory consolidation. During this phase, the brain detoxifies, hormones are regulated, and tissues repair themselves, making deep sleep essential for overall health and vitality.

In **Vedanta**, Sushupti is viewed as a state of **Ananda** (bliss), where the individual self is closest to experiencing the **Atman** (pure consciousness) without the distractions of mental activities. Though there is no conscious awareness in this state, the experience is still one of profound peace and contentment. The mind's usual turmoil and desires are absent, and in this momentary cessation of duality, the individual unknowingly touches upon the essence of the Self.

The **Mandukya Upanishad** describes Sushupti as **Prajna**, a state of undivided consciousness that experiences bliss without desires or dreams. It states, "The third quarter is Prajna, whose sphere is deep sleep, where one neither desires nor dreams." In this state, there is no division between subject and object, self and other. Consciousness is unified, resting in its purest form, though the individual is not aware of this unity.

Though deep sleep offers a fleeting connection to the Atman, it remains incomplete because the individual is not consciously aware of this connection. In other words, Sushupti represents the potential for spiritual realization, but without conscious recognition, it is merely a state of rest. However, the bliss experienced in Sushupti is a reminder of the deep peace inherent in the Self, which can be fully realized in the transcendental state of **Turiya**.

Sushupti, therefore, is both a necessary part of physical existence and a spiritual clue, pointing toward the deeper, undisturbed consciousness that underlies all states of being. It is the calm before the full realization of the Self, where the ego and mind are temporarily dissolved, allowing a glimpse—albeit unconscious—of pure awareness.

4. Turiya: The Transcendental State

Turiya, often referred to as the "fourth" state of consciousness, transcends the limitations of the waking (Jagrat), dreaming (Svapna), and deep sleep (Sushupti) states. Unlike these previous states, Turiya is a state of **pure, unconditioned awareness**, where dualities such as subject and object, self and other, disappear. In Turiya, the individual experiences complete oneness with **Brahman**, the universal consciousness. This state is regarded as the ultimate goal of spiritual realization, the point at which the individual soul (Atman) merges with the infinite cosmic reality.

In Turiya, the mind is no longer active in its usual sense, nor is it absent, as in deep sleep. Instead, it is fully absorbed in pure consciousness, free from the ego's identification with the body or the mind. This state is one of **supreme bliss** (Ananda) and **universal knowledge** (Sat-Chit-Ananda), where all boundaries dissolve, and one attains a direct realization of the Self as eternal, unchanging, and limitless.

Throughout history, **saints and sages** have described Turiya as the pinnacle of spiritual experience. In this state, there is no time, space, or causality—only the eternal present. It is attained through deep meditation, contemplation, and self-realization, where the individual gradually transcends the fluctuations of the mind and the distractions of the material world.

In **neuroscience**, Turiya is often likened to the brain state observed during **deep meditation**, where brainwave patterns shift to **gamma waves**, indicating heightened awareness and unity. Gamma waves are associated with peak mental clarity, focused attention, and an expanded sense of consciousness. During deep meditation, practitioners report feelings of profound peace, interconnectedness, and a sense of timelessness—all of which echo the descriptions of Turiya in the spiritual texts.

The **Mandukya Upanishad** offers a profound description of Turiya, stating, "It is neither inward nor outward consciousness… it is pure, peaceful, blissful, and non-dual. This is the Atman, and it is to be realized." Here, Turiya is seen as the essence of the Self, the ultimate reality that is beyond the play of illusion (Maya) and the fluctuations of the mind. Turiya is the **substratum** of all states of consciousness, the silent witness that remains unchanged and eternal beneath the ever-shifting experiences of waking, dreaming, and deep sleep.

Swami Vivekananda beautifully articulated Turiya as the **witness** of the other three states, stating, "Turiya is the witness of the waking, dreaming, and sleeping states. It is pure consciousness itself." Vivekananda emphasizes that while we pass through the other three states, Turiya remains constant and unchanging. It is not a separate state to be "achieved," but the ground of being that is ever-present, even when we are unaware of it.

Turiya is the ultimate realization of one's true nature. It is the **goal of life**, as recognized in Vedanta, where the soul's journey is aimed at transcending ignorance and realizing its unity with Brahman. Through spiritual practices like meditation, self-inquiry, and devotion, one can gradually experience the transition from the external world of form and duality to the inner realm of non-dual awareness, culminating in the blissful realization of Turiya.

Integration: The Journey of Consciousness

The four states of consciousness represent a profound journey from the external world of sensory perception to the internal realm of pure awareness. This journey, outlined in the **Mandukya Upanishad**, guides individuals toward realizing the **Atman** (the true self) and its oneness with **Brahman** (the ultimate reality). By understanding and transcending these states, we uncover the deeper truths of existence and consciousness.

In the waking state, we are immersed in the physical world, identifying with the body and engaging with external reality. The journey inward begins as we transition into the dreaming state, where consciousness shifts from the external to the internal, exploring the subconscious mind. The deep sleep state takes us further, offering a temporary experience of undivided consciousness, where the mind and ego dissolve, and we rest in blissful ignorance. However, the culmination of this journey lies in **Turiya**, the state of pure, non-dual awareness, where the individual transcends the limitations of the mind and body to experience oneness with the cosmos.

The wisdom of the **Mandukya Upanishad** illuminates this path, describing each state as a reflection of the broader, cosmic journey toward enlightenment. In modern times, scientific advancements offer a unique perspective, bridging ancient spiritual teachings with contemporary understanding. Studies in **neurobiology** and **quantum physics** explore the nature of consciousness, suggesting that the states described in the Upanishads are not merely philosophical concepts but are deeply connected to the brain's functioning and the fundamental nature of reality.

Meditation, **yoga**, and **mindfulness** practices are essential tools for individuals seeking to explore and transcend these states. Through regular practice, one can quiet the mind, withdraw from the external distractions of the waking state, and access the deeper layers of consciousness. These practices help in the gradual unveiling of Turiya, where one experiences the **unity of all existence** and the boundless nature of the Self.

Modern **quantum physics** and studies in **consciousness** hint at the interconnectedness of all things, resonating with the non-dual philosophy of Vedanta. For instance, theories about quantum entanglement and the observer effect echo the spiritual understanding that consciousness is fundamental to the fabric of reality. In **neuroscience**, the exploration of different brainwave patterns during various states of meditation and sleep provides insights into how the mind and consciousness function at deeper levels.

This merging of ancient wisdom and modern science offers a rich, multidimensional perspective on the nature of reality. As we continue to explore the **mysteries of consciousness**, both through spiritual practices and scientific inquiry, we come closer to understanding our place in the cosmos. Ultimately, the journey through the four states of consciousness is not just about understanding the mind but about realizing the boundless, eternal nature of the **Self**, culminating in the blissful awareness of Turiya.

This integration of Vedic teachings with modern insights is a powerful guide for those on the spiritual path, showing us that the quest for understanding consciousness is as ancient as it is modern—and that it is a journey toward the infinite, ever-present truth within us.

Conclusion

The four states of consciousness are fundamental to understanding the nature of the self and the universe. Each state offers a unique perspective on reality, with Turiya standing as the ultimate realization of unity with the cosmos. By integrating ancient teachings with modern science, we can deepen our understanding of consciousness and its role in spiritual growth.

10

The Seven Major Chakras

The practice of yoga is deeply intertwined with the understanding and harmonization of the subtle energies within the body. At the core of this energy system are the seven major chakras, which are believed to be the energy centers that influence physical, emotional, and spiritual well-being. However, beyond these, there are additional, lesser-known chakras distributed throughout the body that play significant roles in the subtle energy system, bringing the total number to **114 chakras**.

Each chakra corresponds to specific aspects of life and consciousness, and balancing these chakras through yoga can lead to holistic healing and self-realization.

The Concept of Chakras: An Overview

The term *chakra* comes from the Sanskrit word meaning "wheel" or "disk." According to yogic philosophy, chakras are spinning wheels of energy located along the spine, starting from the base of the spine and extending to the crown of the head. The seven major chakras are the root, sacral, solar plexus, heart, throat, third eye, and crown chakras. Each chakra governs specific physical, emotional, and spiritual aspects of life.

The earliest references to chakras can be found in ancient Indian texts such as the *Vedas* and the *Upanishads*. The *Shat-Chakra-Nirupana*, a 16th-century Sanskrit text, provides a detailed description of the chakras and their associated deities, elements, and mantras. In the modern era, chakras have been studied and explored by spiritual leaders, psychologists, and energy healers, making them a vital part of holistic wellness practices.

Understanding the Chakras: The 7 Major Energy Centers

1. Muladhara Chakra (Root Chakra)

- **Location**: Base of the spine (perineum area)
- **Color**: Red
- **Element**: Earth
- **Function:** Governs survival instincts, stability, physical vitality, and a sense of security
- **Mantra**: Lam
- **Associated Areas**: Legs, feet, bones, large intestine, adrenal glands

The **Muladhara Chakra**, also known as the Root Chakra, is the foundational energy center in the body. It is the grounding force that connects us to the Earth and governs our most basic needs for survival, including safety, food, shelter, and physical well-being.

Balanced Root Chakra: When the Muladhara Chakra is balanced, you feel secure, grounded, and stable in your life. There is a deep sense of physical and emotional well-being. You are more confident, have a strong will, and can make decisions without fear. Physiologically, your digestion, lower back, and legs feel strong and healthy. A balanced root chakra is associated with the qualities of trust, stability, and self-sufficiency. You feel present in your body and connected to the Earth.

Imbalanced Root Chakra: When the Muladhara Chakra is imbalanced, you may experience fear, anxiety, restlessness, and a lack of stability. This can manifest as insecurity about finances, relationships, or career, and a constant feeling of being unsettled. Physically, imbalances in this chakra may result in problems with the lower body, such as lower back pain, constipation, fatigue, and issues in the legs and feet. Emotionally, a blocked Root Chakra can lead to excessive worry, feeling "stuck" in life, or an overwhelming need for control. Imbalances may lead to hoarding behaviours, overeating, or materialism as ways to seek security.

How to Balance the Muladhara Chakra

Balancing the Root Chakra is essential for overall well-being. Practices that create a sense of groundedness and physical connection to the Earth are most effective.

Grounding Exercises: Grounding, also known as earthing, involves connecting physically with the earth. Walking barefoot on natural surfaces like grass, sand, or soil can help reconnect with the Earth's energy. Research has shown that grounding can reduce stress, improve mood, and enhance feelings of stability and security. For instance, a study published in the *Journal of Alternative and Complementary Medicine* indicated that individuals practicing grounding exercises reported a significant reduction in anxiety and an increased sense of well-being.

Yoga Poses: Certain yoga postures that stimulate the lower body can help activate and balance the Muladhara Chakra. Poses such as **Tadasana (Mountain Pose), Vrikshasana (Tree Pose), Malasana**

(Squat Pose), and **Virabhadrasana (Warrior I)** focus on grounding the body and stabilizing the lower limbs. A 2018 study from the *Journal of Evidence-Based Complementary & Alternative Medicine* found that yoga practices targeting the root chakra significantly reduced stress and promoted emotional balance.

Meditation and Visualization: Meditation focused on the Muladhara Chakra often involves chanting the mantra **"Lam"** or visualizing a vibrant red light at the base of the spine. Regular meditation helps calm the mind, reduce anxiety, and restore balance to this energy center. While meditating, you can visualize yourself being rooted to the ground, with strong, deep roots connecting you to the earth. This can create a sense of security and grounding.

Breathing Techniques (Pranayama): Deep, slow breathing techniques, such as **Ujjayi Breath** or **Nadi Shodhana (Alternate Nostril Breathing)**, can help balance the Root Chakra. These techniques calm the nervous system and bring attention to the body, creating a sense of stability. Conscious breathing while focusing on the base of the spine is particularly effective for reconnecting with this chakra.

Nutrition: Since the Root Chakra is associated with the Earth element, consuming foods that grow close to the earth can support its balance. Root vegetables like potatoes, carrots, beets, as well as protein-rich foods such as beans and lentils, help stabilize this chakra. Eating mindfully and consciously can further enhance feelings of grounding.

Affirmations: Affirmations can help shift thought patterns and promote balance in the Root Chakra. Examples include:

- "I am safe and secure."

- "I am grounded and connected to the Earth."
- "I trust in the process of life."

Crystals: Stones and crystals like **Red Jasper, Black Tourmaline,** and **Hematite** are believed to resonate with the Root Chakra. Holding these crystals during meditation or keeping them in your living space can assist in grounding and stabilizing the energy flow.

Aromatherapy: Essential oils such as **Patchouli, Cedarwood,** and **Sandalwood** are grounding scents that support the Muladhara Chakra. These oils can be diffused, added to baths, or applied to the skin to promote a sense of calm and stability.

I would advise against spending your hard-earned money on crystals and aromatherapy. The methods mentioned before crystals, will be sufficient.

Conclusion

The Muladhara Chakra is the foundation upon which all other chakras rest, and its balance is crucial for physical, emotional, and spiritual well-being. By engaging in grounding exercises, yoga, meditation, and incorporating mindful dietary and lifestyle choices, you can bring balance to this chakra, creating a sense of security and stability in your life.

2. **Swadhisthana Chakra (Sacral Chakra)**

- **Location**: Lower abdomen, just below the navel
- **Color**: Orange
- **Element**: Water

- **Key Concepts**: Creativity, pleasure, emotions, sexuality
- **Function:** Controls creativity, sexuality, sensuality, emotional expression, and pleasure
- **Mantra**: Vam
- **Associated Areas**: Reproductive organs, kidneys, bladder

The **Swadhisthana Chakra**, or Sacral Chakra, is the second energy center in the human body, deeply connected to emotions, desires, pleasure, and creative expression. As the chakra associated with the water element, it represents fluidity, adaptability, and the flow of emotions and creativity. The word "Swadhisthana" means "one's own abode" or "dwelling place of the self," symbolizing the seat of the subconscious mind and emotional body.

Balanced Sacral Chakra: When the Swadhisthana Chakra is in balance, you experience emotional harmony, healthy relationships, and the ability to enjoy life's pleasures without attachment. You are creative, passionate, and confident in expressing your desires. Sexuality is viewed in a positive light, and there's a healthy flow of emotions. You are able to experience intimacy, joy, and connection with others. Creativity flows effortlessly, and you are open to new experiences and ideas.

Imbalanced Sacral Chakra: An imbalanced Swadhisthana Chakra can lead to emotional instability, sexual dysfunction, and difficulties in relationships. On a physical level, you may experience issues with the reproductive organs, urinary system, or lower back. Emotionally, imbalance in this chakra can manifest as fear of intimacy, guilt, shame, or an overindulgence in sensual pleasures. You may feel creatively blocked, disconnected from your emotions, or overly dependent on others for validation and emotional security. Conversely, excessive energy in this chakra may lead to impulsive behaviours, addiction, or overindulgence in sensory pleasures. In extreme cases, it can cause emotional turbulence, jealousy, or possessiveness in relationships.

How to Balance the Swadhisthana Chakra

Balancing the Sacral Chakra involves reconnecting with your emotions, embracing creativity, and allowing pleasure into your life in a balanced way. Since this chakra is tied to the water element, practices that encourage fluidity and emotional release are most beneficial.

Movement and Dance: As the chakra of fluidity, rhythmic movement, particularly dancing, helps to unblock the energy of the Swadhisthana. Dance and free-form movement release stored emotions and allow the creative energy to flow freely through the body. Dancing to music that makes you feel joyful and expressive can be especially beneficial for this chakra.

Yoga Poses: Certain yoga postures can help activate the Swadhisthana Chakra by opening the hips and lower abdomen, which is where this chakra resides. Poses like **Baddha Konasana (Bound Angle Pose)**, **Upavistha Konasana (Seated Wide-Legged Forward Fold)**, and **Bhujangasana (Cobra Pose)** are effective for stimulating this chakra. These poses encourage openness in the pelvic region and stimulate emotional release and creative flow.

Meditation and Visualization: Meditating on the Swadhisthana Chakra involves focusing on the colour orange and visualizing a warm, glowing orange light swirling in the lower abdomen. Chanting the mantra **"Vam"** during meditation can help to activate and balance this energy center. Visualization of water—such as imagining yourself standing by a calm river or in the ocean—can help connect with the fluid nature of this chakra. This helps in releasing emotional blockages and bringing emotional fluidity.

Creative Expression: Since the Swadhisthana Chakra is closely tied to creativity, engaging in artistic activities like painting, writing, or music can help bring it into balance. When this chakra is blocked, creative energy may feel stagnant, so allowing yourself to create without judgment or expectation can reignite that flow. Embrace creative hobbies, even if they are outside your usual activities, as they help awaken the creative energy within.

Emotional Awareness and Release: Emotional healing is essential for balancing the Sacral Chakra. Journaling about your emotions, practicing self-awareness, and allowing yourself to fully feel and express your emotions—whether they be joy, sadness, or anger—can clear blockages. Avoid suppressing emotions, as doing so can lead to an energetic build-up. Instead, practice emotional release through safe outlets such as crying, talking with a trusted friend, or practicing mindfulness to observe and let go of negative emotional patterns.

Breathing Exercises (Pranayama): Deep, rhythmic breathing that engages the lower abdomen, such as **Belly Breathing** or **Kapalabhati (Skull-Shining Breath)**, helps bring awareness to the lower body and energizes the Swadhisthana Chakra. These techniques help improve circulation and release tension stored in the lower abdominal area, allowing for a smoother flow of energy.

Nutrition: Foods that are rich in water content, such as oranges, melons, berries, and coconut water, can nourish the Sacral Chakra. Additionally, foods that support the reproductive system, like nuts, seeds, and healthy fats, also help balance this energy center. Orange-coloured foods like carrots, mangoes, and papayas resonate with the chakra's colour and can help restore balance.

Affirmations: Affirmations can help shift negative thought patterns related to creativity, pleasure, and emotions. Examples of affirmations to balance the Sacral Chakra include:

- "I embrace pleasure and abundance."
- "I am creative and inspired."
- "I allow my emotions to flow freely and joyfully."

Crystals: Crystals like **Carnelian, Orange Calcite**, and **Moonstone** resonate with the Swadhisthana Chakra. Using these crystals in meditation, placing them on your lower abdomen, or carrying them with you can help balance the energy of this chakra. Carnelian, in particular, is known for stimulating creativity and boosting emotional health.

Aromatherapy: Essential oils such as **Ylang Ylang, Sandalwood**, and **Rose** are associated with balancing the Sacral Chakra. These oils enhance emotional well-being, sensuality, and creativity, helping to bring harmony to this energy center. Diffusing these scents, adding them to a bath, or using them in a massage can promote a more balanced Swadhisthana Chakra.

Conclusion

The Swadhisthana Chakra is the seat of emotional balance, creativity, and sensual pleasure. By actively engaging in creative expression, emotional awareness, and balancing physical and energetic practices, you can bring harmony to this chakra, leading to a life filled with more joy, healthy relationships, and a balanced approach to desires. The teachings of the **Yoga Sutras of Patanjali** remind us of the importance of self-control over desires and emotions, and by balancing this chakra, we find equilibrium between indulgence and discipline, creativity and control.

3. Manipura Chakra (Solar Plexus Chakra)

- **Location**: Upper abdomen, between the navel and the diaphragm
- **Color**: Yellow
- **Element**: Fire
- **Key Concepts**: Power, will, self-esteem, confidence, personal identity
- **Function:** Governs personal power, self-esteem, confidence, and self-discipline
- **Mantra**: Ram
- **Associated Areas**: Digestive system, pancreas, liver, stomach

The **Manipura Chakra**, also known as the Solar Plexus Chakra, is the center of personal power and will. "Manipura" translates to "city of jewels," symbolizing the precious nature of our self-worth and empowerment. This chakra represents the fire element, which is linked to transformation, energy, and drive. It is through the energy of Manipura that we manifest our goals, assert our willpower, and gain confidence in our abilities.

Balanced Manipura Chakra: When the Manipura Chakra is balanced, you feel confident, in control, and have a strong sense of self-worth. You possess a healthy level of self-esteem, inner strength, and determination, allowing you to assert yourself and make decisions with clarity. You trust your ability to take action and achieve your goals. On a physical level, a balanced solar plexus chakra promotes healthy digestion, balanced metabolism, and strong energy levels. Emotionally, a balanced chakra fosters independence, a sense of purpose, and the ability to lead with confidence.

Imbalanced Manipura Chakra: An imbalance in the Solar Plexus Chakra can manifest as low self-esteem, lack of confidence, or a need for excessive control. If underactive, this chakra can lead to feelings of powerlessness, insecurity, or a victim mentality. You may experience difficulty making decisions, lack motivation, or feel a sense of inadequacy. Physically, this can result in digestive issues, chronic fatigue, or problems with the pancreas or liver. On the other hand, if overactive, you may become domineering, controlling, or overly critical of yourself and others. This can lead to anger, perfectionism, or aggression, as well as physical issues like ulcers, acid reflux, or hypertension.

How to Balance the Manipura Chakra

Balancing the Solar Plexus Chakra requires practices that strengthen self-worth, ignite inner fire, and develop self-discipline. Techniques that stimulate the digestive system, enhance metabolism, and boost personal empowerment are particularly beneficial.

Core-Strengthening Yoga: Yoga poses that stimulate the core region and strengthen the abdominal muscles are ideal for balancing the Manipura Chakra. Poses such as **Navasana (Boat Pose), Utkatasana (Chair Pose), Dhanurasana (Bow Pose)**, and **Plank Pose** activate and energize the solar plexus region, helping to build physical strength and increase confidence. A study published in *Frontiers in Psychology* found that yoga practices focused on the core improved self-esteem and personal empowerment in participants. The physical engagement of the core area stimulates the fire element within the body, which can ignite willpower and determination.

Meditation and Visualization: Meditating on the Manipura Chakra involves focusing on the colour yellow and visualizing a bright, radiant sun at the solar plexus. Chanting the mantra **"Ram"** while meditating can help activate and balance this chakra. Visualizing the energy of a fire burning brightly in the stomach area helps to clear blockages and enhance feelings of empowerment. This fire symbolizes the transformation of doubts and insecurities into confidence and self-assertion.

Pranayama (Breathing Techniques): Kapalabhati (Skull-Shining Breath) and **Bhastrika (Bellows Breath)** are powerful breathing exercises that energize the body and stimulate the Manipura Chakra. These techniques invigorate the digestive system, improve circulation, and promote clarity of mind, which strengthens personal willpower. By practicing these breaths, you can awaken the dormant energy within the solar plexus and develop greater focus and discipline.

Affirmations for Self-Empowerment: Using positive affirmations can help rewire negative thought patterns and foster a stronger sense of self-worth. Examples of affirmations for the Manipura Chakra include:

- "I am confident and worthy of success."
- "I honour the power within me."
- "I trust myself to take action and manifest my goals."

Repeating these affirmations regularly can help rebuild confidence and encourage self-empowerment.

Healthy Diet for Digestive Balance: Since the Manipura Chakra governs the digestive system, consuming foods that support healthy digestion and metabolism is key. Incorporate warm, easy-to-digest foods such as whole grains, legumes, ginger, and turmeric. Avoid heavy, overly processed foods that may disrupt digestion. Yellow-coloured foods such as corn, bananas, and pineapples resonate with the energy of the solar plexus and can be included to help activate this chakra.

Building Self-Discipline: As the center of willpower, the Manipura Chakra thrives on practices that enhance self-discipline. Setting small, achievable goals and committing to daily routines, such as exercising or mindful eating, strengthens this chakra. The **Bhagavad Gita** emphasizes the importance of self-discipline, and developing a daily practice, whether through yoga, meditation, or healthy habits, directly correlates with a balanced Manipura Chakra.

Crystals for Confidence: Crystals such as **Citrine**, **Tiger's Eye**, and **Amber** are associated with the Solar Plexus Chakra and help amplify self-confidence and personal power. Citrine, known as the "stone of abundance," helps increase energy and motivation, while Tiger's Eye is believed to enhance courage and mental clarity. You can meditate with these stones, carry them with you, or place them on your solar plexus during relaxation to boost the chakra's energy.

Aromatherapy for Willpower: Essential oils such as **Lemon, Peppermint**, and **Ginger** are invigorating and help stimulate the Manipura Chakra. These oils can be diffused, used in massages, or applied to the skin to awaken energy and promote feelings of personal empowerment. The sharp, energizing scents of these oils resonate with the fire element, enhancing focus and motivation.

Conclusion

The **Manipura Chakra** is the powerhouse of personal strength, self-esteem, and determination. When balanced, it allows you to step into your power, take control of your life, and pursue your goals with confidence. By engaging in practices that strengthen the core, empower the mind, and support healthy digestion, you can bring this energy center into alignment and unlock your full potential.

4. Anahata Chakra (Heart Chakra)

- **Location**: Center of the chest
- **Color**: Green
- **Element**: Air
- **Key Concepts**: Love, compassion, connection, forgiveness, emotional balance
- **Function:** Regulates love, compassion, emotional connection, forgiveness, and empathy
- **Mantra**: Yam
- **Associated Areas**: Heart, lungs, circulatory system, shoulders, arms, and hands

The **Anahata Chakra**, also known as the Heart Chakra, is the fourth energy center and acts as the bridge between the lower, more physical chakras and the higher, more spiritual chakras. "Anahata" means "unstruck" or "unbeaten," symbolizing a pure, unwavering love that is not affected by external conditions. It is through this chakra that we cultivate unconditional love, compassion, and deep emotional connections with others. The air element associated with Anahata reflects its expansive, open nature, which allows love and empathy to flow freely.

Balanced Anahata Chakra: When the Anahata Chakra is balanced, you experience unconditional love for yourself and others. You are open, empathetic, compassionate, and able to give and receive love freely. Forgiveness and emotional healing come naturally, and you are able to form deep, meaningful connections. A balanced heart chakra also promotes physical health in the heart and circulatory system, contributing to a sense of emotional peace and well-being. You feel a sense of oneness with the world, cultivating harmony and understanding in your relationships.

Imbalanced Anahata Chakra: An imbalance in the heart chakra can manifest in two ways: underactive or overactive.

- **Underactive Heart Chakra**: You may experience feelings of isolation, jealousy, or difficulty in trusting others. Emotional wounds may cause you to guard your heart, making it hard to connect with others on a deeper level. This can lead to emotional withdrawal, lack of empathy, or a sense of being disconnected from love. Physically, an underactive Anahata Chakra can result in heart or lung issues, high blood pressure, and poor circulation.

- **Overactive Heart Chakra**: When the heart chakra is overstimulated, you may become overly self-sacrificing or dependent on others for emotional validation. You might find it difficult to maintain healthy boundaries, leading to co-dependency or losing your sense of self in relationships. Overactive energy can manifest as possessiveness or an overwhelming need to please others. Physically, this may cause heart palpitations, shortness of breath, or anxiety.

How to Balance the Anahata Chakra

Balancing the Heart Chakra involves opening up to love and compassion while healing past emotional wounds. Practices that promote connection, forgiveness, and emotional healing are ideal for bringing harmony to Anahata.

Heart-Opening Yoga Poses: Yoga poses that expand the chest and open the heart area are highly beneficial for balancing the Anahata Chakra. Postures like **Ustrasana (Camel Pose), Bhujangasana (Cobra Pose), Matsyasana (Fish Pose)**, and **Setu Bandhasana (Bridge Pose)** open the heart space, stimulate the chest and lungs, and promote a sense of emotional release. These poses also engage the back, shoulders, and arms, encouraging openness and allowing the heart energy to flow freely.

Meditation and Visualization: Meditating on the Anahata Chakra involves focusing on the colour green and visualizing a radiant, green light at the center of your chest. Chanting the mantra **"Yam"** helps activate and align the heart chakra. You can also visualize an expanding energy of love and compassion, filling your entire body and extending to those around you. This practice fosters feelings of connection and deep emotional healing. Guided meditations that focus on self-love, forgiveness, and compassion can further promote heart chakra balance.

Cultivating Love and Gratitude: Cultivating positive emotions such as love, gratitude, and compassion is essential for balancing the heart chakra. A study by the **HeartMath Institute** demonstrated that generating feelings of love and gratitude enhances coherence between the heart and brain, leading to better emotional health and overall well-being. Practices such as journaling about what you are grateful for, expressing love to those around you, and engaging in random acts of kindness can help open the heart chakra and increase emotional flow.

Breathing Exercises (Pranayama): Deep, slow, and mindful breathing practices help balance the Anahata Chakra by stimulating the lungs and promoting relaxation. **Anulom Vilom (Alternate Nostril Breathing)** and **Dirga Pranayama (Three-Part Breath)** are excellent for calming the mind and opening the heart. These techniques bring awareness to the breath and encourage a sense of inner peace, which allows love and compassion to flow more freely.

Forgiveness and Emotional Release: Healing past emotional wounds and practicing forgiveness are crucial for balancing the heart chakra. Holding onto grudges, resentment, or past trauma can block the flow of love and prevent the heart chakra from functioning properly. Engage in forgiveness practices, whether through journaling, therapy, or talking with loved ones. Releasing emotional pain can open the space for new, loving energy to enter.

Affirmations for Compassion and Love: Using positive affirmations helps in reprogramming the subconscious mind to promote love, compassion, and self-acceptance. Examples of heart chakra affirmations include:

- "I am open to giving and receiving love."
- "I forgive myself and others with ease."
- "My heart is full of compassion, love, and gratitude."

Heart-Healthy Diet: Since the Anahata Chakra is associated with the heart and lungs, it is beneficial to consume heart-healthy foods. Green, leafy vegetables such as spinach, kale, and broccoli are especially nourishing for this chakra. Foods rich in antioxidants, like berries, and those that support cardiovascular health, such as avocados, nuts, and seeds, also promote heart chakra balance.

Crystals for Healing and Compassion: Crystals like **Rose Quartz, Green Aventurine**, and **Emerald** are strongly associated with the Heart Chakra. Rose Quartz is known as the stone of unconditional love and helps heal emotional wounds, while Green Aventurine promotes emotional healing and growth. Placing these crystals on the heart chakra during meditation or carrying them with you can help open and balance Anahata's energy.

Aromatherapy for Emotional Balance: Essential oils such as **Rose, Lavender**, and **Eucalyptus** are linked to the heart chakra and promote emotional healing and balance. These oils can be diffused, added to baths, or used in massage to support emotional well-being. Rose oil, in particular, has long been associated with the energy of unconditional love and compassion, helping to open the heart and heal emotional wounds.

Conclusion

The **Anahata Chakra** is the center of love, compassion, and emotional connection. Balancing this chakra enables you to cultivate unconditional love, compassion, and empathy for yourself and others. The ancient wisdom of the **Hatha Yoga Pradipika** aligns with modern research from the **HeartMath Institute**, highlighting the transformative power of the heart. By engaging in practices that open the heart space, encourage forgiveness, and foster connection, you can bring harmony to this chakra and lead a life filled with love, peace, and emotional well-being.

5. Vishuddha Chakra (Throat Chakra)

- **Location**: Throat
- **Color**: Blue
- **Element**: Ether (Space)
- **Key Concepts**: Communication, self-expression, authenticity, truth, creativity
- **Function:** Governs communication, self-expression, truthfulness, and creative expression
- **Mantra**: Ham
- **Associated Areas**: Throat, neck, mouth, thyroid, vocal cords, jaw

The **Vishuddha Chakra**, also known as the Throat Chakra, is the center of communication and self-expression. "Vishuddha" means "purity," reflecting the importance of clear and honest communication in our interactions. As the element of ether (space) governs this chakra, it represents openness, expansion, and the infinite possibilities that arise when we speak our truth. The energy of Vishuddha allows us to express our authentic selves, articulate our thoughts, and communicate in a way that resonates with our inner truth.

Balanced Vishuddha Chakra: A balanced Throat Chakra allows for clear, effective, and authentic communication. You are able to express yourself confidently and truthfully, listen actively to others, and communicate with compassion. Creativity flows freely, and you feel empowered to voice your opinions, thoughts, and emotions without fear of judgment. Physically, a balanced throat chakra supports a healthy thyroid, clear vocal cords, and overall wellness in the throat, neck, and mouth areas. This balance also enhances your ability to align with your higher truth and speak from a place of integrity.

Imbalanced Vishuddha Chakra: When the Vishuddha Chakra is out of balance, communication and self-expression become difficult.

- **Underactive Throat Chakra**: You may struggle with speaking up, expressing yourself, or finding the right words to articulate your thoughts. This can lead to feelings of insecurity, shyness, or fear of judgment. You may suppress your emotions, avoid conversations, or feel misunderstood. Physically, this can manifest as a sore throat, laryngitis, thyroid issues, or neck stiffness.

- **Overactive Throat Chakra**: An overactive Throat Chakra may cause excessive talking, gossiping, or dominating conversations without listening to others. This imbalance can manifest as a tendency to interrupt, manipulate through words, or be overly critical or harsh. Physically, an overactive chakra may result in throat infections, vocal strain, jaw tension, or hyperthyroidism.

How to Balance the Vishuddha Chakra

Balancing the Throat Chakra requires practices that enhance communication skills, encourage authenticity, and promote clarity in self-expression. It also involves working on both listening and speaking with mindfulness and truth.

Throat-Opening Yoga Poses: Yoga poses that open and stretch the throat and neck area are effective in balancing the Vishuddha Chakra. Poses like **Matsyasana (Fish Pose), Sarvangasana (Shoulder Stand), Setu Bandhasana (Bridge Pose)**, and **Ustrasana (Camel Pose)** help stimulate the throat and clear any energetic blockages. **Jalandhara Bandha (Throat Lock)**, as described in the **Hatha Yoga Pradipika**, is a powerful technique for purifying and balancing the throat chakra. It involves contracting the throat and holding the breath, creating space for the expression of truth.

Mantra Chanting and Sound Therapy: Chanting the mantra **"Ham"**, associated with the Throat Chakra, helps to vibrate the throat region and activate Vishuddha's energy. Singing, chanting, or simply humming can be incredibly beneficial for clearing blockages in the throat chakra. Sound therapy, such as using **Tibetan singing bowls** or **tuning forks** that resonate with the frequency of the Vishuddha Chakra, can also help bring it into balance.

Mindful Communication and Active Listening: To balance Vishuddha, practice mindful communication by speaking thoughtfully, with awareness of your words and their impact on others. Engaging in conversations with honesty and kindness promotes harmony in this chakra. Equally important is active listening—being fully present when others speak and giving them the space to express themselves without interruption. This balanced exchange of speaking and listening fosters healthy communication and helps develop empathy.

Journaling and Self-Reflection: Writing is an excellent way to express thoughts and emotions, especially when verbal expression is challenging. Journaling about your feelings, experiences, and inner truth allows you to release suppressed emotions and gain clarity about your thoughts. It can help you become more aware of your communication patterns and areas where you might need to improve self-expression.

Affirmations for Authenticity and Communication: Positive affirmations can help rewire your subconscious and promote authentic self-expression. Examples of affirmations for the Throat Chakra include:

- "I speak my truth clearly and confidently."

- "I express myself with honesty and compassion."
- "I listen to others with an open heart and mind."

Repeating these affirmations daily helps you align with the energy of Vishuddha, creating space for clear and authentic communication.

Pranayama (Breathing Exercises): Breathing exercises that engage the throat area are excellent for clearing blockages in the Vishuddha Chakra. **Ujjayi Pranayama (Ocean Breath)**, in which you constrict the back of the throat slightly while breathing, creates a soothing sound and promotes calmness, helping to balance the throat chakra. This breath is often used in yoga to create focus and bring awareness to the present moment, assisting in aligning communication with inner truth.

Creative Expression: Since Vishuddha governs creativity, engaging in creative activities like singing, painting, writing, or public speaking helps balance this chakra. These forms of self-expression provide a safe space for you to express your thoughts, emotions, and inner truth. When you allow your creativity to flow, you release any energetic blockages and open yourself to the fullness of self-expression.

Crystals for Clarity and Expression: Crystals such as **Blue Lace Agate, Aquamarine**, and **Sodalite** are closely associated with the Throat Chakra and can help enhance communication and clarity. Blue Lace Agate promotes calm and clear expression, while Aquamarine encourages truthful communication. Carrying these stones, meditating with them, or placing them on the throat area can amplify the energy of Vishuddha and promote balance.

Aromatherapy for Expression: Essential oils like **Lavender, Peppermint**, and **Eucalyptus** are excellent for soothing and opening the throat chakra. These oils can be diffused, applied as a neck massage, or used in baths to promote relaxation and encourage clarity in communication. Eucalyptus, in particular, helps clear the throat area, improving the flow of energy in Vishuddha.

Conclusion

The **Vishuddha Chakra** is the gateway to authentic communication and self-expression. Balancing this chakra allows you to speak your truth clearly and confidently while being mindful of others. Ancient yogic practices such as **Jalandhara Bandha**, combined with modern techniques like **speech therapy integrated with throat-focused yoga**, offer powerful tools for enhancing communication skills. The **Hatha Yoga Pradipika** and other yogic texts remind us that purification of this chakra is essential for clear and truthful expression. By practicing mindful communication, engaging in creative expression, and using techniques that support the throat chakra, you can align with your highest truth and communicate with authenticity and clarity.

6. Ajna Chakra (Third Eye Chakra)

- **Location**: Between the eyebrows (center of the forehead)
- **Color**: Indigo
- **Element**: Light
- **Key Concepts**: Intuition, wisdom, insight, inner vision, perception
- **Function**: Governs intuition, wisdom, psychic abilities, spiritual insight, and inner vision
- **Mantra**: Om
- **Associated Areas**: Eyes, brain, pineal gland, nervous system

The **Ajna Chakra**, or Third Eye Chakra, is the sixth energy center and is regarded as the seat of intuition, wisdom, and spiritual insight.

"Ajna" means "command" or "perceive," symbolizing the ability to command inner wisdom and perceive the truth beyond the physical senses. This chakra is often associated with the **pineal gland**, which is linked to spiritual awakening and heightened states of awareness. It governs our ability to see beyond the material world, providing clarity, inner knowing, and access to higher consciousness. The element of light symbolizes the illumination of truth and higher understanding that comes with the activation of this chakra.

Balanced Ajna Chakra: When the Ajna Chakra is balanced, you have a strong sense of intuition and inner knowing. You experience clarity of thought, wisdom, and insight into the nature of reality. A balanced Third Eye Chakra enables you to trust your intuition, make wise decisions, and perceive situations with deeper understanding. This chakra also enhances imagination, creativity, and spiritual awareness, allowing for profound inner experiences. You may have vivid dreams, heightened perception, and a clear connection to your higher self. Physically, a balanced Ajna Chakra promotes healthy vision, mental clarity, and a well-functioning nervous system.

Imbalanced Ajna Chakra: Imbalances in the Third Eye Chakra can manifest in several ways:

- **Underactive Ajna Chakra**: You may feel disconnected from your intuition, experience confusion, or find it difficult to trust your inner guidance. An underactive Ajna Chakra can cause a lack of focus, poor memory, or indecisiveness. You might struggle with seeing the bigger picture or feeling lost in day-to-day concerns. Physically, this imbalance may result in headaches, vision problems, or sleep disturbances.

- **Overactive Ajna Chakra**: An overactive Ajna Chakra can cause an overwhelming flood of thoughts or psychic experiences, leading to anxiety or difficulty distinguishing between imagination and reality. You may become overly attached to abstract ideas or spiritual concepts, leading to detachment from the material world. Overstimulation of the Third Eye can also lead to difficulty concentrating, vivid nightmares, or hallucinations.

How to Balance the Ajna Chakra

Balancing the Third Eye Chakra requires practices that promote mental clarity, enhance intuition, and support spiritual growth. It involves cultivating inner stillness and deepening your connection to your higher consciousness.

Meditation for Clarity and Intuition: Meditation is one of the most powerful tools for activating and balancing the Ajna Chakra. Focused meditation on the **Third Eye** or practicing **Candle Gazing (Trataka)** can help stimulate this chakra. Trataka involves gazing at a candle flame or a point of focus, which improves concentration, clears mental clutter, and enhances inner vision. Meditation with the mantra **"Om"**, the universal sound of creation, aligns your energy with higher consciousness and awakens the Third Eye.

Visualization and Inner Reflection: Visualizing a deep indigo light at the center of your forehead during meditation helps activate the Ajna Chakra. You can also visualize this light expanding outward, illuminating your mind and bringing clarity to your thoughts. Engaging in self-reflection and introspection allows you to tune in to your inner wisdom, making it easier to access your intuition and higher awareness. Regular contemplation of your thoughts and beliefs helps clear mental blockages and bring balance to this chakra.

Mindfulness and Observation: Practicing mindfulness in your daily life brings awareness to your thoughts, emotions, and perceptions. By observing your reactions and thoughts without judgment, you strengthen your ability to perceive the truth beyond the surface. This mindful observation opens the door to deeper insight and helps balance the Ajna Chakra by promoting clarity and wisdom.

Pranayama (Breathwork) for Mental Clarity: Breathing exercises that engage the mind and promote calmness are effective in balancing the Ajna Chakra. **Nadi Shodhana (Alternate Nostril Breathing)** is particularly beneficial as it balances the left and right hemispheres of the brain, enhancing mental clarity and focus. This pranayama also purifies the nadis (energy channels), promoting the free flow of energy through the Third Eye and aligning your inner vision.

Chanting and Sound Therapy: Chanting the mantra **"Om"** during meditation or throughout the day helps activate the Third Eye and align your consciousness with universal wisdom. The vibration of "Om" resonates with the frequency of the Ajna Chakra, clearing mental fog and promoting spiritual insight. Sound therapy using **singing bowls** or **binaural beats** tuned to the frequency of the Third Eye Chakra (around 144 Hz) can also aid in bringing balance to this energy center.

Affirmations for Intuition and Wisdom: Affirmations are a powerful way to reprogram your subconscious mind and align with the energy of the Third Eye Chakra. Examples of affirmations include:

- "I trust my intuition and inner wisdom."
- "I see clearly and perceive truth beyond illusions."
- "My mind is open, and I am connected to higher consciousness."

Regularly repeating these affirmations helps strengthen your intuition and bring clarity to your thoughts.

Yoga Poses for Insight and Focus: Yoga poses that bring awareness to the Third Eye Chakra are excellent for enhancing concentration and intuition. Poses such as **Balasana (Child's Pose), Adho Mukha Svanasana (Downward-Facing Dog)**, and **Viparita Karani (Legs-Up-the-Wall Pose)** encourage circulation to the head and stimulate the Third Eye. These poses also promote relaxation and help clear mental blockages.

Crystal Healing for Clarity and Insight: Crystals like **Amethyst, Lapis Lazuli**, and **Sodalite** are associated with the Ajna Chakra and help enhance spiritual insight and intuition. Amethyst is known for its calming and spiritually enlightening properties, while Lapis Lazuli promotes inner vision and self-awareness. Placing these crystals on the Third Eye during meditation or keeping them close to you throughout the day can help bring balance to this chakra.

Aromatherapy for Spiritual Awakening: Essential oils such as **Sandalwood, Lavender**, and **Frankincense** are known to support the activation of the Third Eye Chakra. These oils promote relaxation, mental clarity, and spiritual awareness. Using them in a diffuser or applying them topically during meditation can help stimulate your intuition and inner vision.

Conclusion

The **Ajna Chakra** is the center of intuition, inner wisdom, and spiritual insight. A balanced Third Eye Chakra allows you to perceive truth, trust your intuition, and connect with higher consciousness. Ancient yogic texts such as the **Shiva Samhita** emphasize the significance of awakening the Third Eye to transcend duality and achieve spiritual enlightenment. Modern practices like meditation, trataka, and pranayama help activate and balance the Ajna Chakra, promoting mental clarity and a deeper connection to your inner wisdom. By integrating these practices, you can unlock the full potential of your intuition and experience profound spiritual growth.

7. Sahasrara Chakra (Crown Chakra)

- **Location**: Top of the head (Crown)
- **Color**: Violet or White
- **Element**: Cosmic Energy (Akasha)
- **Function:** Governs spiritual connection, enlightenment, and oneness with the universe
- **Mantra**: Om (or Silence)
- **Associated Areas**: Brain, nervous system, pineal gland

The **Sahasrara Chakra**, also known as the Crown Chakra, is the seventh and highest energy center in the body. It symbolizes pure consciousness and the ultimate connection to the divine and the universe. The word "Sahasrara" means "thousand-petaled," representing the lotus flower with a thousand petals, a metaphor for the expansion of spiritual awareness and the limitless nature of consciousness. The element associated with the Sahasrara is cosmic energy, also called **Akasha** or **Brahman**, representing the vast, infinite energy of the universe. This chakra transcends individual identity and ego, offering a state of pure awareness and unity with all that exists.

Balanced Sahasrara Chakra: When the Sahasrara Chakra is balanced, one experiences a deep sense of spiritual connection, peace, and fulfillment. It represents the awakening of higher consciousness and the realization of one's oneness with the universe. A balanced Crown Chakra leads to feelings of profound joy, clarity, and inner peace, along with a sense of purpose and alignment with the higher self. Individuals with an open Sahasrara feel a deep connection to divine consciousness, often leading to moments of bliss, spiritual insight, and transcendence. This chakra, when balanced, also harmonizes the lower chakras, allowing the entire energy system to function optimally.

Imbalanced Sahasrara Chakra:

- **Underactive Sahasrara Chakra:** An underactive Crown Chakra can manifest as feelings of isolation, disconnection, and purposelessness. It may lead to a lack of spiritual awareness or a sense of being cut off from the higher self and the universe. This imbalance can also cause mental fog, rigid thinking, and scepticism toward spiritual matters. People may feel stuck in materialistic pursuits without a deeper understanding of their life's purpose.

- **Overactive Sahasrara Chakra:** An overactive Crown Chakra can lead to detachment from the physical world and an overwhelming focus on spiritual matters at the expense of everyday life. Individuals may feel disoriented, ungrounded, or excessively "in the clouds," leading to difficulties functioning in daily tasks. This state can also manifest as spiritual narcissism, where the individual becomes overly obsessed with spiritual experiences or concepts and neglects practical responsibilities.

How to Balance the Sahasrara Chakra:

Balancing the Sahasrara Chakra involves practices that enhance spiritual awareness, foster a sense of oneness, and bring clarity and serenity to the mind. It also requires balancing the lower chakras to create a stable foundation for spiritual growth.

Meditation for Enlightenment: **Meditation** is the primary practice for balancing and activating the Sahasrara Chakra. Meditative practices that focus on silence, stillness, and awareness of the present moment help awaken the Crown Chakra. **Silent meditation**, focusing on the infinite, or contemplating concepts like oneness with the universe can help open this chakra. Guided visualizations of divine light descending into the crown can also enhance spiritual connection.

Connection with Universal Consciousness: Cultivating an awareness of your connection to all beings and the universe fosters the expansion of the Sahasrara Chakra. Practices such as **bhakti yoga** (devotion), where one surrenders to a higher power, or **jnana yoga** (wisdom), where one seeks to understand the nature of reality, are powerful ways to connect with divine consciousness. These practices lead to a sense of unity and dissolve the ego, allowing the divine flow of energy through the Crown Chakra.

Affirmations for Divine Connection: Affirmations are a simple yet powerful way to align your thoughts with the energy of the Sahasrara Chakra. Examples of affirmations include:

- "I am connected to the divine source of the universe."
- "I am one with all that is."
- "I trust the higher wisdom that flows through me."

Regularly repeating these affirmations brings awareness to your spiritual connection and enhances the flow of divine energy.

Breathwork and Pranayama: Pranayama practices like **Bhramari (Bee Breath)** can help calm the mind and activate the Sahasrara Chakra. This breathwork technique creates a gentle vibration in the brain, promoting mental clarity and spiritual awareness. **Kundalini**

pranayama practices that guide energy upward through the chakras, from the base of the spine to the crown of the head, are also effective in awakening this chakra.

Yoga Poses for Alignment and Peace: Yoga poses that focus on stillness and relaxation can support the activation of the Sahasrara Chakra. **Savasana (Corpse Pose)**, where you completely relax the body and focus on the breath, helps cultivate inner peace and spiritual openness. **Padmasana (Lotus Pose)** is also traditionally associated with the Crown Chakra, symbolizing the blossoming of spiritual awareness. Gentle inversions like **Viparita Karani (Legs-Up-the-Wall Pose)** can also encourage energy flow to the head, promoting a connection to the divine.

Crystals for Spiritual Expansion: Crystals like **Clear Quartz**, **Amethyst**, and **Selenite** are closely associated with the Sahasrara Chakra. Clear Quartz is known as the "master healer" and helps in amplifying spiritual energy and clarity. Amethyst fosters spiritual growth and promotes serenity, while Selenite is believed to open the gateway to higher consciousness. Meditating with these crystals or placing them near your head while you sleep can help balance the Crown Chakra.

Aromatherapy for Divine Awakening: Essential oils such as **Frankincense**, **Myrrh**, and **Lotus** are excellent for enhancing the spiritual connection associated with the Sahasrara Chakra. These oils promote a sense of tranquillity and divine awareness. Using them in a diffuser or during meditation can create a sacred atmosphere and help open the Crown Chakra.

Sound Therapy and Chanting Om: The sound **"Om"** resonates with the Sahasrara Chakra and is often considered the universal sound of creation. Chanting "Om" during meditation or listening to **binaural beats** tuned to the Crown Chakra's frequency (around 963 Hz) can help activate and balance this chakra. The vibration of Om aligns your consciousness with the infinite, promoting peace, clarity, and spiritual enlightenment.

Contemplation of Oneness: Engage in contemplative practices that explore the concept of oneness with the universe. Ancient texts like the **Upanishads** speak of the Sahasrara as the doorway to **Brahman** (the ultimate reality). Reading sacred texts or engaging in deep philosophical reflection can help stimulate the Sahasrara Chakra and bring about a greater sense of connection to the divine.

Conclusion

The **Sahasrara Chakra** represents the highest level of spiritual connection and consciousness. A balanced Crown Chakra allows you to experience unity with the universe, inner peace, and spiritual enlightenment. Ancient scriptures like the **Upanishads** and **Yoga Sutras** speak of the Sahasrara as the portal to the ultimate reality, **Brahman**, where the individual self merges with universal consciousness. By engaging in meditative practices, pranayama, yoga, and spiritual reflection, you can activate the Sahasrara Chakra and unlock the profound wisdom and bliss that come with this ultimate spiritual awakening.

The Mystical Significance of 144,000

The number 144,000 holds profound significance in both yogic teachings and biblical symbolism, representing spiritual awakening and perfection. In the yogic system, the chakras are energy centers, each with a specific number of petals that symbolize the levels of consciousness and spiritual energy within an individual. These chakras serve as gateways to higher levels of awareness, and the number of petals associated with each chakra plays an important role in spiritual awakening.

The **Root Chakra (Muladhara)** has **4 petals**, symbolizing the foundation of stability and security. The **Sacral Chakra (Svadhisthana)** has **6 petals**, the **Solar Plexus Chakra (Manipura)**, with **10 petals**, the **Heart Chakra (Anahata)** has **12 petals**, while the **Throat Chakra (Vishuddha)** has **16 petals**.

When you add the petals of these chakras — 4, 6, 10, 12, and 16 — you get a total of **48 petals**. The **Ajna Chakra (Third Eye)**, which is often referred to as the seat of intuition and higher perception, is traditionally described as having **2 petals**. However, in esoteric interpretations, it is understood to be **two times as powerful** as the lower chakras, symbolically doubling its petals to **48** to reflect its heightened significance in spiritual ascension. This doubling suggests the Ajna Chakra transcends the duality of rational and intuitive understanding, uniting these aspects into a higher, singular perception.

Adding the 48 petals of the Ajna Chakra to the total of 48 petals from the lower chakras results in **96 petals**.

The **Crown Chakra (Sahasrara)**, the highest chakra located at the top of the head, is traditionally described as having **1,000 petals**, symbolizing the ultimate state of spiritual awakening and enlightenment, where the individual experiences union with the divine. The 1,000 petals of the Crown Chakra represent a state of complete transcendence, far beyond the material world.

In spiritual numerology, the total number of petals (96) is often linked with the number **144**, which is a significant number in many spiritual traditions. This number is then multiplied by the **1,000 petals** of the Crown Chakra, yielding **144,000** — the same number mentioned in the Bible's Book of Revelation (7:4), where it refers to a group of spiritually "sealed" individuals chosen by God.

The number **144,000** appears in several spiritual, esoteric, and religious contexts beyond the Bible, often symbolizing spiritual awakening, completion, or transformation. While the most well-known reference is in the Book of Revelation, other traditions and theories also invoke this number or have concepts resonating with its symbolic meaning. Here are some examples:

1. Mayan Calendar and Prophecy

In Mayan mythology, the number 144,000 is said to be significant in the context of cosmic cycles. The Mayan "baktun" is a period of 144,000 days, which represents a full cycle of creation. The end of a baktun was believed to mark a significant shift in consciousness or transformation. The number 144,000 here indicates not just a passage of time but also points to an era of renewal, transformation, and spiritual awakening.

2. Kabbalah (Jewish Mysticism)

In **Kabbalistic teachings**, certain numerological interpretations suggest that the number 144,000 holds mystical significance related to the concept of **Tikkun Olam** (the spiritual repair of the world). Although not directly referenced as 144,000, the process of repairing and refining spiritual energy to return it to its divine source resonates with the idea of spiritual transformation that the number signifies in other traditions.

3. Theosophy and Esoteric Christianity

Theosophy, an esoteric philosophical system that draws from various religious traditions, views 144,000 as significant in the context of spiritual evolution. In Theosophical teachings, it is believed that humanity is evolving through cycles, and 144,000 represents the souls that are ready for ascension or enlightenment. This echoes similar ideas from the Book of Revelation but with a more universal application, suggesting that these souls are spread across different races, cultures, and belief systems.

4. Freemasonry and Secret Societies

Freemasonry and other secret societies sometimes reference the number 144,000 in their symbolic language and rituals. Although the specifics can vary, it is often used to represent an elite group of initiates who have achieved a higher level of spiritual or esoteric knowledge. The idea here parallels the biblical concept of a chosen group but extends it to encompass those who have reached advanced stages of enlightenment through secret teachings.

Chakras and *Pheres* in Hindu Weddings

In a traditional Hindu wedding, the couple takes seven sacred steps around the fire (*saptapadi*), known as *pheres*, which symbolize vows of partnership and mutual responsibility. Each step resonates with deeper spiritual significance, paralleling the progression through the seven chakras. For example, the first *phere* is often about nourishment and provision, linked to the *Muladhara* (Root Chakra), which governs survival and security. As the couple progresses through the *pheres*, they move towards the higher chakras, such as the *Anahata* (Heart Chakra), representing unconditional love, and finally towards spiritual union, aligning with the *Sahasrara* (Crown Chakra), symbolizing divine consciousness. Thus, the *pheres* are not just physical rituals but also energetic steps towards deeper unity on a spiritual level.

Chakras and the Colors of the Rainbow

The seven chakras are traditionally associated with specific colors that correspond to the seven colors of the rainbow. Starting from red at the *Muladhara* chakra to violet at the *Sahasrara* chakra, this spectrum symbolizes the progression of energy from the most grounded, material aspects of existence to the highest states of spiritual awareness. The rainbow itself, with its natural progression from denser to lighter frequencies, can be seen as a visual metaphor for this energetic journey. Just as the rainbow appears after rain as a bridge between earth and sky, the chakras serve as a bridge between the physical body and the realms of consciousness, harmonizing the individual with cosmic energies.

Chakras and the Concept of Heavens

In Hindu cosmology, the concept of heavens or *lokas* represents various planes of existence, each corresponding to different levels of spiritual evolution. These realms can be seen as analogous to the chakras, with lower heavens representing more material planes and the higher heavens embodying subtler, spiritual realms. For example, *Bhurloka* is associated with earthly existence and survival, reflecting the energy of the *Muladhara* chakra. Higher realms, such as *Brahmaloka*, correspond to spiritual transcendence, resonating with the energy of the *Sahasrara* chakra. As a person evolves spiritually, they move through these realms, just as energy ascends through the chakras, leading ultimately to liberation and unity with the divine.

Integrating Yoga and Chakra Healing

Incorporating chakra-focused yoga practices into your daily routine can help harmonize your physical, emotional, and spiritual energies. Whether you are seeking to overcome personal challenges or elevate your spiritual consciousness, working with the chakras offers a pathway to holistic well-being. Various styles of yoga, such as Kundalini Yoga and Hatha Yoga, emphasize chakra activation as a means to awaken the dormant energy known as Kundalini, discussed later in this book, which is believed to lie coiled at the base of the spine.

Additionally, I want to emphasize that if you are seeking external help in healing or balancing chakras then it is crucial to remain vigilant in identifying and steering clear of impostor tantrics and harmful practices. True spiritual healers operate with integrity, respect, and a commitment to guiding inner transformation, without ever crossing ethical boundaries. A significant red flag to be aware of is when a so-called tantric insists on unnecessary physical contact, particularly touching private areas, under the pretext that it is essential for healing. Genuine chakra healing and energy work focus primarily on the flow of energy, meditation, and alignment of the body, mind, and spirit, typically without any invasive physical contact.

Authentic practices are rooted in ancient teachings that emphasize purity, respect, and non-harm. If something feels inappropriate or makes you uncomfortable, trust your intuition. It is essential to seek guidance from reputable, trustworthy sources or spiritual communities to avoid exploitation and ensure that the sanctity of your spiritual journey is preserved.

Conclusion: Yoga as a Path to Energetic Balance

Yoga and the chakras offer a profound journey of self-discovery, healing, and transformation. By understanding the seven major chakras and their corresponding yoga practices, one can cultivate balance, strength, and a deeper connection with the self and the universe. Drawing from both ancient wisdom and modern research, this chapter serves as a guide to exploring the subtle energies within and unlocking your fullest potential.

11

Aura

The concept of the *aura*—an energy field surrounding the human body—has fascinated spiritual seekers, healers, and scientists alike. Often described as a luminous glow or field that radiates around the physical body, the aura reflects our physical, emotional, mental, and spiritual states. Rooted in various ancient traditions, from the Vedic texts to modern metaphysical teachings, the aura is considered an essential aspect of human existence, linking the physical body with the subtle energies.

This chapter explores the nature of the aura, its layers, colors, and significance. By understanding the aura, we can gain insight into our well-being and the subtle energies that influence our daily lives.

The Nature of the Aura

The aura is often visualized as a multi-layered field of energy surrounding the physical body. Each layer corresponds to a different aspect of our being: the physical, emotional, mental, and spiritual. The health of the aura is believed to directly impact the health of the individual, and disruptions in the aura can manifest as physical or emotional imbalances.

The Vedic texts and the Upanishads describe the aura as the *Tejas* or radiance emanating from the individual, representing the vital force or *prana* within. In the *Brihadaranyaka Upanishad* (2.1.20), it is stated, "One becomes radiant when the inner consciousness is pure, and the life force shines through."

Modern metaphysical traditions also emphasize the aura, with practices such as Reiki, energy healing, and chakra balancing aimed at cleansing and strengthening it. Research in biofield science, a field that studies the energy fields around living beings, supports the existence of a measurable energy field surrounding the body.

The Layers of the Aura

1. **Physical Layer**
2. **Emotional Layer**
3. **Mental Layer**
4. **Spiritual Layers**

Let's understand each and every layer.

1. Physical Layer

The physical layer, or the *etheric body*, is the closest to the physical body and directly corresponds to our physical sensations, health, and vitality. It acts as a blueprint of our physical body and is sensitive to our lifestyle choices, like diet, exercise, and stress levels.

Research in biophoton emission—conducted by scientists like Dr. Fritz-Albert Popp at the International Institute of Biophysics—

demonstrates that living cells emit weak light. This could be interpreted as evidence of the physical layer, or the bioenergetic field, which interacts with our body's biological functions.

Regular yoga, especially Hatha Yoga and Pranayama (breathing exercises), purifies and strengthens this layer by improving circulation, oxygen flow, and reducing toxins, ultimately leading to enhanced vitality. Yoga postures open energy pathways (*nadis*), allowing life force (*prana*) to flow freely, which is reflected in a strong physical aura.

2. Emotional Layer

The emotional layer exists just beyond the physical, fluctuating with our emotional states. It vibrates with the emotional energy we experience, often manifesting as colors that shift based on whether we're experiencing joy, anger, love, or sadness.

The colors in this layer may change frequently, depending on emotional fluctuations. For instance, feelings of love and compassion are often represented by vibrant pink or green hues, while anger or frustration may appear as darker shades, such as red or gray.

Emotional healing practices, like Emotional Freedom Technique (EFT), meditation, or Pranayama (especially *Nadi Shodhana* or alternate nostril breathing), can balance and cleanse the emotional body. *Patanjali's Yoga Sutras* offer emotional regulation tools, emphasizing equanimity and compassion (Sutra 1.33) as means to cleanse the emotional field. When emotional blockages are resolved, the aura radiates more harmoniously.

3. Mental Layer

This layer governs thoughts, belief systems, and mental clarity. It holds the energy of intellectual activity, logic, and thought patterns, which can either be constructive or self-limiting.

Recent neuroscience research, including Dr. Joe Dispenza's work on neuroplasticity, shows how thought patterns and emotional reactions can alter brain structures. This is directly tied to the mental aura, where toxic thinking clouds clarity, while positive, mindful thinking creates a bright, clear mental field.

Mindfulness practices, positive affirmations, and *Jnana Yoga* (the yoga of wisdom) can help clear negative thought patterns, leading to a healthier mental aura. For example, repeating affirmations such as "I am worthy" or "I am at peace" shifts the energy within the mental layer, helping align thoughts with positive mental states.

4. Spiritual Layers

Beyond the physical, emotional, and mental layers, the spiritual layers of the aura represent our deeper connection with higher consciousness and the universal divine energy.

There are several sub-layers within the spiritual realm, including the *Astral, Etheric Template, Celestial,* and *Causal* bodies, each becoming more subtle as one progresses toward higher consciousness. These layers are associated with intuition, spiritual purpose, and divine awareness, often accessed through deeper spiritual practices.

The teachings of the *Kena Upanishad* (1.4) describe the ineffable nature of Brahman—the ultimate reality beyond sensory perception. This resonates with the energy of the spiritual layers, which transcend ordinary awareness and connect to the divine source. Through meditation, prayer, or Bhakti Yoga (devotion), one can nourish these layers and increase spiritual radiance.

Practices such as *Kundalini Yoga* and *Dhyana* (meditation) enhance the spiritual aura, increasing one's sense of oneness with the universe. Individuals who consistently engage in such practices develop a more luminous, expansive aura, indicating their deep spiritual connection and enlightenment.

The Colors of the Aura and Their Meanings

The colors of the aura are believed to represent various qualities, emotions, and spiritual states. Understanding these colors can provide insight into the current state of an individual's energy.

1. **Red:** Represents vitality, strength, and physical energy. A strong red aura often indicates a grounded and active person.

   Athletes or individuals engaged in physical labour may exhibit red auras due to their physical exertion and energy output.

2. **Orange:** Connected to creativity, joy, and enthusiasm. A bright orange aura signifies a person who is creative and emotionally balanced.

   Studies in color therapy, such as those published in the *Journal of Alternative and Complementary Medicine*, suggest that orange tones can stimulate creativity and vitality, correlating with the aura's emotional layer.

3. **Yellow:** Reflects mental clarity, intellect, and optimism. A bright yellow aura often appears in individuals who are mentally focused and positive.

   Scholars, writers, and individuals involved in intellectual work may have a prominent yellow aura.

4. **Green:** Associated with healing, growth, and balance. A strong green aura indicates compassion, healing abilities, and a connection to nature.

   Healers, doctors, and those who work closely with nature may exhibit a green aura, representing their nurturing and healing energies.

5. **Blue:** Represents communication, intuition, and calmness. A vibrant blue aura signifies someone who is spiritually connected and communicates with clarity and truth.

   In the *Bhagavad Gita* (10.33), Lord Krishna says, "Of letters, I am the letter A." This divine connection to sound and communication is often reflected in the blue aura of spiritual teachers and communicators.

6. **Indigo and Violet:** Linked to spiritual awareness, intuition, and higher consciousness. A bright violet aura indicates a person who is deeply spiritual and connected to the divine.

   Mystics, spiritual leaders, and advanced meditators often display these colors in their aura, reflecting their heightened spiritual awareness.

Real-Life Applications

Energy Healing Practices

Reiki, a form of energy healing developed by Dr. Mikao Usui, works directly with the aura to promote physical, emotional, and spiritual healing. Practitioners often observe changes in the aura as a person undergoes healing.

In one documented case, a person suffering from chronic stress experienced a significant change in their aura after a series of Reiki sessions, moving from dark, muted tones to brighter, vibrant colors, indicating restored vitality and emotional balance.

Scientific Research

The *Biofield Hypothesis*, proposed by researchers like Dr. Beverly Rubik, suggests that the human energy field, or aura, can be measured and manipulated to promote healing. Studies have shown that energy fields can influence cellular processes, supporting the idea that the aura plays a vital role in health and well-being.

Dr. Rubik's research on the biofield emphasizes that "The human biofield serves as a bridge between the physical and subtle bodies, influencing both health and consciousness."

Aura Cleansing and Strengthening Techniques

Cleansing and strengthening the aura is essential for maintaining a balanced energy field that promotes physical, emotional, and spiritual well-being. Various holistic techniques can be used to purify and energize the aura, creating harmony in all layers.

1. Meditation

Meditation is one of the most powerful and accessible tools for aura cleansing and strengthening. It works on multiple layers of the aura by fostering mental clarity, emotional equilibrium, and a deep connection to spiritual energy.

Chakra Meditation: This form of meditation involves focusing on the body's seven main energy centers (chakras). By visualizing the cleansing and alignment of these centers, one can remove blockages in the energy field, promoting a free flow of energy through the aura. For example, focusing on the heart chakra (*Anahata*) can release emotional baggage, enhancing the emotional layer of the aura, while the crown chakra (*Sahasrara*) meditation boosts spiritual energy.

Pranayama (Breathwork): Practices like *Kapalabhati* (skull-shining breath) or *Nadi Shodhana* (alternate nostril breathing) directly influence the aura by regulating the flow of *prana* (life force) through the subtle body. These techniques purify and energize the aura by balancing the internal energy system. With regular practice, the aura becomes brighter and more resilient, reflecting increased vitality and mental calmness.

Mindfulness Meditation: Through the practice of mindfulness, where one stays present and aware, negative thought patterns and emotional blockages are released from the mental and emotional layers. This enhances the overall vibrancy of the aura and leads to greater emotional and mental clarity.

2. Crystals and Gemstones

Crystals and gemstones have been used throughout history to influence the aura. These stones are believed to interact with and strengthen the energy field, each resonating with different vibrations that promote healing, protection, and spiritual growth.

Clear Quartz: Known as the "master healer," clear quartz is highly versatile and can amplify energy, making it ideal for overall aura cleansing. It absorbs negative energy and can be programmed with specific intentions for personal healing. Clear quartz can enhance clarity in the mental layer and heighten spiritual awareness by working on the higher spiritual layers of the aura.

Amethyst: This stone resonates with the higher chakras—especially the third eye (*Ajna*) and crown chakras—making it effective for spiritual protection and enhancing intuition. Amethyst clears out mental fog and negativity from the emotional and mental layers, fostering calmness, emotional stability, and spiritual clarity. It can also protect the aura from external energetic disruptions.

Black Tourmaline: Often used for grounding and protection, black tourmaline shields the aura from negative energies and electromagnetic pollution. It works on the physical and emotional layers, offering a layer of protection against toxic emotional or environmental influences.

To use these crystals for aura cleansing, one can meditate with them, wear them as jewellery, or place them in living spaces. Crystals can be used to create a protective and nurturing energy field around the body, enhancing the strength of the aura.

3. Sound Healing

Sound is a powerful tool for clearing and balancing the aura, as certain frequencies and vibrations resonate with the subtle energy body. These sounds help dislodge stagnant or negative energies and restore harmony to the aura.

Tibetan Singing Bowls: These ancient instruments produce deep, resonant tones that can penetrate the aura, shaking loose negative energy and restoring balance across all layers. The sound vibrations from the bowls create harmonious waves that cleanse and revitalize the energy field, often resulting in feelings of deep relaxation and spiritual awakening.

Mantra Chanting: Chanting sacred sounds, such as "Om" (often considered the sound of the universe), can align the physical, mental, and spiritual energies of the aura. The repetitive vibrations of these sounds harmonize the aura's frequencies, dissolving energetic blockages and promoting spiritual connection. Specific mantras, like "Gayatri" or "Maha Mrityunjaya," are believed to invoke divine protection and cleansing, enhancing the aura's spiritual layers.

Tuning Forks: Tuning forks calibrated to specific frequencies, like 432 Hz or 528 Hz, can be used for aura cleansing. These frequencies are known to harmonize and reset the body's natural vibrational state, aligning the aura's layers. This method is especially effective for recalibrating the mental and spiritual layers.

By immersing oneself in sound therapy, the aura can be cleared of energetic clutter, and the body's subtle energies can come into alignment. This promotes not only a balanced aura but also an overall sense of harmony and well-being.

Additional Techniques

Salt Baths: Immersing the body in saltwater, especially with sea salt or Epsom salts, is known to purify and cleanse the aura by absorbing negative energies. This technique works primarily on the physical and emotional layers, allowing a sense of renewal and detoxification.

Smudging with Sage or Palo Santo: These sacred herbs have been used for centuries in various cultures to purify energy. The smoke from burning sage or Palo Santo cleanses the aura, removing negative energies and allowing positive energy to flow freely.

Sun and Moon Exposure: Spending time in natural sunlight or moonlight can naturally recharge and strengthen the aura. The sun invigorates the physical and mental layers, while the moon enhances the emotional and spiritual layers.

Aura cleansing and strengthening are vital for maintaining an energetic balance in the body. Regular practice of these techniques helps protect against negative influences, boosts vitality, and deepens one's connection to their higher self. By integrating meditation, crystals, sound healing, and other methods, the aura remains radiant and resilient.

Conclusion

The aura is a profound reflection of our physical, emotional, mental, and spiritual states. By understanding and working with the aura, we can enhance our well-being, promote healing, and deepen our spiritual practice. This chapter has explored the nature of the aura, its layers, colors, and significance, drawing on ancient wisdom, modern research, and real-life examples to provide a comprehensive understanding of this vital aspect of our subtle anatomy.

12

Nadis

In the ancient system of yoga, the subtle body is as significant as the physical body. Central to this subtle anatomy are the *nadis*, the channels through which *prana* (vital energy) flows. The concept of nadis is foundational in yoga, Ayurveda, and tantric traditions, and understanding them is essential for those pursuing spiritual practices aimed at awakening higher consciousness.

The Meaning and Importance of Nadis

The word *nadi* comes from the Sanskrit root *nad*, which means "motion" or "flow." Nadis are often described as channels or conduits of prana, the life force that sustains all living beings. According to yogic tradition, there are 72,000 nadis in the human body, although only a few are considered of primary importance. These nadis form a complex network, carrying energy to every part of the body, much like the veins and arteries in the physical body. Veins are physical structures in the gross (physical) body responsible for transporting blood. They are part of the circulatory system and can be observed and measured directly.

Nadis, on the other hand, are considered part of the subtle body in various Eastern spiritual and yogic traditions. They are thought to be channels through which vital energy (prana) flows. Nadis are not physically observable but are believed to exist on a more subtle, energetic level.

So, veins and nadis represent different aspects of human anatomy: the former pertains to the physical realm, while the latter is associated with the subtle or energetic body.

The ancient texts, such as the *Hatha Yoga Pradipika* and the *Gheranda Samhita*, emphasize the purification of nadis as a prerequisite for awakening kundalini energy. The blockage or imbalance in the flow of energy through the nadis can lead to physical and mental ailments, whereas free-flowing nadis contribute to health, vitality, and spiritual awakening.

The Three Principal Nadis

1. **Ida Nadi**
2. **Pingala Nadi**
3. **Sushumna Nadi**

Let's understand these 3 important nadis.

1. Ida Nadi: The Channel of Lunar Energy

Ida Nadi is one of the three primary energy channels (*nadis*) in the yogic tradition, running along the left side of the spine. It corresponds to

Chandra Nadi, or lunar energy, which is considered cooling, calming, and introspective. The function of *Ida Nadi* is closely related to the parasympathetic nervous system, which governs rest, relaxation, and the body's ability to regenerate. Its activation encourages a state of mental tranquillity, emotional balance, and receptivity, making it essential for introspective and meditative practices.

Connection to Lunar Energy and Intuition

Just as the moon reflects calm, cooling light, *Ida Nadi* embodies the qualities of passivity, cooling energy, and calmness. It is the counterpart to *Pingala Nadi*, which represents solar energy. While *Pingala* is active and energizing, *Ida* is passive, soothing, and introspective. These qualities make *Ida Nadi* crucial for the development of intuition, creativity, and emotional balance.

Calmness and Relaxation: When *Ida Nadi* is dominant, the mind and body enter a state of rest and recovery. This is the energy that allows you to relax, sleep deeply, and reflect.

Intuition and Creativity: The lunar energy flowing through *Ida* fosters deeper insights, creativity, and intuition. It enhances the ability to connect with the subconscious mind and is often associated with creative problem-solving and emotional intelligence.

Association with the Parasympathetic Nervous System

Physiologically, *Ida Nadi* governs the parasympathetic nervous system (PNS), which is responsible for "rest and digest" functions. The PNS promotes activities that occur when the body is at rest, including the conservation of energy, slowing down the heart rate, and increasing digestive processes. When *Ida Nadi* is activated, the body experiences a sense of calm, and the mind becomes more receptive, reflective, and contemplative.

In contrast, over-activation of *Pingala Nadi* (the sympathetic nervous system) can lead to stress, anxiety, and an overactive mind. Balancing these two nadis is key to maintaining both physical and mental health, with *Ida Nadi* acting as a counterbalance to the stress and overactivity of modern life.

Pranayama Techniques for Ida Nadi Activation

Chandra Bhedana (Left Nostril Breathing)

Chandra Bhedana, also known as Left Nostril Breathing, is one of the most effective pranayama techniques for activating *Ida Nadi*. This practice draws in cool, lunar energy through the left nostril, promoting relaxation and mental clarity.

How to Practice Chandra Bhedana

- Sit in a comfortable position with the spine straight.
- Close your right nostril with your thumb.
- Inhale deeply through your left nostril.
- After the inhale, close your left nostril and exhale through the right.
- Repeat this process for 5–10 minutes, focusing on the cooling effect of the breath.

This practice activates *Ida Nadi*, balancing the body's energies and calming the mind. It is particularly beneficial during times of stress, anxiety, or when you feel mentally overworked.

Nadi Shodhana (Alternate Nostril Breathing)

While *Chandra Bhedana* focuses specifically on *Ida Nadi*, *Nadi Shodhana* (Alternate Nostril Breathing) balances both *Ida* and *Pingala Nadis*. This technique is ideal for harmonizing both the lunar and solar energies, ensuring that neither becomes overly dominant.

I have discussed how to practice Nadi Shodhana in the **Sushumna** section.

Nadi Shodhana purifies both nadis, clearing blockages and allowing prana (life force) to flow freely. This practice harmonizes the mind, balancing both intuition (through *Ida*) and logic (through *Pingala*).

Hatha Yoga and Ida Nadi

The word *Hatha* itself represents the balance between the sun (*Ha*, or *Pingala*) and the moon (*Tha*, or *Ida*). Many Hatha Yoga practices are designed to bring harmony between these two opposing energies. By practicing postures (asanas) and breathwork in unison, the practitioner can balance the physical and energetic body.

Moon Salutation (Chandra Namaskar): While Sun Salutation (Surya Namaskar) is widely known, the Moon Salutation sequence focuses on calming and grounding the body. It enhances the cooling effects of *Ida Nadi* and is often practiced in the evening or during times when a more restorative yoga practice is needed.

Restorative and Yin Yoga: These slow-paced, meditative forms of yoga help stimulate *Ida Nadi* by promoting deep relaxation and inward focus. As they emphasize longer holds in poses, the parasympathetic nervous system is activated, aligning with *Ida Nadi's* qualities of receptivity and calmness.

Ida Nadi and the Chakras

The *chakras* are energy centers along the spine, and *Ida Nadi* interacts with these energy centers as it flows through the body. *Ida* and *Pingala*

Nadis spiral around the central channel, *Sushumna Nadi*, crossing each other at certain points where the chakras reside.

Each chakra has both masculine (solar, active) and feminine (lunar, passive) aspects, and the balance of *Ida* and *Pingala* influences their energy.

Key Chakras Affected by Ida Nadi

Muladhara (Root Chakra): Located at the base of the spine, the *Muladhara* chakra governs survival, stability, and security. A balanced *Ida Nadi* can help keep the root chakra grounded and calm, preventing fear and anxiety. When *Ida* is overactive in this area, it may cause sluggishness, while underactivity can lead to restlessness or insecurity.

Svadhisthana (Sacral Chakra): Located in the lower abdomen, the *Svadhisthana* chakra governs creativity, pleasure, and emotional well-being. As *Ida Nadi* connects with this chakra, it supports the flow of emotions and creativity. A balanced *Ida* in this area promotes a healthy relationship with emotional expression and fluidity, while imbalance can cause emotional suppression or overwhelming emotional experiences.

Ajna (Third Eye Chakra): The *Ajna* chakra, located between the eyebrows, is the center of intuition, insight, and inner wisdom. Since *Ida Nadi* is closely linked to intuition and the subconscious mind, its energy is especially important at this chakra. Activation of *Ida Nadi* helps open the third eye, enhancing clarity, perception, and intuitive abilities. Many meditative practices aim to harmonize *Ida* and *Pingala* at this chakra to achieve a deep state of awareness and spiritual insight.

Impact on Mental and Emotional Well-Being

When *Ida Nadi* is in balance, it promotes emotional well-being and mental calmness. Many mental health benefits are associated with the activation of *Ida Nadi*:

Stress and Anxiety Management: Activating *Ida Nadi* helps manage stress by promoting the body's relaxation response. The calming energy of *Ida* brings balance to the mind, reducing anxiety and mental agitation. As *Ida Nadi* stimulates the parasympathetic nervous system, it helps counteract the effects of stress by slowing down heart rate, lowering blood pressure, and calming the mind.

Mental Clarity and Reflection: *Ida Nadi* is the pathway to deeper mental clarity. When active, it allows for more profound inner reflection, fostering self-awareness, creativity, and a better understanding of oneself. This is why many yogic practitioners focus on balancing *Ida* during times of meditation, as it opens the mind to new insights and helps unlock the subconscious.

Emotional Balance: By calming the nervous system, *Ida Nadi* supports emotional balance. It helps individuals deal with emotional challenges, ensuring that emotions like anger, frustration, or sadness do not overwhelm them. It also encourages compassion, receptivity, and empathy, making it essential for nurturing emotional intelligence.

Ida Nadi and the Subconscious Mind

Swami Satyananda Saraswati, in *Kundalini Tantra*, describes *Ida Nadi* as the "source of mental and emotional comfort and a pathway to the subconscious mind." This connection to the subconscious highlights *Ida Nadi's* role in accessing deeper layers of consciousness that are normally hidden from everyday awareness. When *Ida Nadi* is active and balanced, individuals often experience vivid dreams, heightened creativity, and intuitive insights.

Since *Ida* governs introspection and inner awareness, it is often activated during deep states of meditation and contemplation, leading practitioners into the deeper realms of the subconscious. Through the purification and activation of *Ida Nadi*, one can unlock hidden mental patterns, work through emotional blockages, and ultimately move toward a higher state of consciousness.

Conclusion

Ida Nadi represents the cool, reflective, and calming lunar energy within the body. Through the practice of pranayama techniques like *Chandra Bhedana* and *Nadi Shodhana*, you can activate and balance *Ida Nadi*, bringing relaxation, mental clarity, and emotional stability into your life. By fostering a healthy balance between *Ida* and *Pingala*, you can achieve a state of harmony, both within yourself and with the world around you.

2. Pingala Nadi: The Channel of Solar Energy

In the yogic tradition, *Pingala Nadi* is one of the three primary energy channels (*nadis*) in the body, running along the right side of the spine, and corresponding to solar energy (*Surya Nadi*). It is the counterpart of *Ida Nadi*, which carries lunar energy, and the two work together to balance the mind and body. While *Ida* governs calmness, intuition, and introspection, *Pingala* represents the active, logical, and physical side of existence.

Association with Solar Energy

Pingala Nadi is closely associated with the sun's vibrant, warming, and stimulating energy. Its qualities reflect dynamism, vitality, and outward-directed focus. This energy channel is linked with:

- **Activity and Action**
- **Logic and Rational Thinking**
- **Physical Strength and Vitality**
- **Alertness and Stimulation**

The sun-like quality of *Pingala Nadi* brings heat, energy, and dynamism into the body and mind. It governs the right side of the body and the left hemisphere of the brain, which is responsible for logical thinking, analysis, and problem-solving.

Physiological and Mental Impact

Pingala Nadi corresponds to the *sympathetic nervous system*, which is responsible for the body's "fight or flight" response. This system stimulates physical activity, increases alertness, and prepares the body for action by elevating the heart rate, increasing blood flow to muscles, and releasing adrenaline.

When *Pingala Nadi* is active, it brings vitality and sharp mental focus, making it ideal for tasks that require logic, reasoning, and decision-making. However, overactivity in *Pingala* can lead to restlessness or difficulty relaxing, overthinking or anxiety, physical tension, particularly in the form of increased heart rate, shallow breathing, or digestive issues related to stress, while an underactive *Pingala* can result in lethargy or mental dullness.

Pranayama and Pingala Nadi

Surya Bhedana (Right Nostril Breathing)

One of the key practices to activate *Pingala Nadi* is *Surya Bhedana Pranayama*, also known as Right Nostril Breathing. This technique stimulates the solar energy in the body, increasing physical energy and mental sharpness. It is particularly useful when you need to increase alertness or overcome fatigue.

How to Practice Surya Bhedana:

- Sit comfortably in a meditative posture with your spine straight.

- Close your left nostril with your ring finger and inhale deeply through your right nostril.

- After a full inhale, close the right nostril and exhale through the left.

- Repeat this process for 5–10 minutes. This technique stimulates the active, solar energy of *Pingala Nadi*, promoting alertness and energy.

Scientific Perspective

Modern research has explored the effects of pranayama, particularly alternate nostril breathing, on the autonomic nervous system. A study published in the *Journal of Clinical and Diagnostic Research* showed that alternate nostril breathing can improve autonomic functions such as heart rate variability and overall cardiovascular health. This balancing effect enhances the body's ability to adapt to stress and maintain homeostasis, supporting both physical and mental health. Through practices that activate and balance *Pingala Nadi*, such as *Surya Bhedana*, individuals can tap into the energy reserves of their bodies, improving focus, decision-making, and physical endurance.

Pingala Nadi and the Chakras

Like *Ida Nadi*, *Pingala Nadi* interacts with the body's *chakras* as it spirals around the *Sushumna Nadi* (the central energy channel). *Pingala's* energy affects each chakra, bringing active, solar energy into these centers of vitality and transformation.

Key Chakras Influenced by Pingala Nadi

Manipura (Solar Plexus Chakra): Located in the area of the navel, the *Manipura* chakra is the energy center of power, will, and vitality. *Pingala Nadi* is strongly connected to this chakra, as both represent solar energy and dynamic power. When *Pingala* is balanced, it energizes *Manipura*, helping to foster confidence, personal strength, and the ability to take decisive action.

Muladhara (Root Chakra): The *Muladhara* chakra governs physical stability and survival, and when balanced by *Pingala*, it strengthens physical endurance and groundedness. A strong *Pingala Nadi* at this chakra can provide the energy needed for physical strength, ensuring security and grounding.

Ajna (Third Eye Chakra): At the *Ajna* chakra, where *Pingala* and *Ida* meet, the energy of logical thinking and intuition come together. A balanced *Pingala* ensures clarity of thought, allowing one to channel logic and mental sharpness into decision-making. When the *Ajna* chakra is harmonized, it provides vision, insight, and the ability to integrate reason and intuition.

Balancing Pingala Nadi

While *Pingala Nadi* represents essential qualities for an active and productive life, balancing it with *Ida* ensures that energy is directed efficiently without overstimulation. To harmonize *Pingala*, practices that cool and calm the body are essential.

Chandra Bhedana (Left Nostril Breathing): As the counterpart to *Surya Bhedana*, *Chandra Bhedana* stimulates *Ida Nadi* to bring balance to overactive solar energy. Practicing this after high-energy tasks, like intense work or exercise, helps calm the body and prevent burnout.

Restorative Yoga: Incorporating restorative or yin-style yoga helps balance the active energies of *Pingala*. Poses like *Child's Pose* (Balasana) and *Reclining Bound Angle Pose* (Supta Baddha Konasana) soothe the nervous system and allow *Pingala* to rest, preventing it from becoming overactive.

Alternate Nostril Breathing: Regular practice of *Nadi Shodhana* ensures that both *Ida* and *Pingala* are balanced, keeping the body's solar and lunar energies in harmony. This practice can be done daily for a few minutes to ensure that neither channel becomes too dominant.

Conclusion

Pingala Nadi plays a crucial role in energizing the body and sharpening the mind. By harnessing its solar energy through practices like *Surya Bhedana* and maintaining its balance with calming techniques, you can experience greater vitality, alertness, and mental clarity. However, balance is key—ensuring *Pingala* works in harmony with *Ida Nadi* fosters a holistic approach to health, blending action with reflection and logic with intuition.

2. Sushumna Nadi: The Central Channel of Spiritual Awakening

Sushumna Nadi is the most important and sacred energy channel in the human body, running along the central axis of the spine, from the *Muladhara* (Root Chakra) at the base, all the way to the *Sahasrara* (Crown Chakra) at the top of the head. It is considered the pathway for the awakening of *kundalini* energy, which is the dormant spiritual energy located at the base of the spine. The activation and ascent of this energy through *Sushumna Nadi* is regarded as the ultimate goal of many yogic practices, leading to spiritual enlightenment and self-realization.

Integration of Ida and Pingala Energies

While *Ida Nadi* governs the lunar energy, and *Pingala Nadi* governs the solar energy, *Sushumna Nadi* represents the harmonious balance and integration of these two opposing forces. It is only when both *Ida* (left) and *Pingala* (right) nadis are purified and balanced that energy can flow freely through *Sushumna*. This state of balance between the lunar and solar forces allows the practitioner to transcend duality and enter a state of unity and spiritual insight.

In the context of yoga and spiritual awakening, *Sushumna Nadi* is often described as the channel through which one can achieve liberation from the cycles of birth and death (*moksha*) by realizing their true, divine nature.

Role of Kundalini Energy

At the base of the spine lies the dormant *kundalini* energy, often symbolized as a coiled serpent. Through deep and consistent yogic practices, this energy can be awakened and begins to rise through

Sushumna Nadi. As it ascends, it activates the seven main chakras, opening the individual to deeper states of awareness, ultimately leading to union with the divine at the *Sahasrara* (Crown Chakra).

The awakening of *kundalini* energy is not a casual experience. It requires careful preparation of the body, mind, and energy channels, as well as the guidance of a knowledgeable teacher. Improper practices or premature awakening of *kundalini* can result in imbalance or physical and mental disturbances.

Clearing Sushumna Nadi: Path to Spiritual Enlightenment

For *Sushumna Nadi* to be activated, it must first be cleared of any blockages or impurities. This process of purification is essential, as blockages in *Sushumna* can prevent the ascent of *kundalini* and the experience of higher consciousness. Ancient yogic texts like the *Hatha Yoga Pradipika* emphasize the importance of purifying *Sushumna Nadi* through the consistent practice of pranayama (breath control), meditation, and other advanced techniques.

The *Hatha Yoga Pradipika* (2.4) states:

"When the *Sushumna Nadi* is free from impurities by the constant practice of pranayama, then the mind becomes fit for concentration, and the mind awakens the kundalini energy."

This quote underlines that the activation of *Sushumna Nadi* is not just about physical purification but also about mental and emotional clarity. When the nadi is purified, the mind naturally becomes still and focused, making it a suitable vehicle for the ascent of *kundalini.*

Practices for Awakening Sushumna Nadi

1. Deep Meditation

Meditation is one of the most powerful tools for clearing *Sushumna Nadi* and awakening *kundalini*. Through regular meditation, the mind becomes calm, focused, and detached from external distractions, allowing the practitioner to concentrate on the inner flow of energy. During meditation, one can focus on the spine and visualize the energy rising through *Sushumna Nadi* from the base to the crown, facilitating the eventual ascent of *kundalini*.

2. Nadi Shodhana (Alternate Nostril Breathing)

Nadi Shodhana is a pranayama practice specifically designed to balance and purify *Ida* and *Pingala Nadis*. By alternating the breath between the left and right nostrils, the practice harmonizes the lunar and solar energies in the body. Once the energies of *Ida* and *Pingala* are balanced, energy can flow through *Sushumna Nadi* without obstruction. Regular practice of *Nadi Shodhana* helps clear blockages in the nadis and prepares the mind for deeper concentration.

How to Practice Nadi Shodhana

- **Find a Comfortable Position**: Sit in a quiet place in a comfortable position, with your spine straight. You can sit cross-legged on the floor or in a chair.

- **Preparation**: Close your eyes and take a few deep breaths to center yourself. Focus on your breath and allow any distractions to fade away.

- **Hand Position**: Use your right hand to form a mudra. You can use Vishnu Mudra (fold your index and middle fingers down, keeping the ring and little fingers extended).

- **Begin the Practice:**
    - Close your right nostril with your right thumb.
    - Inhale deeply through your left nostril.
    - Close the left nostril with your ring finger, and release your right nostril.
    - Exhale through the right nostril.
    - Inhale through the right nostril, close it with your thumb, and release your left nostril.
    - Exhale through the left nostril.

- **Continue the Cycle**: Repeat this process for several minutes, maintaining a steady, relaxed rhythm. Focus on the flow of energy through the Sushumna channel as you balance the left (Ida) and right (Pingala) nadis.

- **Conclude the Practice**: After several rounds, allow your breath to return to normal. Sit in silence for a moment, feeling the effects of your practice.

- **Reflect**: Take a moment to observe any sensations or shifts in energy within your body.

3. Advanced Pranayama Techniques

Once a practitioner is experienced in basic pranayama practices like *Nadi Shodhana*, more advanced techniques like *Kumbhaka* (breath retention) can be introduced. Breath retention is believed to intensify the internal energy flow, further purifying the nadis and encouraging the upward movement of energy through *Sushumna*.

Kumbhaka (Breath Retention): In this practice, the practitioner inhales deeply, holds the breath, and then exhales after a controlled pause. The breath retention creates internal pressure, driving the prana (life force) into the central channel (*Sushumna*) and stimulating the *kundalini* energy.

Bhastrika Pranayama: This is a dynamic pranayama technique that involves forceful inhalations and exhalations. It is known for generating heat in the body and activating the pranic energy needed for *Sushumna Nadi*. After practicing *Bhastrika*, practitioners may feel an increased flow of energy through the spine, preparing *Sushumna* for higher states of consciousness.

4. Bandhas (Energy Locks)

Bandhas are specific body locks used in conjunction with pranayama to direct energy into *Sushumna Nadi*. The three main bandhas are:

- **Mula Bandha (Root Lock)**: This involves contracting the muscles at the base of the spine (pelvic floor), directing energy upward toward *Sushumna Nadi*. It is often practiced during pranayama or meditation to activate the root chakra and encourage the rise of *kundalini*.

- **Uddiyana Bandha (Abdominal Lock)**: Here, the abdomen is drawn inward and upward, creating a vacuum that directs energy upward into *Sushumna*. It is particularly effective for clearing blockages in the lower chakras.

- **Jalandhara Bandha (Chin Lock)**: This lock is performed by tucking the chin toward the chest. It helps to direct the upward flow of energy through the upper chakras, especially toward the *Ajna* and *Sahasrara* chakras.

Sushumna Nadi and the Chakras

As *Sushumna Nadi* runs through the spine, it intersects with each of the seven main chakras, serving as the highway through which the awakened *kundalini* energy travels. The opening of each chakra signifies a deeper level of spiritual awakening:

- **Muladhara (Root Chakra)**: When *Sushumna* is clear at the base, it enables the dormant *kundalini* energy to begin its upward journey.

- **Svadhisthana (Sacral Chakra)**: As energy rises through the sacral chakra, it brings creativity and emotional balance.

- **Manipura (Solar Plexus Chakra)**: At the navel center, the rise of energy ignites personal power and confidence.

- **Anahata (Heart Chakra)**: Here, the energy opens the heart, fostering compassion and unconditional love.

- **Vishuddha (Throat Chakra)**: As energy moves through the throat chakra, it enhances communication and self-expression.

- **Ajna (Third Eye Chakra)**: The opening of the third eye awakens intuition and insight, allowing for the transcendence of duality.

- **Sahasrara (Crown Chakra)**: The final stage of *kundalini* awakening occurs at the crown chakra, leading to the experience of *samadhi* (spiritual union) and self-realization.

Sushumna Nadi: The Pinnacle of Yogic Practice

In yogic traditions, the awakening of *Sushumna Nadi* and the ascent of *kundalini* are considered the pinnacle of spiritual practice. It is believed that when *kundalini* rises through *Sushumna Nadi*, it dissolves the ego, transcends the material world, and leads to *samadhi*—a state of complete union with the divine.

However, it is important to remember that awakening *Sushumna Nadi* is a gradual and delicate process that requires discipline, patience, and proper guidance. The body, mind, and energy channels must be carefully prepared through consistent practice, purity of lifestyle, and devotion.

Ganga, Yamuna, and Saraswati

In yogic tradition, the rivers **Ganga**, **Yamuna**, and the hidden **Saraswati** are symbolically linked to these three most significant nadis.

Ida nadi is metaphorically linked to the river **Yamuna**, which flows in the northern plains of India and is revered for its nourishing and life-giving properties. Ida is responsible for the more reflective and introspective aspects of the mind, mirroring the gentle flow of the Yamuna.

Pingala corresponds to the river **Ganga**, the holiest of rivers, known for its purifying and cleansing powers. Just as the Ganga is revered for its ability to wash away impurities, Pingala is believed to purify the body and mind through its vital and energizing force.

Sushumna Nadi, which is associated with the river **Saraswati**, an ancient river said to flow beneath the surface. Saraswati represents the hidden, subtle knowledge that underpins creation. Similarly, the Sushumna Nadi is the central channel through which kundalini energy rises, bringing spiritual awakening and profound understanding.

The **Triveni Sangam**, where these rivers converge, mirrors the union of these nadis within the body, symbolizing the balance of physical, mental, and spiritual energies essential for higher consciousness and spiritual awakening.

Krishna and His 16,108 Wives

The connection between Lord Krishna, the concept of 16,108 nadis, and the mystical elements of his life—such as his marriage to 16,108 women, the enchanting sound of his flute, and the divine dance of the Gopis—can be understood deeply through the symbolism of yoga, energy, and the soul's journey toward union with the Divine. An additional layer of meaning comes from the linguistic and symbolic similarity between the Sanskrit word *nadi* (energy channel) and the Hindi word *nari* (woman), which enhances the esoteric interpretation of Krishna's consorts and their relationship to the energy channels in yogic tradition.

In Hindu scriptures, Krishna's marriage to 16,108 women (*naris*) has often been viewed as a profound metaphor for the mastery of subtle energy channels (*nadis*) within the human body. The *Hatha Yoga Pradipika* and other yogic texts describe 72,000 nadis, with 16,108 of these being specifically highlighted in certain esoteric traditions. Just as Krishna is said to have lovingly cared for and nurtured his 16,108 consorts, this can be seen as a symbolic representation of the yogi's ability to master and balance the flow of prana through these nadis.

The word *nari* in Hindi, meaning "woman," bears a striking resemblance to the Sanskrit *nadi*, which means "channel" or "stream." This linguistic connection adds a deeper symbolic layer to the story of

Krishna's relationship with the 16,108 women. In this interpretation, each *nari* or woman in the story can be seen as an embodiment of a *nadi*, an energy channel. Krishna's ability to harmonize his relationship with all his *naris* reflects the yogi's path of mastering the movement of prana within each nadi. The union with each wife symbolizes spiritual mastery over each nadi, leading to spiritual liberation (moksha).

The Flute and the Dance of the Gopis: Nadis, and the Soul's Journey

The sound of Krishna's flute, which captivated the Gopis and drew them into the divine dance **(Rasa Lila)**, is another potent symbol in this esoteric framework. In yogic philosophy, the flute's melody represents the *anahata nada*—the **unstruck sound** or divine vibration that resonates within the subtle body. This inner sound is experienced as the prana moves through the nadis, much like how Krishna's flute called out to the Gopis, symbolizing the soul's yearning for union with the Divine.

In this context, the Gopis, like Krishna's wives, can also be seen as representing the soul's relationship with the nadis. Each Gopi, responding to the call of Krishna's flute, symbolizes the prana's movement through a particular nadi, drawn toward divine connection. The Rasa Lila, their joyful dance with Krishna, is a metaphor for the harmonious movement of prana through the nadis, leading to blissful spiritual states. Just as the Gopis danced in perfect synchrony with Krishna, a yogi experiences the inner dance of prana moving through the nadis in perfect rhythm, leading to a state of union with Krishna, who represents the supreme consciousness.

Krishna, the Soul, and the Dance of the Nadis and Naris

Krishna, in this mystical understanding, represents the supreme Self, the Divine, or universal consciousness. The soul, represented by the Gopis and the *naris* in Krishna's life, is constantly seeking reunion with this divine consciousness. The 16,108 *naris* are not just symbolic of women but represent the subtle channels of energy (*nadis*) through which the prana flows. When all these nadis are mastered, harmonized, and aligned, the soul experiences a state of blissful union with Krishna.

The sound of the flute, calling the Gopis into the divine dance, is akin to the inner call of the soul to awaken and respond to the divine vibration that flows through the nadis. The Gopis' dance represents the dynamic and joyful movement of prana through these channels, leading the soul toward the ultimate union with Krishna. This dance is a metaphor for the spiritual practice of yoga, where the prana moves through the nadis like a divine melody, and the soul, much like the Gopis, is drawn into a blissful state of union with the Divine.

The Nadi-Nari Connection: Uniting the Feminine and the Energetic

The similarity between the words *nadi* and *nari* emphasizes the sacred feminine aspect of energy in yogic practice. In this sense, the *naris* in Krishna's life are a reflection of the subtle energy channels within each individual. Just as Krishna harmonized and nurtured his relationships with each of his 16,108 wives, a yogi must master and balance the energy within the nadis. The journey to spiritual union is a process of nurturing and awakening the divine feminine energy within, symbolized by the *naris* or women in Krishna's life.

Ultimately, Krishna's relationship with the 16,108 *naris* and the Gopis is a profound allegory for the soul's journey to unite with the Divine through the mastery of the nadis. The flute's sound is the inner call of the Divine, the Gopis' dance represents the movement of prana through the nadis, and the union with Krishna symbolizes the final merging of the soul with the supreme consciousness. The subtle linguistic connection between *nadi* and *nari* further reinforces the sacred bond between energy and the feminine, highlighting the importance of balancing these energies on the spiritual path.

The Science Behind Nadis and Energy Channels

While the concept of *nadis* is deeply rooted in ancient yogic and spiritual traditions, modern science offers analogous frameworks that reflect the idea of energy flow within the human body. In yogic philosophy, *nadis* are described as subtle energy channels through which *prana* (life force) flows, facilitating physical, mental, and spiritual vitality. Although invisible to the physical eye, these channels are crucial to the overall functioning of the human organism. Interestingly, contemporary scientific fields, such as neurobiology, biofield science, and energy medicine, have proposed models that share similarities with these ancient concepts.

Nadis and the Nervous System: Bridging Ancient and Modern Understanding

One of the closest parallels between the ancient concept of *nadis* and modern science lies in the functioning of the nervous system. The nervous system transmits electrical impulses throughout the body, coordinating bodily functions such as movement, sensation, and autonomic processes. This intricate network of nerves is akin to the *nadis* in that both systems are vital pathways of communication and energy transmission, albeit at different levels of existence.

Electrical Impulses and Subtle Energy: In the yogic tradition, the *nadis* are considered pathways for the flow of *prana*, the subtle life force energy that sustains physical and mental vitality. Similarly, the nervous system relies on electrical impulses that travel through neurons, enabling communication between the brain and the rest of the body. These electrical impulses are the body's way of transmitting energy at a biological level, while the *nadis* facilitate the movement of subtle energy, which, though not measurable in conventional scientific terms, is believed to influence overall health and consciousness.

Sympathetic and Parasympathetic Systems: The traditional descriptions of *Pingala Nadi* (solar energy) and *Ida Nadi* (lunar energy) align with the modern understanding of the sympathetic and parasympathetic nervous systems, respectively. *Pingala* is associated with activation, alertness, and physical energy—paralleling the sympathetic nervous system, which governs the body's "fight or flight" response. *Ida*, on the other hand, represents calming, introspective, and restorative energies, akin to the parasympathetic nervous system, which manages "rest and digest" functions. Together, these systems create balance in the body, much like the balanced flow of *Ida* and *Pingala* facilitates harmony in the yogic understanding.

Scientific Evidence for Energy Channels and Biofields

Though modern science does not yet have a complete understanding of subtle energy systems like *nadis*, research in complementary and alternative medicine has provided evidence supporting the existence of energy fields that influence health and well-being. One of the leading fields investigating this is **biofield science**, which studies the body's electromagnetic and subtle energy fields.

Energy Medicine and Biofield Science: Institutions such as the *National Center for Complementary and Integrative Health* **(NCCIH)** have recognized the importance of exploring the human biofield. While the biofield has not been fully mapped or understood, emerging studies suggest that it plays a critical role in maintaining health and balance. For example, techniques like **acupuncture**, which targets *meridians* (energy pathways) similar to the *nadis* in yoga, have demonstrated measurable physiological effects. Studies show that acupuncture can reduce pain, regulate stress hormones, and influence the autonomic nervous system. The effects of these treatments suggest that manipulating subtle energy pathways—whether we call them *meridians* or *nadis*—can bring about tangible health benefits.

Acupuncture and Energy Meridians: Acupuncture, a core practice in Traditional Chinese Medicine (TCM), is based on the stimulation of energy meridians to treat various physical and psychological conditions. Although meridians are not directly observable, modern research has documented their effects on the human body. Studies using technologies such as functional MRI (fMRI) have shown changes in brain activity after acupuncture treatment, as well as reductions in pain and stress. These effects may provide a scientific framework to understand the *nadi* system, as both traditions believe that the flow of energy through these channels affects overall health.

Research Evidence: Pranayama and Its Impact on the Physical Body

Several scientific studies have begun to explore the physiological effects of yogic practices that target the *nadis*, particularly through pranayama (breathing techniques). For example, a study published in the **International Journal of Yoga** examined the physiological impact of pranayama techniques that specifically aim to balance the flow of *prana* through *Ida*, *Pingala*, and *Sushumna Nadis*. The results demonstrated that these practices had profound effects on various physical markers of health.

Pranayama and Cardiovascular Health: The study found that pranayama practices, especially alternate nostril breathing (*Nadi Shodhana*), significantly reduced blood pressure, lowered the respiratory rate, and improved heart rate variability. These findings suggest that by balancing the flow of *prana* through the *nadis*, pranayama has a direct impact on the cardiovascular and respiratory systems, promoting relaxation, reducing stress, and enhancing overall physiological well-being.

Impact on the Autonomic Nervous System: Pranayama has also been shown to positively influence the autonomic nervous system, which controls involuntary bodily functions such as heart rate, digestion, and respiratory rhythm. By activating specific *nadis* through breath control, practitioners can engage the parasympathetic response, lowering stress and promoting relaxation. These effects demonstrate how the subtle body (*nadis*) and physical body (nervous system) are intricately connected, with practices like pranayama serving as a bridge between the two.

Mind-Body Connection: Another aspect of the research highlights the profound connection between the subtle and physical bodies. By targeting the flow of energy through the *nadis*, pranayama and other yogic techniques help regulate not just the physical body but also the mind. The reduction in stress markers, such as cortisol levels, suggests that manipulating subtle energy through the *nadis* directly impacts emotional well-being, providing a deeper sense of calm and clarity.

Real-Life Applications

The concept of *nadis* extends beyond the spiritual and meditative practices of yoga into holistic health systems such as Ayurveda, where the balance of these subtle energy channels is considered essential for maintaining physical, mental, and emotional well-being. In Ayurvedic medicine, the flow of *prana* (life energy) through the *nadis* is assessed to determine an individual's health, and any disruption in this flow is seen as a precursor to illness. The focus on restoring the balance of energy in the *nadis* forms the basis for many healing practices that aim to treat the root causes of diseases, rather than merely alleviating symptoms.

Nadis in Ayurveda: The Pathway to Health

In Ayurveda, the traditional Indian system of medicine, *prana* is viewed as the vital life force that sustains all living beings. It moves through the *nadis* in a similar way that blood flows through veins or nerves transmit signals in the body. Ayurvedic practitioners evaluate the state of the *nadis* during diagnostic procedures, paying attention to how *prana* circulates within the body. Imbalances or blockages in the flow of *prana* are thought to lead to disease, just as blockages in blood vessels can cause physical ailments.

Diagnosis of Health Conditions: When an Ayurvedic practitioner assesses a patient's health, they often look for signs of imbalance in the *nadis*. This might involve taking the pulse (*nadi pariksha*), where they can feel subtle variations in the pulse that indicate how *prana* is flowing through the body. An imbalance in *Ida Nadi*, for instance, might manifest as mental disturbances such as anxiety or insomnia, while an overactive *Pingala Nadi* could lead to physical symptoms such as hypertension or excessive stress.

Physical Manifestation of Nadis Imbalance: Imbalances in the *nadis* are believed to manifest in the physical body as illnesses or discomfort. For example, if *Ida Nadi* (which governs the parasympathetic nervous system) is underactive, an individual may experience fatigue, depression, or a lack of motivation. On the other hand, an overactive *Pingala Nadi* (which governs the sympathetic nervous system) may lead to stress-related conditions such as high blood pressure, digestive problems, or difficulty sleeping.

By identifying the dominant or imbalanced *nadi* in a person, Ayurvedic treatments aim to restore the harmonious flow of *prana*, ensuring that both *Ida* and *Pingala Nadis* are balanced to maintain health and prevent illness.

In his work as a holistic health practitioner, Dr. Vasant Lad emphasizes the role of nadis in diagnosing health conditions. He describes how imbalances in the nadis can lead to various diseases, and through practices such as Marma therapy (Ayurvedic acupressure) and pranayama, the flow of prana can be restored, leading to healing.

Ayurvedic Perspective on Disease and Nadis Imbalance

Ayurveda views disease as a result of imbalances in the body's *doshas* (biological energies) and disruptions in the flow of *prana* through the *nadis*. An Ayurvedic practitioner assesses the *dosha* type (Vata, Pitta, Kapha) and how the *nadis* are functioning. For instance, Vata imbalances often correlate with disruptions in *Ida Nadi*, leading to anxiety, restlessness, and insomnia. Similarly, Pitta imbalances, which manifest as inflammation or anger, may be tied to overactivity in *Pingala Nadi*.

Restoring Balance Through Treatment: Treatments in Ayurveda aim to restore balance by clearing blockages in the *nadis* and promoting the smooth flow of *prana*. This can be achieved through a combination of therapies such as herbal remedies, diet modifications, meditation, and specialized practices like **panchakarma**, a detoxification and rejuvenation process that purifies the body's energy channels.

In Ayurveda, prevention is key. Regular practices of *pranayama* and yoga are recommended not just as cures for illness, but as daily practices to keep the *nadis* functioning optimally. This holistic approach to health ensures that energy flows freely throughout the body, preventing stagnation that could lead to physical or emotional disease.

Beyond Ayurveda: Integration of Nadis in Other Holistic Practices

The concept of *nadis* has also found resonance in other holistic and complementary health practices. For example, **Reiki**, a Japanese form of energy healing, works with the body's energy fields in a way that aligns with the *nadis* concept. Practitioners channel universal life force energy (*qi* or *ki*) to clear blockages and restore the balance of energy in the body, helping to alleviate physical pain and emotional distress.

Chakra and Nadi Healing: In the broader context of energy healing, *nadis* are also associated with the **chakras**—energy centers in the body. Many healing modalities focus on balancing the chakras and, by extension, the *nadis*. For example, yoga practices that focus on opening specific chakras are believed to clear the corresponding *nadis*, allowing *prana* to flow freely and resulting in better overall health.

Conclusion

The *nadis*, though subtle and invisible to the naked eye, form the intricate network through which prana, or vital life force, flows. They are not mere physiological structures but rather channels of energy that connect the physical, mental, and spiritual dimensions of our being.

Functioning as conduits for prana, the nadis influence every aspect of our existence—from the rhythm of our breath and the clarity of our mind to the awakening of higher states of awareness. When these energy pathways are balanced and flowing harmoniously, the individual experiences physical well-being, mental clarity, emotional balance, and spiritual awakening. Blockages or imbalances, on the other hand, can manifest as disease, mental unrest, or spiritual stagnation.

In essence, the nadis serve as the hidden framework that supports the journey of spiritual evolution, guiding the practitioner from a limited, ego-centered awareness to the boundless experience of universal consciousness.

13

The Five Principal Kleshas

In the vast landscape of yoga philosophy, the concept of *Kleshas* holds significant importance. The term *Klesha* is derived from the Sanskrit root "klis," which means "to cause pain" or "to suffer." These Kleshas are considered the five principal afflictions or obstacles that cloud the mind and prevent us from attaining liberation (moksha). Understanding and overcoming these Kleshas is crucial in the journey towards self-realization.

The five principal Kleshas are:

1. **Avidya** (Ignorance)
2. **Asmita** (Egoism)
3. **Raga** (Attachment)
4. **Dvesha** (Aversion)
5. **Abhinivesha** (Clinging to Life)

These Kleshas are outlined in the *Yoga Sutras* of Patanjali, specifically in Chapter 2, Sutras 3-9. They represent the root causes of human suffering and form the foundation for the cycles of pain and pleasure in life. By addressing these Kleshas, one can transcend the dualities of existence and move towards a state of equanimity.

1. Avidya (Ignorance)

Avidya, or ignorance, is considered the root cause of all other Kleshas. It is the fundamental misperception of reality, where one mistakes the impermanent for the permanent, the impure for the pure, and the non-Self for the Self.

Patanjali defines Avidya in Yoga Sutra 2.5, "Ignorance is perceiving the non-eternal, impure, painful, and non-Self as eternal, pure, pleasurable, and the Self."

Avidya can be compared to a veil that obscures the true nature of reality. It is like mistaking a rope for a snake in dim light—an illusion that causes fear and suffering. Examples of Avidya can be seen in our daily lives when we chase material wealth or relationships, believing they will provide permanent happiness. In reality, these are temporary and can lead to suffering when they are lost or change.

Statistics on mental health can provide insight into the prevalence of Avidya in modern society. According to a 2020 report by the *World Health Organization*, over 264 million people globally suffer from depression, often driven by unfulfilled desires and misperceptions of happiness. This illustrates how ignorance can manifest as mental distress when we fail to recognize the transient nature of life.

Many people identify with their physical bodies, professions, or social roles. This identification leads to suffering when these aspects of life inevitably change or end.

The Bhagavad Gita (2.16) states, "The unreal has no existence, and the real never ceases to be; the seers of truth have concluded the same about both."

Swami Vivekananda emphasized, "All the misery we have is caused by this false idea of attachment, by our identifying ourselves with the body."

2. Asmita (Egoism)

Asmita, or egoism, is the identification of the Self with the mind and body. It is the false notion of "I-ness" or individuality, where one believes the ego to be the true Self. This leads to a sense of separation from others and the world, causing feelings of pride, superiority, and inferiority.

Patanjali addresses Asmita in Yoga Sutra 2.6, "Egoism is the identification of the power of seeing with the instrument of seeing."

Asmita manifests in various forms, such as the desire for recognition, validation, and success. For instance, in the corporate world, individuals often derive their sense of self-worth from their job titles or achievements. When these external identifiers are threatened or removed, it can lead to a crisis of identity, anxiety, or depression.

Real-life examples of Asmita can be seen in the lives of celebrities or public figures who struggle with their sense of self after losing fame or fortune. The attachment to the ego can lead to suffering when the illusion of individuality is challenged. In spiritual practice, overcoming Asmita involves dissolving the ego and recognizing the oneness of all beings.

The Ashtavakra Gita (1.11) asserts, "The wise person speaks neither in praise nor in blame of the world. Always maintaining an attitude of indifference, he sees the ego as being in all things."

3. Raga (Attachment)

Raga refers to attachment or desire for pleasurable experiences. It is the clinging to sensory pleasures, relationships, and material possessions, which creates a cycle of craving and dissatisfaction.

Patanjali discusses Raga in Yoga Sutra 2.7, "Attachment is that which follows identification with pleasurable experiences."

Raga can be understood as the force that drives consumerism and the constant pursuit of happiness through external means. Examples of Raga are evident in addiction to technology, social media, or even substances, where individuals seek repeated pleasure but often end up trapped in a cycle of dependency.

Statistics on addiction highlight the impact of Raga on society. According to a report by the *National Institute on Drug Abuse*, approximately 20.4 million people in the United States alone suffered from substance use disorders in 2019. This underscores the pervasiveness of attachment to sensory pleasures and the resulting suffering.

The *Buddha* said, "Attachment is the root of suffering," emphasizing that clinging to impermanent things leads to inevitable pain.

4. Dvesha (Aversion)

Dvesha is the opposite of Raga—it is aversion or avoidance of unpleasant experiences. It is the tendency to push away or reject what we dislike or fear, leading to resentment, anger, and suffering.

Patanjali defines Dvesha in Yoga Sutra 2.8, "Aversion is that which follows identification with painful experiences."

Dvesha can manifest in various ways, from avoiding difficult conversations or situations to holding grudges and harbouring resentment. For example, an individual who has been hurt in a relationship may develop an aversion to intimacy, which can prevent them from forming meaningful connections in the future.

Events like conflicts and wars can be seen as macro-level manifestations of Dvesha, where aversion to different ideologies or groups leads to violence and suffering. Overcoming Dvesha involves cultivating acceptance and equanimity in the face of discomfort and pain.

The *Dalai Lama* teaches, "We can never obtain peace in the outer world until we make peace with ourselves," suggesting that overcoming aversion is key to inner peace.

5. Abhinivesha (Clinging to Life)

Abhinivesha is the fear of death and the clinging to life. It is the deep-rooted instinct for self-preservation that drives much of human behaviour. This fear is not limited to the physical death of the body but extends to the fear of loss, change, and the unknown.

Patanjali explains Abhinivesha in Yoga Sutra 2.9, "Clinging to life, flowing by its own potency, is established even in the wise."

Abhinivesha is considered one of the most powerful Kleshas because it is deeply ingrained in the subconscious mind. Examples of

Abhinivesha are seen in our fear of aging, illness, and loss of loved ones. The desire to hold onto life and avoid change can lead to anxiety and resistance to the natural flow of existence.

In spiritual practice, overcoming Abhinivesha involves embracing the impermanence of life and accepting the inevitability of death. This can be seen in the teachings of the Buddha, who emphasized the importance of mindfulness of death (maranasati) as a way to transcend the fear of mortality.

The Bhagavad Gita (2.27) teaches, "For one who has taken birth, death is certain; and for one who is dead, birth is certain. Therefore, in the unavoidable discharge of your duty, you should not lament."

Practical Strategies for Overcoming the Kleshas

In yogic philosophy, the *kleshas* are mental afflictions or obstacles that cloud the mind and lead to suffering. Overcoming these kleshas requires conscious effort, self-awareness, and a commitment to spiritual growth. Below are some practical strategies rooted in yogic teachings to help transcend the influence of the kleshas:

1. Self-Study (Svadhyaya)

Svadhyaya, or self-study, is an essential practice for developing self-awareness and overcoming the root cause of the kleshas—*avidya* (ignorance). This practice involves both the study of sacred texts and the introspective examination of one's own thoughts, actions, and motivations.

Study of Sacred Texts: Engaging with ancient yogic texts like the *Yoga Sutras of Patanjali*, the *Bhagavad Gita*, and the *Upanishads* provides wisdom and insight into the nature of the mind and the kleshas. These texts offer guidance on how to live a life free from mental afflictions, with lessons that can be applied to modern life.

Self-Reflection: Regular self-reflection helps uncover patterns of behaviour influenced by the kleshas. Keeping a journal, for example, can be a powerful tool for tracking emotional reactions, desires, and fears. This heightened self-awareness brings the unconscious drivers of behaviour to light, helping one make conscious, informed choices rather than acting on autopilot.

Through *svadhyaya*, one develops discernment (*viveka*), allowing them to see the kleshas as fleeting mental states rather than absolute truths, thus breaking their hold over the mind.

2. Meditation (Dhyana)

Meditation is a cornerstone of yogic practice that offers a direct method for observing the mind and dissolving the influence of the kleshas. By quieting the mental chatter, meditation creates space between the mind's impulses and reactions, enabling one to witness the arising of the kleshas without becoming entangled in them.

Observing the Kleshas: During meditation, one can practice *mindful observation* or *witness consciousness (sakshi bhava)*, observing the thoughts, emotions, and desires as they arise. By not identifying with them, the practitioner gradually weakens the power of the kleshas. For example, when the klesha of attachment (*raga*) surfaces, one can observe the desire without acting on it, realizing its transient nature.

Mindful Breathing: Techniques like *Anapanasati* (mindfulness of breath) or *Soham* meditation help stabilize the mind and bring it back to the present moment when kleshas like *asmita* (egoism) or *dvesha* (aversion) arise. Over time, this detachment from reactive thought patterns reduces their influence, allowing the practitioner to act from a place of calm and clarity.

Through regular meditation, the mind becomes more peaceful and less susceptible to the fluctuations that give rise to the kleshas.

3. Detachment (Vairagya)

Vairagya—the practice of non-attachment—is a key principle in yoga for overcoming the kleshas. It involves recognizing the impermanent nature of all things and letting go of cravings, aversions, and identification with the ego. This is particularly effective for overcoming *raga* (attachment) and *dvesha* (aversion), which are born out of the tendency to cling to pleasure and avoid pain.

Understanding Impermanence: Yoga teaches that nothing in the material world is permanent. By deeply reflecting on this truth, one can loosen the grip of attachment and aversion. For example, when desires arise, remind yourself that the object of desire is impermanent, as is the pleasure associated with it. This perspective cultivates *vairagya*, helping you let go more easily.

Non-Attachment in Daily Life: Practice detachment by learning to let go of outcomes. Whether in work, relationships, or personal goals, focus on the process rather than the result. When the ego clings to specific outcomes, it creates suffering. Detaching from the need for external validation or success alleviates the pressure of *asmita* (egoism) and reduces emotional turbulence.

Through *vairagya*, one becomes less reactive to life's highs and lows, cultivating equanimity and mental peace.

4. Mindfulness

Mindfulness, or *smriti*, is the practice of maintaining awareness of the present moment and observing one's thoughts, emotions, and actions without judgment. This practice helps counteract the kleshas by bringing unconscious reactions into conscious awareness.

Daily Awareness: By cultivating mindfulness in daily activities—such as eating, walking, or engaging in conversation—you become more attuned to the subtle ways the kleshas manifest. For example, you might notice that a strong attachment to certain foods (raga) or aversion to specific tasks (dvesha) influences your decisions. Becoming aware of these influences is the first step in overcoming them.

Noticing the Kleshas in Action: Mindfulness helps prevent the kleshas from taking root. For instance, if you are mindful during a disagreement, you can recognize when the ego (*asmita*) flares up and choose not to react with anger. Instead, you might respond from a place of calmness and detachment, avoiding unnecessary conflict.

Body Awareness: Kleshas often manifest as physical tension or discomfort in the body. Practicing mindfulness of bodily sensations helps you recognize when emotions like fear (*abhinivesha*) or aversion (*dvesha*) are influencing your posture or breath. Releasing this physical tension can also help dissolve the associated mental klesha.

By integrating mindfulness into daily life, one gains the ability to respond to situations with clarity and balance, reducing the grip of the kleshas on the mind.

Conclusion

The five Kleshas are powerful forces that shape human experience and contribute to the cycles of suffering. By understanding and addressing these afflictions, one can begin to unravel the layers of ignorance, egoism, attachment, aversion, and fear that cloud the mind. The path of yoga provides tools and practices to overcome these Kleshas, leading to a state of clarity, peace, and ultimately, liberation.

In the words of Swami Vivekananda, "The greatest religion is to be true to your own nature. Have faith in yourselves!" This faith and inner strength allow us to confront and transcend the Kleshas, moving closer to the realization of our true nature.

14

Vishaya and Vikara

In the journey of self-realization, one of the significant challenges is the struggle with **Vishaya** (sense objects) and **Vikara** (mental disturbances or modifications). These elements often obstruct the spiritual path, making it crucial to understand their nature, effects, and methods to transcend them. This chapter explores the intricate relationship between Vishaya and Vikara, providing insights on how to conquer them using ancient wisdom and modern understanding.

Vishaya: The World of Sense Objects

In Sanskrit, *Vishaya* refers to the objects of the senses—sight, sound, taste, touch, and smell—that captivate and bind the mind. The external world constantly bombards us with stimuli, and our senses are naturally drawn to these objects. While sensory engagement is essential for survival, excessive attachment to these sensory objects leads to bondage.

The mind's attachment to these sense objects creates desires, which in turn lead to a cycle of pleasure and pain, fulfillment and disappointment. In the Bhagavad Gita, Lord Krishna warns:

The Bhagavad Gita (2.62) describes the process of attachment to Vishaya succinctly, "When a person constantly thinks about objects, attachment to them arises; from attachment, desire is born, and from desire, anger arises."

This verse highlights the chain reaction that begins with sensory indulgence. Continuous engagement with sensory objects can foster attachment (Sanga), which in turn generates desire (Kama). This unfulfilled desire can lead to frustration, anger, and ultimately suffering.

In today's context, Vishaya can be likened to the over-consumption of media, social networking, and materialistic pursuits. For example, a person constantly checking social media may develop an attachment to the validation received through likes and comments. This attachment can lead to a cycle of desire for more validation, resulting in mental disturbances when such validation is not forthcoming.

A modern study on materialism conducted by psychologists Tim Kasser and Richard M. Ryan reveals that individuals who place a high value on material possessions (Vishaya) report lower levels of well-being and higher levels of distress, anxiety, and depression. This aligns with the ancient understanding that an obsession with external objects leads to mental instability and suffering.

Vikara: Mental Disturbances and Modifications

Vikara are the mental disturbances or modifications that arise from the interaction of the mind with sense objects. In other words, *Vikara* refers to the distortions or modifications of the mind that arise due to unrestrained attachment to *Vishaya*. These disturbances can manifest as desires, anger, fear, jealousy, pride, and various other emotions that cloud the mind and obstruct spiritual progress.

One of the primary forms of *Vikara* is *Krodha* (Anger), which stems from unfulfilled desires (Kama). The *Bhagavad Gita* (2.63) warns about the consequences of this, "From anger comes delusion; from delusion, confusion of memory; from confusion of memory, the destruction of intellect; and from the destruction of intellect, one perishes."

This sequence illustrates how mental distortions lead to the gradual degradation of wisdom and, ultimately, self-destruction.

History provides numerous examples of how unchecked desires and mental distortions have led to the downfall of powerful leaders. Take, for instance, the story of King Ravana from the *Ramayana*. Despite being a highly learned and powerful king, Ravana's uncontrolled desire for Sita led him to his downfall. His attachment to *Vishaya* clouded his judgment, and his mind became filled with *Vikara* (lust, anger, and pride). Eventually, his distorted mind led to his destruction in the epic battle against Lord Rama.

Another real-life example of Vikara could be the case of a successful business-person who, despite achieving material success, feels unfulfilled and constantly agitated. This mental disturbance may stem from an insatiable desire for more wealth or recognition, illustrating how Vikara can disrupt even those who appear to have everything.

Swami Vivekananda once said, "The mind is but the subtle part of the body. The body is the grosser part of the mind." This highlights the deep connection between the mind (and its disturbances) and our overall well-being.

Conquering Vishaya and Vikara

Now you understand that, *Vishaya* refers to sensory objects or worldly pleasures, while *Vikara* signifies mental disturbances or negative tendencies, such as anger, greed, and lust, that arise in response to sense objects. The ancient sages of India recognized the challenges posed by *Vishaya* and *Vikara* and offered practical strategies to conquer them, purify the mind, and lead it toward higher spiritual pursuits, ultimately attaining liberation (*moksha*). Below are several key methods that have been emphasized in ancient texts and teachings:

1. Mindfulness and Awareness

Mindfulness is the first and perhaps most essential tool for conquering *Vishaya* and *Vikara*. By developing mindfulness, one cultivates the ability to observe the arising of desires and disturbances without becoming entangled in them. This is a form of self-awareness that prevents the mind from getting swept away by sense objects or emotional upheavals.

Vipassana Meditation: A powerful method for cultivating mindfulness is *Vipassana* meditation, which involves observing the flow of thoughts and bodily sensations with detachment and equanimity. When desires for sensory pleasures (*Vishaya*) arise or when negative mental states (*Vikara*) surface, the practice of mindfulness allows one to simply observe them without reacting. Over time, this practice dissolves the attachment to sense objects and mental disturbances, helping to purify the mind.

Self-Observation: In daily life, maintaining moment-to-moment awareness of how *Vishaya* influences your thoughts and actions can help break habitual responses. For example, when faced with an object of desire, such as food or material possessions, mindfulness allows you to pause and evaluate whether the craving is necessary or merely a passing impulse. This awareness weakens the grip of *Vikara* on the mind.

2. Detachment (Vairagya)

The concept of *Vairagya*, or detachment, is central to the teachings of the *Bhagavad Gita* and other yogic texts. *Vairagya* means cultivating a sense of inner freedom from the pull of sensory objects (*Vishaya*). This detachment is not about renouncing the world entirely but involves a mental state of non-attachment—where one is not swayed by pleasure or pain, desire or aversion.

Non-Attachment to Outcomes: In the *Bhagavad Gita*, Krishna teaches Arjuna the art of *Karma Yoga*, performing one's duties without attachment to the fruits of action. By practicing detachment from results, you can reduce the mental disturbances (*Vikara*) caused by both success and failure, pleasure and pain. The mind becomes steady and focused, free from anxiety and craving.

Detaching from Desires: Recognizing the impermanence of sensory experiences helps weaken attachments to sense objects. For example, when faced with a strong desire for material pleasure, you can reflect on the temporary nature of that satisfaction. Over time, this practice of detachment reduces the influence of *Vishaya* on the mind.

3. Cultivating the Opposite Thought (Pratipaksha Bhavana)

The technique of *Pratipaksha Bhavana*, mentioned in Patanjali's *Yoga Sutras* (2.33), is a powerful mental practice for overcoming negative emotions and tendencies (*Vikara*). This involves consciously replacing harmful thoughts with their positive counterparts. By doing so, the mind becomes trained to reject negative tendencies and cultivate positive virtues.

Replacing Negative Emotions: For example, if anger arises, you consciously generate thoughts of compassion or forgiveness. When jealousy surfaces, you cultivate thoughts of kindness and joy for others' success. By repeating this practice, the mind gradually becomes conditioned to respond with positivity rather than negativity.

Reprogramming the Mind: *Pratipaksha Bhavana* is essentially a form of cognitive restructuring, where habitual responses like greed, anger, or lust (*Vikara*) are replaced with generosity, patience, and purity. This continuous reprogramming of the mind weakens the hold of *Vikara* and helps redirect mental energy toward higher, more virtuous pursuits.

4. Discrimination (Viveka)

Viveka, or discriminative wisdom, is the ability to discern between the real and the unreal, the eternal and the transient. This wisdom is essential for overcoming both *Vishaya* and *Vikara,* as it allows the practitioner to see sense pleasures and mental disturbances for what they are—fleeting, impermanent, and ultimately unsatisfying.

Discerning the Real from the Unreal: Through constant reflection, one can recognize that sense objects (*Vishaya*) and the pleasures they bring are temporary and cannot provide lasting fulfillment. On the other hand, the eternal nature of the Self (*Atman*) is the only source of true peace and joy. By focusing on this truth, one can transcend attachment to *Vishaya* and avoid being swayed by *Vikara*.

Reflections from Sacred Texts: The *Vivekachudamani* of Adi Shankaracharya emphasizes the importance of discrimination between the eternal and the transient. By constantly reminding oneself that material pleasures are ephemeral and that the true nature of the Self is changeless, one cultivates detachment and overcomes mental afflictions.

5. Spiritual Practice (Sadhana)

Consistent spiritual practice, or *Sadhana*, is crucial for purifying the mind and gradually overcoming the influence of *Vishaya* and *Vikara*. Various yogic practices provide a structured approach to conquering these obstacles.

Ashtanga Yoga: The eight limbs of yoga—*Yama* (ethical discipline), *Niyama* (personal observances), *Asana* (postures), *Pranayama* (breath control), *Pratyahara* (withdrawal of senses), *Dharana* (concentration), *Dhyana* (meditation), and *Samadhi* (union)—offer a comprehensive system for purifying the mind and overcoming the distractions of *Vishaya* and *Vikara*. Each limb progressively leads the practitioner inward, away from the external world of sense objects and toward the inner realization of the Self.

Karma Yoga: The path of selfless action helps reduce attachment to outcomes and purifies the mind of selfish desires, which are the root cause of *Vishaya* and *Vikara*. By performing duties with the attitude of service to the divine, the practitioner gradually dissolves egoism (*asmita*) and overcomes worldly temptations.

6. Company of the Wise (Satsang)

Association with spiritually-minded individuals (*Satsang*) and regular study of sacred texts provides inspiration and guidance on the spiritual path. The presence of wise teachers and like-minded seekers can help burn away the seeds of desire and strengthen the resolve to overcome mental disturbances.

Inspiration from Saints and Teachers: The *Srimad Bhagavatam* and other scriptures emphasize that the company of saints and sages can have a transformative effect on the mind. Listening to their teachings and being in their presence helps align one's mind with spiritual goals, reducing the distractions caused by *Vishaya* and *Vikara*.

Sacred Study and Reflection: Regular study of scriptures, such as the *Upanishads*, the *Bhagavad Gita*, and the *Yoga Sutras*, reminds the practitioner of the higher purpose of life and provides methods for overcoming the pitfalls of worldly desires and mental disturbances.

Conclusion

The path to self-realization is often hindered by the allure of Vishaya and the turmoil of Vikara. However, with the right understanding, awareness, and practice, one can overcome these obstacles and progress towards inner peace and liberation. The teachings of the ancient scriptures, combined with modern mindfulness practices, provide a robust framework for conquering Vishaya and Vikara, leading to a life of harmony and spiritual fulfillment.

15

Conquering the Obstacles with Yoga

The path of yoga is not without its challenges. As practitioners' journey toward self-realization, they inevitably encounter obstacles that can hinder progress—be they physical, mental, emotional, or spiritual. The ancient yogic texts offer profound insights into these obstacles and provide methods to overcome them. By integrating these teachings into daily life, one can not only address these challenges but also transform them into stepping stones toward spiritual growth and inner peace.

The Nature of Obstacles in Yoga

In the *Yoga Sutras of Patanjali* (1.30), Patanjali identifies nine primary obstacles that hinder spiritual progress:

1. **Vyadhi** (Physical Illness)
2. **Styana** (Mental Laziness)
3. **Samshaya** (Doubt)
4. **Pramada** (Carelessness)
5. **Alasya** (Laziness)

6. **Avirati** (Sensory Distractions)
7. **Bhrantidarshana** (Delusion)
8. **Alabdhabhumikatva** (Inability to Reach the Next Stage)
9. **Anavasthitatva** (Instability in Progress)

1. Conquering Physical Illness (Vyadhi)

In yoga and Ayurveda, **Vyadhi** represents an imbalance in the body, which can result from poor lifestyle choices, environmental factors, or inherent weaknesses in the body. It may manifest as anything from minor ailments like fatigue or headaches to chronic diseases. According to yoga philosophy, physical health is crucial for mental clarity and spiritual growth because the body serves as a vessel for the mind and spirit.

Causes of Vyadhi (Physical Illness)

Poor Lifestyle Choices: Unhealthy eating habits, lack of physical activity, improper sleep, and high-stress levels can weaken the body and lead to illness.

Imbalance in the Doshas: In Ayurveda, it is believed that physical illness arises due to an imbalance in the three doshas (Vata, Pitta, and Kapha). Each person has a unique constitution, and maintaining balance among these elements is key to preventing illness.

Environmental Factors: Pollution, toxins, and exposure to harmful substances can contribute to physical ailments.

Weak Immune System: A compromised immune system, whether due to genetics or lifestyle factors, can make the body more susceptible to illness.

Mental and Emotional Stress: Chronic stress, anxiety, and emotional instability weaken the body's resilience, making it more prone to physical disorders.

Karma and Samskaras: In yogic philosophy, some illnesses are also believed to be the result of past karmic actions or impressions (Samskaras) that manifest in this life.

Methods to Conquer Physical Illness (Vyadhi)

1. Prevention through a Balanced Lifestyle

Diet (Ahara): Eating a balanced, nutritious diet that suits your body constitution is key to maintaining health. In Ayurveda, foods should be chosen based on your dosha to balance the elements in the body. A diet rich in fresh fruits, vegetables, whole grains, and healthy fats supports the immune system and prevents disease.

Exercise (Vyayama): Regular physical activity keeps the body strong, flexible, and resilient. Yoga asanas (postures) are particularly effective because they not only strengthen the body but also harmonize the energy flow (prana) within, helping prevent illness.

Adequate Rest (Nidra): Proper sleep is crucial for healing and maintaining physical health. Lack of sleep can weaken the immune system and increase vulnerability to illness.

Stress Management: Managing mental and emotional stress through techniques like meditation, pranayama (breath control), and mindfulness helps maintain overall health and prevent stress-related illnesses.

2. Yoga Practices for Healing

Asanas (Postures): Regular practice of yoga postures enhances flexibility, strengthens the muscles, improves circulation, and balances the body's systems. Some specific asanas, such as **Shavasana (Corpse Pose)**, **Balasana (Child's Pose)**, and **Viparita Karani (Legs-Up-the-Wall Pose)**, are restorative and help the body heal from illness.

Pranayama (Breathing Exercises): Pranayama techniques such as **Nadi Shodhana (Alternate Nostril Breathing)** and **Kapalabhati (Skull Shining Breath)** help regulate the flow of prana (life force) in the body. These techniques strengthen the respiratory and immune systems, purify the body, and promote healing.

Meditation and Relaxation: Meditation helps reduce stress and calm the nervous system, promoting physical healing. Techniques like **Yoga Nidra** (Yogic Sleep) allow deep relaxation, which is essential for healing from illness.

3. Ayurvedic Approach to Healing

Dosha Balancing: Understanding your constitution (Prakriti) and any imbalances in your doshas (Vata, Pitta, Kapha) helps tailor a lifestyle that prevents illness. For example, a Vata imbalance might be treated with warm, grounding foods and calming practices, while a Pitta imbalance may require cooling foods and stress-reducing techniques.

Herbal Remedies: Ayurveda recommends various herbs such as **Ashwagandha, Tulsi, Turmeric**, and **Ginger** for boosting immunity and restoring balance. These herbs help in reducing inflammation, detoxifying the body, and supporting the healing process.

Panchakarma: Panchakarma is a detoxification therapy in Ayurveda designed to cleanse the body of toxins (Ama) that accumulate due to poor diet and lifestyle. This process strengthens the immune system and promotes overall well-being.

4. Strengthening the Immune System

Immune-Boosting Foods: Include foods rich in vitamins, minerals, and antioxidants, such as **Citrus Fruits** (rich in vitamin C), **Ginger**, **Turmeric**, **Leafy Greens**, and **Almonds**. These help strengthen the body's natural defences.

Hydration: Drinking plenty of water is essential for flushing out toxins, keeping the body hydrated, and ensuring the smooth functioning of the immune system.

Sunlight and Fresh Air: Exposure to sunlight (for vitamin D) and fresh air is important for maintaining immune health and preventing infections.

5. Mental and Emotional Healing

Mind-Body Connection: Healing physical illness often requires addressing the mental and emotional aspects of well-being. Practices such as journaling, counselling, and emotional release can help clear the mind and promote physical healing.

Positive Thinking: Maintaining a positive mindset and avoiding negative emotions such as fear, anger, or anxiety can speed up the healing process. Yoga philosophy teaches that the mind has a powerful influence over the body, and cultivating a calm, positive attitude helps the body heal more effectively.

Self-Compassion and Patience: Recovery from illness requires patience and a compassionate attitude toward oneself. Avoid being overly critical or anxious about the healing process.

6. Spiritual Perspective on Illness

In spiritual practices, illness is sometimes seen as an opportunity for **self-reflection** and **spiritual growth**. It can be a reminder to slow down, focus inward, and deepen your connection with your true self.

Karma and Healing: According to karma theory, some illnesses may be karmic in origin. However, through conscious living, spiritual practice, and right actions, one can reduce the impact of past karma and promote healing on all levels—physical, mental, and spiritual.

Overcoming Vyadhi in Daily Life

To conquer physical illness and prevent it from becoming a hindrance, it's important to:

Listen to your body: Pay attention to early signs of fatigue or imbalance and take steps to address them before they escalate.

Practice preventive care: Adopt a lifestyle that emphasizes prevention through healthy habits, mindfulness, and regular self-care.

Seek appropriate medical attention: While yoga and holistic practices are powerful, don't hesitate to seek medical advice when necessary. Integrating traditional medicine with holistic practices can create a comprehensive approach to health.

The *Bhagavad Gita* (2.47) emphasizes the importance of action, "You have the right to perform your prescribed duties, but you are not entitled to the fruits of your actions." This teaching encourages practitioners to continue their yoga practices regardless of temporary physical setbacks, focusing on effort rather than outcomes.

Conquering **Vyadhi** is about maintaining a balance between body, mind, and spirit. Through proper diet, exercise, rest, stress management, and spiritual practices, it is possible to strengthen the body's resilience, prevent illness, and promote healing when illness arises. A healthy body is crucial for a clear, focused mind and continued progress on the path of self-discipline and spiritual growth.

2. Conquering Mental Laziness (Styana) and Doubt (Samshaya)

Styana refers to a state of inertia, a lack of willpower, or resistance to action, especially when it comes to activities that require mental effort or self-discipline. It manifests as procrastination, lack of enthusiasm, or feeling overwhelmed by tasks.

Causes of Mental Laziness

Fear of failure: People may avoid action because they fear not being good enough or failing.

Lack of clarity: Not having a clear purpose or direction can lead to confusion and stagnation.

Overstimulation: Modern life, with its constant distractions from technology, often contributes to a scattered mind.

Excessive comfort: A life of convenience can dull the motivation to challenge oneself or grow.

Burnout: Overexertion without proper rest can lead to a sense of exhaustion and reluctance to take action.

Methods to Overcome Mental Laziness

Set Clear Goals: Having a clear sense of purpose and breaking it down into smaller, actionable tasks can ignite a sense of direction. Start by focusing on what matters most.

Discipline and Routine: Creating a structured routine and sticking to it can help combat inertia. A disciplined mind develops momentum, making it easier to engage in activities even when motivation is low.

Mindfulness Practices: Meditation and mindfulness practices help cultivate awareness of one's thoughts and habits, enabling the individual to recognize laziness as it arises and choose to act differently.

Self-Compassion: It's essential to be kind to yourself during the process. Mental laziness often stems from overwhelming pressure. Compassion allows for better handling of setbacks, encouraging persistence.

Physical Exercise: Physical activity stimulates mental clarity, improves mood, and energizes the body. Regular exercise can break the cycle of lethargy.

Accountability: Sharing your goals with others or working with a mentor can provide the external motivation needed to stay on track.

Samshaya refers to the state of indecision, uncertainty, or scepticism, especially regarding one's abilities, beliefs, or the path they are following. In spiritual contexts, Samshaya can be paralyzing, preventing a person from progressing on their journey toward self-realization or achieving their goals.

Causes of Doubt

Lack of Knowledge: Insufficient understanding or experience often leads to doubt. When you don't have enough information, it's natural to feel uncertain.

Negative Past Experiences: Previous failures or setbacks can create self-doubt, making you question your abilities or the likelihood of success.

External Influences: Criticism or negative feedback from others can reinforce self-doubt and hesitation.

Fear of Change: Doubt often arises when you are moving out of your comfort zone or venturing into the unknown.

Internal Conflict: Conflicting values or beliefs can create inner tension, making it difficult to fully commit to a path or decision.

Methods to Overcome Doubt

Gain Knowledge and Clarity: Deepening your understanding through study, research, or guidance from experienced individuals can help dispel uncertainty. When you have clear knowledge, your conviction strengthens.

Self-Affirmation and Positive Thinking: Reinforce belief in your abilities by focusing on past successes and positive qualities. Visualization and positive affirmations can build confidence.

Start Small and Build Confidence: Taking small steps toward a goal allows for gradual building of confidence. Small achievements can reinforce your belief in your path and abilities.

Seek Guidance: Working with a mentor, teacher, or trusted advisor can provide clarity and help you navigate moments of doubt. They can offer reassurance and a broader perspective.

Practice Detachment: In yoga philosophy, detachment (Vairagya) involves letting go of the attachment to outcomes. When you focus more on the process and less on the results, doubt naturally diminishes.

Meditation and Introspection: Regular meditation fosters a deeper connection with your inner self, helping to dissolve mental turbulence and providing clarity. Introspection allows you to examine the root causes of doubt and address them.

Spiritual Perspective on Samshaya

In texts like the *Bhagavad Gita*, doubt is seen as one of the greatest hindrances to spiritual growth. It is said that those who are filled with doubt are never at peace and fail to attain true knowledge or self-realization. Krishna advises that one must conquer doubt through direct experience, knowledge, and faith in oneself and the teachings of the scriptures.

In the *Yoga Sutras* (1.20), Patanjali offers the antidote to doubt, "By cultivating faith, vigour, memory, and discernment, the practitioner overcomes these obstacles." This verse highlights the importance of perseverance and faith on the path of yoga.

Integrating Both in Practice

To conquer both **Styana** (mental laziness) and **Samshaya** (doubt), a balance of discipline, self-inquiry, and guided learning is essential.

Sadhana (Spiritual Practice): Consistent engagement in spiritual practices like meditation, yoga, and self-study (Svadhyaya) can help eliminate these obstacles by cultivating focus, clarity, and inner strength.

Commitment to Growth: A commitment to lifelong learning and growth can fuel the energy needed to overcome mental laziness and strengthen one's resolve in the face of doubt.

3. Conquering Sensory Distractions (Avirati) and Carelessness (Pramada)

Avirati refers to the tendency of the senses to be constantly drawn toward external objects and pleasures, leading to a lack of restraint or indulgence in sensory gratification. This restlessness prevents the mind from focusing inward and attaining deeper states of meditation or mindfulness.

Causes of Sensory Distractions

External Stimuli: Modern life is full of distractions such as technology, entertainment, social media, and consumer culture that constantly attract attention.

Cravings and Desires: The mind is naturally inclined toward seeking pleasurable experiences, which can lead to a habit of chasing fleeting sensory gratification.

Lack of Mindfulness: When we act on autopilot, we are more likely to be drawn into sensory distractions because we lack awareness of our thoughts and actions.

Habitual Patterns: Over time, repeated indulgence in sensory pleasures can become habitual, making it harder to break free from these distractions.

Methods to Overcome Sensory Distractions

Mindfulness and Awareness: Cultivating awareness of the present moment helps identify when the senses are being pulled outward. By recognizing distractions early, you can consciously choose to redirect attention.

Sensory Withdrawal (Pratyahara): In yoga, Pratyahara is the practice of withdrawing the senses from external objects and focusing them inward. This can be practiced during meditation or in daily life by reducing external stimuli and creating a calm environment.

Moderation and Restraint: Practicing moderation (Brahmacharya) in sensory experiences can help reduce their hold on the mind. This doesn't mean complete renunciation but finding a balanced approach to engage with the senses mindfully.

Create an Intentional Environment: Removing or minimizing distractions in your surroundings, such as limiting screen time or organizing your space for clarity, can reduce the frequency of sensory interruptions.

Focus on Purpose: Having a clear sense of purpose or direction helps align the mind with meaningful goals, making sensory distractions less appealing. When your energy is directed toward higher objectives, distractions lose their power.

Meditation: Regular meditation strengthens the mind's ability to stay focused and resist being pulled by the senses. With practice, the mind becomes less reactive to external stimuli and more centered.

Pramada refers to negligence, inattentiveness, or a lack of awareness in one's actions and thoughts. It is the failure to maintain mindfulness and discipline, leading to errors, missed opportunities, or a weakening of one's progress.

Causes of Carelessness

Lack of Focus: Without clear attention to what one is doing, it is easy to make mistakes or forget important details.

Overconfidence: When someone assumes they know what to do or has done something many times before, they may become careless, thinking that full attention isn't necessary.

Fatigue or Burnout: When you are tired or overwhelmed, attention tends to waver, leading to a lack of focus and careless actions.

Disorganization: Mental or physical clutter can create an environment where carelessness thrives, as there is little clarity or order in thought or action.

Procrastination: When tasks are rushed due to delays, carelessness often creeps in as attention to detail is sacrificed for speed.

Methods to Overcome Carelessness

Cultivate Awareness and Presence: The antidote to carelessness is mindfulness. Bringing full awareness to each action, no matter how small, ensures that you perform tasks carefully and with intention.

Slow Down: Often, carelessness arises from trying to rush through tasks. Slowing down allows for more attention to detail and reduces the chance of mistakes.

Establish Good Habits: Creating disciplined routines for daily tasks can help avoid carelessness. When you practice mindfulness in every activity, from eating to working, you build a foundation of attentiveness.

Take Breaks: Fatigue can lead to carelessness, so taking breaks and resting ensures that your mind and body remain alert and attentive.

Accountability and Reflection: Regularly reflecting on your actions and seeking feedback from others can help identify moments of carelessness and provide opportunities to improve.

Practice Humility: Recognize that carelessness often stems from overconfidence or a lack of proper attention. Practicing humility helps maintain awareness of one's limitations and encourages greater care in everything you do.

Integrating Both in Practice

To effectively overcome both **Avirati (sensory distractions)** and **Pramada (carelessness)**, cultivating **mindfulness** and **self-discipline** is key. Here's how they can be integrated into daily practice:

Mindful Living: Practice bringing your awareness to every activity, whether it is as simple as eating or as complex as a work task. This mindfulness helps reduce distractions and prevents careless errors.

Routine and Discipline: Establish a daily routine that includes time for reflection, meditation, or introspection. This helps strengthen the mind against distractions and reinforces attentive behaviour.

Detachment from Results: In both cases, focusing on the process rather than the outcome is crucial. When you're detached from the result, sensory distractions lose their allure, and carelessness is less likely to arise because the process itself becomes important.

Meditation for Clarity: Regular meditation practices help in developing greater control over the senses (Pratyahara) and cultivating mindfulness, which directly counters both Avirati and Pramada.

Balance: Create a balance between external engagements and internal reflection. By limiting external stimuli, especially when they become excessive, and focusing on careful, mindful action, you create harmony within and around you.

The teachings of Swami Vivekananda emphasize the importance of controlling the senses. He famously stated, "Take up one idea. Make that one idea your life—think of it, dream of it, live on that idea." His life exemplifies dedication to a higher purpose, unaffected by the distractions of the material world.

The Bhagavad Gita (6.5) advises, "Let a man lift himself by his own self; let him not degrade himself." This teaching encourages practitioners to cultivate self-awareness and self-discipline, avoiding carelessness and sensory distractions that hinder progress.

In summary, conquering **Avirati** and **Pramada** is about developing mindfulness, restraint, and attentiveness to every moment. With consistent effort, these obstacles can be minimized, allowing for greater focus, clarity, and inner peace.

4. Conquering Delusion (Bhrantidarshana) and Inability to Progress (Alabdhabhumikatva)

Bhrantidarshana refers to a false or distorted perception of reality. It is the inability to see things clearly, either about oneself, the world, or the path to spiritual liberation. Delusion can manifest as misconceptions, false beliefs, or illusions, leading to confusion and misdirection. This prevents the practitioner from progressing because they are operating under a flawed understanding of truth.

Causes of Delusion

Ignorance (Avidya): Ignorance is considered the root of all delusion. It arises from the misidentification of the self with the body, mind, and external world, rather than recognizing the deeper, true self.

Attachment and Desire: Strong attachment to material objects, people, or ideas clouds judgment and leads to distorted thinking. Desire creates emotional turbulence, making it difficult to see clearly.

Ego (Asmita): The ego creates a false sense of self, leading to delusions of grandeur, superiority, or inferiority. It blinds the individual to the truth of their interconnectedness with the world and others.

External Influences: Social conditioning, cultural beliefs, and misinformation can also lead to false perceptions of reality.

Mental Conditioning: Repeated patterns of thought or deep-rooted samskaras (mental impressions) from past experiences can perpetuate delusion.

Methods to Overcome Delusion

Self-Inquiry (Jnana Yoga): Engage in regular self-inquiry and reflection to question and dismantle false beliefs. Ask yourself, "Who am I?" to strip away layers of delusion and ego-driven thoughts. This process helps one move closer to the true understanding of self (Atman).

Study of Scriptures (Svadhyaya): Reading and reflecting on spiritual texts like the *Bhagavad Gita*, *Yoga Sutras*, and other wisdom literature can help correct misunderstandings and provide a clearer perspective. These texts often point out common misconceptions and guide practitioners toward truth.

Guidance from a Guru or Teacher: A teacher can help point out where you may be caught in delusion. They offer an external perspective that can shed light on blind spots, providing correction and insight to clarify confusion.

Meditation for Clarity: Regular meditation cultivates a calm and focused mind, allowing one to see things as they are, rather than through the lens of attachment, desire, or fear. It enhances discernment (Viveka) and helps one distinguish between the real (Sat) and the unreal (Asat).

Detachment (Vairagya): Practicing detachment from outcomes, possessions, and rigid ideas of identity reduces the likelihood of getting caught in delusion. When the mind is free from excessive attachments, it is more receptive to truth.

Cultivating Discernment (Viveka): Developing the power of discernment is essential in overcoming delusion. This means constantly evaluating your perceptions and thoughts to determine whether they are rooted in truth or illusion. Viveka helps in distinguishing what is eternal (truth) from what is temporary (illusion).

Satsang (Association with Wise Company): Surrounding yourself with people who are on the same spiritual path or who possess greater wisdom can help prevent falling into delusion. These individuals act as mirrors, reflecting where you may be off-course.

2. Inability to Progress (Alabdhabhumikatva)

Alabdhabhumikatva refers to the inability to achieve or reach the next stage of development in one's practice, despite continuous effort. This could manifest as a feeling of being "stuck" or stagnant in your spiritual or personal growth. It is the frustration of putting in effort but not seeing the results, which can lead to doubt, frustration, or a sense of failure.

Causes of Inability to Progress

Impatience: Expecting immediate results and becoming discouraged when they don't materialize.

Inconsistent Effort: Lack of regularity in practice or discipline can lead to slow or no progress.

Mental or Emotional Blockages: Unresolved emotional issues or mental conditioning may prevent you from moving forward.

Attachment to Results: Being overly attached to the outcome of your efforts can create frustration when progress doesn't happen as expected.

Lack of Clarity: Not having a clear sense of direction or purpose in practice can make it difficult to know how to proceed.

Methods to Overcome Inability to Progress

Patience and Perseverance (Shraddha): Cultivating patience is key when progress seems slow or nonexistent. Trust that growth happens at its own pace, and that continuous effort will eventually bear fruit. Shraddha, or faith, in your path and practice helps sustain you through periods of stagnation.

Consistent Practice (Abhyasa): Regular, dedicated practice is essential for overcoming the inability to progress. Whether it's meditation, yoga, or self-inquiry, progress is often the result of long-term, steady effort. Abhyasa involves commitment to practice, even when progress is not immediately visible.

Self-Discipline (Tapas): Tapas refers to the discipline required to purify the mind and body through effort. When progress stalls, strengthening self-discipline can help overcome laziness or resistance that may be blocking advancement.

Seek Guidance: If you're feeling stuck, seek advice from a teacher, mentor, or community. Sometimes, an outside perspective can help you identify what might be holding you back and suggest ways to move forward.

Break the Routine: If the same practices have been yielding no progress, consider changing your approach. Sometimes a fresh perspective, a new technique, or altering your routine can open up new paths for progress.

Let Go of Attachments to Results: The more you focus on achieving a certain level of progress, the harder it can become to attain it. Practice detaching from the results of your actions and focus on the process itself. This helps create mental space for growth.

Clear Emotional and Mental Blocks: Unresolved emotional issues, fear, or mental conditioning can block progress. Work on emotional healing through counselling, therapy, or reflective practices. Meditation helps in dissolving these blockages by bringing unresolved issues to the surface and allowing them to be processed.

Refining Intention (Sankalpa): Reassess your intention or goal. Sometimes the inability to progress arises from unclear or conflicting intentions. Clarifying what you are working toward can provide renewed motivation and direction.

Focus on Inner Growth: Progress is not always visible on the surface. Instead of looking for external markers of success, pay attention to internal shifts such as greater calmness, increased clarity, or deeper compassion. These subtle changes often precede more tangible results.

Integrating the Two in Practice

Both **Bhrantidarshana (Delusion)** and **Alabdhabhumikatva (Inability to Progress)** are deeply intertwined, as delusion often clouds one's perception of progress, and the inability to progress can be due to misconceptions about the path itself. Overcoming these requires:

Self-awareness and Reflection: Regular introspection is essential to identify where delusion might be clouding your judgment or where progress is being hindered. Journaling, meditation, and self-inquiry can help bring clarity.

Balanced Approach: Cultivating a balanced approach to practice that includes both effort and detachment from results helps keep you moving forward without falling into frustration or delusion.

Trust in the Process: Understanding that both delusion and the inability to progress are natural parts of the spiritual journey helps maintain faith in the process. Progress is often non-linear, and periods of stagnation or confusion can be valuable for deeper growth.

The *Mundaka Upanishad* (2.2.8) teaches, "The wise, having realized the Self, leave behind both joy and sorrow." This wisdom points to the importance of self-realization in overcoming the illusions and obstacles of the mind.

5. Conquering Instability in Progress (Anavasthitatva)

Anavasthitatva is often experienced as a lack of steadiness or commitment after making initial advancements. It reflects the challenge of sustaining the fruits of one's practice, whether in spiritual disciplines, meditation, yoga, or other personal development efforts. The person may reach a certain level of achievement or insight but finds it difficult to remain in that elevated state due to various distractions, challenges, or internal barriers.

Common Causes of Instability

Lack of Consistent Practice: Once progress is made, there may be a tendency to become complacent, leading to irregularity in practice.

External Distractions: Life events, responsibilities, or environmental influences can pull attention away from the spiritual path or self-improvement goals.

Mental Fatigue or Stress: Constant effort without proper rest or self-care can lead to burnout, making it difficult to maintain progress.

Emotional Turbulence: Emotional upheavals like anger, fear, or grief can disturb inner stability and cause regressions.

Overconfidence or Ego: Reaching a certain level of progress may cause the ego to inflate, leading to overconfidence or complacency, which can destabilize further growth.

Attachment to Results: Being overly fixated on results can cause frustration when they aren't achieved, leading to instability and backsliding.

Lack of Clear Direction: When the next steps in personal or spiritual growth are unclear, it can cause confusion or wandering off the path.

Methods to Conquer Instability in Progress (Anavasthitatva)

1. Establish a Steady Routine (Abhyasa)

Consistency is Key: The *Yoga Sutras* emphasize the importance of **Abhyasa**, or consistent, long-term practice, as essential for stability. To maintain progress, develop a regular routine for your practice, whether it's meditation, yoga, or any form of self-discipline.

Daily Discipline: Set aside specific times each day for your practice. Whether you feel inspired or not, continuing the practice in a disciplined manner helps prevent regression.

Gradual Progression: Avoid overwhelming yourself by taking on too much at once. Gradual, steady advancement ensures long-lasting progress.

2. Mindfulness and Awareness (Dhyana)

Stay Present: Meditation and mindfulness help keep the mind steady and focused on the present moment. This can reduce the impact of distractions and help you maintain inner peace.

Observe the Mind: Develop awareness of your thoughts, emotions, and actions. Notice when you're slipping back into old habits or losing focus, and gently guide yourself back on track.

Daily Meditation: A regular meditation practice helps cultivate mental clarity and emotional stability, reducing the likelihood of falling back into unstable patterns.

3. Reaffirm Your Intentions (Sankalpa)

Set Clear Intentions: Having a strong, clear intention or purpose for your spiritual or personal practice can help you stay focused. Remind yourself of your long-term goals and why you started the journey in the first place.

Recommit Regularly: Reaffirm your commitment to your path by regularly reflecting on your intentions and goals. This creates a mental anchor to keep you steady during challenging times.

4. Detachment from Results (Vairagya)

Practice Non-Attachment: Vairagya, or detachment from outcomes, is crucial to maintain stability in progress. When you become overly attached to achieving specific results, the frustration of not reaching them can destabilize your progress. Instead, focus on the effort and let go of expectations about outcomes.

Let Go of the Ego: Avoid becoming overly attached to the sense of accomplishment or the notion of having "arrived." Recognize that spiritual growth is a continuous journey, not a final destination.

5. Balance Between Effort and Rest

Pacing Your Progress: Recognize the need for balance between intense practice (Tapas) and rest. Burnout often leads to instability because the mind and body need time to integrate the progress made.

Rest and Recuperation: Take breaks when necessary to rest and recharge. Just as the body needs rest after physical exertion, the mind needs downtime to consolidate spiritual and personal growth.

6. Strengthen Emotional Resilience

Manage Emotions: Emotional instability is one of the major causes of backsliding in spiritual practice. Practices like Pranayama (breath control), journaling, and talking with trusted mentors or peers can help process emotions and maintain emotional balance.

Regular Self-Reflection: Engage in regular self-inquiry to address any unresolved emotional issues that might destabilize your progress. By processing emotions healthily, you reduce the likelihood of emotional turbulence pulling you off course.

7. Seek Support from a Community (Satsang)

Connect with Like-Minded People: Surround yourself with a community of practitioners or individuals who share similar goals. Being part of a spiritual or personal development community (Satsang) provides external support and motivation, helping you stay consistent.

Accountability: Share your goals and progress with a mentor, teacher, or peer group. Accountability helps maintain stability in progress by providing external encouragement and guidance.

8. Grounding Practices

Physical Grounding: Engage in grounding physical activities like walking in nature, practicing grounding yoga postures (like Tadasana, Mountain Pose), or simply spending time in nature. Grounding practices help keep the mind and body stable.

Stay Humble: Humility helps prevent the ego from destabilizing progress. Recognize that growth is an ongoing process and that periods of regression or instability are natural. Staying humble keeps you receptive to learning and improvement.

9. Reassess and Refine Your Practice

Adaptability: If you notice your progress becoming unstable, it may be a sign that your practice needs adjustment. Perhaps the techniques you are using are no longer appropriate for your current state, or new practices might be needed to address emerging challenges.

Consult a Teacher: Sometimes instability occurs because you've outgrown a certain phase of practice. Seeking guidance from a more experienced teacher can help you refine your approach and find new techniques to deepen your practice.

10. Stay Open to Change

Non-Resistance to Change: Accept that life is dynamic and progress in any area of life, including spirituality, is not linear. Embrace the ebb and flow of growth. When setbacks occur, use them as opportunities for learning rather than allowing them to destabilize your practice.

Spiritual Flexibility: Be willing to adjust your expectations and practices as life circumstances change. Flexibility in practice helps sustain progress when faced with new challenges.

B.K.S. Iyengar, the founder of Iyengar Yoga, is a prime example of perseverance and dedication. Despite numerous health challenges and setbacks, he continued his practice and went on to become one of the most influential yoga teachers of the 20th century. His teachings emphasize the importance of discipline and dedication to the path.

Conquering **Anavasthitatva (Instability in Progress)** requires a combination of consistent practice, mental discipline, emotional resilience, and adaptability. Maintaining progress is not just about effort but also about developing the inner capacity to remain steady in the face of challenges. By cultivating patience, non-attachment, mindfulness, and humility, and by staying grounded in purpose and practice, you can sustain the progress you've achieved and continue advancing on your spiritual and personal path.

Stability comes not from reaching an endpoint but from learning how to remain anchored as you move forward.

16

The Self (Atman)

The concept of the Self, or Atman, is central to Hindu philosophy, representing the innermost essence of an individual beyond the physical body, emotions, and mind. Unlike the transient ego, the Atman is the eternal core of existence—pure consciousness. Understanding the Atman is key to spiritual liberation (moksha), where one transcends the cycle of birth and death (samsara) by realizing their divine nature. Hindu philosophy teaches that the individual Self (Atman) and the universal consciousness (Brahman) are one, expressed by the Vedic dictum: **"Tat Tvam Asi"**— "Thou art that." The Atman is formless, infinite, and the silent witness behind all experiences.

The Nature of Atman: Beyond the Ego

To fully grasp the profound nature of *Atman*, it is essential to first distinguish it from the ego, or *Ahamkara*. While the *Atman* represents the pure, unchanging essence of the Self, *Ahamkara*—literally meaning the "I-maker"—is the sense of individuality that arises when we identify with the body, mind, and emotions. It is the construct that shapes our personality and personal identity, giving us the perception of being separate from others and the world.

In everyday life, most people operate from the level of *Ahamkara*. This is the ego that constantly defines who we are through external factors like status, relationships, and achievements. It thrives on comparison, attachment, and desires, often leading to a life filled with conflict, stress, and dissatisfaction. The ego seeks validation and security through transient experiences, which is why no matter how much we acquire or achieve, the sense of fulfillment remains elusive.

The spiritual journey, however, calls us to transcend *Ahamkara* and uncover the deeper reality of the *Atman*. This transition from ego to Self is the essence of spiritual practice. It involves shedding the layers of identification with the physical and mental realms and rediscovering our true nature. Ancient yogic texts describe this as a path of unlearning—releasing the conditioning and false perceptions that bind us to the material world.

Yoga, meditation, and self-inquiry are powerful tools on this journey, as they help quiet the mind and dissolve the illusions created by *Ahamkara*. Through these practices, the seeker learns to witness their thoughts, emotions, and sensations without attachment, understanding that these are impermanent aspects of the human experience. Over time, this witnessing leads to the realization that the true Self, the *Atman*, is beyond these fleeting states of being.

The transition from *Ahamkara* to *Atman* is not a rejection of the ego but a harmonization of it. As the ego's grip loosens, one no longer feels a need to defend or inflate their identity. Instead, life is lived from a place of inner stillness, where the boundaries between self and other dissolve. In this state, the individual perceives themselves as part of the greater whole, and their actions become an expression of unity and love.

This journey from ego to Self is not merely theoretical; it is experiential. It unfolds gradually through consistent spiritual practice and inner reflection. In the next section, we will explore specific methods and techniques that help facilitate this transformation, allowing us to live from the level of *Atman* and experience true freedom from the limiting grasp of *Ahamkara*.

The *Atman* is pure consciousness, the eternal witness that transcends the ego and individuality. According to the Upanishads, the *Atman* is indestructible and unchangeable. The *Brihadaranyaka Upanishad* (4.4.5) states, "This Self is indeed Brahman, and all the gods worship this Self."

Here, the concept of *Atman* is intricately connected to Brahman, the universal consciousness. The realization of one's true nature as *Atman* is synonymous with recognizing that the individual self (Jiva) and the universal self (Brahman) are one and the same. This realization is central to the path of Jnana Yoga, where knowledge and wisdom are the means to liberation (Moksha).

The Atman in the Bhagavad Gita

The Bhagavad Gita serves as a profound philosophical and spiritual guide, offering deep insights into the nature of the Self, or Atman. In Chapter 2, Verse 20, Lord Krishna articulates a fundamental truth: "The Self is never born, nor does it die; it is not that having been, it ceases to exist. The Self is unborn, eternal, everlasting, and primeval. Even though the body is slain, the Self is not killed."

This verse encapsulates the essence of the Atman as timeless and immutable, transcending the limitations of physical existence. Krishna's teachings emphasize that the Atman is beyond the transient nature of the body, which is subject to decay and death. While the physical form may perish, the Atman remains untouched, eternal, and unchanging, highlighting a crucial aspect of Vedantic philosophy: the distinction between the temporary and the everlasting.

The Bhagavad Gita underscores the importance of realizing the Self as the ultimate purpose of life. This realization is not merely an intellectual exercise; it is a transformative understanding that can lead to profound shifts in one's perception of reality. By recognizing the eternal nature of the Atman, individuals can transcend the fears and attachments that often bind them to the material world. The realization of the Self serves as a powerful antidote to the anxieties of existence, illuminating the path toward liberation (moksha).

Furthermore, this understanding encourages a sense of detachment from the fruits of one's actions. When one identifies with the Atman rather than the ephemeral aspects of life, they can engage with the world without being overly attached to outcomes. This principle of selfless action, or karma yoga, is a recurring theme in the Gita, guiding individuals to act in alignment with their true nature.

In essence, the teachings of the Bhagavad Gita invite us to embark on a journey of self-discovery, urging us to delve deep into the nature of our being. By awakening to the truth of the Atman, we can cultivate inner peace, resilience, and a sense of unity with the cosmos. This profound knowledge not only aids in personal transformation but also contributes to a greater understanding of our interconnectedness with all of existence, ultimately guiding us toward the liberation that is the birthright of every soul.

Atman in Different Yogic Paths

Various yogic paths, while differing in their methods and focus, all aim at the same goal: realizing the Atman, the true essence of one's being, which transcends the limitations of body, mind, and ego. Each path offers a unique approach to this realization, tailored to the tendencies and inclinations of different seekers.

Jnana Yoga (Path of Knowledge)

Here, the seeker engages in intellectual and philosophical inquiry to realize the Atman (true self) through direct knowledge. This path involves deep self-inquiry, known as Atma-Vichara, where the seeker questions the nature of reality, the self, and the universe, aiming to distinguish between the **real** (Atman/Brahman) and the **unreal** (Maya/illusion). The ultimate goal is to transcend ignorance (Avidya) and realize one's identity with the infinite consciousness (Brahman).

This process often involves studying sacred texts (such as the Upanishads), reflecting on their teachings, and meditating on the truths revealed, guided by the practice of discernment (Viveka) and dispassion (Vairagya). Through rigorous contemplation, the seeker breaks free from ego and illusion, ultimately attaining self-realization and liberation (Moksha).

Bhakti Yoga (Path of Devotion)

In this path, the devotee focuses on devotion and love for a personal god or divine presence, which can be seen as either external (a deity like Krishna, Rama, or any chosen form of God) or internal (the Atman as the divine self). The practice involves surrendering one's ego and desires to the divine, cultivating love, and seeing the divine presence in everything.

In the context of the Atman, which represents the true self, some Bhakti traditions might view the Atman as an expression of the divine, leading the devotee to experience God within themselves. However, many forms of Bhakti Yoga focus more on an external relationship with a deity, emphasizing loving devotion, service, and emotional connection.

Karma Yoga (Path of Action)

This approach involves selfless service (known as *Nishkama Karma*) without attachment to the outcomes. Practitioners engage in their duties and actions with the intention of serving a higher purpose or the divine, without selfish desires or concern for personal gain. This approach aligns with the teaching of the Bhagavad Gita, where Lord Krishna advises performing one's duty with dedication, but to relinquish attachment to the fruits of that labour.

In this way, practitioners of Karma Yoga gradually purify their minds and reduce egoistic tendencies, leading them to realize the Atman (true self) as part of the divine order. The key is to act with awareness and dedication, but to surrender the results to a higher will.

Raja Yoga (Path of Meditation)

This method involves meditation and mental discipline to experience the *Atman* directly. The ultimate goal of Raja Yoga is to transcend the fluctuations of the mind and experience the Atman in its pure, undisturbed state.

Scientific Perspectives on Consciousness

While the concept of Atman has long been a cornerstone of spiritual philosophy, modern science, particularly in fields like neuroscience and quantum physics, is beginning to explore the nature of consciousness, though it remains one of the most enigmatic topics in scientific inquiry. Consciousness is central to understanding reality, and many scientists are now questioning the traditional materialist view that confines consciousness strictly to brain activity. Some emerging theories suggest that consciousness might be more than just a byproduct of neuronal processes—it could be a fundamental aspect of the universe itself, resonating with ancient philosophical ideas like the Atman.

Quantum Physics and Consciousness

Quantum physics has challenged many classical ideas about the nature of reality, leading to intriguing speculations about the role of consciousness in the physical world. Some interpretations of quantum mechanics suggest that consciousness might be involved in the "collapse" of the wave function—the transition from potentiality (where multiple outcomes exist simultaneously) to actuality (where one outcome is realized). This aligns with ancient Indian philosophical views that consciousness, or the Atman, is not merely confined to individual beings but is a pervasive, unifying force underlying all of reality.

Schrödinger and Vedantic Parallels

Prominent physicist and philosopher **Erwin Schrödinger**, one of the pioneers of quantum mechanics, held views that strikingly resemble Vedantic philosophy. He questioned the common perception of individual minds being separate and distinct entities. In his philosophical writings, Schrödinger argued that **consciousness is**

singular and that the apparent multiplicity of individual minds is an illusion. In his words, "The overall number of minds is just one. In truth, there is only one mind."

This idea mirrors the Vedantic concept of **Atman**, which posits that the true self (Atman) in each being is not separate but is part of a singular, universal consciousness (Brahman). Just as Schrödinger suggested that individual consciousnesses are facets of one unified mind, Vedanta teaches that the diversity of individual selves is an illusion (Maya), and in reality, there is only one undivided consciousness that pervades all existence.

Integrated Information Theory (IIT)

Another scientific approach exploring consciousness is **Integrated Information Theory (IIT)**, which suggests that consciousness arises from the way information is processed and integrated within a system. IIT posits that consciousness is a fundamental property of systems that are highly interconnected and complex, much like the human brain. However, the theory allows for the possibility that consciousness might exist in varying degrees in all entities, not just in humans, offering a modern parallel to the ancient idea that consciousness is not limited to individual brains but pervades all of existence, much like the Atman.

Consciousness as a Fundamental Force

Some scientists propose that consciousness is a **fundamental force** of the universe, akin to gravity or electromagnetism. According to this view, consciousness is not something that "emerges" from brain activity, but instead, it is a basic feature of the cosmos, embedded in the very fabric of reality. This perspective brings science closer to the spiritual idea that consciousness is a primary, non-derivative reality, consistent with the Atman concept found in Vedanta, which posits that consciousness is the ultimate essence of all beings and the universe itself.

The Hard Problem of Consciousness

Despite these advances, science continues to grapple with what philosopher **David Chalmers** calls the **"hard problem"** of **consciousness**: how and why subjective experiences (qualia) arise from physical processes in the brain. While neuroscience can explain certain functions like perception and memory, it remains a mystery how the feeling of being aware or conscious of these experiences emerges. This "hard problem" echoes the metaphysical questions explored in Vedantic philosophy, where consciousness (Atman) is considered self-evident, beyond empirical analysis, and is not reducible to physical explanations.

Conclusion

Though modern science is still far from fully understanding consciousness, some scientific perspectives suggest that it may not be limited to the brain but instead could be a fundamental aspect of reality, mirroring the ancient spiritual teachings of Vedanta. Thinkers like Erwin Schrödinger bridge the gap between science and spirituality by proposing that the multiplicity of consciousness is an illusion, resonating with the idea that Atman, the true self, is singular and universal. As scientific inquiry continues, it may further unravel the mysteries of consciousness, bringing us closer to understanding the profound connections between ancient wisdom and contemporary science.

Experiencing the Self: Meditation and Practices

To truly experience the Self (Atman), spiritual traditions across the world emphasize inner practices such as meditation, self-inquiry, and detachment from material desires. These practices are designed to quiet the restless mind, reduce attachment to the transient world, and help the practitioner access a deeper, more direct experience of their true nature.

Meditation on the Atman

Meditation is a powerful tool in the quest to experience the Atman. When the mind is still, free from the distractions of thoughts and sensory inputs, one can tap into pure awareness—the unchanging essence of being. Meditation on the nature of the Atman allows individuals to step back from their identification with the body, mind, and ego, and instead recognize their true self as eternal and formless.

This meditative practice often involves focusing on concepts such as:

- **Nirguna Brahman**: The formless, attributeless reality that underlies everything, which corresponds to the Atman within each individual.

- **Witness Consciousness (Sakshi)**: Cultivating awareness of oneself as the detached observer of thoughts, feelings, and sensory experiences without becoming entangled in them.

As meditation deepens, one can experience moments of non-duality, where the sense of separation between the self and the universe dissolves, revealing the unity of all existence.

Self-Inquiry (Atma-Vichara)

Another core practice to realize the Self is **Atma-Vichara**, or self-inquiry, popularized by sages such as Ramana Maharshi. This method involves continually asking the question, "Who am I?" Not seeking a verbal answer, the practice instead directs the seeker inward, away from the superficial layers of identity—such as body, emotions, and intellect—and toward the pure awareness that remains. This persistent questioning gradually breaks down false identifications and leads to the direct realization that the Self is not the ego, but the eternal Atman.

The process of self-inquiry requires patience and commitment. Over time, it dismantles deeply ingrained illusions about the nature of the self, helping the practitioner transcend the ego and experience the Atman as their fundamental essence.

Detachment from Material Desires (Vairagya)

In addition to meditation and self-inquiry, **detachment** from material desires is key to experiencing the Self. Spiritual teachings emphasize that as long as individuals are attached to the physical world—its pleasures, possessions, and status—they remain caught in the cycle of suffering and ignorance (Avidya). By cultivating **Vairagya** (dispassion), one can break free from this attachment, clearing the path to experience the Atman.

This detachment does not mean rejecting the material world entirely, but rather shifting one's relationship with it. A person can still engage in worldly activities while maintaining inner detachment, recognizing that the true source of peace and fulfillment lies within, not in external circumstances. This mental shift helps liberate the mind from cravings and aversions, allowing it to focus on the unchanging, eternal reality of the Self.

The Story of Sage Ashtavakra: A Model of Self-Realization

The life and teachings of the great sage **Ashtavakra** serve as a profound example of realizing the Self. Even as a child, Ashtavakra had an advanced understanding of the Atman, being well-versed in the scriptures. His story is a reminder that self-realization is not bound by age, social status, or conventional wisdom, but comes through inner clarity and wisdom.

In the famous dialogue between Ashtavakra and King Janaka, known as the **Ashtavakra Gita**, Ashtavakra expounds on the nature of the Self and the means to liberation. He teaches that liberation (Moksha) is not achieved through elaborate rituals or external practices, but through the **direct experience** of one's true nature as Atman. He stresses that the self is ever-free, and it is only ignorance (Avidya) that binds one to the illusion of separation.

Ashtavakra's teachings are notable for their simplicity and clarity. He does not encourage complex practices but rather focuses on the essential truth that one is already liberated; the only task is to **realize** this by looking inward. He famously says, "You are the one observer of this ever-changing world. Knowing this, cease striving, let go of illusion, and find inner peace."

Key Lessons from Ashtavakra's Teachings

Self-Realization as the Ultimate Truth: The *Ashtavakra Gita* emphasizes that self-realization, the recognition of one's true nature, is the highest goal. Ashtavakra teaches that each person is, at their core, pure, infinite, and beyond physical and mental limitations. Unlike the body and mind, which are transient, the self is eternal and unchanging. Understanding this helps one transcend fears and anxieties linked to the body and mind.

Liberation Through Inner Detachment: True liberation, according to Ashtavakra, comes from detaching oneself from worldly desires, attachments, and aversions. He advises practicing non-attachment to outcomes, as attachment only binds the mind and creates suffering. This is not the same as physical renunciation but involves mental detachment—a freedom within, regardless of external circumstances.

Illusory Nature of the World (Maya): Ashtavakra teaches that the world is an illusion, or *maya*, and that attachment to this illusion binds us in cycles of suffering and rebirth. By seeing through this illusion and recognizing the self as beyond the material, one achieves liberation. Recognizing this illusory nature enables a person to move through life without becoming entangled in fleeting experiences and desires.

Non-Identification with Body and Mind: He emphasizes the difference between the self and the mind or body. Ashtavakra teaches that identifying oneself with these transient aspects leads to misery. True self-realization involves seeing oneself as the consciousness that observes all experiences. This principle aligns with the philosophy of Advaita (non-duality), where the self is one with the universe and not limited by the individual body or ego.

Acceptance and Equanimity: The path to freedom also involves acceptance of all things, as they are, without resistance or desire for control. Ashtavakra encourages equanimity in both pain and pleasure, success and failure. This acceptance fosters inner peace and freedom from the disturbances created by reactive emotions, allowing one to remain calm and centered in any situation.

Embracing Simplicity and Stillness: Ashtavakra promotes a life of inner simplicity, where one need not engage in constant mental or external striving. He emphasizes that spiritual freedom arises in stillness—when the mind is calm and silent, and there's no compulsion to seek outside validation or achievements. Through stillness, one realizes that true happiness is innate and does not rely on external factors.

Living Without Judgments and Labels: Ashtavakra advises not to label experiences, people, or oneself. When we drop labels, we move beyond judgments and see things as they are—neutral, transient experiences. This opens up the possibility of a liberated life where one is free from conditioning and expectations. Living without judgment cultivates compassion, self-love, and a greater sense of unity with all beings.

The Power of Witness Consciousness: He encourages embracing a "witness" attitude, observing thoughts and feelings without getting entangled in them. By practicing this witness consciousness, one can rise above mental patterns and ego-based reactions. Witnessing the mind as separate from oneself dissolves the attachments that lead to suffering and reveals the self as pure awareness.

Experiencing the Self is not a distant goal but an ever-present reality waiting to be realized through meditation, self-inquiry, and detachment. Whether through the stillness of meditation, the probing questions of self-inquiry, or the dispassion cultivated by detachment, these practices lead the seeker inward to the ultimate truth—the Atman. The story of Ashtavakra and his discourse with King Janaka reinforces that the realization of the Self is within everyone's reach, and that it is simplicity, clarity, and inner focus that reveal the eternal nature of the Atman.

Atman and the Modern World

In today's fast-paced and materialistic world, the pursuit of external achievements and success often overshadows the deeper quest for inner truth and self-realization. People are conditioned to focus on wealth, status, and personal accomplishments, creating an environment where mental well-being is frequently neglected. However, the teachings of **Atman**—the realization of the eternal, unchanging self—are more relevant than ever in helping individuals find lasting peace, contentment, and a higher sense of purpose amidst the chaos.

The Relevance of Atman in the Modern World

Modern life is filled with distractions, from constant connectivity through technology to the pressures of work, relationships, and social expectations. While external accomplishments provide temporary satisfaction, they often leave a sense of incompleteness, fuelling a cycle of desire and dissatisfaction. The ancient concept of the **Atman** teaches that true fulfillment comes not from external sources but from realizing one's true nature, which is beyond material existence and worldly attachments.

According to the **American Psychological Association (APA)**, meditation has been linked to measurable reductions in stress, anxiety, and depression. One study revealed that **39% of adults** who regularly practice meditation reported increased emotional well-being, which includes greater feelings of calm, improved focus, and enhanced self-awareness. This modern research points to the **transformative power of meditation** and introspection, echoing the ancient teachings of Atman, which emphasize the importance of inner stillness and self-reflection for realizing the true self.

Conclusion: The Ultimate Realization

The realization of *Atman* is not merely an intellectual understanding but an experiential truth. It is the recognition that the individual self is inseparable from the universal consciousness, leading to the dissolution of ego and the attainment of ultimate freedom. The journey to discovering *Atman* is the journey to realizing our true nature, beyond the illusions of the material world.

As Swami Vivekananda beautifully expressed, "Each soul is potentially divine. The goal is to manifest this divinity within by controlling nature, external and internal." This manifestation of divinity is the realization of the Atman.

17

Ego vs. Self

The distinction between ego and self is a fundamental concept in spiritual and psychological traditions. While the ego is often associated with the false self, rooted in identification with the body, mind, desires, attachments and external achievements, the self (Atman) represents the true essence of a being, the unchanging and eternal consciousness, that transcends the ego. This chapter explores the intricate relationship between ego and self, offering insights into how understanding this duality is essential for spiritual growth and self-realization.

The Nature of Ego

The ego, in the context of spirituality and psychology, is the sense of "I" or individual identity that is shaped by one's thoughts, emotions, memories, and external experiences. It is the aspect of consciousness that identifies with the physical body and the mind, leading to a sense of separateness from others and the world. In psychological terms, the ego helps us navigate the world and manage our personal and social identities, but when unchecked, it can lead to suffering, conflict, and a distorted sense of self.

In Sanskrit, the ego is often referred to as *Ahamkara*, meaning "the I-maker." It is the construct that gives rise to the notion of individuality, distinct from the universal consciousness.

A person may identify strongly with their job title, social status, or possessions. This identification forms the ego, which can lead to feelings of pride, attachment, or insecurity when these external factors are threatened or lost.

The Self (Atman) in Contrast

The self (Atman) is the true, unchanging essence of a being, beyond the ego. It is the eternal consciousness that underlies all existence, free from the limitations of the physical body and mind. Unlike the ego, which is transient and changeable, the self is eternal and unbounded. Recognizing that our true nature is not confined to the individual identity but is connected to the universal consciousness (Brahman).

The *Bhagavad Gita* (2.20) describes the self as "never born, eternal, ever-existing, and primeval. It is not slain when the body is slain." This verse emphasizes the immortality and permanence of the self, in contrast to the transient nature of the ego.

The *Mandukya Upanishad* (1.2) describes the self as "unseen, beyond empirical reality, beyond the senses, and incomprehensible." It is that which underlies all experience but remains untouched by it.

The Illusion of the Ego: Maya

The ego operates within the realm of *Maya*, the illusory force that veils the true nature of reality. In Vedanta, Maya is often described as the cosmic illusion that distorts our perception of the world, causing us to mistake the transient for the eternal, the individual self for the infinite. Within this framework, the ego — our sense of individuality, of "I" — is perhaps the most potent manifestation of Maya. It leads to the mistaken belief that the ego is the true self, creating a state of ignorance or *avidya*, where we lose sight of our real essence, which is pure consciousness, the *Atman*.

Swami Vivekananda, a revered spiritual leader, once remarked, **"The whole life is a succession of dreams. My ambition is to be a conscious dreamer, that is all."** This profound quote sheds light on the nature of the ego-driven life, where individuals live as if within a dream, mistaking the ephemeral for the real. Just as in a dream we believe in the experiences we have, only to wake and realize their unreality, so too do we live under the sway of Maya, identifying with our egoic thoughts, emotions, and desires as if they define who we are. To become a **"conscious dreamer"** is to awaken from the illusion of the ego, to live with awareness that what we call reality is but a fleeting shadow of the ultimate truth.

One of the clearest illustrations of this concept is the famous story from Vedanta philosophy about the rope and the snake. In the dark, a person may mistake a rope lying on the ground for a snake and react with fear. The misperception causes an immediate emotional and physical response, driven by the illusion. But when light is shed on the situation, the person sees the rope for what it truly is, and the fear dissipates. The snake never existed; it was a projection of the mind, a false reality born of ignorance.

In much the same way, the ego is the illusion that conceals our true self, the *Atman*. The fear, attachment, and desires we experience are like the imagined snake, compelling us to act and react in ways that deepen our identification with the ego. But when the light of wisdom and self-inquiry shines upon our consciousness, the ego's illusory nature is revealed, and we recognize that we are not the limited being we once thought we were. Just as the rope is always a rope, never a snake, we are always the Atman, never the ego — it is only our perception, clouded by Maya, that deceives us.

This realization is the cornerstone of spiritual awakening. As long as we are enmeshed in the ego, we live in the world of duality — of pleasure and pain, success and failure, hope and fear. But by seeing through the illusion, we begin to experience the unity of existence, where the *Brahman* (the ultimate reality) is all there is, and the individual ego is a mere flicker of light in the vast ocean of consciousness. In essence, the journey of spiritual awakening is the process of dissolving the ego, transcending Maya, and recognizing our oneness with the infinite.

The Conflict Between Ego and Self

The tension between ego and self lies at the heart of the spiritual journey. The ego, with its constant cravings for recognition and control, pulls us away from the realization of the self. The more we identify with the ego, the more we remain trapped in the cycle of desires, fears, and suffering. In contrast, identifying with the self leads to liberation (moksha), inner peace, and the dissolution of the ego's illusory power.

In the *Bhagavad Gita* (2.47-48), Krishna advises Arjuna to perform his duties without attachment to the results, emphasizing the importance of transcending the ego's desires. By detaching from the fruits of action, one can align with the true self and experience peace.

Modern research in neuroscience shows that individuals who practice mindfulness and meditation, which often involve reducing egoic tendencies, exhibit higher levels of well-being, reduced stress, and increased empathy.

The Consequences of Ego-Identification

Living in identification with the ego leads to various negative outcomes, including suffering, anxiety, and a sense of incompleteness. The ego is never satisfied, always seeking more validation, recognition, and material possessions. This constant craving leads to a cycle of desire and disappointment.

Psychological research has shown that people with high levels of ego involvement tend to experience greater stress, anxiety, and depression. Their self-worth is tied to external factors, making them vulnerable to emotional disturbances when these factors are challenged or lost.

In the corporate world, individuals who identify strongly with their job titles may experience an identity crisis upon retirement or job loss. Their sense of self-worth, tied to their professional achievements, crumbles when these external markers are no longer present.

The Role of the Ego in Spiritual Growth and Evolution

Interestingly, the ego is not something to be entirely eradicated; rather, it can be transformed and used as a tool for growth. The ego, when disciplined and aligned with higher awareness, becomes a servant to the self rather than its master. This transformation allows the individual to function in the world without losing touch with their deeper essence.

While the ego is often seen as an obstacle to spiritual growth, it also plays a crucial role in the process of evolution. The ego's challenges and conflicts serve as catalysts for the search for the self. Without the ego's limitations, one might never seek the deeper truths of existence.

Carl Jung, a Swiss psychiatrist and psychoanalyst, noted, "One does not become enlightened by imagining figures of light, but by making the darkness conscious." This emphasizes the importance of confronting and understanding the ego as a necessary step in spiritual growth.

Real-Life Spiritual Teachings

Throughout history, spiritual leaders, mystics, and sages have embodied the journey of transcending the ego, offering living examples of self-realization and the boundless potential of the human spirit. These figures are not just mythological characters or distant ideals but are individuals who have walked among us, offering us a glimpse into the profound state of inner freedom and enlightenment.

One of the most well-known stories of such transcendence is that of **Siddhartha Gautama,** known to the world as the Buddha. His journey towards enlightenment is a timeless narrative of spiritual discovery and liberation. After years of extreme self-denial, however, Siddhartha realized that neither indulgence nor self-mortification held the key to enlightenment. This revelation led him to embrace what he called the **Middle Way**—a path of balance that transcended both attachment to the physical world and the rejection of the body. It was under the Bodhi tree, in a moment of profound clarity, that he awakened to the truth of **Anatta**—the realization of the non-self, the dissolution of the ego, and the understanding of the interconnectedness of all life. In this moment, he became the Buddha, and his teachings have since illuminated the path for countless others seeking to transcend the egoic self.

Another deeply inspiring example of ego transcendence is found in the life of **Saint Teresa of Avila,** a Spanish mystic and one of the greatest spiritual figures of the Catholic tradition. Born in the 16th century, Teresa struggled for many years with the tension between her human desires and her spiritual calling. Her early years in religious life were marked by ego-driven aspirations—seeking recognition, success, and approval in her spiritual endeavours. However, as she deepened her practice of prayer and inner contemplation, Teresa experienced what she described as an "inner castle"—a metaphor for the soul's journey toward union with the divine. In her seminal work, *The Interior Castle,* she articulates the stages of this journey, where she moved through the layers of the ego, shedding her attachments to worldly desires and ego-driven spirituality. Her writings reveal that as she progressed through these stages, she moved closer to what she called **mystical union**—a state of being in which the individual self dissolves into the divine self, or **Atman**. In this union, the ego no longer holds sway, and the individual experiences a direct, unmediated connection with the divine. Saint Teresa's life and works continue to inspire those on the path of spiritual awakening, reminding us that the transcendence of the ego is not only possible but leads to the highest form of self-realization.

Both the Buddha and Saint Teresa represent distinct cultural and religious traditions, yet their journeys share a common thread: the recognition that the ego, while an essential aspect of human experience, is ultimately an illusion that must be transcended in the pursuit of higher consciousness. Their lives show us that true spiritual growth does not lie in external achievements or ego-driven aspirations, but in the dissolution of the self, leading to an experience of unity with all that is.

Their stories invite us to reflect on our own lives, urging us to ask: How can we move beyond the limits of the ego, and what does it mean to live in a state of union with the self or the divine?

Conclusion

The journey from ego to self is the essence of spiritual evolution. By understanding the nature of the ego and its distinction from the self, individuals can embark on the path of self-realization. The ultimate goal is to transcend the ego and realize the true self, leading to a life of inner peace, fulfillment, and liberation.

18

Karma and Reincarnations

The concept of *karma* and *reincarnation* form the cornerstone of many spiritual traditions, particularly within Hinduism, Buddhism, and Jainism. These doctrines explain the interconnectedness of actions and their consequences, extending across multiple lifetimes. This chapter delves into the intricate relationship between karma and reincarnation, exploring how actions in one life influence the circumstances of subsequent births.

Understanding Karma: The Law of Cause and Effect

Karma, derived from the Sanskrit word *karman*, means "action" or "deed." In the spiritual context, karma refers to the universal law of cause and effect, where every action has corresponding consequences. These consequences are not limited to a single lifetime but can manifest across multiple incarnations.

Karma operates on three levels—thought, word, and deed. Every action, whether physical, verbal, or mental, contributes to an individual's karma, influencing their future experiences.

If a person performs selfless acts of kindness, they accumulate positive karma, which may lead to favourable circumstances in future lives. Conversely, harmful actions generate negative karma, which can result in suffering or challenges in subsequent incarnations.

The Bhagavad Gita (4.17) states, "The intricacies of action are very hard to understand. Therefore, one should know properly what action is, what forbidden action is, and what inaction is." This verse highlights the complexity of karma and the importance of discerning right from wrong actions.

The Cycle of Samsara: Birth, Death, and Rebirth

Samsara refers to the continuous cycle of birth, death, and rebirth, driven by the law of karma. According to this doctrine, the soul (Atman) undergoes countless *punarjanma* (incarnations), each shaped by the karma accumulated in previous lives. The ultimate goal of spiritual practice is to break free from this cycle and achieve liberation (Moksha).

The cycle of samsara is often depicted as a wheel, symbolizing the repetitive nature of existence. Each rotation of the wheel represents a new life, with the soul bound by the consequences of past actions.

A person who has lived a life of greed and selfishness may be reborn in circumstances that challenge them to overcome these tendencies. Conversely, a person who has cultivated virtues such as compassion and selflessness may experience more favourable conditions in their next life.

In the Bhagavad Gita (2.22), Krishna explains, "As a person sheds worn-out garments and wears new ones, likewise, the soul casts off its worn-out body and enters a new one." This verse beautifully illustrates the soul's journey through different incarnations.

The *Brihadaranyaka Upanishad* (4.4.5) states, "As a man acts, so he becomes. As is his desire, so is his destiny." This verse emphasizes that the nature of one's desires and actions directly shape their future incarnations.

Real-Life Spiritual Teachings

Throughout history, various spiritual figures have exemplified the principles of karma and reincarnation, providing insights into these profound concepts.

The story of King Bharata, as narrated in the *Bhagavata Purana*, serves as a powerful illustration of karma and reincarnation. Despite his spiritual achievements, King Bharata became attached to a deer during his final days, leading to his rebirth as a deer in his next life. This story underscores the importance of detachment and the far-reaching consequences of one's actions.

The Tibetan practice of identifying reincarnated lamas, known as tulkus, is a living example of belief in reincarnation. After the death of a lama, a search is conducted to find the child believed to be the lama's reincarnation, based on signs, memories, and behaviours from the previous life.

Swami Vivekananda stated, "Samsara is the infinite dream of Maya, from which we wake up only when we reach self-knowledge." This highlights the illusory nature of the world and the importance of spiritual awakening to escape the cycle of *samsara*.

Studies on near-death experiences and past-life regression therapy suggest that many individuals have memories of previous lives, supporting the idea of reincarnation across various cultures.

A 2018 *Pew Research Center* survey found that nearly a third of U.S. adults believe in reincarnation, reflecting the growing interest in Eastern philosophies and the concept of karma.

The past-life regression work of Dr. Brian Weiss, a prominent psychiatrist, has brought the concept of reincarnation into the mainstream. His book *Many Lives, Many Masters* documents his experiences with patients who recalled previous lifetimes during hypnotherapy, offering compelling evidence of reincarnation.

Types of Karma

In Hindu philosophy, karma is categorized into three types, each playing a unique role in the cycle of birth and actions.

- **Sanchita Karma**: The accumulated karma from all previous lives. This is the storehouse of actions that have not yet borne fruit.

- **Prarabdha Karma**: The portion of sanchita karma that is ripe and will manifest in the present life. It is this karma that determines the circumstances of one's current incarnation.

- **Agami Karma**: The future karma that will be created by actions performed in the present life, impacting future incarnations.

The *Yoga Vasistha* (3.7.27) explains, "Whatever man does in this life becomes the cause of his future birth." This verse emphasizes the interconnectedness of actions across lifetimes.

The Role of Karma in Reincarnation

Karma dictates the circumstances of reincarnation. Positive actions lead to favourable births, while negative actions result in challenging conditions. The soul takes birth in various forms—human, animal, or even divine—based on its karmic debts and merits.

The *Chandogya Upanishad* (5.10.7) describes how a person who performs virtuous deeds is reborn into a good family, enjoys wealth, and gains happiness, while one who performs negative deeds is born into a difficult life, with suffering and challenges.

The Bhagavad Gita (14.15) also touches on the idea of reincarnation into lower life forms, "When one dies in the mode of passion, he takes birth among those engaged in fruitive activities; and when one dies in the mode of ignorance, he takes birth in the animal kingdom." Here, Lord Krishna explains that a person who dies in ignorance may take birth in lower life forms, including animals. This is connected to the idea that the soul's next form is determined by the dominant qualities (gunas) present in their life.

In Buddhist tradition, the story of Milarepa, a Tibetan saint, demonstrates how karma can influence future lives. After committing serious wrongdoings in his youth, Milarepa (known as a murderer when he was a young man) suffered immensely, but through spiritual practice, he purified his karma and attained enlightenment within a single lifetime.

The Role of Free Will and Destiny

While karma plays a significant role in shaping an individual's destiny, the concept of free will is also vital. Spiritual traditions often teach that while past karma influences one's circumstances, individuals possess the free will to shape their responses and create new karma.

The balance between free will and destiny is delicate. While one cannot change the karma that has already been set into motion, they have the power to create positive karma through righteous actions in the present.

A person born into difficult circumstances due to past karma still has the ability to choose how they respond to their situation. By exercising compassion, patience, and wisdom, they can create positive karma that will influence future lives.

Swami Vivekananda once said, "We are responsible for what we are, and whatever we wish ourselves to be, we have the power to make ourselves." This quote highlights the empowering aspect of free will within the framework of karma.

Liberation from the Cycle: Moksha

The ultimate goal of spiritual practice is to transcend the cycle of karma and reincarnation, achieving liberation (Moksha). Moksha is the state of realizing the self's true nature, free from the bonds of karma and the cycles of birth and death.

Moksha is not merely an escape from suffering but a realization of one's unity with the infinite consciousness. It is the culmination of spiritual evolution, where the soul is no longer bound by the consequences of past actions.

The Bhagavad Gita (2.51) states, "The wise, engaged in devotion, renounce the fruits of action. Freed from the bonds of birth, they go to the abode beyond all evil." This verse emphasizes the path of renunciation and the attainment of liberation.

Conclusion

The interplay between karma and reincarnation offers profound insights into the nature of existence, emphasizing the importance of conscious actions and spiritual practice. By understanding the cycles of birth and actions, individuals can navigate their spiritual journey with greater awareness, ultimately seeking liberation from the endless cycle of samsara.

19

Non-Violence

Yoga, in its truest essence, is more than a practice of postures; it is a philosophy of life, a spiritual path that leads to the union of body, mind, and soul. At the core of this philosophy lies the principle of *Ahimsa*—non-violence. Ahimsa is not merely the absence of physical violence but encompasses non-harming thoughts, words, and actions. This chapter delves into the profound connection between yoga and non-violence, exploring the historical roots, modern interpretations, and practical implications of living a life grounded in this essential yogic value.

Ahimsa in the Yoga Sutras of Patanjali

Ahimsa, or non-violence, holds a foundational place in the philosophy and practice of yoga, with its earliest and most prominent mention in Patanjali's *Yoga Sutras*. It is the first of the five Yamas (ethical restraints) in the second limb of the eightfold path of yoga. Patanjali emphasizes Ahimsa as the bedrock upon which all other practices of yoga rest. He declares in *Yoga Sutras* 2.35: "Ahimsa pratishthayam tat sannidhau vaira tyagah," meaning, "When one is firmly established in non-violence, all hostility ceases in their presence."

This profound verse conveys the transformative nature of Ahimsa. It is not merely the avoidance of physical harm but also extends to thoughts, words, and intentions. Patanjali suggests that a person who is firmly grounded in non-violence radiates an aura of peace so powerful that it affects everyone and everything around them. In their presence, aggression and hostility dissolve naturally, without the need for confrontation or coercion.

Imagine a yogi who has practiced Ahimsa for years, integrating non-violence not only into their actions but also into their thoughts and speech. When this individual enters a room where tensions are high, conflicts may arise, or tempers are flaring, their presence alone has the potential to calm the environment. Without saying a word, the energy they carry creates a shift, diffusing the anger and aggression around them. This yogi doesn't engage in debates or force peace upon others; instead, their inner state of harmony permeates the space, inspiring others to let go of their hostility. This is the deeper essence of Ahimsa that Patanjali speaks of—its power to not only transform the self but also to influence the world around in subtle yet profound ways.

Ahimsa thus acts as a catalyst for personal and collective transformation, setting the tone for all other yogic principles to flourish. By establishing non-violence within, a yogi can positively impact not just their immediate relationships, but potentially the larger social fabric.

The Roots of Ahimsa in Ancient Indian Traditions

The concept of *Ahimsa* is deeply woven into the fabric of ancient Indian philosophies and spiritual traditions. It transcends mere physical non-violence, extending to thoughts and words, emphasizing compassion, kindness, and the recognition of the interconnectedness of all life. While *Ahimsa* is predominantly associated with Hinduism, Buddhism, and Jainism, its influence permeates other aspects of Indian thought and practice, forming a cornerstone for moral and spiritual conduct.

In **Hinduism**, *Ahimsa* is revered as a vital virtue for those seeking spiritual growth and self-realization. The Bhagavad Gita, lists *Ahimsa* as a key attribute for individuals striving for inner transformation and enlightenment. In Chapter 16, Verse 2, it states: "Ahimsa satyam akrodhas tyagah shantir apaisunam," which translates to, "Non-violence, truthfulness, freedom from anger, renunciation, serenity, and aversion to fault-finding."

This verse emphasizes that non-violence is not just an action, but a mindset and an approach to life. It underlines that peace and harmony are cultivated through patience, truth, and the ability to rise above anger. In this light, *Ahimsa* becomes more than just refraining from physical harm; it is about nurturing a life of integrity, balance, and love for all beings, aligning with the ultimate goal of achieving *moksha* (liberation).

In **Jainism**, *Ahimsa* stands as the highest ethical principle, far surpassing all others in importance. It forms the foundation of Jain ethical and spiritual practice, to the extent that the religion is often described as being entirely centered around the concept of non-violence. The *Acaranga Sutra*, one of the oldest Jain texts, profoundly articulates this principle: "All beings desire to live. No one wishes to be harmed. Therefore, no one should cause harm to any living being."

This encapsulates the Jain belief that all living beings, from humans to the smallest microorganisms, possess a soul, and therefore deserve respect and compassion. To uphold *Ahimsa*, Jains practice extreme care to avoid causing harm to any form of life, even going as far as to sweep the ground before walking or wearing face coverings to avoid unintentionally harming insects. This is also why Jainism encourages strict vegetarianism or veganism, as a commitment to reducing harm in every aspect of life.

Similarly, **Buddhism** embraces *Ahimsa* as a foundational ethical precept. The Buddha taught that non-violence is essential for developing compassion (karuna) and loving-kindness (metta) towards all beings. *Ahimsa* is a reflection of the interconnected nature of existence in Buddhist thought—since all beings are part of the same cycle of life, death, and rebirth, harming others only perpetuates suffering for all.

The practice of non-violence in Buddhism extends beyond mere actions to include one's speech and thoughts. Practitioners are encouraged to cultivate *right speech*—free from hurtful words and malicious intent—and *right mindfulness*, ensuring that their inner landscape is free from anger, hatred, or ill will. In this way, *Ahimsa* helps reduce suffering for oneself and others, guiding practitioners toward the ultimate goal of *nirvana*, the cessation of all suffering.

One of the most visible expressions of *Ahimsa* in these traditions is the practice of **vegetarianism**. For many Hindus, Buddhists, and Jains, adhering to a vegetarian or vegan diet is a direct reflection of their commitment to non-violence. By abstaining from consuming animal products, they minimize harm to sentient beings and seek to live in harmony with the natural world. The act of eating becomes a spiritual practice, reinforcing the broader values of empathy, mindfulness, and respect for life.

When we look into the eyes of an animal, we see a soul full of life, a being that feels love, fear, joy, and pain just as we do. These creatures trust us with their lives, unaware of the fate that may await them. To take that life for a momentary taste or fleeting satisfaction is to end something sacred—an existence as valuable as our own. Every life is a unique expression of the universe, and by killing animals for food, we sever that precious connection, silencing the gentle breath of beings who only wish to live, as we do. Compassion is the language of the heart, and choosing not to harm those who cannot defend themselves is the most profound expression of love and empathy.

Some may wonder why it is acceptable to eat plants when they too are alive. But there is a profound difference between plants and animals. Plants, though living, do not have a central nervous system or the capacity to feel pain in the same way animals do. Their purpose in the ecosystem is intertwined with giving life—providing nourishment to sustain other beings. When we consume plant-based foods, we are partaking in a cycle that allows life to flourish without causing unnecessary suffering. The earth offers her abundance, and by accepting it with gratitude and respect, we honour the delicate balance of nature. We can live, thrive, and nurture ourselves on the gifts of the earth without taking the life of a creature whose only wish is to live in peace.

By choosing a vegetarian lifestyle, we become guardians of life rather than destroyers of it. We embrace a way of living that recognizes the beauty and sanctity of all beings. Each time we sit down to eat, we have the power to make a choice that speaks volumes about who we are and the kind of world we wish to create. It is not about denying ourselves pleasure but about finding a deeper joy in knowing that no blood was spilled, no pain endured, and no life ended for the food on our plates. This is how we truly nourish our souls—through compassion, kindness, and an unwavering respect for the life that surrounds us.

In this context, *Ahimsa* is not just a philosophical ideal but a practical guide to everyday living. Whether through the food they consume, the way they speak, or their approach to interpersonal relationships, individuals practicing *Ahimsa* strive to create a ripple effect of peace and compassion throughout the world.

In ancient times, the concept of vegetarianism was prevalent among many warrior cultures, a testament to their strength and discipline. Contrary to modern stereotypes that associate meat consumption with physical power, several renowned ancient warriors and athletes followed plant-based diets. Among them were the Roman gladiators, who were known to subsist primarily on a vegetarian diet. These fierce fighters, often referred to as **"hordearii,"** or **"barley eaters,"** consumed grains like barley, wheat, and legumes as their staple foods. Historical records and modern scientific analyses of their bones reveal high levels of strontium, which is consistent with a diet rich in plant-based proteins. Their vegetarian lifestyle was not only a choice for sustenance but also played a role in their physical endurance, strength, and rapid recovery after intense combat in the arena.

Similarly, in ancient Greece and Rome, vegetarianism was embraced by certain athletes who partook in the Olympics and other competitive sports. Many of these athletes avoided meat, adhering instead to diets rich in fruits, vegetables, and grains, believing that it would maintain a balance of mind and body. Greek philosopher Pythagoras, a staunch advocate of vegetarianism, influenced a number of his followers, including athletes, to avoid meat consumption. His teachings suggested that abstaining from animal products promoted harmony with nature and enhanced physical and mental performance.

The adoption of plant-based diets by warriors and athletes in ancient civilizations highlights the deep connection between physical prowess and disciplined dietary practices. Their vegetarian diets, rich in nutrients and high in energy, fueled their intense training and combat, showcasing that plant-based eating was not a limitation but rather a strength.

In today's context, *Ahimsa* continues to inspire movements related to animal rights, environmental conservation, and social justice. It serves as a reminder that the pursuit of peace, both internally and externally, begins with the simple but profound choice to refrain from causing harm in all its forms. By aligning our actions, words, and thoughts with the principle of *Ahimsa*, we can contribute to a more compassionate, equitable, and harmonious world.

Non-Violence in Modern Yoga Practices

In the modern world, the practice of Ahimsa has taken on new dimensions. As yoga has become popularized in the West, the focus has often been on physical asanas, with less emphasis on the ethical and philosophical foundations. However, many contemporary yoga practitioners and teachers are re-emphasizing the importance of Ahimsa as a guiding principle in daily life.

Ahimsa in modern yoga can manifest in various ways, including:

Dietary Choices: Many yoga practitioners adopt a vegetarian or vegan diet, rooted in the desire to avoid harm to animals.

Environmental Awareness: Practicing Ahimsa also extends to how we treat the environment. Eco-conscious choices such as reducing waste, using sustainable products, and supporting environmental causes are considered acts of non-violence towards the planet.

Mental and Emotional Non-Violence: Modern interpretations of Ahimsa also focus on self-compassion and the avoidance of harmful thoughts and self-criticism. This is reflected in the growing popularity of mindfulness practices, which encourage non-judgmental awareness and self-acceptance.

According to a 2019 study by the *Yoga Alliance*, over 70% of yoga practitioners in the U.S. reported that their practice had made them more aware of their impact on the environment and encouraged them to adopt more sustainable habits.

A study published in the *Journal of Positive Psychology* (2015) found that individuals who practiced loving-kindness meditation experienced increased positive emotions, decreased negative emotions, and improved psychological well-being.

Many yoga practitioners choose a plant-based diet as an expression of non-violence, avoiding harm to animals. According to a 2021 report by the *Plant-Based Foods Association*, the plant-based food market in the United States grew by 27%, indicating a growing awareness of the ethical implications of dietary choices among yoga practitioners and the general public.

Non-Violence in Action: Case Studies and Events

Throughout history, the principle of *Ahimsa* (non-violence) has been a transformative force, driving profound social change and inspiring movements for justice, peace, and environmental stewardship. From compassionate leadership to grassroots activism, these case studies illustrate the enduring power of non-violence in action.

The Dalai Lama: A Living Embodiment of Compassionate Leadership

His Holiness the Dalai Lama stands as a beacon of *Ahimsa*, embodying the principle in his words, actions, and leadership. Despite enduring decades of political persecution, exile from his homeland of Tibet, and witnessing the suffering of his people, the Dalai Lama has consistently upheld non-violence as the only path to true peace and reconciliation. His teachings stress that non-violence is not merely the absence of physical harm but the active cultivation of compassion, understanding, and empathy toward all beings, including those who may be seen as enemies.

The Dalai Lama's leadership reminds us that true strength lies in compassion, not in retaliation or aggression. His unwavering commitment to peaceful resistance, even in the face of adversity, exemplifies the power of *Ahimsa* to create harmony in a world often divided by violence and conflict. Through his advocacy for compassion and human connection, he continues to inspire individuals and nations alike to resolve differences through dialogue and kindness rather than violence.

The Black Lives Matter Movement: Non-Violent Protest for Racial Justice

The Black Lives Matter (BLM) movement, which emerged in response to systemic racism and police violence against Black communities, draws heavily from the legacy of non-violent civil rights protests. Figures such as Martin Luther King Jr., a key leader of the American civil rights movement, advocated for peaceful resistance and were themselves influenced by Mahatma Gandhi's philosophy of *Ahimsa*. King famously said, "Nonviolence is a powerful and just weapon which cuts without wounding and ennobles the man who wields it."

Although some BLM protests have escalated into violence, it is essential to remember that the core message of the movement is one of non-violent resistance. At its heart, BLM seeks to challenge deeply entrenched systems of racial inequality through peaceful protests, awareness campaigns, and calls for systemic reform. By echoing the non-violent methods of past civil rights movements, BLM demonstrates how *Ahimsa* can be a potent tool in dismantling structures of injustice without perpetuating cycles of hatred and harm.

Environmental Activism and Ahimsa: Protecting the Earth through Peaceful Action

Environmental movements like Extinction Rebellion and Fridays for Future have taken the principles of *Ahimsa* and extended them to the natural world. These movements recognize that non-violence must also include the protection of our planet, acknowledging the deep interconnectedness between human well-being and the health of the Earth. By engaging in peaceful demonstrations, sit-ins, and acts of civil disobedience, environmental activists aim to draw attention to the urgent need for climate action without resorting to violence.

Extinction Rebellion, in particular, promotes the idea that the harm we inflict on the environment is a form of violence—violence against future generations and all living beings that depend on a healthy ecosystem. Their commitment to non-violent protest reflects an understanding that true environmental justice cannot be achieved through destruction but rather through the compassionate defense of the natural world. Similarly, Fridays for Future, inspired by Greta Thunberg, uses peaceful demonstrations to demand that world leaders take responsibility for the climate crisis and enact policies that protect the planet for future generations.

In this way, these environmental movements highlight the importance of applying *Ahimsa* to our relationship with the Earth. They challenge us to consider how our actions, even those that seem distant or disconnected, can cause harm and suffering to the planet and its inhabitants. By embracing non-violence, they offer a path forward that seeks to heal rather than harm, ensuring that future generations inherit a world where life, in all its forms, can thrive.

Each of these movements—whether for political freedom, racial justice, or environmental sustainability—demonstrates the far-reaching impact of *Ahimsa* when applied to the most pressing issues of our time. Non-violence is not passive; it is an active, courageous choice to confront injustice, protect life, and create a better world without resorting to harm. Whether through compassionate leadership, peaceful protest, or environmental activism, *Ahimsa* continues to be a powerful force for change, reminding us that true progress is made not through violence, but through empathy, understanding, and respect for all beings.

Throughout history, true leadership has never been defined by violence, but by the values of compassion, justice, and the protection of the innocent. Revered figures like **Arjuna, Chhatrapati Shivaji Maharaj, Guru Gobind Singh, and Maharana Pratap** stand as shining examples of warriors who embodied these principles. Their legacies are not marked by the glorification of war but by their deep commitment to non-violence, choosing battle only when all other paths of peace were exhausted. For them, war was a last resort—a necessary response to protect their people, preserve righteousness, and defend the vulnerable from oppression.

Arjuna, for instance, struggled deeply with the idea of engaging in battle during the Mahabharata's Kurukshetra war. His internal conflict was not one of fear but of a moral dilemma, as he did not wish to bring harm to his kin, even when justice demanded it. It was only after Lord Krishna enlightened him on the greater purpose of upholding *dharma*—the cosmic order and righteousness—that he took up arms, not for personal victory, but to restore balance and truth. This was not an act of violence, but one of sacred duty.

Likewise, **Chhatrapati Shivaji Maharaj** is celebrated for his courage, but his strength lay in his compassion and love for his people. He led not out of ambition for conquest, but out of a need to protect his homeland from foreign powers. Shivaji preferred diplomacy and only took up arms when his peaceful efforts failed. Even in war, he upheld strict ethical standards, ensuring the protection of civilians, especially women and children. His battles were fought for survival and freedom, not for the sake of inflicting suffering or asserting dominance.

Guru Gobind Singh, the tenth Sikh Guru, stands as another powerful testament to non-violence in action. Faced with relentless persecution and violence against his people, he only resorted to armed defense when peaceful means were no longer possible. Guru Gobind Singh's founding of the **Khalsa** was not a call to violence but a call to defend justice, equality, and the right to live freely. His teachings stressed that the sword should only be wielded to protect, never to oppress, and that compassion and righteousness were the highest virtues.

Maharana Pratap, the warrior king of Mewar, similarly fought not out of a desire for war but to defend his kingdom from invasion and protect its sovereignty. His refusal to submit to the Mughal Empire was not born from pride or aggression but from a deep commitment to protect his land and culture. His resilience in the face of overwhelming odds was a testament to his courage and sense of duty, rather than a lust for violence.

These figures share a common thread: their battles were always defensive, guided by a moral compass that prioritized justice and the well-being of their people over personal ambition or conquest. Their actions were motivated by compassion, a sense of responsibility, and the need to protect *dharma*. Through their lives, they exemplify the true essence of a warrior—one who fights not out of hatred or aggression, but out of love for humanity and a desire for peace. Their legacies remind us that non-violence is not the absence of action, but the courageous choice to seek justice through compassion and righteousness, even in the face of conflict.

"By cultivating attitudes of friendliness toward the happy, compassion for the unhappy, delight in the virtuous, and disregard toward the wicked, the mind retains its undisturbed calmness" (*Yoga Sutras of Patanjali, Sutra* 1.33)

Challenges of Practicing Ahimsa in the Modern World

The ancient principle of *Ahimsa*, is both profound and simple in theory: it calls for kindness, compassion, and the avoidance of harm toward all living beings. Yet, in today's fast-paced and complex world, practicing *Ahimsa* presents numerous challenges that require conscious effort and deep self-awareness. As violence—whether physical, verbal, or structural—permeates modern society, adhering to the path of non-violence demands not only individual resolve but a rethinking of how we interact with others and with ourselves. This section delves into some of the most significant challenges we face while trying to live by the principles of *Ahimsa*.

Digital Violence: Navigating Non-Violence in Online Spaces

In the digital age, violence is no longer confined to physical interactions. Social media platforms, online forums, and the anonymity of the internet have made digital spaces fertile ground for harassment, bullying, and aggressive discourse. Online "trolling," verbal abuse, and cancel culture have become common, making it increasingly difficult to engage in civil discourse without being drawn into negativity.

Practicing *Ahimsa* in these spaces requires extraordinary mindfulness. It means resisting the urge to respond with anger, hatred, or personal attacks, even when provoked. Instead, it calls for patience, compassion, and empathy, recognizing that behind each online persona is a real person with their own struggles and perspectives. Non-violent engagement online involves not only refraining from harmful behavior but also standing up against digital harassment and fostering respectful, constructive conversations. It requires the courage to be a voice of calm amidst the digital storm, as *Ahimsa* teaches us to break cycles of aggression by responding with love and understanding, even in the most volatile virtual environments.

Structural Violence: Confronting Inequality and Injustice

While *Ahimsa* encourages the avoidance of direct harm, it also calls upon us to challenge the more insidious forms of violence embedded within societal structures. Structural violence refers to the systemic inequalities and injustices that harm individuals and communities, often without immediate or visible aggression. These include poverty, discrimination, racism, sexism, and other forms of marginalization that deny people access to basic rights and opportunities.

Practicing *Ahimsa* in this context means recognizing our role in perpetuating or challenging these structures. It is not enough to avoid personal acts of violence; true *Ahimsa* compels us to actively work toward dismantling the systems that create harm on a broader scale. This can take the form of advocating for social justice, supporting policies that promote equality, or engaging in peaceful activism that calls attention to these injustices. As **Thich Nhat Hanh** eloquently stated, "Non-violence does not mean non-action. It means we act with love and compassion, even in difficult situations." Confronting structural violence is one of the most difficult challenges of modern *Ahimsa* because it requires sustained effort and the willingness to speak out against ingrained systems of harm.

Self-Harm: Cultivating Kindness Toward Ourselves

One of the often-overlooked aspects of *Ahimsa* is the importance of non-violence toward oneself. In a world that is increasingly demanding and competitive, many people struggle with self-critical thoughts, stress, burnout, and unhealthy coping mechanisms. Self-harm may not always take physical forms—it can manifest as negative self-talk, toxic perfectionism, or a lack of self-care. The pressure to meet societal expectations can lead to feelings of inadequacy, leading individuals to harm themselves emotionally or mentally.

Ahimsa teaches that true non-violence begins within. It asks us to treat ourselves with the same compassion, patience, and love that we extend to others. This involves recognizing our own intrinsic worth, practicing self-compassion, and being gentle with ourselves in moments of failure or weakness. Only when we can cultivate inner peace and non-violence can we authentically extend that energy to the outside world. In many ways, practicing *Ahimsa* toward oneself may be the most difficult challenge of all, as it requires deep introspection and a commitment to self-acceptance in a culture that often encourages self-criticism.

Materialism and the Culture of Competition

Another challenge to practicing *Ahimsa* in the modern world is the pervasive culture of materialism and competition. Modern society often glorifies success, wealth, and personal achievement, creating a hyper-competitive environment where people are driven by a desire to outdo one another. This culture of competition can foster envy, greed, and aggression, which run counter to the principles of *Ahimsa*. The pursuit of material wealth often comes at the expense of others, leading to exploitation, environmental harm, and the breakdown of community bonds.

To practice *Ahimsa* in this context, one must resist the temptation to measure success solely by external achievements. Instead, *Ahimsa* encourages a shift toward valuing cooperation, generosity, and the well-being of all. It invites us to cultivate contentment and gratitude for what we have, rather than perpetually striving for more at the expense of others. Living simply, mindfully, and with a sense of responsibility toward others and the planet are crucial aspects of practicing non-violence in a world driven by materialism.

Conclusion: Integrating Ahimsa into Daily Life

Practicing Ahimsa is a lifelong journey that requires conscious effort in every aspect of life. Whether through our interactions with others, our relationship with the environment, or how we treat ourselves, non-violence is a guiding light that leads to inner peace and harmony with the world. Yoga offers the tools to cultivate this awareness and transform our lives, helping us to embody the essence of Ahimsa in a world that desperately needs it.

20

Beyond Caste, Creed, Race, Religion, Gender, Disability, and Place of Birth

Yoga, a timeless practice deeply rooted in the ancient wisdom of India, transcends all social, cultural, and personal divisions. At its true essence, it is an inward journey toward self-realization, a path that guides the practitioner beyond the limitations of superficial identities. Whether we speak of caste, creed, race, religion, gender, disability, or place of birth, yoga offers a universal approach that dissolves these boundaries, reminding us that our true essence lies beyond these external labels.

In its purest form, yoga leads the practitioner toward an experience of oneness, where the dualities and divisions of the outer world lose their grip. It invites the individual to transcend ego and personal identity, discovering the inner self that is untouched by societal constructs. This self is pure consciousness, the essence of existence that resides equally in all beings, beyond any markers of division.

Throughout history, yoga has been practiced by kings and sages, rich and poor, men and women, the able-bodied and those with disabilities. The teachings of the ancient rishis were never restricted by societal hierarchies or norms, for they recognized that the pursuit of truth and inner freedom is a universal aspiration. The message of the Bhagavad Gita, the Upanishads, and the Yoga Sutras of Patanjali is clear: the path of yoga is open to all, regardless of external circumstances. It is a spiritual journey that knows no prejudice.

This chapter delves into how yoga acts as a bridge to unity, not only uniting the body, mind, and spirit within an individual but also fostering a sense of universal connectedness among all beings. By cultivating practices such as compassion, mindfulness, non-attachment, and self-inquiry, yoga enables us to recognize the underlying truth that we are all part of a greater whole. The ancient yogic teachings show us how to live harmoniously in a world of diversity, not by ignoring differences, but by embracing the shared humanity that runs through all people.

In today's world, where divisions and conflicts based on identity are so prevalent, yoga's teachings offer a timeless antidote. By integrating the principles of yoga into daily life, one can break free from the narrow confines of identity-based thinking and step into the expansive realization that we are all expressions of the same universal consciousness. Yoga teaches us to honour the diversity of human experience while recognizing the oneness at the core of all life.

Ultimately, yoga serves as a powerful reminder that beneath the countless labels we wear, we are all one. Through its practice, we can rise above the divisive forces of the outer world and experience the peace, unity, and interconnectedness that lies within us all.

The Universality of Yoga in Ancient Texts

The ancient yogic scriptures, such as the **Upanishads**, the **Bhagavad Gita**, and **Patanjali's Yoga Sutras**, emphasize that spiritual growth and liberation are not confined to any particular group of people. These sacred texts transcend the limitations of caste, creed, gender, and status, focusing instead on the **unity of consciousness** and the **non-dual nature of reality**. According to these teachings, all individuals possess the inherent potential for self-realization, and distinctions based on societal categories hold no significance in the spiritual journey. The essence of yoga, as described in these texts, is universal and accessible to everyone.

The Bhagavad Gita on Equality

The Bhagavad Gita, a revered text in the yogic tradition, explicitly addresses the theme of spiritual equality. In Chapter 5, Verse 18, Lord Krishna shares a profound message on the nature of wisdom and universal perception, "The wise see the same in a learned and humble Brahmin, a cow, an elephant, a dog, and even an outcaste."

This verse highlights that spiritual wisdom—like the practice of yoga—transcends societal divisions. It calls for the recognition of the same divine essence within all beings, regardless of external identities such as caste, species, or social standing. The Bhagavad Gita reinforces that the pursuit of wisdom and self-realization is a path open to every human being, offering a vision of equality that defies the superficial distinctions of the material world.

The Upanishads on the Self

One of the core teachings of the Upanishads is the realization of the self's true nature as identical with the ultimate reality. In the Chandogya

Upanishad (6.8.7), the famous declaration **"Tat Tvam Asi"** (That Thou Art) speaks to the non-dual nature of existence, asserting that the same divine consciousness pervades every individual. This teaching forms the foundation of yogic philosophy, reminding us that our **true self** (Atman) is one with the **supreme reality** (Brahman). The distinctions that humans cling to—based on caste, race, religion, or other social categories—are mere **illusions** of the material world.

The Upanishads encourage practitioners to look beyond these illusions and realize the deeper truth of oneness, which is the essence of yoga. As the individual attains this realization, the false distinctions that create division are dissolved, making way for a life rooted in universal love and unity.

Patanjali's Yoga Sutras: The Path for Everyone

The **Yoga Sutras of Patanjali**, one of the foundational texts of yoga, offer a structured approach to spiritual liberation through **Ashtanga Yoga** (the eightfold path). The eight limbs of yoga—ranging from ethical disciplines (**yama**) and personal observances (**niyama**) to meditation and ultimate absorption in the self (**samadhi**)—are presented as universal principles that can be practiced by anyone, regardless of their background or social status.

Patanjali's teachings are notably inclusive, as they do not limit the practice of yoga to a specific group or sect. Instead, the **yamas** (such as non-violence and truthfulness) and **niyamas** (such as contentment and self-discipline) are universal values meant for the betterment of all human beings. The ultimate goal, **Kaivalya** (liberation), is attainable by anyone willing to follow the path, regardless of their external circumstances.

Yoga Beyond Caste and Creed

Throughout history, India's rigid caste system often imposed barriers to spiritual practices, restricting access to many profound traditions like yoga. However, these barriers were consistently challenged by saints, mystics, and reformers who emphasized that the path of spiritual growth, particularly yoga, transcends caste, creed, and social standing. Yoga, in its essence, is a universal practice aimed at self-realization, available to all who seek it, regardless of societal labels.

The Bhakti Movement: Breaking Caste Barriers

One of the most significant movements that challenged the rigidity of the caste system in India was the **Bhakti Movement**. Arising in medieval India, the Bhakti saints rejected hierarchical structures, asserting that love and devotion to the Divine were the true means to spiritual liberation, not birth or social status. This egalitarian spiritual movement dismantled traditional caste divisions and proclaimed that all individuals, regardless of caste, were equally capable of achieving spiritual union with the Divine.

Prominent saints such as **Kabir**, **Mirabai**, and **Guru Nanak** championed the idea of devotion over societal divisions. **Kabir**, a weaver by caste and a mystic poet, directly criticized the notion of caste-based spirituality. In one of his poems, he posed a profound question, "If caste were what determined one's relationship with God, how could God be the creator of all humanity?"

Kabir's teachings emphasized that the Divine exists beyond the boundaries of human-made distinctions, and that the essence of yoga—spiritual union—could be realized by anyone, regardless of caste. Similarly, **Mirabai**, a princess-turned-saint, renounced her royal status and dedicated herself to Lord Krishna, demonstrating through her life that devotion, not birthright, is the key to spiritual awakening. **Guru Nanak,** the founder of Sikhism, also proclaimed the oneness of humanity and rejected the caste system, advocating for a direct connection with the Divine accessible to all.

These Bhakti saints laid the foundation for a more inclusive understanding of spiritual practice, breaking down the barriers of caste and creed in the pursuit of liberation through yoga and devotion.

Swami Vivekananda: Yoga for the World

In the modern era, **Swami Vivekananda** played a crucial role in reviving and spreading the universal message of yoga beyond the borders of India. As one of the foremost proponents of yoga, he took the ancient practice to the world stage, declaring that yoga belongs not to any particular caste, creed, or religion, but to all of humanity. His teachings and speeches emphasized the intrinsic unity of all beings and the universal nature of spiritual practices like yoga.

At the **Parliament of the World's Religions** in Chicago in 1893, Vivekananda boldly proclaimed, "I am proud to belong to a religion which has taught the world both tolerance and universal acceptance."

In this landmark speech, Vivekananda presented yoga as India's gift to the world, a spiritual science that transcends religious and cultural boundaries. His vision of yoga was inclusive, calling for global unity and harmony. He urged people of all faiths and backgrounds to embrace yoga as a tool for spiritual elevation, irrespective of their identity or belief system.

Swami Vivekananda's influence extended far beyond his native India. By presenting yoga as a universal philosophy and practice, he broke the misconception that yoga was exclusive to Hinduism or a select group of people. Instead, he framed yoga as a **science of the mind and spirit**, available to all individuals, regardless of their background.

Yoga Beyond Race and Religion

Yoga's core teachings transcend the boundaries of race and religion, promoting a sense of unity and interconnectedness among all beings. Rather than belonging to any specific faith or culture, yoga is a **science of the self**, guiding individuals toward spiritual growth and inner transformation. The principles of yoga encourage practitioners to look beyond external differences and discover the shared essence that connects all of humanity. In this way, yoga stands as a universal practice, available to anyone, regardless of their race, religion, or cultural background.

Yoga in Different Religions

Though yoga originated in ancient India within the context of Hindu philosophy, its appeal has extended far beyond its cultural and religious roots. In the modern world, practitioners from various religious backgrounds—including **Christians**, **Muslims**, **Buddhists**, **Jews**, and **spiritual seekers** of all kinds—have embraced yoga for its ability to foster inner peace, self-awareness, and personal transformation.

For instance, in Islam, the **Sufi mystics** have developed meditative practices akin to yoga, focusing on breath control, mindfulness, and ecstatic states to deepen their connection with the Divine. **Christian contemplatives** find parallels between yoga's meditative practices and the silent prayer traditions of monastic Christianity. **Buddhists**, too, resonate with yoga's emphasis on mindfulness, ethical living, and the realization of non-duality, which aligns with the core tenets of their spiritual path.

Yoga's adaptability to different religious and spiritual traditions stems from its **non-dogmatic nature**. Rather than imposing a particular belief system, yoga offers a set of universal tools—such as meditation, breath control, and ethical living—that can be practiced alongside one's faith. The focus is on personal experience and inner growth, making yoga a complement to various spiritual paths while respecting their unique traditions.

International Yoga Day: A Global Celebration

Yoga's universal appeal was globally recognized when the United Nations declared **June 21st** as **International Yoga Day**, a day dedicated to celebrating the practice of yoga worldwide. This event, initiated by India in 2014, highlights yoga's value for **health, well-being**, and fostering **unity** across borders. It serves as a testament to how yoga has transcended cultural and religious differences to become a global phenomenon, embraced by millions of people from diverse backgrounds.

Every year, on International Yoga Day, people from over 190 countries participate in public yoga events, from small community gatherings to large-scale celebrations in major cities. The day showcases the vast reach of yoga, from its humble origins to becoming a **global practice** that unites people across race, religion, and nationality. Statistics show that millions of people join in the celebration, underscoring yoga's significance as a tool for holistic health and harmony in a world increasingly divided by differences.

Yoga Beyond Gender

Yoga transcends gender barriers, offering its profound benefits to people of all genders equally. While traditional yogic texts may reflect the patriarchal norms of their times, modern interpretations and practices of yoga emphasize its **inclusivity** and universality. In the true spirit of yoga, the body and mind are seen as vehicles for spiritual growth, and gender distinctions hold no significance on the path to self-realization.

Women and Yoga

Historically, in many societies, including India, women were often excluded from certain religious and yogic practices. However, throughout history, numerous female saints and yoginis have **broken these barriers** and emerged as pioneers, challenging the gender norms of their time. These women not only practiced yoga but also became spiritual leaders and teachers, spreading the wisdom of yoga and devotion.

For instance, **Andal**, a 9th-century mystic poet, is revered for her devotional hymns and her deep connection to the Divine. **Akka Mahadevi**, a 12th-century yogini and poet, renounced worldly life and followed the path of Shiva, defying societal expectations for women. Similarly, **Lalleshwari**, a 14th-century Kashmiri saint, blended elements of yoga and mysticism in her teachings, living as an ascetic and inspiring countless followers. These women **challenged societal norms** and demonstrated that yoga and spiritual practices were not exclusive to men.

Today, yoga is practiced by millions of women worldwide, who find empowerment, balance, and spiritual growth through its teachings. Yoga provides women with tools for managing both physical and emotional well-being, helping them navigate the pressures of modern life. Research shows that in many countries, **women make up the majority of yoga practitioners**, highlighting its inclusive nature and its ability to meet the needs of women across cultures and societies.

Non-Binary and LGBTQ+ Inclusion

Yoga is for all, including **non-binary** and **LGBTQ+** individuals. The core teachings of yoga, which emphasize **self-awareness** and the discovery of one's **true self** beyond the ego, naturally align with the understanding that all beings transcend societal labels of gender and sexual orientation. Inclusive yoga communities have emerged, embracing diversity and fostering a sense of acceptance for everyone, regardless of their identity.

Inclusive yoga spaces highlight that the practice of yoga is about connecting with the **essence of one's being**, which goes beyond external identities. Yoga allows individuals to explore their inner selves in a **safe, supportive environment**, free from societal constraints and expectations. This approach resonates deeply with the LGBTQ+ community, where many find yoga to be a path of **self-acceptance** and **empowerment**, helping them reconnect with their bodies and minds in healing ways.

Yoga studios, workshops, and online spaces dedicated to **gender inclusivity** have grown in prominence, offering specialized classes and communities where non-binary and LGBTQ+ individuals feel represented and respected. These spaces contribute to the broader understanding that yoga is for **everyone**, and that **gender identity** and **sexual orientation** should never be obstacles to accessing its transformative power.

Yoga for Those with Disabilities

Yoga is a profoundly adaptable practice that transcends physical abilities, offering benefits to individuals with disabilities just as it does to able-bodied practitioners. While traditional yoga might focus on physical postures (asanas), the true essence of yoga—**union of body, mind, and spirit**—is accessible to everyone, including those with physical, intellectual, or sensory disabilities. Yoga accommodates all kinds of bodies and needs, making it a powerful tool for promoting physical, mental, and emotional well-being, even in the face of physical limitations.

Here's a detailed look at how yoga benefits individuals with disabilities, the modifications and approaches used, and the holistic impact it can have.

1. Benefits of Yoga for People with Disabilities

Yoga offers a range of physical, mental, and emotional benefits to individuals with disabilities, often enhancing their quality of life in profound ways. These benefits can include:

Improved Mobility and Flexibility: Modified yoga postures, when adapted for individuals with limited mobility, can help maintain or improve flexibility, range of motion, and joint health.

Increased Strength and Balance: Gentle strengthening exercises within yoga help improve muscle tone and coordination, particularly for those with neurological conditions or physical impairments.

Better Circulation and Respiration: Breath-focused practices, like **pranayama**, help improve lung capacity, blood circulation, and overall oxygenation of the body, which can positively affect those with respiratory issues or limited physical activity.

Stress Relief and Mental Clarity: Yoga offers powerful tools for managing stress and anxiety. The **meditation** and **mindfulness** aspects of yoga can help individuals with disabilities cultivate a deep sense of peace, focus, and mental resilience, especially in dealing with day-to-day challenges.

Enhanced Self-Esteem and Emotional Well-Being: Yoga fosters self-awareness and self-acceptance, which can be particularly empowering for individuals with disabilities. It helps build confidence and emotional strength by shifting focus away from physical limitations toward inner growth.

Sense of Community and Inclusion: Many inclusive yoga communities provide safe, welcoming environments for individuals with disabilities, fostering a sense of connection, support, and belonging.

2. Modifications and Adaptive Yoga

Yoga can be modified to meet the specific needs of individuals with varying disabilities. This adaptability makes yoga a versatile practice that can be tailored to any body, ability, or condition. **Adaptive yoga** is a specialized approach designed to make yoga accessible to those with physical limitations or disabilities, and it often involves:

Chair Yoga: For individuals with limited mobility or balance issues, yoga poses can be performed while seated in a chair or wheelchair. Chair yoga modifies traditional postures, allowing practitioners to stretch, strengthen, and relax while remaining in a stable position.

Props and Supports: The use of props like blocks, straps, bolsters, and cushions helps people with disabilities achieve modified postures safely. These tools provide support and enable practitioners to maintain alignment and balance during the practice.

Assisted Yoga: Some individuals may require assistance from a caregiver, teacher, or physical therapist to help guide them into poses or adjust their bodies in a way that ensures safety and comfort.

Gentle and Restorative Yoga: For those with chronic pain, fatigue, or more severe physical limitations, gentle or restorative yoga practices focus on relaxation, breathwork, and subtle movements to promote healing and stress relief without exerting strain.

Yoga for the Visually or Hearing Impaired: For individuals who are blind or visually impaired, yoga can be taught through verbal cues and tactile adjustments to help guide the body into proper alignment. For those who are hearing impaired, instructors may use sign language, visual aids, or demonstrate poses with exaggerated movements to provide clear guidance.

3. Specific Approaches for Different Disabilities

Here's how yoga can be adapted for different types of disabilities:

Mobility Disabilities (e.g., Spinal Cord Injuries, Paralysis, Amputations): Individuals with limited mobility can practice yoga in a wheelchair or on the floor with the help of props. Seated twists, arm stretches, and mindful breathing exercises are common in adaptive yoga for those with mobility impairments.

Neurological Disorders (e.g., Multiple Sclerosis, Cerebral Palsy, Parkinson's Disease): Yoga can help improve coordination, reduce muscle spasticity, and promote relaxation for individuals with neurological conditions. Modified poses that focus on gentle stretching, balance, and breath awareness are key elements of yoga for these individuals.

Chronic Pain and Fatigue (e.g., Fibromyalgia, Chronic Fatigue Syndrome): Restorative yoga practices, which emphasize relaxation and minimal movement, can help alleviate pain and reduce fatigue. Gentle breathwork and meditation are often incorporated to calm the nervous system and relieve tension.

Intellectual and Developmental Disabilities (e.g., Autism, Down Syndrome): Yoga can enhance body awareness, motor skills, and emotional regulation for individuals with intellectual or developmental disabilities. Yoga for these individuals often involves fun, playful movements, breathing exercises, and a focus on sensory integration.

Visual and Hearing Impairments: Visually impaired individuals can rely on verbal guidance from instructors, while hearing-impaired individuals may benefit from instructors using clear, visual demonstrations of poses. In both cases, the focus remains on the mind-body connection, using whatever senses are available.

4. Yoga Therapy for Rehabilitation

Yoga is increasingly being integrated into rehabilitation programs for individuals recovering from injuries, surgeries, or illnesses. In this context, yoga functions as a therapeutic tool, aiding in recovery by:

Promoting **physical rehabilitation** through gentle, controlled movements that restore strength, flexibility, and mobility.

Supporting **mental rehabilitation** by reducing anxiety, depression, and stress, which are often associated with long-term recovery or chronic conditions.

Encouraging **mind-body awareness**, which helps individuals become more attuned to their bodies' needs and limits, fostering a healthier approach to healing.

Many hospitals, rehabilitation centers, and wellness programs now incorporate yoga therapy as part of a holistic approach to recovery for people with disabilities.

5. Yoga for Mental Health in Disability

People with disabilities often face additional mental health challenges, such as depression, anxiety, or feelings of isolation due to physical limitations or societal barriers. Yoga's holistic approach offers a powerful remedy for mental and emotional well-being by:

Cultivating mindfulness and presence through meditation and breathwork.

Encouraging positive body awareness and acceptance, especially for those struggling with self-esteem issues related to their disability.

Offering tools for managing stress, which can reduce symptoms of anxiety and depression, promoting overall emotional resilience.

6. Yoga for Building Community and Inclusivity

Many yoga communities and teachers are working actively to create more **inclusive spaces** for people with disabilities. Adaptive yoga classes and specialized workshops are increasingly offered in yoga studios, rehabilitation centers, and online platforms. This inclusivity ensures that individuals with disabilities feel **welcomed** and **represented** in the yoga world, fostering a sense of community and shared growth.

Organizations like **Accessible Yoga** and **Yoga for All** are dedicated to promoting accessible practices, training instructors to teach adaptive yoga, and advocating for the rights of people with disabilities in the yoga community.

Yoga Beyond Place of Birth

Yoga transcends geographical boundaries, making it accessible to people across the globe, regardless of their nationality or place of birth. Although yoga originated in India, its teachings and practices have resonated with individuals from various countries and cultures, highlighting its universal appeal. This phenomenon reflects yoga's ability to unite humanity by focusing on inner growth and spiritual realization, rather than external distinctions like nationality.

Yoga's Global Reach

Today, yoga is a global practice, embraced by millions of people from diverse backgrounds. Statistics show that yoga is practiced by over **300 million people worldwide**, a number that continues to grow. From the vibrant streets of New York City to the serene temples of Tokyo, yoga has spread far beyond its Indian roots. Its popularity is not limited to urban centers; even in remote villages in Africa and bustling cities across Europe, yoga has become an integral part of daily life for many.

The **United Nations' declaration of International Yoga Day** on June 21st each year further emphasizes the global significance of yoga.

Celebrated in over 190 countries, this day serves as a reminder that yoga belongs to all of humanity and is not confined to any specific region or culture. The practice of yoga has proven to be a powerful tool for promoting **physical health, mental well-being, and social harmony**, making it a valuable resource for people of all nationalities.

Cultural Adaptations

As yoga has spread globally, it has been adapted to fit the cultural contexts of different countries while maintaining its **core essence**. Whether practiced in a California yoga studio or an ashram in Rishikesh, yoga retains its primary focus on **self-realization**, mindfulness, and the union of body, mind, and spirit. The adaptability of yoga has enabled it to thrive in diverse settings, from corporate wellness programs in the West to traditional spiritual retreats in the East.

In some cultures, yoga has been integrated with other local traditions and practices, creating unique variations that still honor the fundamental principles of yoga. For instance, in the West, many yoga classes combine traditional asanas with modern fitness approaches, such as **power yoga** or **yoga therapy**. Meanwhile, in countries like Japan, yoga is often harmonized with **Zen** and **meditation practices**, creating a distinctive blend that resonates with the local spiritual landscape.

21

The Caste System: Origins, Evolution, and Misconceptions

The caste system, often regarded as one of the most misunderstood and controversial facets of Indian society, has been the subject of extensive debate for centuries. Frequently portrayed as a rigid, hierarchical structure designed to discriminate and segregate, the reality of its origins and evolution is far more nuanced and layered. This chapter seeks to unravel the complexity of the caste system, shedding light on its historical context, its intended purpose, and the ways in which it has been misinterpreted and exploited over time.

Rooted in the ancient Vedic period, the caste system, or *varna* system, was initially conceptualized as a framework to organize society based on natural tendencies, qualities, and professional roles. The four *varnas*—Brahmins (scholars and priests), Kshatriyas (warriors and rulers), Vaishyas (merchants and traders), and Shudras (labourers and service providers)—were designed to promote harmony and cooperation within society, each group contributing to the collective well-being. Contrary to its later rigidification, these categories were originally fluid, and movement between *varnas* was possible based on merit, talent, and personal abilities.

However, over time, the caste system began to deviate from its initial spiritual and societal intentions. A system once meant to align individuals with their natural proclivities and societal roles became rigid and hereditary. This transformation was influenced by several factors, including foreign invasions, socio-political power dynamics, and regional interpretations. By the time colonial powers arrived in India, the system had ossified into a strict hierarchy that fostered social inequality and exclusion, leaving a legacy that continues to affect Indian society today.

Throughout this chapter, we will explore the roots of caste from its early philosophical foundations, drawing on ancient texts like the Vedas, the Manusmriti, and the Bhagavad Gita. We will also consider the perspectives of modern scholars and reformers, who have either criticized or sought to reform the system. These viewpoints, paired with real-world examples and historical analysis, will illuminate the misconceptions that have surrounded the caste system and the ways in which it has been misused for political, economic, and social gain.

By engaging with both the historical and modern realities of caste, this chapter aims to clarify its true nature and encourage a more informed understanding of how such an intricate system was co-opted and distorted over time. In doing so, we hope to shift the narrative from one of mere discrimination to a deeper appreciation of the complexity and transformative potential that still lies at the heart of this ancient framework.

You do not belong to the brahmin or any other caste, you are not at any stage, nor are you anything that the eye can see. You are unattached and formless, the witness of everything - so be happy (*Ashtavakra Gita*, 1.5).

The Origins of the Caste System

The caste system, as understood today, has its roots in the ancient Indian scriptures, particularly the *Rigveda*. One of the earliest references to social stratification appears in the *Purusha Sukta* hymn of the *Rigveda* (10.90), where society is metaphorically divided into four distinct *varnas* (classes), symbolizing different parts of the cosmic being, *Purusha*. This representation was initially a functional division of labour rather than a rigid hierarchy:

1. **Brahmins (Priests and Scholars)** – Representing the mouth, they were responsible for preserving knowledge, performing rituals, and imparting spiritual guidance. Their role was to serve as the intellectual and spiritual foundation of society.

2. **Kshatriyas (Warriors and Kings)** – Representing the arms, Kshatriyas were protectors and rulers. Their primary function was to defend the kingdom, enforce justice, and ensure order and security in society.

3. **Vaishyas (Merchants and Farmers)** – Representing the thighs, Vaishyas were involved in trade, agriculture, and commerce. They ensured the material prosperity and economic stability of the community through their skills in trade and production.

4. **Shudras (Laborers and Service Providers)** – Representing the feet, Shudras were tasked with providing services and manual labor that supported the functioning of society. Their work was seen as essential in maintaining the societal infrastructure.

This original division, known as the *varna* system, was not intended to denote a hierarchy of superiority or inferiority but rather to reflect the diversity of roles essential for the functioning of a balanced society. Each *varna* had its specific responsibilities (*dharma*), and the idea of interdependence among the classes was paramount. Moreover, social mobility between the *varnas* was possible, as individuals were not born into a specific class; instead, they could move between roles based on their qualities and achievements.

I **repeat,** each varna was essential to the functioning of society, and **mobility** between these varnas was **possible**. This division was more about **duties** (dharma) and roles in society than about **birth**.

However, over time, this more fluid and flexible *varna* system gradually transformed into a more rigid, hereditary caste system known as *jaati*. While *varna* referred to broad occupational categories, *jaati* became a much more complex and localized division of society based on birth, with thousands of sub-castes and strict rules governing inter-caste interactions, marriage, and social behaviour. This shift solidified the caste system into an inflexible social structure, limiting social mobility and embedding it deeply into the fabric of Indian society.

The transformation of the *varna* system into the hereditary caste system reflected the evolving dynamics of power, economic changes, and societal norms over centuries, eventually leading to the system that became a defining feature of Indian society during medieval times and even under British colonial rule. The complexity and persistence of the caste system continue to be subjects of study and reform efforts in modern India.

Evolution and Institutionalization of Caste

The transformation of the *varna* system into the rigid caste structure we recognize today was a gradual process that unfolded over centuries, influenced by a variety of socio-political, economic, and religious factors. This shift was especially pronounced during the early medieval period, when texts like the *Dharmashastras* played a pivotal role in shaping and legitimizing caste-based divisions.

Medieval Period: The Dharmashastras and Manusmriti

During the early medieval period, the *Dharmashastras*, a body of legal and ethical texts, began to formalize societal norms, and one of the most influential among them was the *Manusmriti*. This ancient legal text is often cited as having codified and reinforced the division of society based on the *varna* system. In *Manusmriti* (Chapter 1, Verse 31), it is stated, "For the sake of the prosperity of the worlds, He, the most resplendent one, assigned separate duties and occupations to those who sprang from his mouth, arms, thighs, and feet." This verse reflects a religious justification for the division of labour based on symbolic associations with the cosmic being, *Purusha*.

However, the *Manusmriti* also contributed to the growing rigidity of these divisions by assigning strict duties (*dharma*) to each *varna*, making it more difficult for individuals to transcend the roles ascribed to them by birth. What was initially intended as a flexible and functional division became increasingly hereditary, with occupational and social mobility greatly restricted. The codification of caste roles within the *Dharmashastras* and the *Manusmriti* not only justified the system but also institutionalized it, allowing the caste structure to become deeply entrenched in the social and religious fabric of Indian society.

It's important to note that the *Manusmriti* and other *Dharmashastras* were products of their time and context, written to maintain social order within a particular societal framework. Despite this, later interpretations used these texts to justify caste discrimination and inequity, creating a system that was far more rigid than what may have originally been intended.

Colonial Period: The British Reinforcement

The arrival of British colonial rule in India marked a significant turning point in the institutionalization and rigidity of the caste system. Through their administration, the British reinforced and, in some ways, redefined caste distinctions for their own purposes, particularly in relation to governance and control. The British census operations, which began in the late 19th century, classified the Indian population into distinct caste categories, effectively freezing what had been, in some cases, more fluid social dynamics.

Nicholas Dirks, a prominent historian, argues that the modern understanding of caste as a rigid, hierarchical system was largely "constructed" during the colonial period. In his seminal work *Castes of Mind: Colonialism and the Making of Modern India*, Dirks explains how the British sought to simplify and categorize Indian society for administrative convenience. In doing so, they solidified caste identities, often imposing new or rigid classifications that did not necessarily reflect pre-colonial realities. What had been a more complex and localized system of social organization became, under British rule, a simplified and essentialized hierarchy.

The British legal system also contributed to the entrenchment of caste distinctions. Colonial laws were enacted that formalized caste boundaries, making it even more difficult for individuals to move outside of their caste-designated roles. Legal provisions reinforced the notion of caste as a fixed identity, thereby institutionalizing discrimination and limiting social mobility. For example, laws regarding marriage, inheritance, and property often upheld caste distinctions, creating further divisions within Indian society.

The Lasting Legacy

By the time India gained independence in 1947, the caste system had become a deeply ingrained social structure, influenced by centuries of religious codification and nearly two centuries of colonial manipulation. Although modern India has made significant efforts to dismantle caste-based discrimination—through laws such as the abolition of "untouchability" and affirmative action policies—the legacy of this complex historical evolution still affects Indian society today.

The evolution from a flexible *varna* system to a rigid caste structure reveals how social, political, and religious forces can shape and institutionalize inequality, making it difficult to dismantle even in more egalitarian times. Despite these challenges, contemporary movements continue to seek justice and equality, pushing against the historical weight of the caste system.

Misconceptions and Misuses of the Caste System

Over the centuries, the original purpose and intent behind the *varna* system have been overshadowed, resulting in the caste system being associated with discrimination, inequality, and entrenched social hierarchies. Several misconceptions and misuses have distorted the original idea of *varna*, leading to social injustices and misunderstandings about its role in Indian culture and religion.

Caste as a Religious Doctrine

One of the most pervasive misconceptions is that the caste system is an intrinsic part of Hindu religious doctrine. While caste has often been justified through selective interpretations of religious texts, it is primarily a socio-cultural construct that evolved over time, rather than a core spiritual teaching of Hinduism. For example, the *Bhagavad Gita* (4.13) states, "The four *varnas* were created by Me according to the differentiation of *guna* (qualities) and *karma* (actions)." This verse emphasizes that *varna* is based on a **person's qualities and actions, not on their birth**. In its original context, the *varna* system was intended to classify individuals based on their inherent traits and the duties they performed, rather than assigning fixed and hereditary roles.

The rigidity of caste, especially its hereditary nature, is a later development and is not part of the original Vedic teachings. The *varna* system was meant to be dynamic and fluid, with individuals moving between roles based on their capabilities and contributions. Over time, however, socio-political factors and entrenched interests led to the ossification of caste, turning it into a rigid and discriminatory system.

Caste and Untouchability

The practice of untouchability, which led to the severe marginalization of the so-called "lower castes" or Dalits, represents one of the most egregious misuses of the caste system. Untouchability has no foundation in the original Vedic texts or teachings. It is a social evil that developed over time, particularly during the later phases of Indian history. Untouchability was used to isolate and oppress certain groups, often denying them basic human rights and dignity.

Leaders like **Dr. B.R. Ambedkar**, a Dalit himself and the **principal architect of the Indian Constitution**, recognized the deep harm caused by caste-based discrimination and untouchability. Ambedkar's tireless efforts to combat these injustices culminated in the framing of the Indian Constitution, which expressly prohibits caste-based discrimination. Through Articles 15 and 17, the Indian Constitution abolished untouchability and prohibited discrimination on the grounds of caste, ensuring legal protection for the rights and dignity of all citizens.

Despite these constitutional safeguards, caste-based prejudice and the legacy of untouchability continue to persist in various forms in Indian society. The social stigma attached to Dalit communities has proven difficult to eradicate, but ongoing reform efforts and grassroots activism continue to challenge these entrenched biases.

Modern-Day Caste Discrimination

Even though the caste system has been legally dismantled in modern India, caste-based discrimination remains a significant issue. According to the National Crime Records Bureau (NCRB), over 45,935 cases of atrocities against Dalits were reported in 2019 alone. These cases include crimes such as violence, social exclusion, and denial of access to public resources and opportunities, demonstrating that caste-based inequalities persist despite legal protections.

However, there have been concerted efforts to address and reduce caste disparities in modern India. Affirmative action policies, such as the reservation system, have been implemented to provide historically marginalized communities with greater access to education, employment, and political representation. These policies have played a crucial role in uplifting Dalit communities and other marginalized groups, fostering greater social mobility and economic progress.

Despite these measures, the challenge of eradicating caste discrimination is ongoing. While the law prohibits caste-based discrimination, deeply ingrained societal attitudes and prejudices remain, particularly in rural areas where caste-based hierarchies are still prevalent. Nevertheless, social reform movements, increased awareness, and government initiatives continue to challenge caste-based injustices, offering hope for a more equitable future.

Conclusion

The misconceptions and misuses of the caste system have contributed to centuries of social inequality and discrimination in India. The original intent of the *varna* system—a functional division of society based on qualities and actions—was lost as the system transformed into a rigid and hereditary caste hierarchy. The practice of untouchability, an extreme manifestation of this system, has been recognized as a social evil with no basis in religious teachings. While modern legal protections have made significant strides in combating caste-based discrimination, the legacy of the caste system continues to affect Indian society today. Through ongoing efforts in social reform and affirmative action, there is hope that the deep-seated inequalities perpetuated by the caste system can be gradually eradicated.

Reforms and Movements Against Caste Discrimination

Throughout India's history, various social reformers, saints, and spiritual leaders have challenged the caste system and its discriminatory practices, advocating for equality and justice. Their efforts have laid the foundation for a more inclusive and equitable society. Below are some of the key figures and movements that played a critical role in opposing caste-based oppression.

1. Brahmarishi Vashistha

Brahmarishi Vashistha, one of the revered *Saptarishis* (Seven Great Sages) in Hindu tradition, is celebrated for his wisdom, equanimity, and deep understanding of *dharma* (righteousness). As a royal sage (*Rajguru*), he served as a counsellor to several generations of kings from the Ikshvaku dynasty, including Lord Rama, as mentioned in the *Ramayana*. His teachings, especially in the *Yoga Vashistha*, emphasized the transcendence of material and social constructs in pursuit of self-realization and the ultimate truth.

Vashistha's spiritual philosophy suggested that liberation (*moksha*) and wisdom are accessible to all individuals, regardless of societal divisions such as caste. His outlook rejected the notion that spiritual progress and self-realization were confined to a particular group or social class, emphasizing instead the inner journey and the equality of all souls in their pursuit of enlightenment.

2. Saints of the Bhakti Movement

The *Bhakti* movement, which flourished in medieval India, rejected caste distinctions and focused on devotion (*bhakti*) to God as the sole means of attaining salvation. It was a powerful social and spiritual revolution that questioned the rigid social hierarchies enforced by the caste system. Several saints of the *Bhakti* tradition became vocal critics of caste discrimination:

Kabir: A weaver by profession and a poet-saint, Kabir rejected caste distinctions and preached the oneness of humanity and God. His famous *doha* (couplet) **"Jaati na poochho saadhu ki, poochh lijiye gyaan"** (Don't ask the caste of a saint, ask about their wisdom) challenged the very basis of caste-based discrimination, urging people to recognize the inherent wisdom and spiritual equality in all individuals.

Ravidas: A Dalit saint and poet, Ravidas preached against caste discrimination and emphasized that one's connection to God is independent of birth or social status. His message of universal love and equality inspired generations of oppressed communities.

Tukaram: A saint from Maharashtra, Tukaram's devotional poetry expressed his deep disdain for the caste system and emphasized the primacy of devotion to God over social distinctions. His egalitarian message resonated with the masses, particularly the marginalized sections of society.

The *Bhakti* movement played a significant role in breaking down caste barriers, offering a path to spiritual liberation that was open to all, regardless of social standing.

3. Swami Vivekananda

Swami Vivekananda was a towering figure of modern Indian spirituality and a vocal critic of the caste system. He believed in the fundamental divinity of all human beings and rejected any form of discrimination based on caste, creed, or colour. In his speeches, he often stressed the oneness of humanity, declaring, "Man is divine, no matter what caste, creed, or colour."

Vivekananda's vision for India was one of unity and spiritual upliftment, where caste divisions would no longer hold people back. He called upon Indians to transcend the limitations of caste and work towards the spiritual and material progress of the nation. His emphasis on national unity and social reform made him an inspiration for generations of reformers and freedom fighters.

4. Dr. B.R. Ambedkar

Dr. B.R. Ambedkar, the principal architect of the Indian Constitution and a champion of the Dalit community, dedicated his life to fighting against caste-based discrimination. A Dalit himself, Ambedkar was acutely aware of the injustices faced by lower-caste communities and sought to eradicate the caste system altogether. His seminal work *Annihilation of Caste* is a powerful critique of the caste system and its oppressive nature. In this text, Ambedkar argued that caste was the biggest obstacle to India's social and economic progress, and that its eradication was crucial for the country's development.

Ambedkar also played a pivotal role in enshrining constitutional protections against caste-based discrimination. His leadership ensured that the Indian Constitution abolished untouchability (Article 17) and guaranteed equal rights for all citizens, regardless of caste. Ambedkar's advocacy for affirmative action policies, such as reservations in education and employment, has had a lasting impact on improving the social and economic conditions of marginalized communities in India.

5. Mahatma Jyotirao Phule

Mahatma Jyotirao Phule was another influential social reformer who worked tirelessly for the upliftment of marginalized castes. Phule, born into a lower caste, was a strong critic of Brahminical hegemony and caste oppression. He believed that education was the key to social empowerment and dedicated much of his life to spreading education among the lower castes and women, who had been denied access to learning.

Phule founded the Satyashodhak Samaj (Society of Truth Seekers) in 1873, an organization aimed at challenging caste-based oppression and promoting social equality. Through his work, Phule sought to create a more just and egalitarian society where people were not judged by their birth but by their actions and contributions to society.

The Atman: Beyond Caste and Social Distinctions

The *Atman* (Self) is the eternal, unchanging essence within every being. According to the teachings of the *Upanishads* and other foundational spiritual texts, the *Atman* transcends all worldly distinctions, including caste, gender, and social status. In the realm of spiritual realization, there is no division or hierarchy—only unity and oneness.

Atman as Universal: The concept of *Atman* emphasizes that every individual, regardless of their caste or background, possesses the same divine essence. The *Brihadaranyaka Upanishad* (1.4.10) states, **"Aham Brahmasmi"** (I am Brahman), meaning the individual soul (Atman) is identical with the universal consciousness (Brahman). This teaching underscores the idea that the true nature of every being is beyond any superficial identity, including caste.

Yoga for All: Yoga, as a path to self-realization, does not discriminate based on caste. The core purpose of yoga is to unite the individual consciousness with the universal consciousness, and this journey is open to everyone. In the *Bhagavad Gita* (Chapter 5, Verse 18), Krishna declares, "The wise see the same in a learned and humble Brahmin, a cow, an elephant, a dog, and even an outcaste." This verse highlights the equality of all beings in the eyes of the spiritually realized.

Inclusivity of Yoga: The practice of yoga is accessible to all who seek it. It is not confined to any particular group or social status. Yoga is an inward journey, where distinctions like caste, wealth, or occupation become irrelevant. The *Yoga Sutras of Patanjali* focus on self-discipline, meditation, and ethical living, which are universal practices that can be undertaken by anyone, regardless of their social background.

Yoga, in its essence, is a path to realizing the *Atman*, the pure consciousness that resides within all beings. Since the *Atman* is beyond caste, race, or social distinctions, and take on different bodies and bodily identifications through successive births, the practice of yoga is equally open to everyone. The pursuit of spiritual enlightenment through yoga transcends all external labels, focusing instead on the inner journey towards self-realization. In this light, yoga stands as a universal practice, uniting people beyond the constraints of the caste system.

22

Ayurveda

Yoga and Ayurveda, often described as sister sciences, are two ancient Indian disciplines that together form a holistic approach to health, wellness, and spiritual development. Both systems aim at harmonizing the body, mind, and spirit to achieve overall well-being. While Yoga focuses on spiritual evolution and physical postures (asanas), Ayurveda provides insights into bodily constitution, diet, and lifestyle, offering personalized health solutions. In this chapter, we explore how these two systems complement each other and how integrating Yoga and Ayurveda can lead to a balanced and healthy life.

"Ayurveda and Yoga are two sides of the same coin. Ayurveda is the Vedic science of healing for both body and mind. Yoga is the Vedic science of self-realization that depends upon a well-functioning body and mind." – Dr. David Frawley

The Connection Between Yoga and Ayurveda

Yoga and Ayurveda both originated in the Vedic tradition of India and share a common philosophical foundation rooted in the principles of Samkhya. Ayurveda, derived from the Sanskrit words 'Ayus' (life) and 'Veda' (knowledge), translates to "the science of life."

Ayurveda provides the foundation for living in balance with nature by addressing lifestyle, diet, and the mind-body connection, while Yoga offers the practices necessary to maintain that balance through physical, mental, and spiritual exercises. Together, these systems enable one to pursue wellness, self-realization, and liberation (moksha).

Many yoga practitioners turn to Ayurveda to understand their dosha (bodily constitution) and adopt a diet and lifestyle that complements their yoga practice. For example, a Pitta-dominant individual may benefit from cooling and calming yoga practices like restorative yoga, coupled with a Pitta-pacifying diet rich in cooling foods.

The Three Doshas and Their Role in Yoga Practice

Ayurveda, the ancient Indian science of life and healing, categorizes individuals based on three primary constitutional types, or doshas: **Vata, Pitta**, and **Kapha**. These doshas represent varying combinations of the five elements (earth, water, fire, air, and ether) and govern both physiological and psychological functions. Understanding one's unique dosha composition can guide not only dietary and lifestyle choices but also inform a personalized yoga practice aimed at restoring balance and health.

1. Vata Dosha (Air and Ether)

Vata, derived from the elements of air and ether, is one of the three primary doshas in Ayurvedic philosophy, responsible for movement and communication within the body and mind. It governs the subtle aspects of bodily functions such as the nervous system, circulation, respiration, and the flow of thoughts. Its primary attributes are lightness, coldness, dryness, and variability, reflecting the nature of air and space.

Characteristics of Vata: Vata types are often characterized by a lean body frame, quickness in actions, and a love for change and new experiences. They are naturally creative, energetic, and adaptable. Just like the wind, Vata individuals tend to be spontaneous, open-minded, and filled with ideas.

Balanced Vata: When in balance, Vata dosha manifests as clarity of thought, sharp intelligence, creativity, flexibility, and a zest for life. Physically, it supports healthy digestion, smooth joint movement, good circulation, and steady breathing. Emotionally, a balanced Vata promotes enthusiasm, vitality, and the ability to adapt to new situations with ease. Those with a well-balanced Vata tend to be fast learners, quick to grasp concepts, and highly innovative.

Imbalanced Vata: When Vata becomes imbalanced, often due to stress, overexertion, excessive travel, irregular routines, or cold, windy environments, it can manifest as restlessness, anxiety, fear, and a scattered mind. Physically, Vata imbalance can cause dryness in the skin, hair, and body tissues, irregular digestion, bloating, and cold extremities. Symptoms like insomnia, constipation, irregular heartbeats, and joint pain can also arise.

An excessive or aggravated Vata can make one feel ungrounded, anxious, or prone to overthinking. It can create a sense of instability and overwhelm, as if too many things are happening at once, resulting in a lack of focus and direction. The key to managing Vata lies in creating warmth, stability, and regularity in one's daily life, fostering grounding activities, and consuming nourishing, warm, and moist foods to counterbalance its dry, cold, and airy qualities.

For Vata-dominant individuals, **grounding yoga practices** are essential to counterbalance their inherent lightness and instability. Slow, deliberate movements—such as those found in Hatha Yoga—along with restorative poses and long holds in asanas help to calm the mind and settle excessive nervous energy. Practices like **Yin Yoga**, which emphasize stillness, and **Pranayama** techniques like **Nadi Shodhana (alternate nostril breathing)** are excellent for stabilizing Vata. Additionally, warm environments and meditative practices further soothe the overactive Vata constitution.

Establish a regular routine, with consistent times for waking, eating, and sleeping. Avoid overexertion and give yourself ample time for rest and relaxation.

2. Pitta Dosha (Fire and Water)

Pitta dosha is a dynamic energy formed from the fire and water elements in Ayurvedic philosophy. It governs all processes of transformation and metabolism in the body, including digestion, body temperature regulation, and cognitive functions. Pitta's primary qualities are heat, sharpness, intensity, and precision, which influence both the body and mind.

Characteristics of Pitta: Pitta types are often medium-built, with a strong appetite for life. They tend to be focused, driven, and goal-oriented, thriving on challenges and often rising to leadership roles. Pitta individuals exhibit a sharp intellect, are quick learners, and are natural decision-makers. Their fiery energy fuels ambition, confidence, and a sense of purpose.

Balanced Pitta: When Pitta is in balance, it manifests as sharp intelligence, a good digestive fire (Agni), and a clear, focused mind. A balanced Pitta promotes warmth, enthusiasm, courage, and determination. Physically, a healthy Pitta supports a strong metabolism, healthy skin, balanced hormones, and a robust digestive system. It also helps in maintaining mental clarity, sharp decision-making abilities, and the energy to pursue goals with vigour.

A balanced Pitta also brings passion and intensity in a controlled, constructive manner, helping individuals lead with confidence, fairness, and integrity. Emotionally, balanced Pitta encourages a calm sense of achievement, fostering harmony in relationships and a positive approach to life's challenges.

Imbalanced Pitta: When Pitta becomes imbalanced, often due to excessive stress, overworking, exposure to extreme heat, or a diet rich in spicy, acidic foods, it can lead to irritability, anger, and impatience. Physically, an aggravated Pitta can result in inflammation, heartburn, ulcers, skin rashes, and overheating of the body. Individuals may also experience increased perspiration, excessive thirst, and digestive disorders like acidity and indigestion.

Mentally, imbalanced Pitta can create a relentless inner drive that manifests as aggression, frustration, and criticism, both towards oneself and others. The fiery energy becomes too intense, leading to burnout, hyper-competitiveness, and a sense of dissatisfaction, especially when things don't go as planned.

To pacify the excess heat and intensity of Pitta, **cooling and calming yoga practices** are recommended. Practices like **Chandra Namaskar (Moon Salutations)**, which are slower and gentler than traditional Sun Salutations, help to reduce heat in the body. Additionally, incorporating **Sheetali and Sheetkari Pranayama** (cooling breaths) into the practice helps regulate body temperature and calm mental agitation. Forward bends, twists, and hip openers can also release the heat stored in the body, while avoiding excessive competitiveness during yoga helps maintain mental clarity and composure for Pitta types.

Incorporate regular breaks into your schedule, especially when engaged in intense activities or work. Avoid overworking and prioritize rest to prevent burnout. Spend time in cool, calm environments, especially in nature, to balance Pitta's heat.

3. Kapha Dosha (Earth and Water)

Kapha dosha, composed of the earth and water elements, is the force of stability and structure in both the body and mind. It governs the physical form, providing strength, solidity, and endurance. Kapha is responsible for the body's lubrication, ensuring that tissues are well-nourished and joints function smoothly. Its inherent qualities are heaviness, coldness, moisture, and steadiness, which provide a foundation of calm and resilience.

Characteristics of Kapha: Kapha individuals often have a solid, strong, and larger body frame, with a tendency toward slower movement and steady energy. They are typically calm, compassionate, and patient, exuding a sense of groundedness that helps them navigate life's challenges with ease. Their nurturing nature makes them empathetic, reliable, and great caretakers in both personal and professional relationships.

Balanced Kapha: When Kapha is in balance, it supports a strong immune system, healthy joints, and well-lubricated bodily tissues. A balanced Kapha manifests as emotional stability, loyalty, and a calm, peaceful demeanour. Physically, Kapha provides endurance, strength, and a steady, sustainable energy throughout the day.

Mentally, balanced Kapha brings a sense of contentment, emotional security, and patience. Kapha types excel at maintaining lasting relationships, providing a sense of comfort and support to others. Their mental outlook is one of acceptance, kindness, and inner peace, and they are often able to handle stressful situations without being easily disturbed.

Imbalanced Kapha: When Kapha becomes imbalanced, it often results from a sedentary lifestyle, overeating, excessive consumption of sweet or heavy foods, or exposure to cold, damp environments. Physically, Kapha imbalance can manifest as lethargy, weight gain, fluid retention, and slow digestion. There may be a tendency toward congestion, sinus issues, and excessive mucus production.

Emotionally, imbalanced Kapha can lead to feelings of stubbornness, attachment, possessiveness, and emotional stagnation. People with excess Kapha may struggle with depression, lack of motivation, and an overwhelming desire to remain in their comfort zone, resisting change. The heaviness and inertia of imbalanced Kapha can create a sense of sluggishness in both mind and body, making it difficult to feel energized or inspired.

For Kapha-dominant individuals, **stimulating and invigorating yoga practices** are ideal. Dynamic forms of yoga, such as **Vinyasa Flow** or **Ashtanga Yoga,** help to counter the sluggish tendencies of Kapha by increasing heart rate, circulation, and energy. **Sun**

Salutations (Surya Namaskar), backbends, and standing poses like **Warrior I and II** activate Kapha's latent energy, motivating both body and mind. Faster-paced, repetitive sequences combined with invigorating breathwork, such as **Bhastrika Pranayama** (bellows breath), are beneficial in balancing the Kapha dosha by igniting internal fire and movement.

Incorporate regular physical activity to stimulate circulation and combat lethargy. Engage in stimulating and dynamic exercises like jogging, dancing, or vigorous yoga. Avoid oversleeping and try to wake up early to harness the day's active energy.

Seek out warm, dry climates and environments, and avoid cold, damp conditions. Spend time in the sun or in lively, uplifting spaces that encourage movement and motivation.

Influence of External and Internal Factors on Dosha Balance

The balance of the three doshas—**Vata**, **Pitta**, and **Kapha**—according to Ayurveda, is deeply influenced by a variety of external and internal factors such as diet, lifestyle, seasons, age, time of day, and circadian rhythms. Each of these factors can increase or decrease specific doshas in the body, leading to harmony or imbalance. Here's how they affect the doshas:

1. Diet

- **Vata:** Dry, cold, and light foods (e.g., raw vegetables, dry snacks) increase Vata. Warm, oily, and nourishing foods (e.g., soups, stews, grains) help balance Vata.

- **Pitta**: Hot, spicy, oily, and sour foods (e.g., chilies, tomatoes) increase Pitta. Cooling, mildly sweet, and bitter foods (e.g., cucumbers, leafy greens) balance Pitta.

- **Kapha**: Heavy, sweet, and oily foods (e.g., dairy, fried foods) increase Kapha. Light, dry, and spicy foods (e.g., lentils, ginger) help balance Kapha.

2. Lifestyle

- **Vata**: A fast-paced, erratic lifestyle with irregular sleep and eating habits increases Vata. A regular routine with grounding practices (e.g., meditation, calm activities) helps balance it.

- **Pitta**: Competitive, stressful, and intense activities or excessive exposure to heat increase Pitta. A balanced lifestyle with cool environments, calming activities, and regular relaxation helps to balance Pitta.

- **Kapha**: A sedentary, overly restful lifestyle with little activity increases Kapha. A dynamic lifestyle with regular physical activity and mental stimulation balances Kapha.

3. Seasons

- **Vata**: Increases in autumn and early winter, when the weather is dry, cold, and windy. Warm, nourishing, and grounding practices help balance Vata during these seasons.

- **Pitta**: Increases in summer when the weather is hot and humid. Cooling, hydrating, and calming practices help balance Pitta during the heat.

- **Kapha**: Increases in late winter and early spring when the weather is cold, damp, and heavy. Stimulating, warming, and dry practices help balance Kapha during this time.

4. Age

- **Vata**: Increases in old age when the body becomes drier, lighter, and more fragile. Grounding, nourishing, and warming practices are beneficial.

- **Pitta**: Dominates in adulthood (from puberty to middle age), when metabolism, drive, and intensity are strong. Cooling, soothing, and stress-reducing practices help balance Pitta during this phase.

- **Kapha**: Dominates in childhood, when the body is naturally heavier, moister, and stable. Stimulating and warming practices help balance Kapha during this time.

5. Time of Day

- **Vata**: Peaks between **2 AM - 6 AM** and **2 PM - 6 PM**. Calm, grounding activities like yoga or meditation are beneficial during this time.

- **Pitta**: Peaks between **10 AM - 2 PM** and **10 PM - 2 AM**. Eating the largest meal around noon when digestion is strongest helps balance Pitta.

- **Kapha**: Peaks between **6 AM - 10 AM** and **6 PM - 10 PM**. Physical activity in the morning helps balance Kapha, while lighter evening meals are advised.

6. Circadian Rhythm

- The body's natural **circadian rhythm** is the internal clock that regulates the sleep-wake cycle and other physiological processes. Adhering to a consistent daily routine helps balance the doshas:

  Vata: Stability in routine, proper sleep, and meals taken at regular intervals balance Vata.

  Pitta: Avoiding late-night work, exposure to artificial light, and overstimulation helps regulate Pitta.

  Kapha: Stimulating the body during Kapha periods (e.g., morning exercise) prevents sluggishness and imbalance.

By understanding the influences of these factors on your dosha constitution, Ayurveda suggests lifestyle changes and personalized practices to maintain balance, leading to better health and well-being.

Ayurveda and Yoga: A Synergistic Approach to Health

In Ayurveda, balance among the three doshas is considered essential for maintaining health and preventing disease. When one or more doshas become imbalanced, physical or mental ailments can manifest. By understanding one's dominant dosha and using yoga as a tool to bring equilibrium, individuals can prevent these imbalances and promote overall well-being.

Both Ayurveda and yoga emphasize the importance of personalized care and attention to one's constitution. According to the **Charaka Samhita**, one of the foundational texts of Ayurveda, "The equilibrium of the three doshas, the normal state of the tissues (dhatus), the proper functioning of the body waste products (malas), the clarity of the mind, senses, and soul are the factors that sustain the health of an individual." This illustrates how the holistic practices of Ayurveda and yoga complement each other, working together to sustain a balance between mind, body, and spirit.

Modern Research on Ayurveda and Yoga Integration

Recent studies support the powerful effects of integrating Ayurveda and yoga for improving overall health. A study published in the *Journal of Ayurveda and Integrative Medicine* found that individuals who combined Ayurveda and yoga practices experienced significant improvements in managing chronic conditions such as hypertension, diabetes, and anxiety. This synergistic approach not only enhances physical well-being but also cultivates mental and emotional resilience.

As the doshas influence both body and mind, a yoga practice tailored to one's doshic constitution not only enhances flexibility and strength but also harmonizes emotional and mental states, leading to greater peace, vitality, and well-being. By understanding and balancing the unique energies of Vata, Pitta, and Kapha, individuals can unlock the full potential of both their yoga practice and their overall health.

Ayurvedic Principles in Yoga Diet: Nourishing Body and Mind through Food

Ayurveda, one of the oldest systems of natural healing, holds the principle that food is medicine, and a personalized diet plays a crucial role in maintaining balance and health. When integrated with yoga practice, an Ayurvedic diet can enhance physical endurance, mental clarity, emotional stability, and spiritual awareness. By tailoring food choices to one's dosha type, the diet helps in balancing the energies within the body, facilitating overall harmony.

Personalizing Your Diet Based on Dosha

Ayurveda teaches that each individual has a unique constitution dominated by one or a combination of the three doshas—Vata, Pitta, and Kapha. Each dosha influences digestion, metabolism, and energy. By aligning food with one's doshic balance, the body can function optimally, and yoga practice becomes more effective in promoting physical and mental wellness.

1. Vata Dosha: Warm, Moist, and Grounding Foods

Vata, governed by air and ether, is naturally cold, dry, and light. When out of balance, Vata individuals often experience issues like anxiety, dryness, bloating, and restlessness. To counter these effects, Vata-dominant individuals benefit from foods that provide warmth, moisture, and nourishment.

Recommended foods

- **Warm, cooked meals**: Focus on easily digestible and nourishing meals like soups, stews, porridges, and broths. These help counterbalance the cold and dry qualities of Vata.

- **Grains**: Opt for warm, well-cooked grains like rice, quinoa, oats, and millet. These provide stability and grounding for Vata's erratic energy.

- **Root vegetables**: Favor warming and grounding vegetables such as sweet potatoes, carrots, beets, squash, and pumpkin. These are nourishing and help balance Vata's light and airy nature.

- **Healthy fats**: Incorporate oils like ghee, sesame oil, olive oil, and coconut oil, which help lubricate and nourish the dry tendencies of Vata.

- **Dairy**: Warm, spiced milk or dairy products like soft cheese, yogurt (preferably warm and spiced), and ghee can be beneficial, especially when consumed in moderation.

- **Legumes**: Prefer well-cooked lentils, mung beans, and chickpeas, especially in soups or stews. Avoid dry and harder-to-digest legumes like raw beans and peas.

- **Spices**: Mild warming spices such as cinnamon, ginger, cumin, cardamom, turmeric, fennel, and black pepper support digestion and enhance warmth in the body.

- **Fruits**: Sweet, moist fruits like ripe bananas, mangoes, peaches, berries, and cooked apples and pears are excellent for Vata. Avoid overly astringent or dry fruits like raw apples or unripe bananas.

- **Nuts and seeds**: Almonds (soaked and peeled), walnuts, and cashews provide nourishing oils and protein for Vata. Sesame and sunflower seeds are also beneficial.

- **Herbal teas**: Chamomile, ginger, cinnamon, fennel, and liquorice root teas are excellent for calming Vata's anxious and restless tendencies.

By choosing warm and grounding foods, a Vata individual can create stability and improve focus, enhancing both physical yoga practice and mental meditation.

Additional tips

- Eat meals at regular times to provide routine and stability.

- Avoid cold, raw, or dry foods such as salads, crackers, and cold beverages.

- Favor slow-cooked, warm, and moist meals that are easy to digest.

2. Pitta Dosha: Cooling and Calming Foods

Pitta, composed of fire and water elements, is associated with heat, intensity, and sharpness. When Pitta is imbalanced, individuals may experience excessive body heat, inflammation, irritability, and digestive problems like acidity. Cooling and calming foods help to pacify the fiery nature of Pitta and promote mental clarity.

Recommended foods

- **Cooling, hydrating foods**: Incorporate fresh, juicy, and sweet fruits like coconut, watermelon, cucumbers, pears, mangoes, pomegranates, and melons. These naturally reduce Pitta's heat and inflammation.

- **Leafy greens and salads**: Include cooling and bitter vegetables like lettuce, kale, spinach, chard, and arugula. These help balance Pitta's fiery nature. Raw salads can be consumed more frequently by Pittas compared to other doshas.

- **Grains**: Opt for cooling and light grains such as barley, quinoa, basmati rice, oats, and wheat. These provide a grounding energy while avoiding excess heat.

- **Dairy products**: Milk, ghee, and fresh, unsalted butter are soothing and cooling for Pitta when consumed in moderation. Dairy can help counterbalance Pitta's heat but should be consumed cool or at room temperature, rather than hot.

- **Cooling beverages**: Coconut water, herbal teas, and fresh fruit juices are ideal for Pitta. These help hydrate and cool the system.

- **Sweet and bitter vegetables**: Include vegetables like zucchini, asparagus, broccoli, cabbage, celery, and cauliflower. These have a cooling and balancing effect on Pitta's fire element.

- **Legumes**: Lentils, mung beans, and chickpeas are good sources of plant protein for Pitta, but they should be consumed with cooling spices and oils to avoid aggravation.

- **Spices**: Favor cooling spices such as coriander, cilantro, mint, fennel, and turmeric. Avoid excessive use of hot spices like chili, cayenne, and black pepper, which can aggravate Pitta.

- **Nuts and seeds**: Sunflower seeds, pumpkin seeds, and almonds (soaked and peeled) are good in moderation for Pitta, but avoid overly oily or heavy nuts like cashews and peanuts.

- **Oils**: Cooling oils like coconut oil and olive oil are best for Pitta. Minimize the use of heating oils like mustard oil or sesame oil.

- **Herbal teas**: Chamomile, peppermint, rose, liquorice, fennel, and hibiscus teas are excellent for calming and cooling Pitta.

A Pitta-pacifying diet helps reduce the fiery energy, allowing for calm focus during yoga practice and meditation while preventing burnout and agitation.

Additional tips

- Eat meals at regular intervals and avoid skipping meals, as Pittas can become irritable when hungry.

- Avoid excessively spicy, sour, oily, fried, and acidic foods such as tomatoes, garlic, onions, and fermented products (pickles, vinegar).

- Favor cool or room temperature foods over hot or spicy ones.

- Maintain adequate hydration, as Pitta types can quickly become dehydrated due to their heat.

3. Kapha Dosha: Light, Dry, and Warming Foods

Kapha, dominated by the earth and water elements, is naturally heavy, cool, and stable. When out of balance, Kapha individuals may experience sluggishness, weight gain, congestion, and lethargy. To stimulate Kapha energy, the focus should be on light, warming, and dry foods that invigorate the body.

Recommended foods

- **Light, warming foods**: Kapha benefits from light, easily digestible, and warming meals. Steamed or lightly sautéed vegetables, broths, and soups made from vegetables like broccoli, cauliflower, leafy greens, and asparagus are ideal. These foods counterbalance Kapha's heavy and cold nature.

- **Whole grains**: Choose light, dry grains such as barley, millet, quinoa, and buckwheat. These grains help reduce the sluggishness and heaviness associated with Kapha. Avoid heavy and moist grains like wheat and rice, which can further imbalance Kapha.

- **Legumes**: Lentils, black beans, chickpeas, and mung beans are excellent sources of protein for Kapha types. These legumes are drying and light, helping to balance Kapha's tendency toward water retention and lethargy.

- **Pungent spices**: To stimulate digestion and metabolism, include warming spices such as turmeric, ginger, black pepper, cumin, mustard seeds, cayenne pepper, and garlic. These spices help enhance circulation, burn excess fat, and clear congestion in Kapha individuals.

- **Bitter and astringent vegetables**: Favor vegetables like bitter gourds, Brussels sprouts, spinach, kale, and collard greens. These help to reduce Kapha's excess moisture and heaviness, while aiding in detoxification.

- **Fruits**: Opt for light and dry fruits like apples, pears, pomegranates, and berries. Avoid sweet, watery fruits like melons, bananas, avocados, and coconut, which can increase Kapha's heaviness and mucus production.

- **Dairy**: Minimize dairy consumption as it can increase mucus and heaviness in Kapha. If consumed, opt for warm and spiced versions like a small amount of warm, spiced milk or yogurt. Ghee is acceptable in small quantities.

- **Nuts and seeds**: Avoid heavy nuts and seeds like cashews, peanuts, and pistachios. Instead, opt for lighter options such as flaxseeds, sunflower seeds, or very small amounts of almonds (soaked and peeled).

- **Oils**: Use oils sparingly. If necessary, opt for lighter oils like flaxseed or sunflower oil. Avoid heavy oils like coconut and olive oil, which can further aggravate Kapha's heaviness.

- **Herbal teas**: Drink warming herbal teas made from ginger, cinnamon, clove, tulsi (holy basil), or cardamom. These teas help stimulate digestion and metabolism.

Additional tips

- Favor dry, light, and warm foods, and avoid cold, oily, and heavy meals.

- Reduce the consumption of sweet, salty, and sour foods, as these increase Kapha's sluggish and dense qualities.

- Avoid excessive use of dairy, oily, fried, and sugary foods, which can contribute to congestion and lethargy.

- Incorporate plenty of physical movement and avoid overeating, as Kapha types tend to gain weight easily.

Best times to eat: Kapha individuals should prioritize eating their main meal in the middle of the day, avoiding late-night meals. Regular fasting or skipping meals occasionally can help reduce Kapha's sluggishness.

Incorporating light and energizing foods supports Kapha individuals in maintaining vitality and alertness during yoga, countering the natural tendency toward inertia.

The Importance of Diet in Ayurveda and Yoga

Ayurveda views food not just as nourishment for the body, but as an essential component for mental and spiritual well-being. A proper diet creates harmony between body and mind, allowing individuals to better focus on their yoga practice and meditation. As an ancient Ayurvedic proverb states: "When diet is wrong, medicine is of no use. When diet is correct, medicine is of no need."

This quote underscores the importance of preventive health through diet. By aligning diet with one's dosha, individuals can avoid imbalances that lead to disease, reducing the need for medical interventions.

Modern Research on the Integration of Yoga and Ayurveda

Recent research highlights the powerful synergy between Ayurveda and yoga in promoting health and well-being. A 2019 study published in the *Journal of Ayurveda and Integrative Medicine* showed that individuals who practiced both yoga and Ayurvedic lifestyle modifications experienced a **32% reduction in perceived stress levels** after 12 weeks. The study also noted improvements in physical health, emotional resilience, and overall life satisfaction.

This research validates the ancient wisdom of Ayurveda, where a balanced diet tailored to an individual's constitution, combined with regular yoga practice, results in enhanced vitality and reduced stress. This holistic approach allows for a more harmonious and fulfilling life, supporting both personal growth and spiritual evolution.

Yoga Therapy and Ayurvedic Treatments

Ayurveda offers therapeutic treatments like Panchakarma (a detoxification process) to cleanse the body and mind, often recommended before starting an intense yoga practice. Combining yoga with Ayurvedic therapies maximizes their healing potential, addressing the root causes of imbalances.

A person with high stress levels and insomnia might benefit from Ayurvedic treatments like Shirodhara (pouring warm oil on the forehead) to calm the mind, followed by restorative yoga practices like Yoga Nidra for deep relaxation.

A patient suffering from anxiety, which is often associated with a Vata imbalance, might be recommended a Yoga practice focusing on slow, grounding asanas, along with Ayurvedic treatments such as Abhyanga (oil massage) with warm sesame oil and a Vata-pacifying diet.

Research conducted at the *National Institute of Ayurveda* in Jaipur, India, demonstrated that patients undergoing Panchakarma therapy followed by a tailored yoga program showed significant improvements in their mental and physical health.

The Role of Pranayama and Meditation in Ayurveda

Ayurveda recognizes the importance of controlling prana (life force) for maintaining health. Pranayama, the yogic practice of breath control, helps balance the doshas and energize the body. For example, Kapalbhati Pranayama is often recommended for Kapha types to stimulate the metabolic fire, while Anulom Vilom (alternate nostril breathing) balances Vata and Pitta doshas.

"Pranayama is the gateway to controlling the mind, senses, and body. It is the foundation of health and spiritual growth." – Hatha Yoga Pradipika.

Meditation is another essential practice in both Yoga and Ayurveda, used to calm the mind, reduce stress, and enhance mental clarity. Ayurvedic meditation practices focus on balancing the doshas through mindfulness, mantra chanting, and visualization techniques.

The Bhagavad Gita (6.5) states, "One must elevate, not degrade, oneself by one's own mind. The mind alone is the friend as well as the enemy of the self."

Conclusion: Integrating Yoga and Ayurveda for Holistic Health

The integration of Yoga and Ayurveda offers a complete system for achieving physical, mental, and spiritual well-being. Yoga provides the tools for spiritual growth, while Ayurveda offers the wisdom for maintaining a healthy body and mind. By understanding your dosha, incorporating personalized yoga practices, and following an Ayurvedic diet and lifestyle, you can achieve harmony and balance in life.

"Ayurveda is the science, and Yoga is the practice of the science. Together, they work to elevate the body, mind, and spirit." – Dr. Robert Svoboda.

23

Traits of a Realized Yogi

The ultimate goal of spiritual practice is self-realization, where one transcends the limitations of the ego and realizes their true nature as the *Atman* (the Self). A realized yogi embodies the highest state of consciousness, displaying qualities that reflect deep inner peace, wisdom, compassion, and unity with all existence. This chapter explores the profound traits that characterize such a being, as described in ancient scriptures and witnessed in the lives of enlightened masters. These traits are not theoretical ideals but lived realities, backed by examples, events, and wisdom from revered texts.

Inner Peace and Equanimity (Samatva)

One of the foremost traits of a realized yogi is unshakable inner peace and equanimity. This inner state is marked by an unshakable calmness and composure that remains unaffected by the ever-changing circumstances of life. A realized yogi dwells in a serene space where emotions like joy and sorrow, success and failure, are seen merely as passing waves on the surface of an ocean that remains vast and tranquil beneath.

This profound equanimity arises from a deep, experiential understanding that all worldly experiences are impermanent, like clouds drifting across the sky, while the true self, the Atman, remains eternally unaffected and unperturbed. Such insight allows the yogi to transcend reactive patterns of pleasure and pain, desire and aversion, anchoring themselves in a steady awareness that is beyond dualities.

The Bhagavad Gita eloquently captures this essence of equanimity. In verse 2.48, Krishna advises Arjuna, saying: "Perform your duty equably, abandoning all attachment to success or failure. Such equanimity is called yoga." Here, the Gita underscores that the real essence of yoga is in the ability to remain balanced and detached while actively engaging in life's duties.

Further expanding on this, the Gita in verse 2.56 describes a realized person as one "whose mind is undisturbed in the midst of sorrow, whose thirst for pleasures has altogether disappeared, and who is free from attachment, fear, and anger." This state of being allows the yogi to witness life with equanimity, unshaken by grief, untouched by cravings, and devoid of the fear and anger that arise from clinging to the impermanent.

Such a yogi lives fully in the present moment, without the desire to alter it for personal gain or the fear of losing it. This quality of acceptance brings a rare kind of freedom, where the realized yogi embraces all situations — whether pleasant or unpleasant — as opportunities for growth and understanding. They transcend personal likes and dislikes, seeing every experience as a manifestation of the Divine, unfolding perfectly in its own way.

By cultivating equanimity, the yogi aligns with the rhythms of the universe, flowing with life rather than resisting it. This leads to a state of inner peace so profound that even the most turbulent storms of existence cannot disturb their center. In this manner, the realized yogi exemplifies the true spirit of yoga, which is to remain centered and equanimous amidst all of life's myriad fluctuations.

The life of Sri Ramana Maharshi exemplifies this trait. Despite facing severe illness and personal challenges, he remained in a state of inner peace, radiating calm and compassion to all who came into contact with him.

Compassion (Karuna) and Universal Love (Maitri)

A realized yogi experiences profound compassion and love for all beings. This universal love arises from the understanding that all living beings are manifestations of the same divine consciousness. The boundaries of self and others dissolve, and the yogi sees the divine in every form of life.

The Upanishads beautifully convey this truth. The Isha Upanishad (Verse 6) states, "He who sees all beings in his own self, and his own self in all beings, no longer hates anyone." This verse underscores the unity that is experienced by a realized soul, where universal love and compassion naturally arise as a reflection of one's oneness with the cosmos.

Similarly, the Bhagavad Gita (12.13-14) highlights this with the words, "One who is free from malice towards all beings, friendly and compassionate, free from possessiveness and ego, balanced in happiness and distress, forgiving, and ever content – that devotee is dear to me." Here, Krishna outlines the qualities that endear one to the

Divine, emphasizing that compassion and love are inseparable from the path of spiritual realization.

Yogananda once said, "The more we extend our love to others, the closer we approach God." His life was a testament to universal love, which he spread through his teachings in the West.

In the Buddhist tradition, the Dhammapada teaches in Verse 1.5, "Hatred does not cease by hatred, but only by love; this is the eternal rule." This profound teaching encapsulates the essence of compassion that Buddha practiced throughout his life. His path of the Four Noble Truths and the Noble Eightfold Path centers on reducing the suffering of all sentient beings, an aspiration rooted in profound compassion.

The Dalai Lama, a living embodiment of compassion, has maintained a compassionate outlook despite being in exile for decades. In his approach to the Chinese government's treatment of Tibet, he advocates for peace, forgiveness, and understanding, rather than hostility or retaliation. His commitment to promoting compassion as a universal virtue transcends religious and cultural boundaries, inspiring millions around the world.

Detachment (Vairagya)

Vairagya is often misunderstood as indifference or lack of care, but in its true essence, it is much deeper and more profound. Detachment, for a realized yogi, does not mean withdrawal from life or a disinterest in the world. Rather, it is the ability to engage fully in life without being entangled by desires, emotions, or the outcomes of one's actions. This detachment arises from the understanding that true fulfillment and happiness are internal states, not dependent on external circumstances, possessions, or relationships. It is a wisdom that comes from knowing the transient nature of the material world.

A yogi, who embodies *Vairagya*, remains active in the world, performing all duties and responsibilities, but does so with a sense of freedom. This freedom is not from actions themselves but from the *attachment* to the results of those actions. In this sense, the yogi's actions are driven by pure intention, guided by selflessness and a higher purpose, not by egoic desires or expectations.

This concept is beautifully captured in the Bhagavad Gita, where Lord Krishna advises Arjuna in verse 2.47: "You have a right to perform your duty, but not to the fruits of your actions." This teaching forms the foundation of *Karma Yoga*—the yoga of selfless action. The yogi performs all actions with dedication, precision, and care, but remains detached from the results, whether they bring success or failure, pleasure or pain.

Such detachment does not imply a lack of feeling or care for the world. On the contrary, it empowers the yogi to act with greater compassion, clarity, and strength. Without the burden of expectation, the mind becomes calm, balanced, and more effective in its efforts. This state of mental equilibrium is known as *sthitaprajna*, a quality of inner steadiness that enables one to remain unaffected by life's dualities—such as praise and criticism, gain and loss, or joy and sorrow.

Moreover, *Vairagya* is a state cultivated over time through deep practice and introspection. It is born from the realization that all external objects, relationships, and experiences are fleeting. A yogi knows that attaching one's happiness to these transient things only leads to suffering. Instead, they cultivate an inner connection with the

Self (*Atman*), the eternal consciousness that is beyond change and unaffected by the fluctuations of the outer world.

This spiritual detachment fosters a profound sense of peace and freedom. The yogi does not deny the beauty or value of life but understands it from a perspective of wholeness, where nothing external can disturb the inherent joy that resides within. Thus, the yogi lives in the world fully engaged, but inwardly remains untouched, like a lotus flower that thrives in water but remains unsullied by it.

Swami Vivekananda, who tirelessly worked to spread the message of Vedanta in the West, remained detached from fame and recognition. He saw himself merely as an instrument of the divine, serving humanity without any desire for personal gain.

Wisdom and Discrimination (Viveka)

Viveka, often translated as the power of discrimination, is one of the most vital qualities for a realized yogi. It represents the ability to distinguish between what is real and unreal, permanent and impermanent, eternal and fleeting. This clarity is not just an intellectual understanding but a profound wisdom arising from deep spiritual insight and direct experience of the true nature of the Self (*Atman*).

For a yogi, *Viveka* serves as an inner compass that guides their thoughts, actions, and decisions. It allows them to see through the illusions (*maya*) of the material world, recognizing that the pleasures, pains, and possessions of this world are temporary and ultimately incapable of providing lasting fulfillment. The yogi, through the lens of *viveka*, understands that the ultimate reality lies beyond the transient—residing in the eternal, unchanging essence of pure consciousness.

The *Ashtavakra Gita*, a profound philosophical scripture, captures the essence of this discrimination in its opening verse (1.3): "You are not the body, nor is the body yours, nor are you the doer of actions. You are pure consciousness, the witness of all." This verse articulates a key realization that comes through *viveka*: the understanding that the body, mind, and all material aspects of existence are not the true self. They are merely instruments through which consciousness experiences the world. The yogi, through deep meditation and self-inquiry, transcends identification with the body and mind and rests in the awareness of being the pure, witnessing consciousness.

This wisdom radically shifts how the yogi relates to the world. When the fleeting nature of material objects is fully understood, the yogi naturally ceases to chase after them, realizing that no amount of worldly success or sensory pleasure can touch the bliss of the Self. This clarity brings about deep peace, equanimity, and a sense of detachment from the ups and downs of life, which are seen as part of the dance of *Prakriti* (nature) but not affecting the true Self.

Adi Shankaracharya, the great Indian philosopher and the most influential figure in Advaita Vedanta, emphasized *viveka* as the first step toward self-realization. According to Shankaracharya, without this ability to discriminate between the real (*Sat*) and the unreal (*Asat*), one cannot embark on the path of liberation. In his famous text *Vivekachudamani* (The Crest Jewel of Discrimination), he highlights the critical role that *viveka* plays in freeing oneself from ignorance and bondage. For Shankaracharya, the mind's tendency to cling to the transient—mistaking the body, mind, and world as one's true identity—is the root cause of suffering. Only through the discrimination of the eternal from the non-eternal can one begin to move toward liberation.

Viveka is not an abstract or passive quality; it is an active practice that a yogi must cultivate throughout their life. In every moment, the yogi exercises this discernment—whether making decisions, interacting with others, or engaging with the world. The yogi's wisdom is sharpened by contemplation, meditation, and the guidance of spiritual teachings. Over time, this discrimination becomes so refined that the yogi is able to see through the veils of illusion instantly, recognizing the underlying truth of all experiences: that they are fleeting reflections of the unchanging Self.

Furthermore, *viveka* is not just about rejecting the material world but about perceiving it accurately. The yogi doesn't shun the world but sees it for what it is—a temporary manifestation that serves as a field of experience for spiritual growth. The world becomes a playground for the yogi, not a trap. Understanding the impermanence of the body, mind, and emotions allows the yogi to act in the world with greater freedom and detachment, knowing that their true essence is beyond all such limitations.

J. Krishnamurti's discourses, which shook the foundations of traditional religious beliefs, also exemplify this wisdom. His famous quote, "Truth is a pathless land," encapsulates the essence of non-dogmatic realization.

Contentment (Santosha)

Contentment is a hallmark of a realized yogi. It is not merely a passive acceptance of life's circumstances, but an active state of inner peace and fulfillment that arises from the deep understanding that the Self is complete and whole, beyond any need for external validation or material acquisitions. In the state of *Santosha*, the yogi remains unwavering, no matter the external conditions, because their happiness is rooted in the realization that true contentment is an inner state, independent of the transient nature of the world.

For most people, happiness is conditioned by external factors—wealth, relationships, achievements, and sensory pleasures. However, these sources of joy are impermanent and inevitably lead to dissatisfaction, as the mind always craves more or fears loss. In contrast, the yogi who has attained *Santosha* transcends this cycle of desire and craving. They realize that lasting joy comes from within, not from any external achievement or possession. This deep contentment is the fruit of a mind that has been quieted through spiritual practice and self-awareness.

The Yoga Sutras of Patanjali highlight the importance of *Santosha* as a key practice on the yogic path. In Sutra 2.42, Patanjali states: "From contentment, supreme joy is attained." This supreme joy, or *paramananda*, is not a fleeting emotional state but a profound and lasting sense of well-being that pervades the yogi's life. It is the natural state of the Self, experienced when the mind is no longer agitated by desires, fears, or attachments. Through the practice of *Santosha*, the yogi learns to find happiness in the present moment, regardless of circumstances.

The realization of *Santosha* comes from the understanding that the true Self (*Atman*) is already whole and perfect. The material world, with all its ups and downs, cannot add to or diminish the completeness of the Self. This knowledge brings an end to the restless search for external fulfillment. The yogi, rooted in the awareness of their divine nature, naturally experiences contentment in every situation. Whether in abundance or scarcity, success or failure, the yogi remains steady and satisfied, knowing that nothing outside can touch the essence of who they truly are.

A shining example of *Santosha* in action is seen in the life of Mata Amritanandamayi, affectionately known as Amma. Despite leading an incredibly active life, tirelessly serving millions of people around the world, Amma radiates an unshakeable peace, love, and joy. She embodies *Santosha* by living in the present moment with full awareness, remaining free from attachment to outcomes while pouring love and compassion into every action. Her contentment is not born of external conditions but is a reflection of her profound inner connection to the divine.

Amma's life demonstrates that *Santosha* does not imply inaction or withdrawal from the world. On the contrary, a realized yogi can be deeply engaged in life's activities, performing service, helping others, and navigating life's challenges, all while remaining inwardly at peace. The yogi's contentment becomes a source of inspiration and strength for those around them, as their calm presence and joyful demeanour touch the lives of others in profound ways.

In practical terms, *Santosha* can be cultivated by accepting life as it comes, without resistance or expectation. This does not mean complacency but rather embracing each moment with gratitude and grace, understanding that every experience is an opportunity for growth and self-realization. The yogi practices seeing the perfection in the present moment, even in adversity, knowing that the challenges of life are temporary and that their true nature is untouched by external circumstances.

Ultimately, *Santosha* is the key to liberation from suffering. As long as one seeks happiness in the external world, dissatisfaction is inevitable. But when contentment is found within, the yogi lives in a state of unshakeable peace, regardless of life's fluctuations. This inner joy, born from the realization of the Self, becomes the yogi's natural state, leading them to experience life in its fullest, with a heart full of gratitude, compassion, and love.

Swami Sivananda exemplified contentment. Despite a life of simplicity and austerity, he radiated happiness and inspired thousands with his teachings on inner contentment.

Humility (Vinamrata) and Simplicity (Sadagi)

Humility (*Vinamrata*) and simplicity (*Sadagi*) are two key virtues that naturally arise in a realized yogi, who has transcended the ego and the need for external validation. For the yogi, the sense of self is no longer tied to personal accomplishments, recognition, or status. Instead, the yogi's identity is grounded in the realization of the *Atman*—the pure, eternal Self that is beyond all worldly distinctions and accolades. As a result, the yogi embraces a life of humility, knowing that the ego's desires for praise and recognition are mere illusions, and simplicity, focusing on service and selfless action.

Humility, in the context of a yogic life, does not mean self-deprecation or a low opinion of oneself. Rather, it is the recognition that the ego, with all its desires for power, status, and praise, is a false construct. A realized yogi knows that the true Self is beyond the temporary identities that the world projects onto us. This deeper understanding allows the yogi to act without the need for acknowledgment or reward. Whether engaged in service, spiritual practice, or daily life, the yogi's actions flow from a place of selflessness and surrender to the divine, not from a desire for personal gain.

The Bhagavad Gita (13.8) offers profound insight into this quality: "Humility, modesty, non-violence, patience, honesty—these qualities, O Arjuna, are born of true knowledge." Here, humility is linked to wisdom and understanding. When one realizes the vastness of the Self and the illusory nature of the ego, humility naturally follows. The yogi becomes humble not because they diminish themselves but because they see themselves as part of a greater whole, understanding that all beings are equal manifestations of the same divine consciousness.

Simplicity (*Sadagi*) is closely tied to humility. A realized yogi leads a life free from unnecessary complications, extravagance, or attachment to material possessions. This simplicity is not born of deprivation but from a deep contentment with what is truly essential. The yogi recognizes that the accumulation of wealth, objects, or social status does not lead to fulfillment. Instead, true peace comes from living in alignment with one's highest purpose and maintaining clarity of mind, free from distractions.

Simplicity is also reflected in the yogi's thoughts, actions, and interactions with others. Without the burden of pride, greed, or vanity, the yogi interacts with others from a place of authenticity and sincerity.

Their simplicity makes them approachable, compassionate, and grounded. They do not seek to impress or dominate but live in harmony with the world around them, using only what is needed and serving others with a pure heart.

In practice, *Vinamrata* and *Sadagi* are cultivated through the continuous surrender of the ego. By consciously letting go of pride, competition, and the need for recognition, the yogi opens themselves to the flow of divine grace. This allows them to serve others without expectation, offering their work as a form of worship. Similarly, simplicity is practiced by focusing on the essentials, whether in material possessions, thoughts, or lifestyle, and by maintaining a heart that is uncluttered by desires.

Ultimately, humility and simplicity are qualities that reflect the yogi's inner freedom. Having realized the nature of the Self, the yogi no longer needs the trappings of the ego or the material world to feel complete. They are content in their being, and this contentment is expressed outwardly through humble, selfless, and simple living. This state of being allows the yogi to move through the world with grace, wisdom, and compassion, serving as a beacon of light and truth for others.

Fearlessness (Abhaya)

Fearlessness, or *Abhaya*, is a natural quality of the realized yogi who has transcended the illusion of the body and the material world. For most people, fear is rooted in attachment—whether it is attachment to the body, relationships, wealth, or status. Fear arises from the belief that these external aspects of life can be lost, harmed, or destroyed.

However, once a yogi realizes their true nature as the *Atman*—the eternal, unchanging self—they no longer identify with the fleeting aspects of material existence. This profound understanding dissolves all fear, allowing the yogi to live with courage, grace, and unshakable inner peace.

The *Atman* is the pure consciousness that is beyond birth and death, untouched by the changing conditions of the world. The realized yogi understands that the body and mind are temporary vehicles through which consciousness experiences life, but they are not the essence of one's true being. The yogi's realization of this eternal nature eradicates the fear of death and loss, for they know that the *Atman* remains untouched by time, disease, or destruction.

The *Mundaka Upanishad* (2.2.8) declares, "The knower of the self goes beyond sorrow and fear." This verse encapsulates the essence of fearlessness. Once the yogi gains direct knowledge of the *Self*, they understand that all forms of fear are rooted in illusion. The fear of death, failure, or suffering is based on the mistaken identification with the body and the ego. By knowing the *Atman*, the yogi sees that there is nothing to fear because the true Self is beyond harm, eternal, and ever-blissful.

This state of *Abhaya* allows the yogi to face life's challenges with extraordinary strength and calmness. Whether confronted by personal difficulties, physical danger, or existential threats, the realized yogi remains anchored in the knowledge of their divine nature. Fearlessness is not the absence of challenges but the ability to meet them without being consumed by anxiety, doubt, or worry. The yogi understands that all external circumstances are part of the changing play of *Prakriti* (nature) and that their true essence remains unscathed.

The Bhagavad Gita also emphasizes the quality of fearlessness as essential to spiritual growth. In chapter 16, fearlessness is listed as one of the divine qualities (*Daivi Sampat*) that lead to liberation. Lord Krishna encourages Arjuna to rise above fear by realizing his divine nature, highlighting that courage and fearlessness come from a deep connection to the Self.

Fearlessness is not recklessness or arrogance but a quiet confidence born of spiritual insight. The realized yogi does not engage in dangerous or harmful activities out of egoic bravado; instead, they face life with clarity and wisdom, knowing that the source of their strength is the eternal Self. This inner peace allows them to take bold actions when necessary, to speak the truth without fear of judgment, and to walk the path of righteousness even in the face of adversity.

As the yogi lets go of attachment to the material world and shifts their awareness to the eternal Self, fear naturally dissolves. The yogi sees that life and death, gain and loss, pleasure and pain are all part of the play of duality, and their true essence remains beyond these fluctuations.

In daily life, this fearlessness translates into the ability to take risks without being paralyzed by fear of failure, to express love and compassion without fearing rejection, and to pursue truth and justice without worrying about consequences. The yogi's actions are grounded in a higher understanding, and this spiritual insight frees them from the limiting grip of fear.

Absence of Desire (Nishkama)

The concept of *nishkama*—acting without desire—is central to many spiritual traditions, particularly in yoga and Vedanta. A realized yogi is one who has transcended the dualities of attraction and aversion, desire and fulfillment. For such a person, the world no longer holds the same allure, as they have realized the transient and ultimately unsatisfactory nature of worldly pursuits.

The Brihadaranyaka Upanishad (4.4.6) describes this as, "He who has no desires, who has renounced all desires, who is free from desires, attains the state of Brahman."

The life of Adi Shankaracharya is a testament to this trait. Despite immense fame and reverence, he remained detached from all materialistic pursuits and focused solely on spiritual work.

In the Bhagavad Gita, Lord Krishna teaches Arjuna about *nishkama karma*—performing one's duties without attachment to the results. This idea reflects the highest state of consciousness where actions are performed not out of desire for personal gain but as an offering, without ego or expectation. It elaborates on the concept of *nishkama karma* in Chapter 3, Verse 19, "Therefore, without being attached to the fruits of activities, one should act as a matter of duty, for by working without attachment one attains the Supreme." This idea teaches that a yogi's actions are free from personal desire, performed for the sake of duty alone, leading to liberation.

Ramana Maharshi, embodied *nishkama*. After his profound spiritual awakening at the age of 16, he lived a life of renunciation and simplicity. He had no personal desires, no attachment to material possessions, and yet was highly active in guiding spiritual seekers. His selfless service to others was done without any expectation or desire, illustrating the ideal of *nishkama*. "Your own Self-Realization is the greatest service you can render the world." — Ramana Maharshi.

Mahavatar Babaji, the immortal yogi of the Himalayas, is revered for his selfless guidance to seekers, remaining hidden from fame while silently aiding humanity.

Research into contentment and minimalism suggests that those who practice desire reduction report higher levels of life satisfaction and well-being.

Non-Duality (Advaita)

A realized yogi embodies the profound experience of *Advaita* or non-duality, a state where the apparent separation between the self and the rest of the universe dissolves completely. In this state, the yogi no longer perceives the world through the lens of dualistic distinctions—such as "self" and "other," "subject" and "object," or "mind" and "matter." Instead, the yogi realizes the fundamental oneness of all existence, understanding that everything is a manifestation of the same divine consciousness.

In ordinary perception, we experience the world through duality, seeing ourselves as separate individuals interacting with an external world. This sense of separateness creates the illusion that we are distinct from others, from nature, and even from the divine. This dualistic view is at the heart of human suffering, as it fosters attachment, fear, and ego. However, through deep spiritual practice and self-realization, the yogi transcends this illusion and directly experiences the non-dual nature of reality.

The essence of *Advaita* is that the universe is a unified field of consciousness. What appears as separate entities—whether people, objects, or natural phenomena—are, in truth, expressions of one underlying reality, which is pure consciousness or the *Brahman*. The realized yogi sees this unity everywhere and in everything. They understand that the body, mind, and the material world are transient and ever-changing, while the *Atman*, the individual soul, is identical with the *Brahman*, the supreme, unchanging consciousness.

The *Mandukya Upanishad* (7) expresses this non-dual realization through the concept of *Turiya*, the "fourth state of consciousness." It states, "That which is indescribable, beyond all thought and speech, the blissful, non-dual self, that is the fourth state (Turiya)." In this verse, *Turiya* represents the ultimate state of awareness, which transcends the three ordinary states of consciousness—waking, dreaming, and deep sleep. In *Turiya*, the yogi abides in a state of pure, undivided awareness, where the distinctions between the observer, the observed, and the act of observation disappear.

This non-dual awareness is beyond intellectual understanding; it is an experiential state that arises when the mind becomes still, and the ego dissolves. The yogi, having transcended the limitations of thought and speech, rests in the direct experience of the *Self* as one with all that exists. This state is often described as "blissful" because it is free from the suffering caused by duality. The yogi no longer experiences the ups and downs of life as separate events affecting an individual ego; instead, they see everything as part of the play (*Lila*) of divine consciousness, perfect and whole in every moment.

In the state of *Advaita*, the yogi sees the divine in everything. There is no longer a sense of separateness between themselves and other beings, between the individual and the universe. This realization leads to spontaneous compassion and love for all living creatures, as the yogi understands that harming another is equivalent to harming oneself. The boundaries that once divided people, races, species, and even life forms dissolve in the light of non-dual awareness.

An example of a realized yogi who lived in the state of non-duality is Ramakrishna Paramahamsa. Ramakrishna often spoke of experiencing the oneness of all beings and the universe, seeing no distinction between himself and others. He would enter states of deep ecstasy, where he perceived the divine in everything around him, from the smallest blade of grass to the infinite cosmos. His teachings on the unity of all religions also reflect his realization of non-duality, as he saw all spiritual paths as leading to the same ultimate truth.

The famous **double-slit experiment**, a cornerstone of quantum mechanics, offers profound insights not just in physics but also in the realm of spirituality. In the experiment, when light or particles such as electrons are shot through two slits, they behave like waves, creating an interference pattern on a screen behind the slits. However, when the particles are observed or measured, they behave like particles, with no interference pattern. This raises a fundamental question: How can the act of observation change the behaviour of particles?

From a spiritual perspective, the double-slit experiment reveals the deep interconnectedness between consciousness and reality. It suggests that the universe does not operate in a fixed, objective manner but is deeply influenced by the observer. In spirituality, this aligns with the idea that **consciousness creates reality**, a concept echoed in many ancient teachings. The way particles behave differently when observed mirrors the understanding that **our awareness shapes our experiences**. Just as the particles change from waves to particles, our perceptions, thoughts, and intentions influence the world around us, blurring the boundary between the observer and the observed.

Furthermore, the experiment invites reflection on the nature of **duality and unity**, a recurring theme in spiritual thought. The particle-wave duality can be seen as a metaphor for the dualities we perceive in life—light and dark, self and other, matter and spirit. However, when we observe the system as a whole, the dualities dissolve, revealing a deeper **unity**. In spiritual terms, this could symbolize the **oneness of existence** beyond the apparent separations we experience through our senses. It speaks to the idea that at the most fundamental level, **everything is interconnected**, and reality is a manifestation of the same underlying energy or consciousness. Thus, the double-slit experiment becomes not just a scientific puzzle but a profound window into the mysteries of existence.

Common Myths or Misconceptions About the Traits of a Realized Yogi

1. Detachment from All Emotions

Myth: A realized yogi is completely detached from all emotions and never feels joy, sadness, or compassion. **Reality:** A realized yogi experiences emotions but is not controlled by them. Their sense of inner peace remains undisturbed, even in the face of emotions.

2. Complete Withdrawal from the World

Myth: Realized yogis abandon all worldly responsibilities and live in complete isolation. **Reality:** While some may choose a reclusive life, many realized beings engage with the world, contributing to society with wisdom, compassion, and service, but without attachment.

3. Miraculous Powers (Siddhis)

Myth: All realized yogis possess supernatural powers like telepathy, levitation, or healing. **Reality:** While spiritual progress can lead to siddhis, they are often seen as distractions from the true goal of self-realization. True yogis rarely use or display such powers, focusing instead on inner freedom.

4. Constant Meditation and Inactivity

Myth: Realized yogis spend all their time in meditation, doing nothing else. **Reality:** A yogi may meditate regularly, but they can also be active and fully present in daily life. The key is that their actions come from a place of awareness and equanimity, not compulsion.

5. Renunciation of Material Possessions

Myth: Realized yogis must give up all material wealth and live in poverty. **Reality:** Realized beings may or may not renounce possessions. What matters is their inner detachment. They do not cling to or define themselves by material wealth.

6. Eternal Calmness and No Problems

Myth: A realized yogi is always calm and never faces challenges. **Reality:** While a realized yogi maintains inner peace, they may still encounter challenges in life. The difference is in their response—they handle difficulties with wisdom and acceptance.

7. Strict Adherence to Ascetic Practices

Myth: A realized yogi must follow strict ascetic practices like fasting, celibacy, and extreme discipline. **Reality:** Realization is not dependent on rigid practices. A realized yogi transcends the need for outward austerities, though they may adopt such practices for their inner discipline.

8. Being Serious and Stern All the Time

Myth: Realized yogis are always serious, somber, and devoid of a sense of humour. **Reality:** Many realized beings exhibit joy, humour, and playfulness. Their lightness comes from being free of ego and worldly attachments.

9. No Need for Physical Body Care

Myth: A realized yogi is indifferent to their body and health. **Reality:** A yogi may be unattached to the body but understands the importance of maintaining it as a vehicle for spiritual practice. They often live in balance, practicing moderation.

10. Immunity to Suffering or Pain

Myth: A realized yogi does not experience physical or mental pain. **Reality:** Realized yogis are not immune to suffering or pain, but they view it with detachment, without identifying with the suffering. They see it as part of the transient nature of the world.

11. Unwavering in a Single Path or Teaching

Myth: A realized yogi must strictly follow one path, tradition, or teacher. **Reality:** Realized yogis transcend specific traditions or teachings, understanding the essence behind them. They may respect and learn from multiple paths, seeing the unity in all.

12. Constant Bliss State

Myth: A realized yogi is always in a state of bliss and ecstasy. **Reality:** A yogi may experience bliss, but more importantly, they live in a state of inner stillness, peace, and contentment that transcends both pleasure and pain.

13. No Family or Social Life

Myth: Realized yogis must leave their families and live an isolated spiritual life. **Reality:** Many realized yogis live within families and social systems. The key difference is their inner non-attachment, allowing them to remain unaffected by worldly relationships.

14. Rigid Moral Codes

Myth: A realized yogi must strictly follow a rigid code of morality or ethical conduct. **Reality:** While realized beings naturally live virtuous lives, their morality is guided by inner wisdom rather than strict external codes. They act spontaneously, based on the context and moment.

15. Beyond Physical Appearance and Health

Myth: Realized yogis neglect their appearance or hygiene as a sign of detachment. **Reality:** Some yogis may care little for appearances, but realization does not require such neglect. Many live hygienically and presentably, knowing that external appearance is irrelevant to their state of being.

16. Immediate Perfection Upon Realization

Myth: The moment someone becomes a realized yogi, they are instantly perfect in all aspects of life. **Reality:** Realization brings inner awakening, but external habits and behaviours may take time to harmonize with the newfound understanding. The integration process can be gradual.

17. Free from Karma

Myth: A realized yogi is free from all past karma and its effects. **Reality:** While a realized yogi is no longer bound by karma or identified with it, the effects of past actions (prarabdha karma) may still play out in their life. However, they remain unaffected and detached.

18. Must Renounce All Desires

Myth: A realized yogi has no desires whatsoever. **Reality:** A yogi may transcend personal, ego-driven desires, but they may still act on universal or compassionate desires, such as helping others or spreading knowledge. These are not based on selfish needs.

19. Never Makes Mistakes

Myth: A realized yogi never makes mistakes or errors in judgment. **Reality:** While realized beings have a higher level of awareness, they can still make practical mistakes in day-to-day life. Realization does not eliminate human fallibility in practical matters.

20. Is Always Young and Physically Strong

Myth: A realized yogi always appears youthful and immune to aging or illness. **Reality:** A yogi's body follows the natural laws of aging and deterioration, but their inner spirit remains free from the limitations of the body. They accept aging and illness without attachment.

21. Complete Control Over All Bodily Functions

Myth: Realized yogis can control every aspect of their body, including breath, heart rate, and digestion at will. **Reality:** Some yogis may develop such control through specific yogic practices, but realization itself does not depend on this. Inner peace and self-realization are independent of physical control.

22. Never Needs Sleep or Food

Myth: A realized yogi transcends basic human needs like sleep and food. **Reality:** While some realized beings may require less sleep or food, they still live within the limitations of the human body. They may practice moderation, but they respect the body's needs.

23. Speaks Only in Parables or Mystical Language

Myth: Realized yogis only speak in cryptic, mystical language, using parables or metaphors. **Reality:** Many realized beings speak clearly and practically, addressing the needs of those around them in plain language. Their wisdom is not about mystery, but about clear understanding.

24. Never Feels Physical Pain

Myth: Realized yogis are immune to physical pain and discomfort. **Reality:** They can experience physical pain like anyone else, but their reaction to pain is different. They don't identify with the pain or suffer psychologically from it, as they understand it as transient.

25. Must Be Celibate

Myth: A realized yogi must be celibate and avoid all forms of sexual expression. **Reality:** While some yogis choose celibacy as part of their path, realization itself is not dependent on celibacy. A realized being may live a balanced life that includes healthy relationships if aligned with their dharma.

26. Free from All Thoughts

Myth: A realized yogi's mind is completely free from all thoughts. **Reality:** Thoughts may still arise in the mind of a realized yogi, but they do not identify with or become entangled in those thoughts. They remain a witness to the mind's activities, rooted in stillness.

27. Possesses a Fixed, Rigid Personality

Myth: Realized yogis have a fixed, predictable personality—either serene, serious, or rigid. **Reality:** Realized beings often have dynamic, unique personalities that are shaped by their individual nature (prakriti). They are fluid and spontaneous, adjusting their responses to different situations.

28. Must Follow a Specific Religion or Tradition

Myth: A realized yogi must belong to a specific religious tradition or follow a certain lineage. **Reality:** Realization transcends religious or cultural boundaries. While some may follow traditional practices, others may not identify with any particular religion, seeing the truth in all paths.

29. Exhibits a Halo or Aura of Light

Myth: A realized yogi is always surrounded by a visible aura or halo of light. **Reality:** While some spiritual traditions describe energetic changes, realization is an inner state of consciousness and does not necessarily manifest as a physical aura. Any outer signs are secondary.

30. Always Silent or Monosyllabic

Myth: Realized yogis prefer silence and speak very little. **Reality:** Some yogis may value silence, but many engage in meaningful conversations and teachings. Their words, however, are often intentional and come from a place of wisdom, rather than idle chatter.

31. Does Not Require Learning or Knowledge

Myth: Once realized, a yogi no longer needs to learn anything new. **Reality:** Realized beings may continue to expand their understanding of the world. They might still read, learn, or seek knowledge, not from a place of ego, but out of natural curiosity or to aid others.

32. Must Always Be in a Meditative Posture

Myth: A realized yogi must constantly be in a meditative posture or display formal yoga postures (asanas). **Reality:** Realized beings can be in any posture—walking, sitting, or lying down—because their awareness is not tied to a particular physical stance. Meditation for them is an ongoing inner state, not just a formal practice.

33. Must Adhere to Traditional Rituals

Myth: A realized yogi must perform traditional rituals or ceremonies to maintain their spiritual state. **Reality:** While some yogis may continue with rituals for their symbolic value, realization is not dependent on external rituals. Many realized beings focus on the direct experience of truth rather than formal practices.

34. Indifferent to the Suffering of Others

Myth: A realized yogi remains indifferent to the suffering of others because they are detached. **Reality:** Realized yogis often exhibit great compassion and care deeply about alleviating suffering. Their detachment means they do not get entangled in the emotional turbulence, but they act out of compassion and wisdom.

35. Must Be a Guru or Spiritual Teacher

Myth: Every realized yogi automatically becomes a spiritual teacher or guru with followers. **Reality:** Not all realized yogis take on the role of a teacher. Some may choose to remain private, without seeking followers or teaching. Realization doesn't necessitate public roles or recognition.

36. Lack of Free Will

Myth: A realized yogi has no free will and is completely surrendered to divine will at all times. **Reality:** A realized yogi acts in harmony with the flow of life and the universe, but this doesn't mean they are incapable of making decisions. Their choices are aligned with a deeper wisdom, rather than egoic desires.

37. Total Rejection of Pleasure or Enjoyment

Myth: A realized yogi completely rejects all forms of physical or sensory pleasure. **Reality:** Realization does not require rejecting pleasure; it simply means not being attached to it. A yogi may enjoy food, art, or other pleasures of life but does so with awareness and non-attachment, without seeking fulfillment through them.

38. Must Look a Certain Way (Long Hair, Beads, Robes, etc.)

Myth: A realized yogi has a distinct appearance, such as wearing robes, growing long hair, or adorning themselves with beads. **Reality:** There is no specific external appearance that defines a realized being. They can look like anyone else, and their realization has nothing to do with their outward dress or physical appearance.

39. Experiences Constant Ecstatic States

Myth: A realized yogi is always in an ecstatic or mystical state of divine union. **Reality:** While yogis may experience moments of ecstasy, they more commonly live in a state of equanimity and inner peace. Realization is not about constant highs, but rather deep inner stability, beyond emotional extremes.

40. Must Renounce All Human Relationships

Myth: A realized yogi must give up all personal relationships, including family and friends, to maintain their spiritual purity. **Reality:** Many realized beings maintain relationships, but they approach them with a sense of detachment and compassion. They don't see relationships as sources of personal fulfillment but rather as part of life's natural flow.

41. Can Never Experience Fear

Myth: A realized yogi is completely free from fear and never experiences it under any circumstances. **Reality:** While a realized yogi may not be dominated by fear, they might still experience moments of fear. The difference lies in their response—they do not identify with or get caught up in it, remaining calm and aware even in challenging situations.

42. Always Has a Dramatic Awakening Experience

Myth: A realized yogi has a dramatic or mystical experience of awakening, like a sudden flash of light or vision. **Reality:** For many, realization is a subtle, gradual unfolding rather than a single, dramatic event. The journey to realization varies for each person, and not all have a profound or mystical awakening moment.

43. A Realized Yogi Has a Superhuman IQ

Myth: A realized yogi possesses extraordinary intellectual abilities, with a genius-level IQ, capable of understanding complex subjects effortlessly. **Reality:** Realization is about spiritual wisdom, not necessarily intellectual brilliance. A realized yogi may or may not have a high IQ or academic knowledge. Spiritual insight is often beyond intellectual understanding, relying on direct experience rather than mental analysis.

44. A Realized Yogi Must Have High EQ to Attain Realization

Myth: One must have high emotional intelligence (EQ)—such as being exceptionally empathetic, socially aware, or emotionally balanced—to become realized. **Reality:** While EQ can aid in understanding oneself and others, realization is not dependent on any particular level of emotional intelligence. It transcends both IQ and EQ, focusing instead on direct knowledge of the Self and freedom from egoic identification.

45. Realization Automatically Enhances IQ and EQ

Myth: Attaining realization will automatically elevate a person's IQ and EQ, making them intellectually sharper and emotionally more intelligent. **Reality:** Realization does not necessarily improve one's IQ or EQ. It brings inner clarity and detachment, which can help one respond wisely to life, but it doesn't directly affect intellectual or emotional capacities. Some yogis may exhibit simple, non-academic wisdom, while others might show heightened emotional empathy, depending on their personality.

24

Jivanmukta and Videhamukta: The Liberated Souls

In the rich spiritual traditions of Vedanta, the concept of liberation (moksha) is the ultimate goal of human existence. Liberation can be achieved while still living in the body, known as *Jivanmukti*, or after leaving the body, known as *Videhamukti*. These two states of liberation, though distinct, represent the pinnacle of spiritual realization, where one transcends the cycle of birth and death (samsara).

Jivanmukta: The Liberated While Living

A *Jivanmukta* is an individual who has attained liberation (moksha) while still living in the physical body, fully liberated from the cycle of birth and death. This state of spiritual freedom transcends worldly dualities and limitations. According to the *Vivekachudamani* (Verse 429) by Adi Shankaracharya, "The Jivanmukta is free from egoism, remains calm, and is unaffected by external circumstances. He is beyond desires and acts with pure wisdom." The realization of the Self, or *Atman*, brings an end to the identification with the body-mind complex, allowing the Jivanmukta to live in the world without being of the world.

For the Jivanmukta, the notion of individuality dissolves, and they experience their oneness with the infinite consciousness (*Brahman*). Even though they continue to engage with the physical world, they do so from a state of total detachment. They witness the world as a passing play of forms and phenomena, fully aware that their true nature is the unchanging, eternal Self.

Scientific Perspective on Self-Realization

Modern research on advanced meditation practitioners offers a glimpse into the neurological changes associated with deep spiritual states, such as those experienced by a Jivanmukta. Studies using brain imaging techniques, such as fMRI and EEG, reveal significant alterations in areas of the brain related to self-referential processing and emotional regulation. In particular, the default mode network (DMN), which is active when the mind is focused on self-oriented thoughts, shows reduced activity during meditation and self-realization experiences. This reduction in self-referential activity mirrors the experience of non-attachment, a key trait of the Jivanmukta, as they transcend the egoic mind.

These findings suggest that the state of *turiya*—the fourth state of consciousness described in the Upanishads, beyond waking, dreaming, and deep sleep—is not just a mystical ideal but has tangible correlates in brain function. For the Jivanmukta, this realization of non-duality translates into a neurological experience where the ego-based mind subsides, and the universal Self shines forth.

Videehamukta: The Liberated After Death

A *Videhamukta* is one who attains liberation after the death of the physical body, achieving ultimate freedom from the cycle of birth, death, and rebirth (*samsara*). In this state, the soul merges completely with *Brahman*, the infinite and unchanging reality, and loses all sense of individual identity. Unlike the *Jivanmukta*, who experiences liberation while still alive, the *Videhamukta* realizes liberation only upon leaving the physical body.

This form of liberation is marked by the dissolution of the soul's remaining subtle attachments to the material world, allowing it to become one with the infinite. The *Mundaka Upanishad* (3.2.9) describes the state of *Videhamukti* through a powerful metaphor: "As rivers, flowing down, merge in the ocean, losing their name and form, so a wise man, freed from name and form, attains the Supreme Being." Here, the river represents the individual soul, which, after its journey through life, loses its distinct identity and merges into the boundless ocean of *Brahman*, the supreme reality.

The Journey Toward Videhamukti

In the process of spiritual evolution, one progresses through various stages of understanding and detachment. While a *Jivanmukta* experiences enlightenment while still embodied, a *Videhamukta* may not attain full realization until the soul departs from the physical form. At the moment of death, all remaining traces of ego, individuality, and worldly attachment are dissolved, allowing the soul to merge into the undivided consciousness of *Brahman*. This final liberation represents the soul's complete and irreversible escape from the cycle of *samsara*.

The *Videhamukta* experiences a state beyond description, beyond even the conceptual limits of bliss or peace. The realized soul, having transcended the limitations of time, space, and causality, is absorbed into the eternal, formless essence of existence. There is no return to the world of duality, no rebirth, and no further individual experience. The soul's journey is complete as it becomes one with the Absolute.

One of the most well-known figures to have attained *Videhamukti* is the sage Yajnavalkya, revered in the *Brihadaranyaka Upanishad*. Yajnavalkya was a great teacher of Vedanta and imparted the highest knowledge of Self-realization to his disciples, revealing the nature of *Atman* and *Brahman*. After completing his earthly duties and imparting the final wisdom to his students, Yajnavalkya renounced his body and merged with the infinite. His example illustrates the path of *Videhamukti*—where a fully realized sage, though enlightened in life, finally dissolves completely into the formless Absolute at the time of death.

Merging with Brahman

The imagery used in the *Mundaka Upanishad* likens the state of *Videhamukti* to rivers flowing into the ocean, losing their individuality in the vastness of the waters. This poetic metaphor beautifully illustrates the process of dissolution that occurs when the soul, having shed its final attachments, returns to its source, Brahman.

In this state, the liberated soul no longer retains any individual identity, name, or form. All attributes that previously defined the soul in the realm of duality—such as desires, fears, and even the notion of personal existence—are dissolved. What remains is pure consciousness, beyond the dualities of life and death, existence and non-existence.

Videhamukti and Liberation Beyond the Physical World

In contrast to the *Jivanmukta*, who functions as a realized being while still interacting with the physical world, the *Videhamukta* is freed from all limitations of physical embodiment. Liberation after death is the soul's final emancipation from the laws of karma and the rebirth cycle. There is no further return to the physical or astral planes of existence.

The soul's individual journey through the illusion of *maya* ends, and it dissolves back into the ultimate reality, where there is no distinction between subject and object, self and other.

In essence, *Videhamukti* is the final destination for those who have realized their true nature but whose ultimate merging with Brahman occurs upon death.

Spiritual Implications

The path to liberation—whether through *Jivanmukti* or *Videhamukti*—is the ultimate culmination of a spiritual seeker's journey. Both states are deeply intertwined with the realization of the Self, or *Atman*, as the non-dual, infinite consciousness that transcends the physical and mental realms. The realization of this truth lies at the heart of liberation in the teachings of Vedanta and various spiritual traditions.

Transcending the Ego: The Path to Liberation

The core of liberation in both *Jivanmukti* and *Videhamukti* lies in transcending the individual ego and realizing one's true nature as the eternal Self, which is identical to *Brahman*, the universal consciousness. The *Mandukya Upanishad* (7) captures the essence of this non-dual realization, stating that *Turiya*, the fourth state of consciousness, is beyond waking, dreaming, and deep sleep. It is the state of pure awareness, where one recognizes that there is no separation between the individual and the universal consciousness. Whether this realization occurs in life or upon death, it leads to the end of all suffering and the dissolution of the ego.

The *Mandukya Upanishad* emphasizes, "There is no second. This is the Self." This direct recognition that one's true essence is non-dual, eternal, and formless is the gateway to liberation. The seeker must transcend identification with the body, mind, emotions, and individual ego to experience unity with the infinite. The *Jivanmukta* does this while living, and the *Videhamukta* achieves this upon death.

Modern research on near-death experiences (NDEs) reveals intriguing parallels with ancient concepts of *Videhamukti* (liberation after death). Many NDE accounts describe merging with an overwhelming light, encountering a vast consciousness, or losing individuality—echoing scriptural descriptions of *Videhamukti*.

For instance, NDEs often include feelings of unity with everything or encounters with a "brilliant light" symbolizing love and truth. This mirrors the *Mundaka Upanishad*'s portrayal of the *Videhamukta* merging with infinite reality, much like rivers losing form in the ocean. Such experiences suggest that death may offer glimpses of liberation, aligning with the idea of *Videhamukti* as the dissolution of ego.

Additionally, NDEs often involve deep peace, detachment from the body, and a sense of non-dual consciousness, highlighting the overlap between spiritual teachings and modern understandings of death and consciousness.

Fear of Moksha

The fear of moksha, merging with Brahman, or *Videhamukti* often stems from the perception of a total loss of individuality, personality, and sense of self. Here are a few perspectives on why this fear arises and how it might be addressed:

Fear of Annihilation of Self

For many, the thought of merging with Brahman seems like a loss of identity. People fear the dissolution of their individual "I" or ego because it feels like erasure, as if their personal experiences, memories, and even consciousness will disappear into nothingness. Addressing this fear often involves recognizing that moksha or merging is not an annihilation but a return to an original, ever-present reality, the pure consciousness that underlies everything.

In the teachings of the Ashtavakra Gita, it's explained that the individual soul (Atman) and Brahman are not truly separate. Rather than being "lost," the self is realized in its truest, most expansive form, beyond limitations, beyond personal suffering, and beyond the ego's concerns. This realization can bring a sense of relief and freedom, rather than fear.

Fear of Letting Go of Attachments

Human nature tends to cling to attachments—relationships, possessions, and even worldly achievements. Moksha signifies a liberation from these attachments, which can seem intimidating because it asks for a detachment from the life and people one cherishes. However, understanding moksha as a deepening love that encompasses everything without grasping can help ease this fear. True liberation doesn't eliminate love but transforms it into a universal, all-encompassing love that transcends individual attachment. This is about expanding one's capacity to love without conditions, without attachment to a particular form.

Misinterpretation of "Void" or "Emptiness"

Some people interpret moksha or merging with Brahman as an entry into a void or emptiness. This can lead to the assumption that moksha results in a state of non-existence. However, Vedantic teachings and texts like the Ashtavakra Gita clarify that moksha is not a nihilistic state. It is, instead, a state of fullness and ultimate reality. The "emptiness" here is often better understood as the absence of ego-driven desires and the suffering they bring. Brahman is fullness, wholeness, and the source of all joy—realizing that merging is into this boundless awareness rather than a void can alleviate the sense of fear.

The Ego's Resistance

The ego thrives on separateness and individuality, so the concept of merging with an all-encompassing oneness can feel like its own "death." It might try to resist the idea of moksha because it doesn't want to relinquish control. But spiritual growth involves understanding that the ego's concerns are transitory. With practices like meditation and self-inquiry, individuals often discover that their true essence—Atman—is untouched by the ego's limitations, fears, and insecurities. Reassuring oneself that moksha is not the ego's end but a realization of a deeper self can create a shift in perspective, making the goal of merging feel safe rather than threatening.

The Unknown and Loss of the Familiar

Moksha represents an ultimate unknown that the human mind can't fully conceptualize. It's natural to feel some trepidation when approaching something so incomprehensible. However, texts like the

Bhagavad Gita and Ashtavakra Gita teach that merging with Brahman is an "unknown" only to the limited mind and not to the true self. By cultivating trust in this unknown, individuals can surrender the mind's fears and embrace moksha as a return home to one's own essence.

Addressing these fears often requires understanding that the path to moksha is not about abandoning or erasing one's life or personality. It's about shedding layers that obscure the reality of our true, infinite nature. Practicing self-inquiry and engaging with teachings that illuminate these truths, like the Ashtavakra Gita, can gradually help one let go of the fear of merging and cultivate a deep desire for liberation.

25

God

The concept of God has been at the heart of human contemplation and spirituality for millennia. Across cultures and civilizations, God represents the ultimate source of creation, sustenance, and dissolution of the universe, often seen as the force that governs all existence. While the characteristics, names, and forms attributed to God vary across religious and philosophical traditions, the core understanding remains consistent: God is the absolute, eternal, and unchanging truth that transcends human understanding and the physical realm.

Throughout history, people have sought to comprehend the divine, often framing God as omnipotent (all-powerful), omniscient (all-knowing), and omnipresent (present everywhere). These attributes reflect humanity's deep yearning to connect with a reality beyond the material world, one that offers meaning, guidance, and a foundation for the order of the cosmos. Yet, this divine essence is often seen as ineffable—beyond the grasp of words or intellect—leading to a variety of interpretations that reflect cultural, geographical, and historical influences.

In some traditions, God is conceived as a personal being, one who listens to prayers, intervenes in human affairs, and establishes moral laws. In others, God is understood as an abstract, formless principle, the ultimate ground of being that is impersonal and beyond any human attributes. Whether personal or impersonal, the divine is almost always viewed as the source from which all life originates and to which it ultimately returns.

In **Hinduism**, the concept of God is both expansive and intricate, reflecting the diversity of beliefs within the tradition. At its core, God is seen as both an impersonal, all-encompassing absolute reality, **Brahman**, and as a personal deity who manifests in various forms to maintain cosmic balance. The **Trimurti**—Brahma (the Creator), Vishnu (the Preserver), and Shiva (the Destroyer)—represents the cyclical nature of creation, preservation, and destruction, essential to the rhythm of the universe.

However, Hinduism also embraces the worship of personal gods and goddesses, such as **Krishna**, **Rama**, **Durga**, and many others, each of whom embodies different qualities and aspects of the divine. Devotion to these deities varies according to individual preference and sectarian tradition, yet all paths ultimately lead to the same truth. The ultimate goal for many Hindus is to realize their unity with **Brahman**, transcending the illusion of separateness (Maya) and attaining spiritual liberation (Moksha).

In exploring the concept of God, we are drawn into the deepest mysteries of existence, touching upon profound questions about creation, purpose, and the nature of reality. These questions have shaped not only religious doctrines but also the philosophical inquiries of countless thinkers across time. Though the interpretations of God are many, the search for the divine—whether through prayer, meditation, or intellectual inquiry—remains a common thread that weaves through the tapestry of human experience.

God in Patanjali Yog Sutra

In Patanjali's *Yoga Sutra*, the concept of God (*Ishvara*) plays a distinctive role, particularly in the context of devotion, surrender, and self-realization. However, Patanjali's view of God differs from the traditional theistic understanding seen in other Hindu texts. Here's how *Ishvara* is presented in the *Yoga Sutra*:

1. Ishvara as a Special Purusha (Spirit)

Patanjali introduces the idea of *Ishvara* in **Sutra 1.24**: "*Ishvara* is a special kind of Purusha (Spirit), untouched by afflictions, actions, the fruits of actions, or desires."

Unlike ordinary souls (*purushas*), *Ishvara* is free from the influence of karma and suffering (*kleshas*). *Ishvara* is eternal, pure, and unaffected by the cycles of birth and rebirth.

2. Ishvara as a Symbol of Perfection

For Patanjali, *Ishvara* serves as an ideal, a symbol of perfect purity, omniscience, and self-liberation. It is not necessary to worship *Ishvara* in a traditional religious sense, but meditating on this concept helps the practitioner focus on the ultimate goal of self-realization.

Ishvara is viewed as a model or archetype for spiritual aspirants, showing what is achievable when one transcends the limitations of the ego and the mind.

3. Ishvara Pranidhana (Surrender to God)

In **Sutra 1.23**, Patanjali highlights one of the practical aspects of *Ishvara*: "*Ishvara Pranidhana*" — surrender to the will of *Ishvara* or complete dedication to the divine, as a means to achieve *samadhi* (self-realization or enlightenment).

Ishvara Pranidhana is one of the **Niyamas** (ethical disciplines) outlined in the second chapter of the *Yoga Sutra*. By surrendering to a higher power, one lets go of the ego and attachments, facilitating the path of liberation.

4. Om as the Representation of Ishvara

Sutra 1.27 states the sound or symbol of *Ishvara* is the syllable *Om* (*Praṇava*).

Chanting or meditating on the sound of *Om* connects the practitioner with the divine and purifies the mind, helping in the concentration needed for higher states of meditation.

5. Ishvara as a Path to Samadhi

Patanjali suggests that meditating on *Ishvara* is one of the methods for attaining *samadhi* (superconsciousness). While the *Yoga Sutra* offers various methods for spiritual progress, such as self-discipline, concentration, and knowledge, the practice of surrendering to *Ishvara* is a devotional path, relying on the grace of the divine for liberation.

6. God in the Context of the Non-Theistic Framework

It's important to note that while Patanjali acknowledges *Ishvara*, the *Yoga Sutra* does not insist on a purely theistic approach. The text offers various non-theistic methods for attaining liberation, the eightfold path (*Ashtanga Yoga*).

Patanjali's approach is flexible, recognizing *Ishvara* as one path among many that a practitioner can take. His system of *yoga* is open to both theists and non-theists alike.

God in Vedanta

In Vedanta, God is fundamentally understood as *Brahman*, the ultimate, indivisible reality that transcends all dualities of existence. Brahman is described as *nirguna* (without attributes) and *nirakara* (without form), indicating its boundless and incomprehensible nature. This infinite consciousness pervades all that exists, yet remains beyond the grasp of the senses or intellect. The Taittiriya Upanishad (2.1) famously defines Brahman as "Satyam Jnanam Anantam Brahma," which translates to truth, knowledge, and infinity. This description highlights the essence of Brahman: an eternal, omniscient, and limitless reality that forms the substratum of everything in the universe.

Vedanta asserts that Brahman is both *immanent* and *transcendent*. Immanence means that Brahman resides within every atom, every being, and every experience. Transcendence signifies that Brahman exists beyond all realms of time, space, and causality, untouched by the material world. Thus, Brahman is at once the deepest core of our existence and the unchanging reality that underlies the entire cosmos.

The Mandukya Upanishad (6) introduces the concept of *Turiya*, the "fourth state" of consciousness, which represents the pure awareness that transcends the waking, dreaming, and deep sleep states. This Turiya is not inward-turned or outward-facing; it is the all-encompassing, serene state of consciousness itself. As the verse says, "That which is beyond all states, the Supreme, is called Turiya. It is neither inward nor outward consciousness, but the pure consciousness that is God." In this way, Vedanta teaches that to realize God is to awaken to our true nature, which is none other than this unconditioned, infinite consciousness.

Sri Ramakrishna – a great mystic of the 19th century, deeply immersed in Vedanta – had direct experiences of this ultimate reality. He described Brahman as an "ocean of consciousness," vast, infinite, and boundless, in which all names and forms dissolve. Ramakrishna's life illustrates the profound harmony between the impersonal formless Brahman and the personal deity. His spiritual experiences ranged from seeing God as *Kali* or *Krishna* (personal forms) to experiencing Brahman in its formless essence. Through his life and teachings, he demonstrated the coexistence of the various dimensions of divine reality.

God in Ashtavakra Gita

The *Ashtavakra Gita*, my absolute favourite, is a profound dialogue between the sage Ashtavakra and King Janaka, focuses on the nature of the Self (*Atman*), pure consciousness, and the ultimate reality (*Brahman*), rather than worshiping or surrendering to a deity. The text is a profound exposition of Advaita Vedanta (non-duality), which teaches that the Self and the Absolute are one and the same.

Here's how the concept of God is understood in the *Ashtavakra Gita*:

1. God as Non-Dual Reality (Brahman)

In the *Ashtavakra Gita*, the ultimate truth is non-dual (*Advaita*), meaning there is no separation between God, the world, and the individual. Everything is a manifestation of the singular, infinite reality called *Brahman*. This is echoed in several verses, like **Ashtavakra Gita 1.3**: "You are not earth, water, fire, or air. Nor are you space. For liberation, know yourself as pure consciousness, the witness of all these." Here, Ashtavakra emphasizes that the individual is not separate from the elements or the world but is the witness of everything, implying unity with the divine consciousness.

2. The Self as God (Atman = Brahman)

The *Ashtavakra Gita* often teaches that the Self (*Atman*) is none other than *Brahman*, the Absolute. There is no external God to be sought or worshiped because the true nature of the individual is divine. This is clearly articulated in **Ashtavakra Gita 1.11**: "You are pure awareness, the witness of all things. Leave the world of appearances behind and be happy." This verse implies that realizing one's own nature as pure awareness (*Atman*) leads to liberation. In this realization, the distinction between God and individual dissolves.

3. No Need for Rituals or Worship

Unlike many other Hindu texts, the *Ashtavakra Gita* does not emphasize rituals, prayers, or devotion to a personal deity. Instead, it teaches that the ultimate goal is self-realization, the understanding that the Self is infinite and free. **Ashtavakra Gita 1.6** expresses this: Right and wrong, pleasure and pain, exist in the mind, not in you, O all-pervading one. You are neither the doer nor the enjoyer. You are ever free." Here, the idea of God as an external force controlling right and wrong or dictating actions is dismissed. Everything is a play of the mind, and the true Self transcends this duality.

4. God Beyond Form and Qualities (Nirguna Brahman)

The concept of God in the *Ashtavakra Gita* aligns with the idea of *Nirguna Brahman*—God without form or attributes. There is no description of a personal God with specific qualities like compassion, love, or wrath. Instead, God is understood as pure consciousness or the unchanging substratum behind the changing world.

This view is aligned with **Ashtavakra Gita 2.18**: "In me, the limitless ocean, let the waves of the world rise and fall as they will. I am neither enhanced nor diminished." In this metaphor, God is like the vast, infinite ocean (*Brahman*), and the world with its dualities is merely waves that rise and fall without affecting the ocean's essential nature.

5. Liberation through Self-Knowledge, Not Devotion

The path to liberation in the *Ashtavakra Gita* is not through devotion (*bhakti*) or surrender to a higher being, but through the direct realization of one's own true nature. The realization that "I am Brahman" or "I am infinite consciousness" leads to liberation (*moksha*). Ashtavakra's teaching is not concerned with a personal relationship with God but with transcending all duality and merging with the infinite. **Ashtavakra Gita 1.8** says: "Bondage is when the mind longs for something, grieves over something, rejects something, holds on to something, feels happy or angry at something. Liberation is when the mind desires nothing, grieves over nothing, rejects nothing, holds on to nothing, and is no longer happy or angry at anything." This understanding of liberation emphasizes inner realization rather than external worship or seeking favour from a deity.

6. Illusion of Duality (Maya)

The *Ashtavakra Gita* also touches upon the concept of *Maya* (illusion) to explain why individuals feel separated from God. The belief in duality—between the self and God, between creation and creator—is seen as an illusion, and once this illusion is pierced through knowledge, the seeker realizes the oneness of existence. In **Ashtavakra Gita 2.4**, it is written: "You are the one observer of all, and in reality, always free. Your bondage is this: You see the observer as something other than this."

God in Bhakti Traditions

In contrast to the abstract and formless Brahman of Vedanta, the *Bhakti* traditions of Hinduism emphasize a deeply personal relationship with God. In Bhakti, God is seen not merely as an infinite consciousness but as a loving, compassionate, and intimate deity who engages with devotees on a personal level. Gods and Deities such as Krishna, Rama, Shiva, and Devi are seen as accessible and relatable forms of the Divine, each embodying unique attributes that evoke devotion and love in their worshippers.

The Bhagavad Gita (9.22) encapsulates this intimate relationship between God and the devotee: "To those who are constantly devoted and who worship Me with love, I give the understanding by which they can come to Me." This verse beautifully expresses the essence of Bhakti – that God responds to sincere devotion by guiding the devotee on the path of spiritual union. Here, the deity is not remote or aloof but actively participates in the devotee's life, offering wisdom, protection, and grace.

The lives of saints like **Mirabai** demonstrate the power of Bhakti. Mirabai, a 16th-century poet-saint, was wholly devoted to Lord Krishna, whom she worshipped not only as a deity but as her beloved. Despite facing immense societal opposition, including from her own royal family, she remained unwavering in her devotion to Krishna. For her, Krishna was not a distant, impersonal God but her closest companion, her lover, and her eternal refuge. Through her devotional songs and poems, she conveyed her longing for union with Krishna, and these compositions continue to inspire countless devotees on the path of Bhakti.

Thus, in Bhakti, the relationship with God becomes a journey of love, surrender, and personal connection, where the devotee seeks divine union not through intellectual understanding but through heartfelt devotion and surrender.

Shaivism, Vaishnavism, and **Shaktism** are three of the primary traditions within Hinduism, each focused on different aspects of the divine and varying philosophical interpretations. Here's an overview:

1. Shaivism

Focus: Shiva is the supreme deity in Shaivism, revered as the creator, preserver, and destroyer.

Philosophy: Shaivism emphasizes inner transformation, asceticism, and self-knowledge as pathways to liberation. Shiva is often associated with both destruction and creation, signifying the cyclic nature of the universe.

Practices: Rituals include meditation, chanting mantras like "Om Namah Shivaya," and worshiping lingams (symbolic representations of Shiva).

Key Texts: The Shiva Purana, Linga Purana, and certain Upanishads like the Kaivalya Upanishad are foundational texts in Shaivism.

Schools of Thought: Shaivism has many branches, including Kashmir Shaivism, Shaiva Siddhanta, and Nath Shaivism, each offering unique perspectives on the nature of reality, consciousness, and the self.

2. Vaishnavism

Focus: Vishnu is the central deity in Vaishnavism, viewed as the preserver of the universe and often depicted with his consort Lakshmi. His avatars, especially Rama and Krishna, are also venerated.

Philosophy: Vaishnavism often emphasizes devotion (bhakti) as a way to attain closeness with God, underlining the idea of divine compassion and grace.

Practices: Bhakti practices like chanting, temple worship, and participating in festivals (e.g., Janmashtami, the birth of Krishna) are central.

Key Texts: The Bhagavad Gita, Vishnu Purana, and Srimad Bhagavatam are key texts in Vaishnavism. The Ramayana and Mahabharata also play a crucial role.

Schools of Thought: Vaishnavism includes multiple sub-traditions, such as Ramanuja's Vishishtadvaita, Madhva's Dvaita, and Chaitanya Mahaprabhu's Gaudiya Vaishnavism, each proposing different understandings of the relationship between God, soul, and the universe.

3. Shaktism

Focus: Shaktism venerates the Divine Feminine or Shakti, the creative energy that manifests as the goddess in various forms like Durga, Kali, and Parvati.

Philosophy: In Shaktism, Shakti is the ultimate reality and the source of all creation, representing both nurturing and destructive aspects. Liberation is achieved by aligning with this primal energy.

Practices: Shakti worship often involves rituals, recitation of mantras, and participation in festivals (e.g., Navaratri). Some sects may also include tantric practices aimed at awakening inner spiritual energy.

Key Texts: The Devi Mahatmya (from the Markandeya Purana), Devi Bhagavata Purana, and various tantric texts are central to Shaktism.

Schools of Thought: Shaktism includes several branches, such as the Sri Vidya tradition, which focuses on the worship of the goddess Lalita Tripurasundari, and various folk traditions that honour local goddesses.

Each of these traditions embraces distinct approaches to divinity:

- **Shaivism** tends to emphasize renunciation and self-inquiry.

- **Vaishnavism** leans towards devotion and surrender to a personal god.

- **Shaktism** explores the dynamism of divine feminine energy and often incorporates tantric elements.

While followers often choose one tradition, Hinduism allows for an inclusive and pluralistic approach, enabling many to revere deities across these paths.

The Philosophical Perspective: Advaita Vedanta and Dvaita Vedanta

Advaita Vedanta is a non-dualistic school of philosophy that teaches the essential oneness of the individual soul (**Atman**) and the ultimate reality, **Brahman**. According to Advaita, the perception of duality—where the self appears separate from God, the universe, or other beings—is an illusion caused by ignorance (**avidya**). This ignorance is what veils the true nature of reality, leading individuals to identify with the limited ego rather than their infinite, divine essence. The core teaching of Advaita Vedanta is that the Atman is, in reality, none other than Brahman, the infinite, unchanging substratum of all that exists.

One of the most famous declarations in Advaita is **"Aham Brahmasmi"** ("I am Brahman"), from the **Brihadaranyaka Upanishad** (1.4.10). This profound statement encapsulates the heart of Advaita philosophy by affirming that the individual's true nature is not a finite, separate being but the infinite, eternal Brahman. Realizing this truth is the key to attaining **moksha** (liberation) from the cycle of birth and death (**samsara**), as it dissolves the false identification with the ego and the material world.

Advaita Vedanta teaches that **Brahman** is not a distant or external entity but the very essence of all existence. Brahman is described as **Sat-Chit-Ananda: existence, consciousness, and bliss**. The individual, deluded by the illusions of the physical world and personal identity, mistakenly perceives themselves as separate from Brahman. Through the practice of **jnana yoga** (the path of knowledge), **self-inquiry** and **meditation**, one gradually dissolves this ignorance, unveiling the ultimate truth that the Atman is identical to Brahman.

Adi Shankaracharya, the most prominent proponent of Advaita Vedanta, emphasized that once the veil of ignorance is removed, the individual realizes that they are not the limited body or mind but the infinite Brahman. As he wrote in his classic text **Vivekachudamani**, "Brahman is existence, consciousness, and bliss. It is one without a second." In this state of self-realization, all dualities—pleasure and pain, success and failure, birth and death—dissolve, and one experiences the profound unity of all existence.

A central part of Advaita Vedanta's teachings is expressed through the **Mahavakyas** (great sayings) found in the Upanishads. These four Mahavakyas convey the essence of Advaita philosophy and the oneness of Atman and Brahman:

1. **Prajnanam Brahma** (Aitareya Upanishad 3.3) – "Consciousness is Brahman." This Mahavakya emphasizes that pure consciousness, the awareness that illuminates all experiences, is the ultimate reality, Brahman. It teaches that the true nature of everything, beyond form and attributes, is this consciousness.

2. **Aham Brahmasmi** (Brihadaranyaka Upanishad 1.4.10) – "I am Brahman." This Mahavakya declares the identity of the individual self (Atman) with Brahman, the infinite reality. It is a direct statement of non-dual realization, revealing that the true nature of the self is not separate from the absolute.

3. **Tat Tvam Asi** (Chandogya Upanishad 6.8.7) – "That Thou Art." This saying is a teaching given by a guru to his disciple, explaining that the individual is not distinct from the ultimate reality. "That" (Brahman) and "thou" (the individual) are one and the same, underscoring the oneness of all existence.

4. **Ayam Atma Brahma** (Mandukya Upanishad 1.2) – "This Self is Brahman." This Mahavakya reveals that the self, when realized in its true essence, is none other than Brahman. It points to the idea that the innermost self of every being is the absolute, transcendent reality.

These Mahavakyas are not just philosophical concepts but are meant to serve as tools for meditation and spiritual realization. By deeply contemplating these great sayings, one can transcend the illusion of separation and experience the non-dual truth that all is one, and that one is Brahman.

Dvaita Vedanta, in contrast, is a dualistic school of thought, founded by the 13th-century philosopher Madhvacharya. Dvaita emphasizes the eternal and irreconcilable distinction between the individual soul (*Atman*) and God (*Brahman*). According to this philosophy, God is a supreme, personal being who governs the universe, and the soul is eternally subordinate to God. Unlike Advaita, which aims to dissolve the sense of separateness, Dvaita maintains that the individual soul and God are distinct, though intimately connected.

In Dvaita, God is worshipped as a personal deity—most often Vishnu or Krishna—who is omnipotent, omniscient, and the source of all creation. The soul, while separate from God, is dependent on divine grace for liberation. Dvaita places emphasis on devotion (*bhakti*) as the means to attain union with God, not through merging but through eternal service and love. Madhvacharya taught that the ultimate goal of life is not to realize one's identity with Brahman but to cultivate a personal, devotional relationship with God.

These two schools of thought offer contrasting yet complementary paths toward spiritual understanding. While Advaita focuses on realizing the oneness of all existence through self-knowledge, Dvaita encourages devotion to a personal God, emphasizing the soul's dependence on divine grace. Both perspectives provide profound insights into the nature of God and the individual soul, offering seekers different paths to spiritual liberation.

God in Other Traditions

God, or the concept of an ultimate reality, is a universal idea found across many religious traditions, each offering its own distinct understanding of the divine. While the approaches and interpretations vary, the quest for understanding the transcendent nature of existence remains central to spiritual inquiry.

In **Christianity**, God is understood as the omnipotent creator and sustainer of the universe, a divine being who embodies **unconditional love, justice, and omniscience**. Central to Christian belief is the doctrine of the **Trinity**, a unique concept of God as one being in three distinct persons: **God the Father** (the creator and source of all life), **God the Son** (Jesus Christ, the saviour of humanity), and **God the Holy Spirit** (the guide, comforter, and sustainer of believers). This triune nature of God is fundamental to Christian theology, expressing the unity and diversity within the Godhead, while affirming that these three persons are co-equal and co-eternal.

God's love for humanity is the foundation of the Christian faith. According to the **Bible**, particularly in the New Testament, God is described as not only just but also profoundly compassionate, seeking an intimate, personal relationship with His creation. This relationship is characterized by divine love that is sacrificial and redemptive, as exemplified in the life and teachings of **Jesus Christ**. Christians believe that God, through Jesus, entered human history to offer salvation and reconciliation with the divine, addressing the problem of sin and spiritual separation. Jesus' death on the cross is seen as the ultimate expression of God's love, offering forgiveness and the promise of eternal life to those who have faith in Him.

The **teachings of Jesus** emphasize love, mercy, and forgiveness as central to human relationships and as a reflection of God's own nature. He taught that believers should love their neighbours as themselves and even extend love to their enemies, echoing the boundless love that God has for all people. Salvation in Christianity is not earned through human efforts alone but is a gift of grace, accessed through faith in Jesus Christ. By trusting in Jesus' redemptive work, believers are reconciled with God and can experience spiritual renewal and eternal life. Through the presence of the Holy Spirit, Christians are guided, strengthened, and sustained in their faith, empowered to live lives of compassion, humility, and service to others.

Ultimately, in Christianity, God is not distant or abstract, but personal and relational, inviting believers into a deep connection with Him through faith, prayer, and the transformative power of divine love.

In **Islam**, God is known as *Allah*, the one and only supreme being, who is both all-powerful and infinitely merciful. Allah is the creator of the universe and the source of all guidance, as revealed through the Quran, the holy scripture of Islam. Central to Islamic belief is the notion of *tawhid*, or the absolute oneness of God. Allah is without form, beyond human comprehension, and is both imminent (closer than one's jugular vein, as described in the Quran) and transcendent. God's mercy and guidance are emphasized, and through submission (*Islam*) to Allah's will, Muslims aim to live in accordance with divine teachings. The five pillars of Islam (faith, prayer, charity, fasting, and pilgrimage) offer practical means for maintaining this connection with Allah.

Sufism, the mystical branch of Islam, offers a deeply personal and experiential approach to understanding God. For Sufis, the relationship with the divine is not confined to formal worship or distant reverence; rather, it is about seeking an intimate and direct connection with God, one that transcends the boundaries of intellect and ritual. Through practices such as **dhikr** (remembrance of God), **meditation**, poetry, music, and intense devotion, Sufis aim to dissolve the ego and experience an overwhelming sense of unity with the divine. This spiritual journey is often described as a path of love, where the devotee seeks to merge with God, recognizing His presence in every aspect of life and creation.

The ultimate goal in Sufism is not merely to worship God but to attain **fana** (annihilation of the self), where the individual ego dissolves, allowing the seeker to experience **baqa** (eternal existence) in God. This is the realization of oneness, where all distinctions between the self and the divine disappear, and the Sufi perceives the divine essence within and around them. As the 13th-century Sufi poet **Rumi** famously expressed, "You are not a drop in the ocean. You are the entire ocean in a drop." This profound metaphor captures the mystical experience of realizing that the divine is not separate from oneself, but that every person, every soul, contains the essence of God within.

For Sufis, God is not a distant, remote being, but the very essence of existence, permeating every atom, every breath, and every moment. The divine is seen in the beauty of nature, the interconnectedness of all living things, and the love that binds the universe together. Sufism teaches that by purifying the heart and cultivating deep inner awareness, one can recognize the divine in everything and experience true spiritual union with God. This mystical journey is often described as an unfolding of love, where the seeker is both a lover and beloved, eternally drawn toward the infinite.

In **Jainism**, there is no belief in a creator God or an omnipotent deity controlling the universe. Instead, the universe is seen as eternal, self-regulating, and governed by natural laws, operating independently without the need for a divine creator or external force. **Jinas** (also called **Tirthankaras**, meaning "ford-makers") are revered as enlightened beings who have transcended the cycle of birth, death, and rebirth (samsara) through their own rigorous spiritual discipline and self-effort, without any divine intervention. The term "ford-makers" symbolizes their role as spiritual guides who have created a "ford" or passage across the river of samsara, helping others navigate the turbulent waters of existence to attain liberation. While they provide an example and a path for others to follow, they are not worshiped as gods, but rather as teachers and exemplars of spiritual achievement.

Jain philosophy places a profound emphasis on **ahimsa** (non-violence), not only in physical actions but also in thoughts and speech. It teaches that every living being possesses a soul (**jiva**) that is inherently divine, with the potential to attain liberation (**moksha**) by shedding accumulated karma. This liberation is not granted by divine grace but is achieved through the individual's own practice of self-discipline, non-attachment, truth, and rigorous asceticism. Jainism underscores that divinity resides within the soul itself, and through personal effort—rather than relying on external forces or deities—perfection and liberation from the cycle of samsara can be realized.

In **Sikhism**, God is known as **Waheguru**, the supreme, omnipresent reality that is both immanent (present within the world and individuals) and transcendent (beyond physical form and comprehension). **Waheguru** is eternal, formless (**Nirankar**), and beyond human understanding, yet manifests within all of creation. Sikh teachings, particularly those of **Guru Nanak** and subsequent Sikh Gurus, emphasize that God is without gender, beyond physical attributes, and cannot be confined to any particular image or form.

Sikhism emphasizes a personal relationship with Waheguru through **Naam Simran** (meditation on God's name), ethical living, and **seva** (selfless service). The practice of selfless love, equality, and devotion to truth are central to the faith. The **Guru Granth Sahib,** the central religious scripture of Sikhism, serves as the eternal Guru, guiding Sikhs towards spiritual wisdom and connection with Waheguru. The essence of Sikh spirituality is that God can be realized through inner contemplation, virtuous actions, and a commitment to justice, compassion, and humility.

Buddhism, unlike many other spiritual traditions, does not center on the belief in a creator God. Instead, its teachings focus on understanding the nature of reality and achieving liberation through the path of self-realization. At the heart of Buddhism is the concept of **Nirvana,** the ultimate state of liberation from **dukkha** (suffering) and the endless cycle of **samsara**—the repetitive cycle of birth, death, and rebirth. Rather than seeking the grace or intervention of a divine being, Buddhists aim to understand and transcend the fundamental causes of suffering by following the teachings of the **Buddha.**

In Buddhism, the goal of spiritual practice is **enlightenment,** which involves realizing the impermanent and interconnected nature of all things. This realization leads to the dissolution of the ego and the abandonment of attachments to worldly desires and illusions. **Nirvana** is often described as a state of profound inner peace, freedom from suffering, and the cessation of all karmic cycles. It is not seen as a place but rather as a transformative experience that marks the end of ignorance and the attainment of ultimate wisdom.

While early **Theravada Buddhism** focuses primarily on the individual's path to enlightenment, **Mahayana Buddhism** offers a more expansive view, incorporating compassion for all beings as central to the path. In Mahayana practices, especially in traditions such as **Pure Land** and **Zen**, devotion to enlightened beings known as **Bodhisattvas** plays a significant role. Bodhisattvas are compassionate beings who, having attained enlightenment, choose to remain within the cycle of samsara to help others reach Nirvana. In the **Pure Land** tradition, for example, devotees seek rebirth in the Pure Land, a realm overseen by the Bodhisattva **Amitabha**, where attaining enlightenment is made easier. In **Zen Buddhism**, while the emphasis is on direct, personal experience of reality through meditation, the guidance of Bodhisattvas or enlightened teachers is still honoured.

In Buddhism, although there is no personal deity to be worshipped, the teachings offer a clear and practical path to understanding the ultimate nature of existence and achieving spiritual liberation. This approach emphasizes self-effort, wisdom, and compassion as essential to attaining the experience of Nirvana and the end of suffering.

These traditions, though distinct in their understanding of God or ultimate reality, reflect a shared human quest to comprehend the divine. Whether through personal devotion, intellectual inquiry, or mystical union, the concept of God serves as a guiding principle, offering different paths to truth and spiritual fulfillment across various cultures and faiths.

Scientific Perspectives on God and Consciousness

Modern science, particularly through the lens of quantum physics and neuroscience, has begun to touch upon questions related to consciousness, which some argue could intersect with the spiritual concept of God. While the scientific method traditionally focuses on material reality, recent developments suggest that consciousness itself may be a fundamental aspect of existence, leading to new insights that resonate with spiritual teachings.

One of the pioneers of quantum mechanics, **Erwin Schrödinger**, made a profound observation about the nature of consciousness, stating, *"Consciousness is a singular of which the plural is unknown."* This suggests that consciousness is not something that can be divided or measured in the way physical objects can be. Schrödinger's assertion resonates with many spiritual traditions, particularly those like Advaita Vedanta, which equate consciousness with the divine. In this view, consciousness is seen as the underlying reality that transcends the dualities of time and space, and the apparent division between individual consciousnesses is illusory. This parallels the Vedantic idea that *Atman* (the individual self) is ultimately one with *Brahman* (the universal self).

In the realm of quantum physics, phenomena like wave-particle duality and quantum entanglement challenge our classical understanding of space, time, and causality. Some interpretations of quantum mechanics propose that the observer's consciousness plays an integral role in determining the outcome of quantum events. While this is still a subject of debate, it hints at the idea that consciousness might be more intertwined with the fabric of reality than previously thought. The notion that the universe requires an observer to manifest reality at a fundamental level has led some to explore the philosophical implications, particularly in relation to the existence of a universal consciousness, or God, that pervades all creation.

Another area where science intersects with spirituality is the study of **near-death experiences (NDEs)**. Many individuals who have had NDEs report encounters with a vast, luminous presence that they often describe as divine. These experiences frequently involve feelings of profound peace, unity, and the dissolution of the ego. Some also report entering a realm that transcends time and space, which aligns with spiritual descriptions of God or ultimate reality. While these experiences are highly subjective and difficult to study scientifically, they offer intriguing insights into the nature of consciousness and its potential continuity beyond physical death.

From a scientific standpoint, some researchers theorize that NDEs are caused by changes in brain chemistry or neurological activity during traumatic events. However, the recurring themes in NDE reports—such as encounters with a divine presence, a life review, or feelings of unconditional love—mirror teachings found in many religious traditions that describe God as an omnipresent consciousness that transcends the individual self.

These reports challenge the materialistic view of consciousness as merely a byproduct of brain activity and open up the possibility that consciousness could exist independently of the body. This aligns with many spiritual teachings, particularly in Vedanta, where consciousness is considered the true essence of the self, rather than a function of the brain.

While modern science has yet to fully understand consciousness or its potential relationship with the divine, the exploration of quantum mechanics, NDEs, and the mysteries of consciousness points to a deeper, more fundamental reality that transcends the material world. This reality, often described in spiritual terms as God, may be intimately connected with the very fabric of existence, suggesting that science and spirituality may ultimately converge in their pursuit of understanding the nature of reality and consciousness.

Experiencing God: The Path to Realization

The realization of God, whether through knowledge (*Jnana*), devotion (*Bhakti*), action (*Karma*), or meditation (*Dhyana*), is the goal of all spiritual practice. The Upanishads describe this realization as the experience of oneness with the divine, where all dualities dissolve and only the infinite remains.

The Bhagavad Gita (4.11) states, "In whatever way people approach Me, I reward them accordingly. Everyone follows My path in all respects." This emphasizes that all paths, when followed sincerely, lead to the realization of God.

Swami Vivekananda, through his intense meditation and selfless service, experienced God as pure consciousness. He famously said, "Each soul is potentially divine. The goal is to manifest this divinity within by controlling nature, external and internal." His life and teachings continue to inspire millions to seek the divine within.

456

Conclusion

The concept of God, whether viewed as a personal deity, the impersonal Brahman, or the ultimate reality, is central to spiritual traditions across the world. Through the teachings of the scriptures, the lives of enlightened beings, and even scientific exploration, humanity continues to seek and experience the divine presence that pervades all existence. Ultimately, God is beyond words and concepts, a reality to be realized through direct experience and inner awakening.

26

Shruti and Smriti

In the vast ocean of Hindu philosophy, the terms *Shruti* and *Smriti* hold great significance. They represent two categories of sacred texts that guide the spiritual and social life of Hindus. Understanding these two concepts is essential for anyone delving into the intricacies of Hinduism, as they form the foundational pillars of Vedic knowledge and dharma (righteousness). This chapter explores the differences, importance, and impact of *Shruti* and *Smriti*, with references to significant texts and traditions.

Shruti: The Eternal Knowledge

Shruti literally means "that which is heard." It refers to the body of knowledge that is considered eternal, divine, and revealed. Unlike other scriptures, *Shruti* texts are believed to have been directly revealed to ancient sages (rishis) during deep meditative states and are therefore considered *apaurusheya* (not of human origin).

The primary texts classified under *Shruti* include the four Vedas—*Rigveda*, *Yajurveda*, *Samaveda*, and *Atharvaveda*—along with the *Brahmanas*, *Aranyakas*, and *Upanishads*. These texts are revered as the highest authority in Hindu philosophy.

The *Rigveda*, the oldest and most venerated of the Vedas, contains hymns dedicated to various deities like Agni (fire), Indra (the king of gods), and Varuna (the cosmic order). Its verses, such as the famous *Gayatri Mantra* (Rigveda 3.62.10), are still recited in daily rituals and spiritual practices.

The Brihadaranyaka Upanishad (1.3.28) presents the renowned teaching, **"Asato ma sadgamaya, tamaso ma jyotir gamaya, mrityor ma amritam gamaya,"** which translates to, "Lead me from the unreal to the real, from darkness to light, from death to immortality." This verse encapsulates the transformative wisdom conveyed through the Shruti texts.

Shruti is considered the ultimate source of spiritual authority in Hinduism. It is regarded as the repository of transcendental knowledge, guiding the pursuit of moksha (liberation). The teachings within the Vedas and Upanishads form the philosophical foundation of various schools of thought, including Vedanta, Sankhya, and Yoga.

Smriti: The Remembered Wisdom

Smriti, in contrast to *Shruti*, means "that which is remembered." These are texts that were composed by sages and scholars, reflecting the practical application of the eternal truths found in *Shruti*. While *Smriti* is also considered sacred, it is secondary in authority to *Shruti* and is adaptable to changing times and circumstances.

The key *Smriti* texts include the *Dharmashastras* (law books), such as the *Manusmriti*, *Yajnavalkya Smriti*, and *Narada Smriti*, as well as the two great epics, the *Ramayana* and the *Mahabharata*. Additionally, the *Puranas, Itihasas,* and the *Agamas* also fall under the category of *Smriti.*

The *Manusmriti* is a well-known *Smriti* text that outlines social, legal, and ethical norms for individuals and society. It has played a significant role in shaping the social order in ancient India, particularly in defining the duties and responsibilities of the four varnas (social classes).

While *Shruti* provides the theoretical framework, *Smriti* offers practical guidance on living a righteous life. It addresses various aspects of life, including ethics, law, social customs, and rituals, making it relevant to day-to-day activities. As *Smriti* evolves over time, it allows for reinterpretation and adaptation to contemporary challenges, ensuring that the eternal principles of *Shruti* are preserved within the context of changing societal norms.

The Relationship between Shruti and Smriti

The relationship between *Shruti* and *Smriti* can be likened to that of a constitution and its bylaws. While *Shruti* represents the immutable and eternal truths of the cosmos, *Smriti* provides the necessary instructions for applying those truths in the temporal world. Traditionally, *Smriti* is expected to conform to the principles of *Shruti*, and where there is a conflict between the two, *Shruti* takes precedence.

The *Bhagavad Gita*, which is part of the *Mahabharata* and hence a *Smriti* text, draws extensively from the *Upanishads* (part of *Shruti*) in its teachings. However, it also provides a practical approach to living in the world through the concept of karma yoga (the yoga of action).

The *Manusmriti* (2.6) asserts, "Vedo'khilo dharmamoolam," meaning "The Vedas are the root of all Dharma." This reinforces the primacy of *Shruti* as the foundational source of spiritual and ethical wisdom, while *Smriti* serves as a guide for implementing these teachings in daily life.

Scholars like Dr. Surendranath Dasgupta and Dr. Radhakrishnan have explored the interplay between *Shruti* and *Smriti* in shaping Indian civilization, noting how the adaptability of *Smriti* allowed Hindu traditions to survive and thrive through the ages, while *Shruti* provided an unchanging spiritual core.

Evolving Nature of Smriti

One of the key aspects of *Smriti* is its ability to evolve and adapt to changing circumstances. Unlike *Shruti*, which remains constant and unalterable, *Smriti* texts are periodically updated and reinterpreted to meet the needs of different eras. This dynamic nature has allowed Hindu society to adjust to various cultural, political, and economic changes over time.

The *Yajnavalkya Smriti* and *Narada Smriti* are later legal texts that offer revisions and updates to the laws presented in the *Manusmriti*, reflecting the changing needs and norms of society.

The adaptability of *Smriti* can be seen in the Hindu Marriage Act of 1955 and the Hindu Succession Act of 1956 in India, which reformulated traditional Hindu laws to address modern concerns such as gender equality and inheritance rights, while still being rooted in *Smriti* traditions.

Spiritual Significance: Harmonizing Shruti and Smriti

In the pursuit of spiritual realization, both *Shruti* and *Smriti* play complementary roles. *Shruti* offers the seeker knowledge of the ultimate reality, guiding them toward moksha, while *Smriti* provides the ethical and ritual framework necessary to live a dharmic life. Together, they create a holistic spiritual path that balances inner realization with outer conduct.

The teachings of *Shruti*, such as the *Mahavakyas* (great sayings) from the Upanishads like "Tat Tvam Asi" (You are That), offer profound insights into the nature of the self. Meanwhile, the *Smriti* texts, such as the *Yogasutras* of Patanjali, provide practical instructions for disciplining the mind and body to realize these truths.

Conclusion

While *Shruti* provides the timeless spiritual wisdom that guides seekers toward liberation, *Smriti* offers practical guidelines for living in accordance with that wisdom. Together, they form a complete and harmonious system that addresses both the transcendent and the immanent aspects of existence.

By understanding and integrating both *Shruti* and *Smriti*, individuals can navigate the complexities of life while remaining aligned with the eternal truths of the universe. Whether through the study of the Vedas and Upanishads or the application of dharma as outlined in the *Smriti* texts, the wisdom of these sacred scriptures continues to illuminate the path for spiritual aspirants.

27

Mantra

A mantra is much more than a mere sound or phrase; it is a profound spiritual tool, often revered as a vehicle for transformation and enlightenment. Typically composed in Sanskrit, the ancient language of the Vedas, mantras have been used for millennia in various spiritual practices to calm the mind, connect with higher consciousness, and channel divine energies. The power of a mantra lies in its vibrational essence—each syllable carries a specific energy that resonates with different aspects of the mind, body, and spirit.

Historically, mantras have been central to sacred traditions, particularly in Hinduism, Buddhism, and Jainism, where they are believed to hold the key to unlocking spiritual potential and guiding practitioners toward inner peace. In Hinduism, mantras like "Om" and the Gayatri Mantra are considered gateways to cosmic consciousness, while in Buddhism, chants such as "Om Mani Padme Hum" invoke compassion and universal love. Jainism also emphasizes mantras for purifying karma and fostering spiritual ascension. Over time, the use of mantras has transcended these traditional boundaries, finding a place in modern spiritual and wellness practices around the world.

In this chapter, we will delve into the multi-layered dimensions of mantras, exploring not only their historical and philosophical significance but also their practical applications in today's fast-paced world. We will examine how chanting or meditating with mantras can cultivate mindfulness, enhance focus, and open the heart to deeper spiritual experiences. Additionally, we will look at how mantras have evolved in modern spirituality, merging ancient wisdom with contemporary practices like yoga, meditation, and sound healing, and continuing to inspire seekers on the path to personal and collective transformation.

The Nature and Purpose of Mantras

The word "mantra" is derived from two Sanskrit roots: *"man"* meaning "mind," and *"tra"* meaning "instrument" or "tool." Essentially, a mantra is an instrument of the mind, designed to support focus, spiritual growth, and the path toward enlightenment. These sacred syllables, sounds, or phrases are considered powerful tools in both ancient and modern spiritual traditions, guiding practitioners toward higher states of consciousness.

Purpose of Mantras

Mental Focus: One of the primary functions of a mantra is to anchor the mind. In the modern world, where distractions abound, mantras help reduce mental chatter and enhance concentration. The rhythmic repetition of a mantra keeps the mind from wandering, enabling practitioners to remain present and centered, a state often sought after in meditation and mindfulness practices.

Spiritual Connection: Mantras serve as a bridge between the practitioner and higher spiritual realities. By chanting or mentally repeating a mantra, one invokes divine energies, which may be experienced as a heightened sense of awareness, connection to the universe, or direct communion with deities or enlightened beings. Different mantras are dedicated to specific aspects of divinity or universal principles, providing a personalized spiritual tool for growth.

Vibrational Impact: Beyond their symbolic meaning, mantras are believed to create specific vibrations that align with cosmic energies. When uttered, mantras vibrate at frequencies that influence the practitioner's energy field, often referred to as the *aura*. These vibrations can calm the mind, balance the body, and awaken the spirit. This vibrational resonance is thought to connect practitioners with the subtle layers of the universe, promoting healing, inner peace, and higher awareness.

As T.K.V. Desikachar beautifully stated, "A mantra is not just a sound but a powerful vibration that transforms our inner reality and connects us with the divine." This profound insight highlights the essence of mantra practice: it is not merely about vocalizing sacred words but about harnessing their transformative vibrations to elevate consciousness and connect with higher spiritual realms.

The Power of Mantras: A Timeless Perspective

As Swami Sivananda beautifully articulated, "Mantras are the seeds of wisdom and spiritual awakening, planted in the fertile soil of our consciousness." This profound statement encapsulates the transformative potential of mantras. Each repetition of a mantra plants a seed within the practitioner's consciousness, nurturing the soul's growth and leading to a deeper understanding of the self and the universe.

The Universal Mantra: "OM" (AUM)

Perhaps the most well-known and widely used mantra is "OM" (also written as AUM). Considered the primal sound from which the universe originated; "OM" symbolizes the essence of all existence. Chanting "OM" aligns the individual with the vibration of the universe, bringing about spiritual unity, a sense of wholeness, and profound inner peace.

It is composed of three Sanskrit phonemes: A, U, and M, which symbolize various aspects of existence.

- **A (अ)**: Represents creation and the waking state.
- **U (उ)**: Symbolizes preservation and the dream state.
- **M (म)**: Denotes dissolution and the deep sleep state.
- **The silence that follows**: Represents the transcendental state, beyond all experiences.

OM encapsulates the essence of Brahman, the ultimate reality in Hindu philosophy. It signifies the unity of the universe and the interconnectedness of all things.

"OM is the sound of the Absolute, the cosmic vibration from which all creation emanates and into which it returns." – Swami Sivananda

"OM is the bridge between the finite and the infinite. It helps us transcend our individual consciousness and merge with the universal consciousness." – Eckhart Tolle

The Mandukya Upanishad, a key text in Hindu philosophy, explains OM as the representation of the entire universe, encompassing all states of consciousness and existence.

Whether used to focus the mind, connect with the divine, or attune oneself to universal vibrations, mantras are invaluable tools on the path to spiritual awakening. In the next sections, we will explore the historical evolution of mantras and how they have been adapted in modern-day practices across various spiritual traditions.

Historical and Scriptural Roots

Mantras have deep historical and scriptural origins in the sacred texts of ancient India. These sacred syllables have been central to spiritual practice for thousands of years, evolving and adapting within various religious and philosophical traditions. Their significance is documented in key texts like the *Vedas*, *Upanishads*, and other revered scriptures, reflecting both their ritualistic and philosophical dimensions.

The Vedas: Sacred Hymns and Ritual Chants

The Vedas, particularly the *Rigveda*, are the earliest known sources of mantras, dating back over several thousand years. The *Rigveda* is a collection of hymns and chants that were primarily used in Vedic rituals and sacrifices to invoke the gods, seek their blessings, and maintain cosmic order. Mantras in the Vedas were seen as potent tools for invoking divine forces, and each one was meticulously constructed to have specific meanings and effects.

These Vedic mantras were typically recited by priests during fire sacrifices (*yajnas*), and their precise pronunciation was believed to be essential for achieving the desired spiritual or material outcomes. The mantras acted as a conduit between the human and the divine, channelling energies to fulfill worldly and cosmic duties. Over time, these mantras became more than just ritualistic chants; they also started to be used for personal spiritual growth and self-purification.

The Upanishads: Mantras as Tools for Meditation and Self-Realization

The philosophical depth of mantras was further explored in the *Upanishads*, where they were linked to meditation, self-realization, and the quest for ultimate truth. The *Upanishads* moved beyond the external rituals of the Vedas, emphasizing the internal spiritual journey of the individual.

In texts like the *Mandukya Upanishad*, mantras such as "OM" are revered not just as sounds, but as profound representations of the universe and consciousness itself. Here, mantras are seen as tools to transcend the material world and connect directly with Brahman—the ultimate reality or universal consciousness. Through the repetition of mantras in meditative practices, individuals were believed to achieve higher states of awareness and even liberation (*moksha*).

The Evolution of Mantras

As time passed, mantras evolved, adapting to various religious and philosophical contexts. From their early use in Vedic rituals, mantras became integral to diverse spiritual traditions like Hinduism, Buddhism, and Jainism. They transitioned from being solely ritualistic to becoming central to meditative, devotional, and yogic practices.

In Hinduism, mantras were woven into devotional practices such as *japa* (repetition of a mantra), *bhakti* (devotion), and *dhyana* (meditation). In Buddhism, mantras became key components of meditation, compassion, and the pursuit of enlightenment, such as the widely known "Om Mani Padme Hum." Jainism also incorporated mantras, emphasizing their use for karma purification and spiritual elevation.

The Gayatri Mantra: An Ancient and Revered Prayer

One of the most ancient and revered mantras in Hinduism is the *Gayatri Mantra*, which appears in the *Rigveda* (Mandala 3.62.10). It is a prayer to Mother Gayatri, invoking her divine light to illuminate the mind and guide the practitioner toward wisdom and clarity:

"Om Bhur Bhuvah Svah,
Tat Savitur Varenyam,
Bhargo Devasya Dhimahi,
Dhiyo Yo Nah Prachodayat."

Translated, it means: "We meditate on the divine light of the radiant source (the Sun deity, or Goddess Gayatri, or Brahman) who is fit to be worshipped, creator of the universe and remover of all sins and ignorance. May that divine light inspire and illuminate our intellect."

This mantra is considered one of the most powerful and essential prayers in Hinduism, representing the light of knowledge, wisdom, and spiritual awakening. There is no milk superior to cow's milk., even so there is no Mantra superior to Gayatri. The recitation of the Gayatri mantra yields the same benefits as chanting all four Vedas along with their Angas. Repeating this single mantra three times daily brings well-being (Kalyan) or liberation (Moksha). Known as the Mantra of the Vedas, Gayatri eradicates sins and bestows excellent health, beauty, strength, vigour, vitality, and a radiant, magnetic aura (Brahmic effulgence).

Gayatri dispels the three types of *Taapa* (suffering) and grants the four *Purusharthas*: Dharma (righteousness), Artha (wealth), Kama (desires), and Moksha (liberation). It dissolves the three Granthis or knots of ignorance—Avidya (ignorance), Kama (desire), and Karma (action). By purifying the mind, Gayatri bestows the Ashta Siddhis (eight spiritual powers), making a person strong and highly intelligent, ultimately leading to liberation from the cycle of birth and death.

I strongly recommend that you chant the mantra of your choice yourself, rather than relying on audio recordings or the recitations of others. The power of mantra lies not only in the sound but in the personal connection and intention behind it. When you chant a mantra, you align your mind, body, and spirit with its vibrational essence, creating a direct and intimate spiritual experience. Listening to pre-recorded or external recitations may have a soothing effect, but it often lacks the profound personal resonance that comes from chanting with mindfulness and intention.

Furthermore, rather than spending your time and resources on external rituals or ceremonies that may not align with your inner journey, focus on the deeper purpose of spiritual practice: transcending the limitations of the mind, intellect, and ego. Rituals can serve as valuable reminders of spiritual ideals, but they often risk becoming mechanical or superficial, diverting attention away from the true goal of self-realization.

Mantras are tools for inward exploration, helping you move beyond the illusions of the conditioned mind and ego-driven desires. By taking ownership of your practice, you cultivate inner discipline, self-awareness, and the capacity to transcend the surface-level distractions of life. Spiritual growth is not about external displays but about deep, personal transformation. Use your energy wisely by focusing on the practices that nurture your inner self, and you will find that the greatest realizations come from within.

The Timeless Power of Mantras

As Swami Prabhupada expressed, "The power of the mantra is not in its words but in its ability to connect us with the divine vibrations of the universe." This highlights the essence of mantra practice—its capacity to transcend the literal meaning of words and tap into the underlying vibrations that resonate with the energies of the cosmos.

Mantras continue to hold a central place in both traditional and modern spiritual practices, acting as a bridge between ancient wisdom and contemporary seekers. In the following sections, we will explore how these mantras have retained their relevance and how their use has expanded in the modern world, from yoga studios to mindfulness practices across the globe.

Types of Mantras

Mantras come in many forms, and their classification varies depending on the spiritual tradition or purpose. There are approximately 25 to 30 distinct types of mantras, with certain traditions merging or expanding these categories based on their focus, such as healing, protection, or devotion to specific deities. While it is beyond the scope of this book to explore each type in detail, here are a few key categories that offer insight into the diversity and power of mantras:

Bija Mantras (Seed Mantras): These are short, single-syllable mantras, often considered the "seeds" of more complex spiritual practices. Each *bija* mantra contains potent spiritual energy in its compact form and resonates with different aspects of the universe and consciousness. For example, "Om" is the most well-known *bija* mantra, representing the essence of the entire cosmos, while other bija mantras like "Kreem," "Shreem," or "Hreem" are used for specific spiritual purposes.

Vedic Mantras: These mantras come from the ancient Vedic texts, such as the *Rigveda, Yajurveda, Samaveda,* and *Atharvaveda.* They are often used in rituals and ceremonies to invoke divine forces, maintain cosmic harmony, and fulfill worldly or spiritual desires. Vedic mantras are typically chanted by priests in precise patterns and with strict rules of pronunciation.

Tantric Mantras: These mantras are used in Tantric practices, where the focus is often on channelling specific energies, awakening kundalini (spiritual energy), and transcending the limitations of the physical world. Tantric mantras can be highly esoteric, combining sound vibrations with specific visualizations, rituals, and meditation techniques aimed at personal transformation and spiritual empowerment.

Saguna Mantras (With Form): Saguna mantras are those that invoke a deity or divine form with specific attributes. For example, the mantra dedicated to Lord Ganesha, "Om Gam Ganapataye Namah," invokes the energy of Ganesha, the remover of obstacles. These mantras help practitioners connect with personal deities, channel their qualities, and deepen devotional practices.

Nirguna Mantras (Without Form): In contrast to *saguna* mantras, *nirguna* mantras focus on the formless aspect of the Divine. They do not invoke specific deities but instead focus on the ultimate reality or universal consciousness. An example is the mantra "Aham Brahmasmi," meaning "I am Brahman," which is used in Advaita Vedanta to realize the oneness of the individual self with the universal consciousness.

Moksha Mantras: These mantras are specifically aimed at liberation (*moksha*), the ultimate goal of spiritual practice. They are used to help the practitioner transcend the cycle of birth and death, realize their true nature, and attain spiritual freedom. The *Mahamrityunjaya Mantra*, also known as the "Death Conquering Mantra," is one example, as it is believed to bestow spiritual liberation and overcome fears of mortality.

The Practice of Mantra Meditation

Mantra meditation is a powerful practice that integrates sound, vibration, and intention to cultivate mindfulness, spiritual awareness, and inner peace. The rhythmic repetition of a sacred sound or phrase helps to focus the mind, transcend distractions, and tap into deeper layers of consciousness. This practice has been used for centuries to purify the mind and align with higher spiritual energies.

Mantra Repetition

Japa: One of the most common forms of mantra meditation is *japa*, the repetitive chanting of a mantra, either silently or audibly. *Japa* is often performed with a mala (prayer beads) to count the number of repetitions, traditionally 108, as this number is considered sacred in many spiritual traditions. The purpose of *japa* is to focus the mind, purify thoughts, and align oneself with divine energies, making it a practice of inner reflection and spiritual development.

In fact, you can make your breath the focal point of your practice, synchronizing your inhalations and exhalations with each repetition of the mantra. This approach can deepen your meditation, enhancing the connection between your breath and the vibrational essence of the mantra.

Alternatively, you may even choose to transcend the use of a mala or breath entirely, allowing the mantra to flow naturally in your mind and heart without any physical aids. The key is to find what resonates best with you, creating a practice that feels authentic and nurturing. Ultimately, the power of mantra meditation lies in your intention, presence, and connection to the sound, regardless of the tools you use.

In Hinduism, for example, devotees frequently chant the mantra "Om Namah Shivaya" to honour Lord Shiva. This mantra is believed to help practitioners attain a state of inner peace, balance, and spiritual enlightenment. It is not just the act of repetition, but the deep connection with the mantra's meaning that allows for the transformation of the self.

As meditation teacher Sharon Salzberg beautifully put it, "Mantra meditation is a journey inward, where each repetition draws us closer to the essence of our being." Every chant is like a step inward, a movement toward inner clarity and self-realization.

Scientific Perspective

Mantra meditation not only holds spiritual benefits but is also recognized for its positive impact on mental health. Scientific research has shown that the regular practice of mantra meditation can reduce stress, lower blood pressure, and improve overall emotional well-being. These benefits are attributed to the calming effect that repetitive sound and focused attention have on the nervous system.

A study published in *Psychosomatic Medicine* found that mantra meditation significantly reduced anxiety and enhanced mood in participants, demonstrating its potential as a therapeutic tool for mental health. The calming rhythm of mantra repetition slows down brain activity, fostering a state of relaxation and reducing the "fight or flight" response that is often triggered by stress.

Additionally, the Transcendental Meditation (TM) technique, which utilizes specific mantras, has been extensively studied for its stress-relieving and cognitive benefits. TM practitioners have reported enhanced focus, emotional stability, and overall well-being. Dr. Herbert Benson, a pioneer in the study of the relaxation response, noted, "The repetition of a mantra can have a profound impact on the brain, altering its activity and fostering a state of tranquillity and focus." These findings align with ancient wisdom that views mantras as powerful tools for self-regulation and inner harmony.

Mantras in Modern Spirituality

In contemporary times, mantras have transcended their traditional religious contexts and found a place in various wellness, mindfulness, and spiritual practices. Whether integrated into yoga, meditation, or holistic healing therapies, mantras are widely used to deepen practice and enhance the practitioner's experience.

Incorporation into Yoga and Meditation: Many yoga classes begin and end with the chanting of a mantra to set the spiritual tone for the practice. Mantras like "Om" are used to center the mind, open the heart, and create a sacred space for both physical and meditative practice. Chanting during yoga enhances focus, aligning breath with intention, and allowing practitioners to experience a more profound connection between body and mind.

Mantras as Wellness Tools: Beyond yoga, mantras have been integrated into modern holistic therapies, where they are used as tools for healing, relaxation, and emotional balance. For example, sound healing therapies often involve the chanting or playing of specific mantras to align the energy centers (chakras) and promote inner healing.

The global popularity of mantra meditation highlights its universal appeal. In today's interconnected world, mantras have transcended cultural and religious boundaries, with practitioners from diverse backgrounds adopting them for their meditative power. This widespread embrace reflects the timeless and adaptable nature of mantras, as they continue to offer spiritual solace and mental clarity to millions.

As Pema Chödrön, a renowned meditation teacher, eloquently states, "The universal nature of mantras speaks to their power to connect us with a deeper aspect of ourselves and the cosmos." The vibrational essence of mantras transcends language and culture, resonating with our innermost being and connecting us to the divine.

Swami Vishnudevananda captures this essence perfectly when he says, "Mantras are the echoes of the divine, guiding us back to our true selves and the infinite." Through their repetition, mantras act as beacons, helping us navigate the complexities of the human experience and return to the simplicity of our higher nature.

Mantra meditation, in both its traditional and modern forms, continues to serve as a gateway to self-awareness, healing, and spiritual growth, offering a profound path toward inner peace and unity with the cosmos.

Conclusion

Mantras are powerful spiritual tools that serve various purposes, from mental focus and emotional balance to spiritual growth and healing. Their rich historical roots and profound impact on modern practices highlight their enduring significance. By understanding and incorporating mantras into our lives, we can connect with deeper layers of consciousness and experience greater harmony and spiritual awakening.

28

Guru: The Guide on the Path of Realization

In the spiritual journey, the figure of the Guru holds a central place. The word *Guru* is derived from two Sanskrit syllables: *Gu*, meaning darkness, and *Ru*, meaning light. Therefore, a Guru is one who dispels the darkness of ignorance and leads the seeker to the light of knowledge. The Guru is seen as an embodiment of divine wisdom, a guide who helps navigate the complexities of spiritual practice and realization.

In the *Guru Gita*, a revered text often chanted in the context of honouring one's Guru, it is said, "Gurur Brahma Gurur Vishnu, Gurur Devo Maheshwara, Guru Sakshat Parabrahma, Tasmai Shri Guruve Namah." (Guru Gita, Verse 2)

This verse emphasizes the Guru's status as not just a teacher but a direct embodiment of the divine itself, guiding the disciple towards realization.

The Necessity of a Guru: Tradition and Practice

In traditional Vedic culture, the role of a Guru is indispensable. Ancient texts like the *Upanishads* are filled with stories of disciples seeking Gurus for initiation into higher knowledge. For instance, in the *Chandogya Upanishad*, we find the story of Satyakama Jabala, who approaches the sage Gautama to become his disciple, despite being of unknown parentage. Gautama accepts him, recognizing his truthfulness, and Satyakama eventually attains realization under his guidance.

Similarly, the Bhagavad Gita speaks of the need for a Guru, "Approach a wise teacher with humility, inquire from them submissively, and render service. The self-realized can impart knowledge because they have seen the truth." (Bhagavad Gita, 4.34)

This verse underscores the traditional belief that a realized teacher is essential for imparting true knowledge, which transcends intellectual understanding.

Gurus in Different Traditions

Hinduism: In Hindu tradition, the Guru-disciple relationship is sacrosanct. The Guru is considered the intermediary between the disciple and the divine. Swami Vivekananda, a disciple of Ramakrishna Paramahamsa, often emphasized the role of the Guru in spiritual practice. He said, "The Guru must be worshipped as God. He is God, he is nothing less than that."

Buddhism: In Buddhism, the Guru, often called a Lama in Tibetan Buddhism, is also seen as essential. The *Dalai Lama* and other spiritual teachers provide guidance on the path to enlightenment. The Buddha himself is considered the supreme teacher or Guru, whose teachings provide the path to liberation.

Sikhism: In Sikhism, the ten Gurus are considered the spiritual leaders who revealed divine wisdom. The *Guru Granth Sahib*, the holy scripture, is also regarded as a Guru. Guru Nanak, the founder of Sikhism, emphasized the importance of a spiritual guide in one's journey to God.

Gurus Beyond the Human Form: Books, Nature, and Inner Guidance

While the tradition of a human Guru is prominent, there are also notable figures who have found guidance in alternative forms. These include books, nature, and inner intuition as their Guru. Here are a few examples:

Sri Aurobindo, a prominent Indian yogi, philosopher, and freedom fighter, regarded inner guidance and the divine as his Guru. He said, "The teacher of the Integral Yoga is the Divine, and the Guru is the Divine. The Guru is not an ordinary man with the ignorant human consciousness."

Ramana Maharshi, one of India's most revered sages, is known for his path of self-inquiry (Atma Vichara). When asked about his Guru, Ramana Maharshi often stated that the self (Atman) was his only teacher. His realization came without the guidance of a traditional human Guru, emphasizing that inner realization is possible for some without an external guide.

Jiddu Krishnamurti rejected the idea of an external Guru entirely, stating that truth is a pathless land and cannot be organized. He advocated self-inquiry and direct perception, encouraging individuals to be their own teachers.

Nature as Guru

Many have found wisdom and guidance in nature. In ancient texts, the sages and rishis often lived in forests and mountains, where nature itself became a teacher. The rhythms of the natural world, the changing seasons, and the harmony of the elements have inspired spiritual seekers for millennia.

An example of this can be seen in the life of *Henry David Thoreau*, the American transcendentalist, who withdrew to Walden Pond to live in simplicity and learn from nature. His book *Walden* became a testament to the idea that nature can be a profound teacher.

Books as Gurus

Sacred texts have often been revered as living Gurus. The *Guru Granth Sahib* in Sikhism is considered a Guru in its own right, providing divine wisdom to its followers. Similarly, the *Bhagavad Gita* is seen as a Guru, guiding seekers on the path of righteousness and self-realization.

Dattatreya and His 24 Gurus: Wisdom in the World Around Us

One of the most profound teachings about the role of a Guru comes from Lord Dattatreya, revered as an incarnation of the Trimurti—Brahma, Vishnu, and Shiva. Dattatreya is often depicted as a wandering sage who found enlightenment through 24 Gurus, none of whom were human. These Gurus were elements of nature, animals, and even aspects of life itself, teaching Dattatreya the deep wisdom inherent in the world. This story illustrates that a Guru need not always be a human teacher; wisdom is available in every corner of existence.

Here are the 24 Gurus of Dattatreya, each offering a unique spiritual lesson:

1. **Earth (Prithvi)**: The earth bears the weight of everything without complaint. From this, Dattatreya learned patience, forbearance, and the virtue of serving others selflessly.

   Teaching: Patience and service.

2. **Water (Apas)**: Water nourishes life and flows without attachment, adapting to every situation. It taught Dattatreya the value of adaptability and purity.

   Teaching: Purity and adaptability.

3. **Fire (Agni)**: Fire consumes everything it touches but remains unaffected by it. This taught Dattatreya about the importance of purity and detachment.

   Teaching: Purity and detachment.

4. **Air (Vayu)**: The wind moves freely, touching everything without becoming attached. Dattatreya learned the lesson of detachment and freedom from desires.

   Teaching: Detachment and freedom.

5. **Sky (Akasha)**: The vast sky represents the infinite nature of the self, unaffected by the activities within it. Dattatreya learned about the all-encompassing nature of the Self (Atman).

Teaching: Infinite nature of the Self.

6. **Sun (Surya)**: The sun shines equally on all, without preference. It taught Dattatreya the value of selfless action and the impartiality of true wisdom.

Teaching: Selflessness and impartiality.

7. **Pigeon**: A pigeon, in its attachment to its young, lost its life trying to save them. From this, Dattatreya learned the dangers of attachment.

Teaching: Dangers of attachment.

8. **Python**: The python waits patiently for food to come to it, teaching Dattatreya the importance of contentment and accepting what life offers.

Teaching: Contentment and patience.

9. **Ocean**: The ocean remains full, regardless of how many rivers flow into it. Dattatreya learned the lesson of equanimity and how to remain undisturbed by external changes.

Teaching: Equanimity and inner fullness.

10. **Moth**: The moth is drawn to fire and perishes in it, teaching Dattatreya about the dangers of uncontrolled senses and desires.

Teaching: Control over desires.

11. **Elephant**: The elephant is lured into captivity by its desire for a female elephant. From this, Dattatreya learned the dangers of uncontrolled lust.

Teaching: Control over lust.

12. **Deer**: The deer is entrapped by hunters due to its attraction to sweet sounds. Dattatreya learned about the dangers of sensual distractions.

Teaching: Dangers of sensory attachments.

13. **Fish**: The fish is caught due to its desire for bait, teaching Dattatreya the peril of greed.

Teaching: Dangers of greed.

14. **Prostitute Pingala**: A courtesan named Pingala, who was always waiting for customers, found peace when she finally gave up her desires. Dattatreya learned the value of renunciation.

Teaching: Peace through renunciation.

15. **Child**: A child lives in the moment and is free from worries. Dattatreya learned about the simplicity and innocence of being content with the present.

Teaching: Living in the present moment.

16. **Maiden**: A young maiden, engaged in housework, learned the importance of solitude when her bangles clanged noisily together, distracting her from her duties. Dattatreya learned that solitude can be essential for inner peace.

Teaching: Value of solitude.

17. **Arrow Maker**: An arrow maker, focused on his craft, was unaware of the king passing by. Dattatreya learned the power of single-pointed concentration.

Teaching: Focus and concentration.

18. **Snake**: The snake lives in solitude, never building a permanent home, moving from one place to another. Dattatreya learned the importance of detachment and the need to live lightly.

Teaching: Detachment and non-attachment to possessions.

19. **Spider**: The spider spins a web from its own body and eventually retracts it. Dattatreya saw this as an allegory for creation and dissolution, learning the impermanence of the world.

Teaching: Impermanence and the cyclic nature of life.

20. **Wasp**: A wasp can become so engrossed in its prey that the prey itself turns into a wasp. Dattatreya learned that one becomes what one constantly contemplates.

Teaching: Power of contemplation and thought.

21. **Moon**: The moon appears to wax and wane, but it remains unchanged. Dattatreya learned that the self is unchanging despite the appearances of change in the material world.

Teaching: The unchanging nature of the self.

22. **Bee**: The bee gathers nectar from many flowers but doesn't harm them, teaching Dattatreya the importance of gathering knowledge from multiple sources without attachment.

   Teaching: Gathering knowledge and non-attachment.

23. **Honey Gatherer**: The honey gatherer takes the honey collected by the bees, symbolizing the futility of hoarding wealth and possessions. Dattatreya learned the importance of simplicity and non-possessiveness.

   Teaching: Non-possessiveness and simplicity.

24. **Vulture**: The vulture, because of its attachment to a piece of meat, attracts other birds who attack it. Dattatreya learned the dangers of holding on to material possessions.

   Teaching: Dangers of attachment to material possessions.

The Evolving Concept of a Guru

While the traditional role of the Guru remains respected, modern trends indicate a shift towards alternative forms of guidance. Studies show that many people now turn to books, online platforms, and even nature for spiritual inspiration.

A survey conducted by the *Pew Research Center* in 2020 found that 29% of Americans describe themselves as "spiritual but not religious," many of whom seek guidance outside organized religion and traditional Gurus.

According to a 2019 report by *Global Wellness Institute*, the self-help industry, including spiritual books and online courses, was valued at $13.2 billion, indicating a growing preference for alternative spiritual guidance.

The Debate: Do You Need a Guru?

The question of whether one needs a Guru remains a topic of debate among spiritual seekers. For some, the presence of a Guru is indispensable. The Guru offers guidance, corrects errors, and provides the blessings necessary for spiritual growth.

For others, the inner Guru, often referred to as *Atma Guru*, is sufficient. They believe that the true teacher resides within, and with deep meditation and self-inquiry, one can access this inner wisdom without the need for an external guide.

The Mundaka Upanishad emphasizes that realization of Brahman (the ultimate reality) can come from within, without external aid, "He who knows this secret finds the self as the self. He has no need of a Guru, nor does he seek it elsewhere." (Mundaka Upanishad, 2.2.4)

Conclusion

Ultimately, whether one finds guidance through a human Guru, sacred texts, nature, or inner wisdom, the essence remains the same—seeking the light of truth. Each path is unique, and each seeker must find what resonates with them. As the spiritual landscape evolves, so too does the concept of the Guru. The traditional reverence for the Guru remains, but so does the recognition that wisdom can come from countless sources, all leading to the same ultimate realization.

In the words of Kabir, the 15th-century Indian mystic poet, "Guru and God both appeared before me. To whom should I prostrate? I bow before my Guru, who introduced me to God."

Kabir's words encapsulate the essence of the Guru's role—whether external or internal, the Guru points to the divine truth that ultimately lies within each of us.

29

Brahma Muhurta: The Sacred Hour of Spiritual Awakening

Brahma Muhurta is considered the most auspicious time of the day in the Vedic tradition. Literally translating to the "time of Brahman," it refers to a specific period that occurs approximately one and a half hours (or two *muhurtas*) before sunrise. This time, usually between 3:30 AM and 5:30 AM, is believed to be the optimal period for spiritual practices such as meditation, yoga, and prayer, as it is when the mind is naturally calm, the environment is serene, and cosmic energies are at their peak.

This sacred hour is often referred to as the "creator's hour" because it is said to be the best time for one to connect with the divine consciousness. The peace of dawn symbolizes the awakening of spiritual awareness, making it an ideal time to focus on self-realization and to draw closer to the ultimate reality, Brahman.

The Science Behind Brahma Muhurta

From a scientific perspective, the environment during *Brahma Muhurta* is rich in oxygen, and the mind is fresh after a night's sleep, making it an ideal time for physical and mental activity. The air is also relatively free from pollution and noise, contributing to a heightened state of concentration and mental clarity.

Studies in circadian biology suggest that early morning light exposure helps regulate the body's internal clock, leading to improved cognitive function and emotional well-being. The quietude of the pre-dawn hours allows for deeper meditation, fostering a state of calm and focus that is difficult to achieve during the busier times of the day.

In modern times, many successful individuals, including entrepreneurs and spiritual leaders, advocate for waking up during *Brahma Muhurta* to align their mind, body, and soul with nature's rhythms. CEOs like Tim Cook of Apple and Howard Schultz (former CEO) of Starbucks are known to rise early, emphasizing the benefits of an early start for productivity and mindfulness.

The Spiritual Importance of Brahma Muhurta

The *Brahma Muhurta* hour has been extolled in various scriptures, including the *Yoga Sutras of Patanjali*, the *Bhagavad Gita*, and numerous Upanishads, as a time of profound spiritual significance. This period is ideal for engaging in sadhana (spiritual practice), as the mind is more receptive to subtle energies, and distractions are minimal.

"The early morning is the time of Brahman. The wise awaken before dawn to meditate, for it is at this time that the mind is still and the energy is highest." (Mundaka Upanishad)

During *Brahma Muhurta*, the vibrations of the earth (the places in the same time zone) are said to be pure, making it easier for spiritual aspirants to tune into higher frequencies and connect with their inner selves.

Sadly, loudspeakers blaring during *Brahma Muhurta* have become a widespread practice by many religious institutions. This time period, is known for its profound tranquillity, with the atmosphere said to be especially conducive to meditation because the thoughts are still and the influence of the ego is diminished, self-introspection, and silent devotion. However, the use of loudspeakers in this sacred time not only disrupts the natural serenity but also raises questions about its alignment with the deeper spiritual objectives these institutions aim to achieve.

Brahma Muhurta is often described as the "ambrosial hours" when the mind is most quiet, the environment most peaceful, and the cosmic energy most aligned for spiritual awakening. Yet, the externalization of religious expression through the use of loudspeakers during this time risks replacing the inward journey with an outward display, one that is more about volume than depth.

True spiritual growth, as taught by sages and scriptures, is an inward process. It is about silencing the distractions of the external world to turn the attention inward, cultivating a connection with one's inner self and, consequently, with the Divine. The noise generated by loudspeakers stands in stark contrast to this idea. Instead of fostering a calm, reflective environment, it often causes discomfort, disturbs those resting, and disrupts the peaceful balance of the natural surroundings.

Moreover, spirituality, at its core, does not require amplification. Whether in the form of prayers, mantras, or religious teachings, the essence of divinity resides in quiet sincerity, not in loud public declarations. Scriptures across traditions emphasize that God is found in the subtleties of existence—in silence, stillness, and deep contemplation. In the Bhagavad Gita, for instance, the concept of *"mounam"* (silence) is considered one of the forms of spiritual discipline. Similarly, many spiritual leaders have highlighted that peace, compassion, and love for all beings are the true markers of devotion, not the decibel levels of one's prayers.

Furthermore, the use of loudspeakers, especially during *Brahma Muhurta*, can create a sense of coercion. It inadvertently imposes a particular religious practice on others who may not share the same beliefs or prefer a different mode of devotion. Instead of fostering harmony, it can lead to resentment or conflict, which is the very antithesis of spiritual teachings.

Religious institutions play a vital role in guiding their communities towards higher consciousness. But to believe that a louder proclamation of faith equates to greater spirituality is a misunderstanding of the divine path. External noise does not bring one closer to God. In fact, it often pulls the seeker away from the quiet, reflective space that is essential for true spiritual realization.

Ultimately, God is found in silence, humility, and genuine intent—not in the volume of one's prayers or rituals. If religious infrastructures truly seek to guide their followers towards enlightenment, they must encourage practices that respect the peace of *Brahma Muhurta* and honour the deeper, quieter journey towards the Divine.

Sandhyas and Transition Periods

The term "Sandhya" means "junction" or "twilight," and it refers to the transitional periods between day and night—specifically **dawn (Pratah Sandhya)** and **dusk (Sayam Sandhya)**. Both of these periods are also considered to be spiritually potent because they mark the transition between different states of nature and consciousness.

Dawn (Pratah Sandhya): This is the period when night transitions into day, often considered a time of awakening for both nature and consciousness. For human consciousness, it mirrors the **hypnopompic state**, when one is moving from the deeper layers of sleep (including REM and deep sleep) toward wakefulness.

Dusk (Sayam Sandhya): This marks the transition from day to night, and it is closely related to the **hypnagogic state**, the period when one transitions from wakefulness to sleep. The **hypnagogic state** is characterized by dreamlike imagery and mental relaxation as the conscious mind begins to disengage.

The connection between these periods and the transition from sleep to wakefulness (and vice versa) is also seen as a metaphor for **the broader transition from ignorance to awareness.** Practitioners link to the development of **lucid dreaming** or **yoga nidra** (yogic sleep).

The Influence of Brahma Muhurta on Ayurveda and Health

In Ayurveda, the ancient system of holistic health, *Brahma Muhurta* is recognized as the most conducive time for mental and physical well-being. According to Ayurvedic principles, waking up at this time aligns the body's internal rhythms with the cycles of nature, which is key to maintaining good health and vitality.

During *Brahma Muhurta*, the *vata* dosha (air and ether elements) is dominant. The qualities of *vata*—lightness, clarity, and expansiveness—are believed to enhance creativity, intuition, and focus. Waking up and engaging in spiritual practices during this time helps balance the *vata* dosha and promotes mental clarity and alertness throughout the day.

Ayurvedic texts, such as the *Ashtanga Hridayam*, recommend rising during *Brahma Muhurta* to practice *dinacharya* (daily routine), which includes oil massage, meditation, and exercise. These practices, when performed during this sacred hour, are said to enhance immunity, improve digestion, and increase longevity.

"To rise early is to align oneself with the cycles of nature, ensuring harmony in mind and body." (Charaka Samhita)

Modern Relevance: How Brahma Muhurta Fits into Today's World

In today's fast-paced world, waking up during *Brahma Muhurta* might seem challenging for many, but its benefits are increasingly being recognized in both spiritual and professional circles. Early risers report increased productivity, a greater sense of well-being, and a deeper connection to their inner selves.

Various mindfulness and wellness movements have also started incorporating the concept of *Brahma Muhurta*, encouraging individuals to embrace the early hours for introspection, creativity, and self-care.

A 2018 study by the University of Colorado Boulder found that early risers are less likely to experience depression and anxiety compared to those who wake up later in the day.

Another study conducted by Harvard Health Publishing suggests that early risers tend to have better sleep quality and greater overall health.

Celebrities and public figures, such as Oprah Winfrey and Jennifer Aniston, have incorporated early morning routines that align with the principles of *Brahma Muhurta*, dedicating this time to meditation, exercise, and reflection.

Practices to Embrace During Brahma Muhurta

To make the most of *Brahma Muhurta*, it is important to engage in activities that foster spiritual and personal growth. Some of the most effective practices include:

Meditation: Begin with deep breathing exercises or *pranayama* to calm the mind and prepare for meditation. Focus on connecting with your higher self, and use this quiet time to reflect on your spiritual journey.

Asanas: Gentle *asanas* during *Brahma Muhurta* help awaken the body and prepare it for the day ahead. *Surya Namaskar* (Sun Salutations) is particularly beneficial.

Mantra Chanting: Reciting mantras or engaging in japa (repetition of a mantra) can help you tap into the divine vibrations of this sacred time.

Reading Sacred Texts: The early morning is an ideal time to read spiritual scriptures such as the *Bhagavad Gita, Upanishads,* or any text that inspires your spiritual growth.

Conclusion: The Eternal Wisdom of Brahma Muhurta

Brahma Muhurta is more than just a time on the clock—it is a gateway to spiritual awakening, mental clarity, and physical well-being. By aligning our daily routines with this sacred hour, we can cultivate a deeper connection with the divine, harmonize our lives with nature's rhythms, and unlock our fullest potential.

Whether through meditation, yoga, or simply quiet reflection, embracing the practice of *Brahma Muhurta* allows us to tap into the ancient wisdom that has guided spiritual seekers for millennia. In today's world, where the demands of daily life often pull us in different directions, starting the day in stillness and peace during *Brahma Muhurta* can be a powerful practice for fostering a balanced and fulfilling life.

However, self-realization is not limited to any specific time or condition. While Brahma Muhurta may be an ideal time for spiritual practices that support self-realization, the experience of realizing one's true nature goes beyond any particular moment or practice. Self-realization can occur in any state of consciousness, whether during moments of stillness, in the midst of activity, or in deep meditation. The true nature of the self, is always present and accessible—it is beyond time, space, and conditions.

30

From Sex to Samadhi

The journey from the base instincts of human existence, such as sexual desire, to the highest state of consciousness, known as *samadhi*, is a profound aspect of spiritual evolution in yoga. This chapter explores the transformation of energy from its most primal expression in sexuality to its highest expression in spiritual enlightenment. The yogic path provides practical tools for sublimating sexual energy (Kundalini) into spiritual energy, ultimately leading to the state of *samadhi*, where the individual self merges with universal consciousness.

The Role of Sexual Energy in Yoga

Sexual energy, also known as *Shakti* or *Kundalini*, is often considered the most potent force within the human body. In the yogic tradition, it is viewed not as something to be suppressed, but as a vital force that can be transformed and elevated for spiritual growth.

Sexual energy holds layers of mystery and potential that often go unspoken in mainstream discussions. In many spiritual traditions, sexual energy is seen as one of the most powerful forms of energy, not just for physical intimacy but as a tool for spiritual growth, healing, and transformation. A secret known to certain tantric and yogic teachings is that when sexual energy is consciously directed, it can fuel creativity, heighten intuition, and even accelerate the kundalini awakening process. By channelling this energy into higher chakras through specific meditative practices, one can experience profound insights, creative breakthroughs, and elevated states of consciousness that might not be accessible otherwise.

Another lesser-known aspect is that sexual energy, when cultivated with awareness, can act as a **healing force**. Ancient practices like Taoist sexual alchemy and Kundalini tantra teach that this energy has a restorative power that can revitalize not only the physical body but also the mind and spirit. When circulated through the body's meridians or energy channels, it clears blockages and aligns the chakras, leading to a balanced state of inner harmony and vitality. This process, known as **microcosmic orbit** in Taoism, is a method of circulating sexual energy that transforms it into a nourishing elixir for the whole system.

Furthermore, sexual energy is often considered a direct pathway to accessing a deeper connection with the universe. The experience of merging energetically with another person is sometimes described as a small glimpse of the universal oneness that many seek on the spiritual path. Advanced practitioners often use this connection as a meditative tool, seeing it as an opportunity to tap into states of pure presence and cosmic unity, far beyond the physical. This secret understanding reframes sexuality not merely as a physical act, but as an exploration of the divine within, allowing individuals to experience the essence of their spiritual being.

Kundalini Energy: The Coiled Serpent

Kundalini refers to the dormant spiritual energy that resides at the base of the spine, in the *Muladhara* chakra. When awakened through specific yogic practices, this energy rises through the chakras, ultimately reaching the *Sahasrara* chakra at the crown of the head, where enlightenment or *samadhi* is attained. The *Hatha Yoga Pradipika* describes Kundalini as "the goddess of speech and the creative power of the universe" (Chapter 3, Verse 105).

The symbolic representation of Kundalini as a coiled serpent highlights its potential power, waiting to be awakened and channelled for spiritual realization.

Sexual Energy as Creative Force

Sexual energy is often associated with creation, not just in the physical sense of procreation, but also as a source of creative expression and vitality. In yoga, this energy is seen as sacred, with the potential to be harnessed and redirected toward higher purposes. The *Tantric* traditions, in particular, explore the sacredness of sexual energy, viewing it as a means of uniting the individual self with the divine.

The Gift of Chakras: Human Potential for Kundalini Awakening

Humans stand unique in the natural order, possessing an intricate system of energy centers known as chakras, which provide a pathway to greater awareness, healing, and spiritual awakening. While all beings share a subtle energy system, the human design includes seven primary chakras aligned along the spine, each corresponding to different aspects of physical, emotional, and spiritual well-being. This complex chakra network not only supports personal growth but also enables us to access and balance the kundalini energy, waiting to be awakened.

This awakening, when nurtured, guides the seeker through stages of enlightenment, offering profound shifts in consciousness and understanding.

Unlike other creatures, humans are endowed with the capacity to intentionally engage in practices like meditation, yoga, and pranayama, which stimulate and harmonize this energy. Each chakra is a gateway to higher planes of experience; as kundalini rises through them, it bestows unique insights and transformative powers, enabling the individual to reach a state of unity and transcendence. This rare opportunity reflects the sacred privilege of human existence, reminding us that through dedicated practice and inner awareness, we can awaken this energy to experience deeper peace, purpose, and connection with the universe.

One intriguing secret about kundalini and the chakras is that the journey isn't as linear as it might seem. While traditional teachings present the awakening as a process of energy moving sequentially through the chakras from the root to the crown, in reality, kundalini can flow dynamically, often jumping or bypassing chakras depending on a person's unique life experiences, karmic influences, and mental readiness. This non-linear awakening can reveal that one doesn't necessarily have to "complete" lower chakras before accessing higher states of consciousness. Instead, flashes of insight or spiritual experiences may occur spontaneously even before the lower chakras are fully balanced.

Another hidden aspect is that each chakra has a **hidden** layer or secret vibration often unknown to most practitioners. For instance, while the heart chakra (Anahata) is commonly associated with love and compassion, its deeper layers unlock access to intuitive wisdom and a profound sense of interconnectedness beyond love alone. When kundalini moves into these subtle dimensions of each chakra, the individual may experience states of heightened awareness that are uniquely their own, often uncovering abilities they never imagined — such as deep empathy, clairvoyance, or even an intuitive grasp of cosmic truths.

Lastly, the true nature of kundalini itself is often hidden. Kundalini is not just a form of energy but is sometimes described as a conscious force or even a personal guide. Some ancient texts and practitioners regard it as a divine presence, a wise intelligence that knows exactly how to heal, balance, and guide the practitioner according to their highest potential. This **living** aspect of kundalini is rarely spoken of openly, as it can only be directly experienced, leaving each practitioner to discover this secret, guiding force on their unique path.

The Yogic Path of Sublimation

Sublimation is the process of transforming and elevating base desires, such as sexual energy, into spiritual energy. Yoga offers various techniques to help practitioners achieve this transformation, allowing them to progress from the material to the spiritual realm.

Brahmacharya: The Practice of Celibacy

One of the key ethical principles in *Patanjali's Yoga Sutras* is Brahmacharya, which is often interpreted as celibacy or control over sexual impulses. Brahmacharya is not merely about abstaining from sexual activity but about conserving and channelling this vital energy toward spiritual pursuits. In Yoga Sutra 2.38, Patanjali states, "By the establishment of Brahmacharya, vigour is gained."

However, Brahmacharya can also be understood in a broader sense, as moderation in all sensual pleasures. It is about mastery over one's desires rather than suppression, leading to inner strength and clarity of mind.

Pranayama: Breath Control for Energy Management

Pranayama (breath control) plays a significant role in controlling and sublimating sexual energy. Techniques such as Nadi Shodhana (alternate nostril breathing) and Kapalabhati (skull-shining breath) help regulate the flow of Prana (life force) within the body, allowing the practitioner to redirect energy away from the lower chakras and toward the higher centers of consciousness.

Research has shown that regular practice of Pranayama can reduce stress and anxiety, which are often linked to uncontrolled desires, including sexual urges. By calming the mind and body, Pranayama helps create the conditions for higher spiritual experiences.

Bandhas and Mudras: Locking and Channelling Energy

In Hatha Yoga, *bandhas* (energy locks) and *mudras* (gestures) are employed to lock and channel energy upward. For instance, *Mula Bandha* (root lock) involves contracting the muscles of the pelvic floor, helping to prevent the dissipation of sexual energy and redirect it toward spiritual growth.

Mudras, such as *Yoni Mudra* (womb gesture), are symbolic hand gestures that can further aid in controlling and channelling energy. These techniques allow practitioners to focus their energy inward, facilitating the process of sublimation.

Swami Vivekananda is a prime example of a yogi who practiced *Brahmacharya* and transformed his vital energy into spiritual power. His teachings emphasized the control of the senses and the sublimation of sexual energy as essential for spiritual progress. His tireless work for humanity and his deep spiritual insights were a result of his disciplined lifestyle, which included the practice of *Brahmacharya*.

From Sex to Samadhi: The Final Destination

Samadhi is the ultimate goal of yoga—a state of complete absorption in the infinite. It is the culmination of the yogic journey, where the individual self merges with universal consciousness. This state of enlightenment transcends all dualities, including the duality of desire and fulfilment.

The Nature of Samadhi

Patanjali describes *Samadhi* in the *Yoga Sutras* as the eighth and final limb of yoga. It is a state of deep meditative absorption where the mind becomes one-pointed, and the ego dissolves. In *Yoga Sutra* 3.3, he defines *Samadhi* as "the state in which the mind becomes one with the object of meditation." This state is beyond all desires, including sexual desire, as the practitioner experiences complete union with the divine.

The Role of Sexual Energy in Achieving Samadhi

Sexual energy, when sublimated, becomes a powerful tool for spiritual transformation. The rise of Kundalini energy through the chakras is often seen as a journey from base desires to higher consciousness. When this energy reaches the *Sahasrara* chakra, the practitioner experiences *samadhi*—the ultimate state of spiritual fulfilment.

The journey from sex to *samadhi* is symbolic of the **transformation of human life from its most primal expression to its most refined**

state. It is a journey that requires discipline, practice, and a deep understanding of the nature of the self.

Conclusion

The journey from sex to *samadhi* is a transformative process that lies at the heart of yoga. By understanding and harnessing sexual energy, practitioners can sublimate this powerful force into spiritual energy, leading to the ultimate realization of *samadhi*. Through the practices of *Brahmacharya*, *Pranayama*, and Kundalini awakening, yoga offers a path to transcend the base desires of the material world and attain the highest state of consciousness. In this journey, every aspect of human experience—from sexuality to spirituality—becomes a stepping stone toward the realization of the divine within.

To achieve self-realization, it is essential to transcend sensual desires, the activities associated with the lower chakras, and an overemphasis on bodily consciousness.

31

Kundalini

Kundalini, a term often encountered in spiritual literature, represents the latent divine energy coiled at the base of the spine in every human being. In Sanskrit, *Kundalini* literally means "coiled serpent," symbolizing the potential energy that lies dormant within each individual. Awakening Kundalini is believed to be a transformative process that can lead to higher states of consciousness, spiritual enlightenment, and ultimately, union with the divine (*samadhi*).

This chapter delves into the concept of Kundalini, its significance in the spiritual journey, and whether it is essential for everyone. We will explore the profound impact of Kundalini on the mind, body, and soul.

Understanding Kundalini: The Dormant Power

As discussed in previous chapter, Kundalini is often depicted as a dormant serpent coiled at the base of the spine, specifically at the *Muladhara* chakra (root chakra). According to yogic tradition, this energy can be awakened through various practices, including meditation, pranayama, asanas, and mantras.

The energy travels through the *Sushumna Nadi*, the central energy channel in the subtle body, and ascends through the seven chakras—*Muladhara, Swadhisthana, Manipura, Anahata, Vishuddha, Ajna,* and *Sahasrara.* The ultimate goal is for the Kundalini to reach the crown chakra (*Sahasrara*), where one experiences union with the divine and realizes the true nature of the self.

The concept of Kundalini is mentioned in ancient Hindu scriptures such as the Upanishads, Hatha Yoga Pradipika, and Shiva Samhita. The Hatha Yoga Pradipika (3.2) states, "When the sleeping Kundalini awakens, then all the lotuses (chakras) and bonds are pierced through. Therefore, when the wise Yogi, having awakened the Kundalini, should attain success by uniting with Shiva."

The Process of Awakening

Kundalini awakening is not merely a physical experience but a profound spiritual transformation. It involves the purification of the nadis (energy channels) and the chakras, leading to a heightened state of awareness and a deep connection with the cosmos.

- **Spontaneous Awakening**: In some cases, Kundalini can awaken spontaneously due to intense spiritual practices, deep emotional experiences, or even without any apparent reason. This sudden awakening can be overwhelming, as the body and mind may not be prepared to handle the surge of energy.

- **Deliberate Awakening**: In contrast, deliberate awakening involves systematic practices under the guidance of an experienced teacher. These practices help prepare the body and mind for the energy's ascent, making the process smoother and safer.

Signs of Kundalini Awakening

The awakening of Kundalini can manifest in various ways, both physically and spiritually. Common signs include:

Physical Sensations: Heat or energy moving through the spine, spontaneous movements, or involuntary yogic postures (*Kriyas*).

Mental and Emotional Changes: Heightened awareness, deep inner peace, or intense emotional upheavals.

Spiritual Experiences: Visions, heightened intuition, or a deep sense of oneness with the universe.

Real-life examples include individuals such as Gopi Krishna, who documented his Kundalini awakening experience in his book *Kundalini: The Evolutionary Energy in Man*. His journey through the process highlighted both the challenges and the spiritual transformation that Kundalini awakening can bring.

Is Kundalini Awakening Important?

The importance of Kundalini awakening varies depending on the spiritual path one follows. For some, it is a crucial aspect of their spiritual journey, while for others, it is not essential. Here's a deeper look:

For the Practitioner of Kundalini Yoga: Kundalini awakening is central to the practice. Kundalini Yoga, emphasizes awakening this energy to achieve spiritual liberation and self-realization. The practice incorporates dynamic breathing techniques, asanas, and mantras to stimulate and balance the energy within.

For Practitioners of Other Paths: In contrast, other yogic paths such as Bhakti Yoga (path of devotion), Jnana Yoga (path of knowledge), and Karma Yoga (path of selfless action) do not emphasize Kundalini awakening as a necessary step toward enlightenment. Saints like Ramana Maharshi, who achieved self-realization through *Atma Vichara* (self-inquiry), did not focus on Kundalini but rather on the direct realization of the self (Atman).

Thus, while Kundalini awakening can accelerate spiritual growth and lead to profound mystical experiences, it is not a prerequisite for spiritual liberation. Enlightenment can be attained through various means, depending on one's temperament and spiritual inclination.

Potential Challenges and Precautions

Kundalini awakening, though transformative, is not without challenges. The sudden surge of energy can cause physical, emotional, and psychological disturbances if not managed properly. Symptoms may include:

Kundalini Syndrome: A condition where the body and mind struggle to cope with the awakened energy, leading to anxiety, depression, or even physical ailments. This is why it is essential to approach Kundalini practices with caution and under the guidance of an experienced teacher.

Preparation and Balance: It is important to purify the mind and body before attempting Kundalini awakening. Practices such as ethical living (Yama and Niyama), regular meditation, and a balanced diet can help prepare the system to handle the energy safely.

Christmas and Santa Claus

In many mystical traditions, Christmas is more than the celebration of the physical birth of Jesus; it signifies the birth of Christ consciousness within. **Christ consciousness** refers to the awakening of a higher, universal awareness that transcends the ego, revealing the divine nature within each individual. This mirrors the spiritual journey of **Kundalini awakening**.

In this view, Christ represents the awakened self, free from the constraints of the ego and in direct communion with the divine. The **birth of Christ** within each individual, therefore, is the birth of their highest potential and spiritual realization.

Santa Claus as a Symbol of Spiritual Guidance

Santa Claus, though often seen as a folkloric figure, holds deeper metaphysical significance. Esoterically, Santa represents the **cosmic forces** that assist the spiritual seeker. His role in distributing gifts aligns with the idea that spiritual practice, devotion, and dedication lead to the reception of spiritual blessings—often referred to as the **gifts of insight, wisdom, love, and enlightenment**.

Santa's descent down the chimney can be compared to the descent of spiritual energy through the spine, often described in yogic traditions as energy flowing through the **Sushumna Nadi** (the central channel of the energy system). This is the same path the awakened Kundalini energy follows as it rises toward the crown chakra, distributing spiritual nourishment along the way.

Santa's **gifts** can be viewed as symbolic of the realizations, heightened awareness, and spiritual abilities attained through the awakening of Kundalini and consistent inner work.

Santa's red suit can also be interpreted as the colour of the **Muladhara chakra**, the root energy center associated with the dormant Kundalini energy, from where the spiritual journey begins.

In this way, Santa Claus becomes a **mythic symbol** representing benevolent cosmic energies or spiritual guides that aid the aspirant on the path of self-realization.

The Winter Solstice and Rebirth of Light

Christmas coincides with the **winter solstice**, the darkest period of the year, marking the return of the light as the days begin to lengthen. This rebirth of light after the longest night is deeply symbolic in mystical traditions, as it parallels the spiritual journey from darkness to light, ignorance to enlightenment.

The **winter solstice** represents the internal state of spiritual dormancy or ignorance, where the divine light within is hidden beneath layers of ego, attachments, and limited perceptions.

The **return of the sun's light** symbolizes the awakening of the Kundalini, where the seeker moves from a state of spiritual ignorance (darkness) toward illumination (light).

Just as the physical sun begins to ascend, bringing warmth and light to the external world, the awakened Kundalini brings **spiritual illumination** to the seeker, enabling them to transcend ignorance and realize their true nature.

Christmas as a Symbolic Journey of Awakening

In both the celebration of Christmas and the process of Kundalini awakening, the overarching theme is **rebirth and transformation**. The spiritual aspirant, like the world at the winter solstice, experiences a profound transition from a state of darkness to light. The **Christ child** born on Christmas symbolizes the **new life** or **divine realization** that comes with the awakening of Kundalini energy, guiding the seeker toward unity with the divine.

Thus, Christmas, in its esoteric interpretation, reflects the spiritual journey of awakening, where the individual recognizes their **divine essence** and aligns with the cosmic forces that nurture and guide them on their path to enlightenment. It is a universal process of rebirth, applicable not only to followers of Christianity but to all spiritual seekers, as it speaks to the awakening of higher consciousness that transcends cultural and religious boundaries.

Pineal Gland

The pineal gland, often called the "third eye," has intrigued mystics and scientists alike due to its mysterious role in spiritual experiences and higher consciousness. This tiny, pinecone-shaped gland is located deep within the brain, and its primary function in modern science is believed to be the regulation of sleep cycles through melatonin production. However, ancient spiritual traditions, like those of India, Egypt, and Taoist China, regard the pineal gland as a portal to other realms and heightened awareness. Here are some fascinating, less commonly known aspects of the pineal gland that remain shrouded in mystery:

Natural Production of DMT: There is speculation and some emerging evidence that the pineal gland may produce trace amounts of DMT (dimethyltryptamine), a powerful psychoactive compound known for inducing profound, sometimes mystical experiences. While scientific confirmation is still ongoing, ancient cultures have long considered the pineal gland to be the "seat of the soul," potentially producing natural psychedelics that facilitate visions, near-death experiences, and altered states of consciousness. This concept aligns with the gland's position at the center of the brain, believed to be connected to higher dimensions of thought and awareness.

Connection with Light and Darkness: The pineal gland is one of the few parts of the brain that is sensitive to light, which makes it an essential part of regulating circadian rhythms. However, ancient yogis and spiritual practitioners discovered that darkness also plays a powerful role in activating this "third eye." Practices involving darkness retreats or spending extended time in dim environments are said to stimulate the pineal gland, allowing practitioners to access visions and inner revelations. These practices supposedly clear mental blockages and heighten intuitive abilities by "switching on" the pineal gland's secret capabilities.

Crystals Within the Pineal Gland: The pineal gland contains microcrystals of calcite, which can generate piezoelectric signals (electrical charges produced by mechanical pressure). This quality means the gland could act as a natural bio-crystal radio receiver, potentially picking up electromagnetic signals or subtle energy fields. Some theorists suggest that this property might allow the pineal gland to act as an antenna for spiritual or other-dimensional information, a concept often explored in esoteric teachings that view the pineal as a bridge between the physical and spiritual realms.

Unlocking Psychic Abilities: Various spiritual traditions hold that a purified and activated pineal gland enhances abilities like clairvoyance, telepathy, and deep intuitive insight. Meditative practices, breathing techniques, and diet adjustments (like minimizing fluoride, which some claim calcifies the gland) are often recommended to stimulate and "detoxify" the pineal gland. Yogic and Tibetan practices specifically emphasize using the pineal gland as a focal point to achieve "samadhi," a state of absolute consciousness where the sense of self merges with the universe.

Pineal Gland and Kundalini Activation: In Kundalini yoga and tantra, the pineal gland is thought to work in harmony with the crown chakra (Sahasrara) and the third eye chakra (Ajna) during kundalini awakening. As kundalini energy rises through the chakras, it's believed to activate the pineal gland, leading to a higher state of awareness and connection to divine consciousness. This process is said to open the individual to inner visions, a deep sense of unity, and a state of pure bliss.

These hidden aspects of the pineal gland reflect its revered status across cultures as a gateway to divine perception and inner wisdom. As scientific and spiritual understandings of the pineal gland evolve, humanity continues to unlock the secrets of this "third eye," revealing its potential to illuminate realms beyond the ordinary mind.

The pineal gland, can be affected by various factors that inhibit its full potential and function. Modern life, in particular, presents many environmental and lifestyle influences that can "block" or hinder the pineal gland, often without us even realizing it. Here are some lesser-known factors that can inhibit its natural functioning, along with insights into how to counteract these blocks:

Fluoride and Calcification: Fluoride, commonly found in tap water and dental products, is believed to accumulate in the pineal gland over time, leading to calcification. This calcification forms hard deposits around the gland, which can restrict its ability to produce melatonin and other important neurochemicals. This is particularly concerning because, when calcified, the pineal gland's sensitivity to light and its overall function are greatly reduced. Reducing exposure to fluoride by using filtered water and fluoride-free products, along with consuming foods high in iodine, magnesium, and boron, is said to help reduce calcification and support pineal health.

Electromagnetic Frequencies (EMFs): The pineal gland is sensitive to electromagnetic frequencies, which are ubiquitous in our modern environment due to devices like cell phones, Wi-Fi routers, and microwaves. Some research suggests that excessive EMF exposure can disrupt the pineal gland's natural rhythms, particularly its production of melatonin, which is vital for sleep and overall brain health. Practicing "digital detoxes," limiting screen time before bed, and keeping devices away from your sleeping area can help reduce EMF exposure and allow the pineal gland to function more optimally.

Excessive Artificial Light Exposure: The pineal gland is directly influenced by the amount of light we're exposed to, which is how it regulates the body's sleep-wake cycle through melatonin production. However, exposure to artificial light, particularly blue light from screens, disrupts this cycle and can inhibit the gland's natural function. Spending time in natural sunlight during the day and minimizing artificial light exposure, especially in the evening, can help the pineal gland maintain its rhythm and produce melatonin at optimal levels.

Poor Diet and Processed Foods: The pineal gland, like the rest of the brain, requires adequate nutrients to function well. Diets high in processed foods, refined sugars, and artificial additives create stress in the body and can lead to inflammation, indirectly affecting the pineal gland. Some reports suggest that a diet high in antioxidants (like berries, leafy greens, and nuts), along with omega-3 fatty acids (found in fish and flaxseeds), can support pineal gland health by reducing oxidative stress and inflammation.

Heavy Metal Accumulation: Heavy metals, particularly mercury and aluminium, can build up in the brain, impacting the pineal gland's ability to function optimally. Mercury exposure, which can come from certain types of seafood, dental fillings, and industrial pollution, is known to affect neurological health and has been linked to pineal gland dysfunction. Engaging in gentle detox methods like consuming cilantro, chlorella, and spirulina, as well as using infrared saunas, can help reduce heavy metal levels in the body and support the pineal gland's functioning.

Negative Emotional Patterns and Stress: Chronic stress and negative emotional patterns may impact the pineal gland's functioning by constantly activating the body's fight-or-flight response, which interferes with melatonin production and pineal regulation. This stress response is known to shift energy resources toward survival mechanisms, leaving little energy for the gland's subtler functions. Meditative practices, mindfulness, and regular relaxation exercises can help reset the nervous system and allow the pineal gland to function in its natural state.

Lack of Spiritual Practice or Introspection: Spiritual traditions hold that a lack of introspection or spiritual practice can dull the pineal gland's energy and functioning. Practices like meditation, yoga, visualization, and sound healing stimulate the pineal gland and the brain's energetic centers, helping to activate and "open" the third eye. These practices not only help clear mental clutter but also stimulate the gland, potentially reversing blockages and fostering greater clarity, insight, and alignment with one's inner self.

Kundalini in Modern Context

In recent times, Kundalini Yoga has gained popularity in the West, particularly due to its introduction by Yogi Bhajan in the 1960s. Celebrities and spiritual seekers alike have embraced Kundalini Yoga for its potential to enhance creativity, improve well-being, and foster spiritual growth.

The phenomenon of Kundalini awakening has also attracted interest from scientists and psychologists. Studies have been conducted to understand the physiological and psychological effects of Kundalini practices, with some researchers suggesting that Kundalini experiences may be linked to altered states of consciousness similar to those observed in near-death experiences or mystical states.

Conclusion: Kundalini—A Path, Not the Only Path

Kundalini awakening can be a powerful catalyst for spiritual growth, but it is not the only path to enlightenment. Different yogic traditions offer various routes to the same goal—union with the divine. Whether one seeks to awaken Kundalini or pursues another spiritual path, the ultimate aim remains the realization of the true self and liberation from the cycle of birth and death (samsara).

The journey of Kundalini awakening is unique to each individual, and while it can lead to profound spiritual experiences, it is essential to approach it with reverence, patience, and proper guidance. In the words of Swami Vivekananda, "The awakening of the Kundalini means that the individual forces are uniting themselves with the cosmic forces. The awakening of the Kundalini is the beginning of spiritual consciousness, and when the Kundalini reaches the brain, one attains Samadhi."

For those drawn to this path, Kundalini offers a transformative journey toward spiritual enlightenment. For others, there are many other ways to reach the ultimate goal of yoga, which is union with the divine.

32

Stories That Inspire

The Story of Ramakrishna Paramahamsa and Totapuri Baba

Ramakrishna Paramahamsa, the mystic saint of 19th-century India, is revered for his deep spiritual experiences and teachings that encompassed various paths of devotion, knowledge, and meditation. One of the most profound and transformative events in his life was his encounter with **Totapuri Baba**, an Advaita Vedanta monk, who guided Ramakrishna from the dualistic (Dvaita) path of devotion to the non-dualistic (Advaita) realization of Brahman.

Ramakrishna's Devotion to Kali

Ramakrishna had spent years as a priest at the Dakshineswar Kali Temple, worshiping the Goddess Kali with deep devotion and intense love. His entire being was consumed by the image of the Divine Mother. He would enter into ecstatic states of communion with her, experiencing visions of Kali in which he saw her as the living embodiment of the universe. For Ramakrishna, Kali was the ultimate reality, and he perceived no difference between the world and the Mother.

However, Ramakrishna's devotion to Kali, while profound, kept him within the framework of duality—where the worshipper and the worshipped were seen as separate. He had yet to experience the non-dualistic reality where all forms dissolve into the infinite, formless Brahman.

The Arrival of Totapuri Baba

Totapuri Baba was a wandering monk of the Advaita Vedanta tradition, which teaches that the ultimate reality is the formless, impersonal Brahman, beyond all dualities and distinctions. When Totapuri arrived at Dakshineswar, he saw in Ramakrishna a seeker of great spiritual potential, but one who had yet to transcend the limitations of duality.

Totapuri offered to initiate Ramakrishna into the path of Advaita, the realization of the non-dual Brahman. Ramakrishna, though initially hesitant, agreed to undergo the initiation, eager to experience this higher state of realization.

The Struggle to Transcend Duality

During the initiation, Totapuri instructed Ramakrishna to meditate on the formless Brahman and to dismiss all forms from his mind, including the beloved image of Kali. However, as Ramakrishna closed his eyes and attempted to meditate on the formless reality, the radiant image of Kali continued to appear before him, preventing him from merging into the infinite.

Frustrated by this inability to go beyond the image of Kali, Ramakrishna expressed his struggle to Totapuri. Totapuri, known for his strict discipline, picked up a piece of glass and pressed it against Ramakrishna's forehead, right between his eyebrows. He instructed

Ramakrishna to focus intensely on this spot (the third eye) and to mentally "cut" through the image of Kali with the sword of knowledge.

The Realization of Brahman

Following Totapuri's instructions with full concentration, Ramakrishna finally managed to shatter the image of Kali in his mind. In that moment, he transcended all forms and entered into a deep state of Samadhi (profound absorption). He realized the ultimate truth of Advaita—the oneness of all existence—and experienced the infinite, formless Brahman, where there is no distinction between the self and the universe.

Ramakrishna remained in this state of Samadhi for three days, completely absorbed in the bliss of non-dual consciousness. He experienced the profound truth that the essence of everything is Brahman, beyond all forms, names, and dualities.

A Harmonious Union of Duality and Non-Duality

Though Ramakrishna realized the ultimate non-dual Brahman through the guidance of Totapuri, he did not abandon his devotion to Kali. After his experience of Advaita, he continued to worship Kali, but with the profound understanding that the formless Brahman and the form of the Divine Mother were one and the same. He recognized that all paths, whether of devotion or knowledge, ultimately lead to the same realization of the divine truth.

This realization became a cornerstone of Ramakrishna's teachings, which emphasized the harmony of all religious paths. He taught that whether one worships God with form or without, all sincere spiritual efforts lead to the same divine truth.

Conclusion

The story of Ramakrishna and Totapuri is a powerful example of the spiritual journey from duality to non-duality. Ramakrishna's experience demonstrates that devotion and knowledge are not mutually exclusive, but can be integrated into a holistic understanding of the divine. His realization of Brahman, under the guidance of Totapuri, transcended the limitations of form and duality, while his continuing devotion to Kali showed that the divine can be experienced in both personal and impersonal forms.

Ramakrishna's teachings continue to inspire spiritual seekers across the world, showing that the ultimate goal of life is the realization of the oneness of all existence, beyond the distinctions of name, form, and belief.

"The same Being whom the dualist calls God, the Vedantist calls Brahman. The being is the same, but the viewpoints are different." – Ramakrishna Paramahamsa

Sant Kabir: The Weaver Saint Who Wove Divine Wisdom

Sant Kabir, one of India's most revered mystic poets and saints, was born in the 15th century in Varanasi. Though the details of his early life are clouded in legend, most agree that he was found as an infant and adopted by a poor Muslim weaver couple, Niru and Nima. Kabir grew up learning the art of weaving, but his heart was set on unravelling the deeper mysteries of existence.

He was deeply inspired by the teachings of the Hindu saint, Swami Ramananda. Kabir's spiritual philosophy developed into a unique blend of devotion (bhakti) and mysticism. Kabir's teachings transcended religious boundaries, drawing inspiration from both Hindu and Islamic traditions, but free from the constraints of both.

He emphasized the unity of all beings and the formless nature of the Divine, calling for love and devotion to the Supreme.

Reviving a Dead Cow

A story involves Kabir reviving a dead cow. When a cow belonging to a Brahmin died, the Brahmin blamed Kabir, accusing him of causing the cow's death. Kabir, known for his compassion, reportedly touched the cow, and it came back to life. This act is seen as symbolic of his divine compassion and his ability to transcend physical reality.

The Miraculous Transformation of the Bed of Thorns

In a display of his tolerance and divine favour, Kabir was once made to sleep on a bed of thorns by those who disapproved of his teachings. However, according to the legend, the bed of thorns transformed into a bed of flowers, leaving him unharmed and peaceful.

Kabir's Defiance of Orthodox Hindu and Islamic Practices

Kabir's teachings and verses often directly challenged the rigid rituals and superstitions of both Hinduism and Islam. He questioned meaningless rituals like idol worship, caste distinctions, pilgrimage, fasting, and animal sacrifices, insisting that true spirituality lies in devotion to a formless God and in righteous living.

For example, in one of his couplets, Kabir says, "Pothi padh padh jag mua, pandit bhaya na koi; Dhai aakhar prem ke, jo padhe so pandit hoye." (The world is dying reading scriptures, but no one becomes a learned one; He alone becomes wise, who understands the two-and-a-half letters of love.)

Through such verses, Kabir mocked the idea that salvation or enlightenment could be achieved through mere reading of scriptures or performing rituals, without a heart filled with love and devotion to God.

Opposition from Both Hindu and Muslim Clergy

Kabir's criticism of established religious practices angered the orthodox clergy of both Hinduism and Islam. Brahmins were upset because Kabir questioned caste divisions and the efficacy of temple rituals, while Muslim clerics were offended by his disdain for external practices like circumcision and observing Ramzan fasts. He refused to follow the rules of either religion strictly, and his message enraged both communities.

It is said that both Hindu and Muslim leaders brought complaints against him to the local king, Sultan Sikander Lodi, accusing Kabir of heresy and misleading the masses.

The Miracle of Escape from Execution

One of the well-known stories associated with Kabir's defiance of orthodoxy concerns an attempt by Sultan Sikander Lodi to have him executed. The story goes that Kabir was arrested and sentenced to death. The sultan ordered that he be drowned in the Ganges, a punishment intended to end his defiance once and for all.

Kabir was bound hand and foot and thrown into the river. However, according to the legend, Kabir did not drown. To everyone's astonishment, he floated on the water, untouched by the death sentence. Some versions of the story say that the ropes miraculously came undone, while others claim that Kabir simply floated away. The people, including the king, were stunned by this display, and Kabir emerged unscathed.

Following this event, the king and his court realized that Kabir's spiritual power was beyond the authority of religious institutions or political force. His survival reinforced his teachings that true spirituality does not need the protection of rituals, dogmas, or human power.

Kabir's Message of Spiritual Unity

Kabir's defiance of religious orthodoxy was rooted in his conviction that true spirituality is found in simplicity, love, and devotion to a formless God, rather than in adherence to rigid customs or ceremonies. He preached a message of unity, asserting that both Hindus and Muslims worshipped the same God, even though they called him by different names.

As Kabir said, "Hindu kahe mohi Ram piyara, Turk kahe Rahiman; Apas mein dou ladi ladi mue, maram na kou jania." which means, "The Hindu says Ram is dear to me, the Turk says Rahim is dear; They both died fighting each other, and no one understood the truth."

Kabir was neither interested in the identity of Ram nor Rahim but in the experience of the divine, which, for him, lay beyond names, rituals, and religious affiliations.

The Miracle of Sant Kabir's Death

Sant Kabir's life was not without challenges. His bold stance against religious hypocrisy and caste discrimination earned him both admirers and enemies. Yet, his devotion to the Divine was unwavering, and his life was filled with miracles that continue to inspire millions.

As Sant Kabir grew old, it became evident that his time on Earth was nearing its end. His disciples, both Hindu and Muslim, gathered around him, each community wanting to claim him as their own. The Hindus believed that Kabir should be cremated according to Hindu rituals, while the Muslims insisted that he should be buried according to Islamic tradition.

Kabir, with his characteristic wit and wisdom, smiled at their disagreement. He lay down peacefully, instructing his followers to cover his body with a white sheet. He assured them that the Divine would reveal the truth.

When Kabir left his physical body, the conflict between the two groups intensified. Unable to come to an agreement, they finally decided to lift the sheet to resolve the matter. But when they did, they were astonished to find that Kabir's body had disappeared. In its place, there lay a heap of fragrant flowers.

Half of the flowers were taken by the Hindus, who performed the cremation, while the other half were buried by the Muslims. In this miraculous event, Kabir transcended religious boundaries even in death, leaving behind a powerful message: The Divine is beyond form, beyond religion, and beyond death.

Kabir's teachings, preserved through his couplets (dohas), continue to inspire countless seekers on the spiritual path. His life serves as a reminder that true devotion is about transcending the divisions of the material world and realizing the oneness of all creation.

Reflection

Sant Kabir's life was a testament to the power of simplicity, devotion, and non-duality. His fearless critique of religious hypocrisy, casteism, and meaningless rituals resonated across communities. Through his words and miracles, he urged humanity to rise above the superficial layers of identity and embrace the Divine within.

For modern seekers, Sant Kabir's teachings offer a timeless guide to living a life of spiritual depth. His story reminds us that the path to realization is not about rigid adherence to rituals but about the sincere pursuit of truth, love, and unity.

Sant Ravidas: The Divine Cobbler Who Mended Souls

Sant Ravidas, also known as Raidas, was a 15th-century mystic, poet, and saint from the Bhakti movement in India. Born into a humble family of cobblers in the city of Varanasi, his life is a testament to the transformative power of devotion, humility, and spiritual realization. Ravidas's life was filled with miraculous events that showcased his deep connection with the divine, making him a revered figure across various religious traditions.

Early Life and Struggles

Ravidas was born to Santokh Das and Kalsa Devi in the village of Seer Govardhanpur near Varanasi. His family belonged to the Chamar community, traditionally engaged in leatherwork. Despite the social stigma attached to his caste, Ravidas displayed a deep spiritual inclination from an early age. He would often meditate, sing devotional songs, and serve the poor and needy with a purity of heart that set him apart.

Even as a young boy, Ravidas was known for his profound wisdom and compassion. However, his spiritual path was not without challenges. The rigid caste system of the time often brought him into conflict with society, but his devotion to God remained unwavering.

Miraculous Encounter with a Brahmin

One of the most famous stories of Sant Ravidas's life revolves around an encounter with a wealthy Brahmin who had ordered shoes from Ravidas. The Brahmin, upon learning that his shoes were made by someone from a lower caste, refused to wear them and scorned Ravidas.

Undeterred by the Brahmin's anger, Ravidas humbly requested him to try the shoes before passing judgment. Reluctantly, the Brahmin complied and, as soon as he put on the shoes, he experienced a divine vision. He saw the feet of Lord Vishnu in the shoes and was overwhelmed by an indescribable sense of peace and connection with the divine. Realizing that Ravidas was no ordinary cobbler, the Brahmin fell at his feet and sought his blessings. This incident spread Ravidas's fame far and wide, attracting people from all castes to seek his wisdom and blessings.

The Miracle of "Man Changa to Kathoti Mein Ganga"

One of the most remarkable miracles associated with Sant Ravidas is the story of how the sacred Ganges River manifested in his humble home. It is said that a group of Brahmins, sceptical of Ravidas's spiritual prowess, challenged him to prove his connection with the divine.

Ravidas, in his characteristic humility, simply replied, "Man changa to kathoti mein Ganga," meaning, "If the mind is pure, then the Ganges flows even in a small vessel." As he spoke these words, a miracle occurred: the sacred Ganges River began to flow from the small vessel (kathoti) in which Ravidas was washing his leather, right in the middle of his workshop.

This miraculous event stunned the Brahmins and all those who witnessed it. It was a powerful reminder that divine grace is not dependent on external rituals or social status, but on the purity of one's heart and mind. The phrase "Man changa to kathoti mein Ganga" became famous and is still quoted today to emphasize the power of inner purity and devotion.

Teachings and Philosophy

Ravidas's teachings emphasized the oneness of all beings and the presence of God within every individual, regardless of caste, creed, or gender. He believed that true devotion lay in inner purity, selfless service, and unwavering faith in God. His verses, written in simple yet profound language, conveyed deep spiritual truths that resonated with people from all walks of life.

One of his most famous hymns is,

"Begumpura, a city without sorrow, where all live in perfect bliss, no one suffers there from any pain, no one feels the sting of misery."

In these lines, Ravidas envisions a utopian society where suffering and discrimination no longer exist—a place of unity and divine peace.

Influence and Legacy

Sant Ravidas's influence transcended his lifetime, and his teachings inspired many, including the renowned saint and poetess Mirabai, who considered him her spiritual guru. His hymns are included in the Guru Granth Sahib, the holy scripture of Sikhism, and continue to be sung by devotees worldwide.

Ravidas's life and teachings challenge the social hierarchies and prejudices that have divided humanity for centuries. He remains a beacon of hope for those who seek to rise above the limitations of caste, creed, and material wealth to realize the divine within.

One of the most enduring aspects of Ravidas's legacy is his vision of Begumpura—a city of eternal bliss, free from the sorrows of the material world. This vision continues to inspire countless devotees, reminding them that spiritual liberation is not a matter of external circumstances but of inner realization.

Conclusion

The life of Sant Ravidas is a shining example of how deep devotion, humility, and spiritual realization can elevate an individual beyond the confines of social constraints. His miracles, teachings, and life experiences continue to inspire millions, reminding us that true spirituality transcends all barriers and is accessible to everyone, regardless of their social or economic status. Ravidas showed that liberation is not a matter of birth or status, but of inner purity and unwavering devotion to the divine.

Sant Jnaneshwar (Dnyaneshwar)

Sant Jnaneshwar, also known as Dnyaneshwar, was a 13th-century Marathi saint, poet, and philosopher, known for his extraordinary wisdom at a young age. He is one of the most revered figures in the Bhakti tradition and played a significant role in making spiritual wisdom accessible to the common people. Jnaneshwar's life was filled with profound teachings, devotional poetry, and miraculous events that continue to inspire countless spiritual seekers.

Early Life and Spiritual Awakening

Jnaneshwar was born in the year 1275 CE in Alandi, near Pune, Maharashtra, to Vithalpant and Rukminibai. His parents had renounced worldly life and taken initiation as sannyasis (renunciates). However, under the orders of their guru, they returned to family life. This unorthodox decision caused social ostracization, and Jnaneshwar and his siblings faced much hardship as a result. Despite these challenges, the young Jnaneshwar displayed an extraordinary spiritual inclination.

From a very early age, Jnaneshwar was immersed in the teachings of the Vedas, Upanishads, and other scriptures, but he also emphasized the need to make this profound wisdom accessible to ordinary people. He believed that spiritual realization was not limited to scholars or the elite but was a birthright of every individual.

Breaking Free from Caste Discrimination

The caste system was deeply entrenched in the social fabric of Gyaneshwar's time, creating divisions that led to discrimination and inequality. Gyaneshwar, however, saw the divine spark within every being and refused to accept the limitations imposed by caste distinctions. He believed that all people, regardless of their caste, were equal in the eyes of God.

This conviction was put to the test when Gyaneshwar, still a young boy, sought the right to undergo the sacred thread ceremony, a ritual typically reserved for Brahmins. The orthodox Brahmin community refused, citing the family's history of social ostracism. Undeterred, Gyaneshwar and his siblings journeyed to Paithan, where they confronted the Brahmins and pleaded their case.

It was during this period that Gyaneshwar composed his first major work, the "Amritanubhava" (The Experience of Nectar), a philosophical treatise that expounded the non-dualistic nature of reality and emphasized the oneness of all beings. In it, he argued that the soul knows no caste, and that devotion to God is the true measure of a person's worth. His wisdom and humility moved many hearts, and eventually, the Brahmins relented, allowing the young Gyaneshwar to undergo the sacred ceremony.

However, Gyaneshwar's disregard for the caste system did not end there. He believed that spiritual teachings should be accessible to all people, regardless of their social status. At a time when sacred knowledge was restricted to Sanskrit-speaking Brahmins, Gyaneshwar boldly decided to write a commentary on the Bhagavad Gita in the Marathi language—the language of the common people. This work, known as the "Gyaneshwari" or "Jnaneshwari," made the profound teachings of the Gita accessible to everyone, breaking down the barriers of caste and education.

The Miraculous Restoration of the Buffalo

One of the most famous miracles associated with Sant Jnaneshwar is the story of the buffalo that spoke the Vedas. As a young boy, Jnaneshwar was often ridiculed by local Brahmins who doubted his spiritual attainments due to his family's controversial background. During one such confrontation, a Brahmin mockingly asked Jnaneshwar to prove his spiritual powers by making a buffalo recite the Vedic mantras.

In response, with calm faith and divine grace, Jnaneshwar gently placed his hand on the buffalo and chanted a sacred mantra. To the amazement of everyone present, the buffalo began to recite the Vedas in a deep, resonant voice. This miraculous event stunned the Brahmins and established Jnaneshwar's divine status among the people. The incident was not only a demonstration of his spiritual power but also a reminder that the divine resides in all creatures, and that true knowledge transcends worldly distinctions.

Writing the Jnaneshwari: Making Wisdom Accessible to All

Sant Jnaneshwar's greatest contribution to the spiritual world was his commentary on the Bhagavad Gita, known as the *Jnaneshwari* (or *Bhavartha Dipika*). Written in Marathi, the vernacular language of the people, this text made the profound teachings of the Gita accessible to everyone, regardless of their education or social standing. It is considered one of the finest works of spiritual literature in India and remains a cornerstone of Marathi spiritual and literary tradition.

In the *Jnaneshwari*, Jnaneshwar explains the essence of the Gita in a simple and poetic manner, emphasizing the importance of devotion (bhakti), selfless action (karma yoga), and spiritual wisdom (jnana yoga). He also speaks of the unity of all life and the presence of the divine in every being. The *Jnaneshwari* continues to be revered as a spiritual guide for seekers across the world.

The Miracle of the Samadhi

Another remarkable event in Jnaneshwar's life is his decision to enter *samadhi* (a state of deep meditation leading to ultimate liberation) at a very young age. At the age of 21, after having completed his mission of spreading spiritual wisdom and having written several works, Jnaneshwar expressed his desire to leave his physical body. He informed his disciples that his time on Earth had come to an end, and he would now enter *samadhi* while still alive.

On the appointed day, Jnaneshwar, accompanied by his disciples and devotees, went to the sacred town of Alandi. There, in a specially prepared underground chamber, he sat in a meditative posture and entered *samadhi*. It is believed that even today, Jnaneshwar remains in this state of deep meditation in the same chamber, radiating spiritual blessings to all those who visit his shrine in Alandi.

This act of voluntary *samadhi* was considered a profound miracle and a testament to Jnaneshwar's mastery over life and death. His samadhi shrine in Alandi remains a major pilgrimage site, drawing thousands of devotees every year who come to seek his blessings and guidance.

Teachings and Philosophy

Sant Jnaneshwar's teachings revolve around the concept of oneness with the divine and the unity of all life. He emphasized that the divine is present in every individual, and spiritual realization is not a distant goal but an ever-present reality. His teachings reflect the essence of the Advaita (non-dual) philosophy, which asserts that there is no separation between the individual soul and the supreme consciousness.

Jnaneshwar also placed great emphasis on the practice of devotion and selfless service. He believed that the path to God could be attained through love, compassion, and surrender. His teachings resonate deeply with the philosophy of the Bhagavad Gita, which advocates for a balanced approach to life, combining knowledge, devotion, and selfless action.

Conclusion

The life of Sant Jnaneshwar is a shining example of spiritual wisdom, humility, and divine grace. His miracles, profound teachings, and contributions to spiritual literature continue to inspire countless seekers on the path of yoga and spirituality. Jnaneshwar's life reminds us that true spiritual realization is not bound by age, caste, or social standing—it is the birthright of every soul that seeks the divine with sincerity and devotion.

Sant Gora Kumbhar: The Devoted Potter

Sant Gora Kumbhar, a prominent saint of the Bhakti movement, was a humble potter from the village of Ter in Maharashtra. His life story is an inspiring example of unwavering devotion, humility, and the miraculous power of faith. Gora Kumbhar's profound connection with Lord Vitthal (an incarnation of Lord Krishna) and his unshakable commitment to his duty as a potter made him a revered figure among the saints of the Bhakti tradition.

Early Life and Devotion

Gora Kumbhar was born into a potter's family, where his occupation was shaping clay pots. Despite the simplicity of his life and the hardships associated with his caste and profession, Gora Kumbhar developed a deep devotion to Lord Vitthal from an early age. His devotion to the Lord was absolute, and he saw his work as a form of worship. Each pot he crafted was shaped with the same devotion he felt toward God.

The name "Kumbhar" means potter, and true to his name, Gora saw God in the clay he worked with every day. His hands may have shaped physical objects, but his heart and mind were ever focused on the divine. His devotion became so intense that he would lose himself in prayer and meditation, forgetting the world around him.

The Miracle of the Broken Pots

One of the most well-known miracles associated with Sant Gora Kumbhar highlights the power of unwavering faith. It is said that on one occasion, Gora Kumbhar was making pots in his workshop while chanting the name of Lord Vitthal. He became so absorbed in his prayers that he didn't realize the pots were being baked in the kiln for too long. By the time he returned to his work, all the pots had cracked and were no longer usable.

Realizing the loss, Gora Kumbhar did not lament. Instead, he calmly continued his work, believing that everything was happening by the will of the Lord. His neighbours and family were puzzled by his calm demeanour, as they knew the loss of these pots would cause him financial hardship.

In a miraculous turn of events, when Gora Kumbhar inspected the broken pots the next morning, he found that they had all been restored to their perfect form. The cracks had disappeared, and the pots were as good as new. This miracle was a sign of divine grace, showing that when one is absorbed in sincere devotion, even material losses are restored through divine intervention.

The Tragic Test of Devotion: The Crushing of His Child

One of the most heart-wrenching episodes in Sant Gora Kumbhar's life is the story of how his intense devotion led to an unimaginable personal tragedy. Gora was so absorbed in his devotion to Lord Vitthal that he was often unaware of the world around him, including his family. On one fateful day, while he was busy working at the potter's wheel, completely engrossed in his chanting and devotion, his young son crawled underneath the wheel.

Unaware of his child's presence, Gora Kumbhar continued to work the wheel, crushing the child under its weight. When his wife came and saw what had happened, she was devastated and accused Gora of being so lost in his devotion that he failed to protect his own son. Gora, though heartbroken, accepted the incident as the will of God, believing that everything that happens is part of the divine plan.

Moved by his unwavering faith and deep remorse, Lord Vitthal himself appeared before Gora Kumbhar and restored his son to life. This miracle not only relieved Gora's grief but also confirmed the depth of his spiritual connection to the divine. It showed that true devotion transcends all worldly attachments, even though the pain of such trials is immense.

Humility and Fellowship with Other Saints

Despite the many miraculous events in his life, Sant Gora Kumbhar remained humble and grounded. His humility and simplicity drew many saints and devotees toward him. Among his closest companions were Sant Tukaram and Sant Namdev, two other prominent saints of the Bhakti movement.

In one famous event, Gora Kumbhar is said to have performed a unique "test" on the saints. During a gathering of saints, Gora playfully placed each of them on his potter's wheel, one by one, to see if they made the right "sound" as a well-formed pot would. His symbolic test was a way of assessing their spiritual purity and devotion. When he placed Sant Namdev on the wheel, he humorously declared that Namdev was still slightly "raw" and needed more spiritual refinement. This playful episode further demonstrated Gora Kumbhar's humility and his light-hearted way of interacting with his fellow saints.

Teachings and Philosophy

Sant Gora Kumbhar's life teaches the importance of humility, devotion, and seeing God in everyday work. He believed that true spirituality lay not in grand rituals or renunciation but in performing one's duties with dedication and seeing the divine in every aspect of life. For him, crafting pots was not just a profession but a form of worship, and every act of creation was a reminder of the divine presence.

His unwavering faith in Lord Vitthal showed that devotion could transcend the greatest of sorrows, even the loss of a child. Gora's life exemplifies how suffering and trials, when accepted with faith, lead to divine grace and transformation.

Conclusion

Sant Gora Kumbhar's life is a profound testament to the power of faith, humility, and devotion. His miracles, such as the restoration of broken pots and the revival of his son, reveal the deep spiritual connection he had with the divine. Through his simple yet devoted life, Gora Kumbhar taught that true spirituality lies in seeing God in every task and surrendering to the divine will, no matter the hardships faced. His story continues to inspire millions, reminding us that devotion can turn even the most ordinary life into one of profound spiritual significance.

Rishi Markandeya: The Eternal Devotee

Rishi Markandeya, a legendary figure in Hindu tradition, is renowned for his unwavering devotion to Lord Shiva and for being blessed with immortality. His story serves as a profound example of how faith and devotion can transcend the boundaries of fate and death itself. Markandeya's life is filled with miraculous events, timeless wisdom, and divine interventions, making him one of the most revered sages in ancient Indian scriptures.

Birth and Prophecy

Markandeya was born to the great sage Mrikandu and his wife Marudvati after they had prayed fervently for a child. Lord Shiva, pleased with their devotion, gave them a choice: they could either have a son who would be wise and virtuous but live only until the age of 16, or they could have a son who would be less intelligent but live a long life. Mrikandu and Marudvati chose the former, valuing spiritual wisdom over longevity, and thus, Markandeya was born.

From a very young age, Markandeya exhibited extraordinary wisdom and devotion to Lord Shiva. However, his parents were aware of the ominous prophecy regarding his early death at the age of 16. Despite knowing this, they nurtured his spiritual inclinations and instilled in him a deep faith in Lord Shiva.

The Miracle of Overcoming Death

As Markandeya approached his 16th year, the time of his destined death drew near. Unaware of his fate, the young sage continued to immerse himself in meditation and devotion to Lord Shiva. On the eve of his 16th birthday, the god of death, Yama, appeared before him to claim his soul, as was foretold by the prophecy.

When Yama approached Markandeya, the young sage was deeply absorbed in prayer, reciting the powerful *Mahamrityunjaya Mantra*, which is a hymn to Lord Shiva for protection against untimely death.

Seeking refuge at the Shiva Linga, Markandeya clung to it with unwavering faith, refusing to surrender to death.

Yama, determined to carry out his duty, cast his noose toward Markandeya, attempting to capture his soul. However, as the noose fell around the Shiva Linga as well, it enraged Lord Shiva. Emerging from the Linga in a burst of light, Shiva struck down Yama with his trident, saving his devotee and granting Markandeya eternal life.

This miraculous intervention by Lord Shiva demonstrated the immense power of devotion and how it can overcome even death. From that moment onward, Markandeya was blessed with immortality, and he is revered as a *chiranjeevi* (one who lives eternally).

Markandeya's Vision of the Cosmic Deluge

Another significant event in the life of Rishi Markandeya is his vision of the cosmic deluge (*pralaya*), which provided him with unparalleled insight into the nature of creation, preservation, and dissolution. According to legend, Lord Vishnu, pleased with Markandeya's devotion, granted him a vision of the dissolution of the universe.

During one of his deep meditations, Markandeya suddenly found himself surrounded by a great flood. The waters of the cosmic deluge engulfed everything in sight, swallowing the heavens, the earth, and all living beings. Markandeya, despite his immense wisdom, felt overwhelmed by the vastness and destructive force of the deluge.

As he floated helplessly in the endless waters, he saw an extraordinary sight: a small banyan leaf floating on the water, with an infant lying on it. This infant was none other than Lord Vishnu in his *Vatsalya* (child) form. The child Vishnu had the entire universe in his mouth and was calmly sucking his thumb. This vision of the child-like Vishnu symbolized the Lord's role as the preserver of the cosmos, even amid its destruction.

This divine revelation filled Markandeya with awe and reinforced his understanding of the eternal nature of the universe and the cyclical process of creation, preservation, and dissolution. The vision granted him a deep realization of the cosmic play of Lord Vishnu and the ultimate truth that the divine sustains everything, even in the face of chaos and dissolution.

Wisdom and Contributions

Markandeya is also credited with composing the *Markandeya Purana*, one of the major Puranic texts that contains a wealth of knowledge on various aspects of life, spirituality, and dharma. The text is a treasure trove of wisdom, detailing the stories of deities, kings, sages, and the principles of righteous living.

The *Markandeya Purana* also contains the famous *Durga Saptashati* (or *Devi Mahatmyam*), a powerful scripture that celebrates the glory of Goddess Durga and her triumph over the forces of evil. This text is still recited with great reverence during the festival of Navaratri, particularly in the worship of the Divine Mother.

Markandeya's teachings emphasize devotion to the divine, the power of faith in overcoming challenges, and the importance of living a righteous and dharmic life. His own life serves as an embodiment of these principles, as he remained steadfast in his devotion despite the inevitability of death.

Conclusion

Rishi Markandeya's life is a testament to the power of unwavering devotion, the grace of the divine, and the ability to transcend even the most formidable obstacles, such as death. His miracles—escaping the clutches of death through Lord Shiva's grace and witnessing the cosmic deluge—have left an indelible mark on Hindu spiritual tradition. Markandeya's eternal life serves as a symbol of immortality, both in a spiritual sense and as a revered figure who continues to inspire seekers of truth and devotion.

Sage Narada and the Nature of Maya

Sage Narada, the celestial wanderer, is known throughout the scriptures as a devoted servant of Lord Vishnu and a divine musician. He was a sage of immense knowledge and wisdom, constantly traveling between realms, chanting the name of Narayana and spreading devotion wherever he went. Despite his deep devotion and spiritual insight, even Narada was not immune to the power of Maya—the illusory force that veils the true nature of reality.

The Question of Maya

One day, as Narada sat in meditation, he began to ponder a profound question that had been troubling him for some time: "What is Maya?" Though he had heard about Maya countless times in the scriptures, he had never fully understood its nature. Was Maya simply an illusion? Or was it a more complex force that bound even the wisest beings to the cycle of birth and death?

With this question in mind, Narada decided to seek the guidance of his beloved Lord Vishnu. He travelled to Vaikuntha, the heavenly abode of Vishnu, where he was greeted with warmth and love by the Lord himself. After offering his respects, Narada humbly asked, "O Lord, you are the knower of all. Please explain to me the true nature of Maya. How does it work, and how can one transcend it?"

Vishnu, with a gentle smile, listened to Narada's question. He knew that this was not a question that could be answered with mere words; it was something that Narada had to experience for himself. Instead of giving a direct explanation, Vishnu chose to teach Narada through an example.

The Divine Play

Vishnu said to Narada, "Come, let us go for a walk." Narada, always eager to follow his Lord, gladly complied. Together, they left Vaikuntha and descended to the earth. As they walked through a serene forest, Vishnu suddenly said, "Narada, I am feeling thirsty. Could you fetch me some water from that nearby village?"

Without hesitation, Narada set off towards the village. As he entered the village, he saw a beautiful young woman drawing water from a well. He approached her and asked for some water. The woman smiled and offered him a drink, and in that moment, something remarkable happened—Narada forgot all about Vishnu's request. Instead, he found himself captivated by the woman's beauty and charm.

Days turned into weeks, and weeks turned into months. Narada became a part of the village, eventually marrying the woman and settling into a peaceful life. They had children together, and Narada became deeply involved in the responsibilities of family life. Years passed, and Narada experienced the joys and sorrows of human existence. He had forgotten his divine mission, lost in the illusion of worldly attachments.

One day, a devastating flood swept through the village, destroying everything in its path. Narada tried to save his wife and children, but he was powerless against the force of nature. As the floodwaters rose, Narada found himself alone, standing on the banks of the river, overwhelmed with grief and despair. In that moment of utter helplessness, he cried out to Vishnu, "O Lord, save me!"

Suddenly, the entire scene vanished. Narada found himself standing in the same forest where he had left Vishnu, holding an empty pot in his hand. Vishnu was standing before him, smiling serenely, as if no time had passed at all.

The Realization

Narada was bewildered. "Lord, what just happened?" he asked in confusion.

Vishnu replied, "Narada, where is the water you went to fetch for me?"

It was then that Narada realized the profound lesson Vishnu had imparted. The entire episode—the village, the marriage, the children, the flood—had all been an illusion created by Vishnu's Maya. In a matter of moments, Narada had been completely immersed in a life that seemed so real, yet it had been nothing more than a play of the mind.

Vishnu said gently, "This is the power of Maya, Narada. It creates an illusion so convincing that even the wisest can become entangled in it. Maya is the force that makes the unreal appear real and the temporary seem permanent. It binds beings to the cycle of samsara—birth, death, and rebirth—by making them forget their true nature. But just as you have now realized the illusory nature of your experience, so too can one transcend Maya by remembering their divine essence and staying devoted to the path of truth."

Narada bowed to Vishnu with deep reverence and gratitude. He now understood that Maya was not merely an illusion but a powerful force that could bind even the most spiritually advanced beings. However, with the grace of the Lord and unwavering devotion, one could see through the veil of Maya and realize the eternal truth.

From that day forward, Narada's devotion to Vishnu became even stronger, and he continued his journey of spreading divine love and wisdom across the universe, ever mindful of the mysterious power of Maya.

Adi Shankaracharya: The Sage Who Revived Vedic Wisdom

Adi Shankaracharya, one of the greatest spiritual reformers and philosophers in Indian history, is known for his role in revitalizing Vedic traditions and establishing Advaita Vedanta (non-dualism) as a central philosophy in Hinduism. Born in the 8th century CE, Shankaracharya's life was filled with profound spiritual insight, miraculous events, and unmatched intellectual prowess, which inspired a widespread spiritual awakening across India. His contributions to spiritual thought continue to inspire seekers to this day.

Early Life and Divine Calling

Shankara was born to devout Brahmin parents, Sivaguru and Aryamba, in the small village of Kaladi in Kerala. His birth itself was seen as a blessing, as his parents had prayed fervently to Lord Shiva for a child.

From a very young age, Shankara displayed an extraordinary intelligence and a deep spiritual inclination. He mastered the Vedas and scriptures by the age of eight, and even at that tender age, he was profoundly aware of the impermanence of the material world.

One of the first miraculous events in Shankaracharya's life occurred when he was still a young boy. During a routine bath in the river, a crocodile grabbed his leg, and Shankara cried out to his mother, asking for permission to take *sannyasa* (renunciation of worldly life). His mother, fearing for his life, granted him permission. At that very moment, the crocodile released him unharmed. This event marked the beginning of Shankara's journey toward becoming a wandering monk and spiritual leader.

Shankaracharya's Mission to Revive Vedic Wisdom

Shankaracharya's mission was clear: to restore the purity of Vedic teachings and to combat the growing influence of ritualistic practices and competing philosophical schools such as Buddhism and Jainism. Traveling across India, he engaged in numerous debates with scholars, challenging philosophical systems that diverged from the essence of the Vedas. His most significant intellectual contribution was the establishment of *Advaita Vedanta*, the philosophy of non-dualism, which asserts that the individual soul (Atman) and the ultimate reality (Brahman) are one and the same.

One of his greatest achievements was his commentaries on the Upanishads, Bhagavad Gita, and Brahmasutras, which clarified the essence of Advaita Vedanta for generations to come. These commentaries are still regarded as foundational texts for the study of Vedanta.

The Miracle of Reviving His Mother

One of the most touching miracles associated with Adi Shankaracharya is the story of how he fulfilled his promise to his mother. After renouncing the worldly life at a young age, Shankara continued his travels and spiritual teachings, but he had promised his mother that he would be with her in her final moments. Many years later, when Aryamba fell seriously ill, Shankara sensed it from afar and returned to Kaladi to be by her side.

At the moment of her passing, in an act of immense grace and love, Shankara recited mantras and performed rites that are said to have granted her liberation (moksha). According to tradition, he also performed a miracle by reviving her for a brief moment to give her a chance to experience the divine light and attain peace. This miracle demonstrated Shankara's profound mastery over life and death, and his compassion for his mother's spiritual well-being.

Defeating Mandana Misra in Debate and the Miracle of Saraswati

One of the most legendary episodes in Shankaracharya's life is his debate with Mandana Misra, a renowned scholar and staunch proponent of the *Purva Mimamsa* school, which emphasized the importance of Vedic rituals. Shankara sought to demonstrate the superiority of the path of knowledge (jnana) and the non-dual philosophy of Advaita Vedanta over ritualism.

The debate was presided over by none other than the goddess Saraswati herself, who took human form as Mandana Misra's wife, Ubhaya Bharati. The two scholars debated for days, and in the end, Shankaracharya triumphed. However, Ubhaya Bharati, as the judge, posed one final challenge to Shankara: a debate on the nuances of household life and the experience of marital relationships—topics beyond the knowledge of a celibate monk.

In response, Shankaracharya is said to have performed a miraculous feat known as *parakaya pravesha* (entering another body). He left his physical body and entered the body of a recently deceased king to experience worldly life. After living in the king's body for a short time and gaining the necessary experience, he returned to his own body and continued the debate with Ubhaya Bharati. His mastery over both knowledge and mystic powers convinced his opponents, and Mandana Misra became one of Shankara's disciples, later known as Sureshvara, a great proponent of Advaita Vedanta.

Establishing the Four Mathas (Monasteries)

Shankaracharya's influence extended beyond intellectual debates. He sought to establish a unified spiritual framework for India by setting up four *mathas* (monastic centers) in the four corners of the subcontinent—Sringeri in the south, Dwaraka in the west, Puri in the east, and Badrinath in the north. These mathas became centers of learning and spiritual practice, and they continue to preserve and propagate the teachings of Advaita Vedanta to this day.

The establishment of these mathas was seen as a miraculous unification of the vast and diverse land of India under one spiritual umbrella. Through these institutions, Shankaracharya ensured that the teachings of Advaita would endure for centuries to come.

The Miracle of Kedarnath

Another famous miracle associated with Adi Shankaracharya occurred at Kedarnath, one of the most sacred pilgrimage sites dedicated to Lord Shiva. According to legend, after completing his pilgrimage,

Shankaracharya disappeared into the sanctum of the Kedarnath temple, attaining final liberation at the age of 32. His disappearance is considered a divine event, and many believe that he continues to reside in an ethereal form at Kedarnath, blessing those who seek him.

Teachings and Philosophy

Adi Shankaracharya's teachings emphasize the oneness of the individual soul (Atman) with the ultimate reality (Brahman). He taught that the world of multiplicity and duality is an illusion (*maya*), and that realization of the non-dual nature of existence leads to liberation (moksha). His teachings are deeply rooted in the Upanishads, which convey the highest truths of Vedanta.

Conclusion

Adi Shankaracharya's life is a shining example of the perfect balance between intellect, devotion, and mysticism. His profound teachings, miraculous events, and deep compassion for humanity transformed the spiritual landscape of India. The miracles of reviving his mother, winning legendary debates, and establishing monastic centers are just a few of the divine acts that reflect his mastery over both the material and spiritual worlds. Even today, Shankaracharya's legacy continues to inspire countless seekers on the path of spiritual awakening.

33

Time to Awaken

In today's fast-paced world, we are surrounded by an endless stream of pleasures and distractions, from the ceaseless notifications of digital media to the pursuit of material success and sensory indulgence. These modern comforts promise happiness and fulfillment, but more often than not, they leave us feeling empty, disconnected, and longing for something deeper. Beneath the surface of this temporary gratification lies a profound truth: the more we chase fleeting pleasures, the further we drift from our true essence, our higher self.

Awakening is not simply about spiritual enlightenment; it is about realizing the contrast between the temporary satisfaction offered by the material world and the eternal bliss that comes from aligning with our higher consciousness. It's an inner journey that leads us from illusion to truth, from restlessness to peace. This chapter delves into the nature of these pleasures—distinguishing between those that serve our growth and those that keep us bound to a cycle of craving and dissatisfaction.

We live in a society where instant gratification has become the norm. From fast food to social media, we are conditioned to expect immediate results, yet this constant chase after 'more' often keeps us imprisoned in lower states of consciousness. Whether it's through the compulsive need to acquire possessions or the endless quest for external validation, we become trapped in a loop that distracts us from our true purpose.

However, the path to awakening is not about renouncing the world but about seeing it for what it truly is. It involves understanding how to rise above the temptations that bind us and choosing actions that bring us closer to our higher self. By embracing ancient wisdom and reflecting on both spiritual traditions and contemporary examples, we will explore practical ways to break free from these shackles and embark on the path to spiritual awakening.

This chapter will guide you in identifying the subtle traps of modern life and offer insights on how to transcend them. Drawing on timeless teachings, it will reveal that true happiness lies not in the transient pleasures of the external world, but in the deep, inner connection with the divine essence within us all. It is time to awaken to our higher potential and step onto the path of lasting peace and fulfillment.

Good and Bad Pleasures

Not all pleasures are harmful to spiritual growth; in fact, some can be essential stepping stones toward higher consciousness when experienced with mindfulness. The true art of living lies in distinguishing between "good" pleasures that uplift the spirit and "bad" pleasures that bind us to the material world, clouding our awareness and diverting us from our inner journey.

Good Pleasures are those that promote long-term well-being, inner fulfillment, and spiritual development. These pleasures are aligned with

Sattva, the quality of purity, balance, and harmony in the ancient yogic tradition. They nurture the soul and foster a deep sense of peace and contentment. For example, the joy that comes from helping others, the deep satisfaction of personal growth, and the serenity experienced during meditation are all forms of good pleasure. These moments of happiness arise from actions that are in alignment with our higher self, contributing to a more meaningful and enriched life.

Scientific studies back up the power of good pleasures. Acts of kindness, for instance, trigger the release of oxytocin, a hormone often referred to as the "love hormone." This chemical fosters feelings of connection, trust, and happiness. According to research conducted by the *University of California, Berkeley*, individuals who regularly engage in altruistic activities report higher levels of life satisfaction and lower levels of stress. These actions not only benefit others but also lead to personal joy and fulfillment, reinforcing the spiritual truth that by lifting others, we too are lifted.

Bad Pleasures, on the other hand, are those rooted in short-term gratification but result in long-term dissatisfaction, suffering, and spiritual bondage. These pleasures are often driven by the *Rajas* (passion, restlessness) and *Tamas* (ignorance, inertia) gunas, which perpetuate the cycle of desire, attachment, and eventual disappointment. Unlike good pleasures, bad pleasures pull us into a loop of craving, where we seek more and more, yet are never truly satisfied.

One of the most pervasive examples of bad pleasure in modern society is digital addiction. With the rise of social media, instant messaging, and on-demand entertainment, the temptation for immediate pleasure is ever-present. However, these distractions often come at a heavy cost. A 2020 study published in the journal *Addiction* found that excessive use of social media, especially among young adults, can lead to heightened feelings of anxiety, depression, and loneliness. What may begin as a harmless scroll through social media can quickly turn into a compulsive habit, pulling individuals away from deeper, more meaningful experiences and keeping them trapped in lower states of consciousness.

Scriptural Insights

The wisdom of ancient texts echoes this understanding of pleasure and its consequences. The *Bhagavad Gita* (2.62-63) offers a timeless warning about the dangers of unchecked desire and attachment. It states:

"While contemplating the objects of the senses, a person develops attachment for them, and from such attachment **lust** develops, and from lust **anger** arises. From anger, **delusion** arises, and from delusion, **bewilderment of memory**. When memory is bewildered, **intelligence is lost**, and when intelligence is lost, one **falls down again** into the material pool."

This profound passage illustrates the slippery slope from innocent desire to the loss of clarity, wisdom, and ultimately, freedom. Attachment breeds a cycle of suffering, pulling us deeper into the material realm and away from the path of self-realization.

Similarly, the *Katha Upanishad* (1.2.2) beautifully contrasts the choice between good and bad pleasures:

"The good is one thing, the pleasant is another. These two, serving different ends, bind man. The **wise** choose the good over the pleasant, while the **foolish** choose the pleasant for worldly gain."

This verse highlights the critical choice each of us faces: to pursue fleeting, worldly pleasures or to seek that which is truly nourishing and enduring. The wise discern between these two paths and choose the good, recognizing that true joy and fulfillment come from living in harmony with our higher purpose, not from chasing the next temporary thrill.

By understanding the distinction between good and bad pleasures, we can make more conscious choices that lead us toward lasting fulfillment. When we cultivate awareness, we begin to see beyond the surface appeal of instant gratification and recognize the deeper, more subtle joys that come from spiritual growth, service to others, and alignment with our higher self. This awareness is key to breaking free from the cycle of desire and attachment, allowing us to experience the profound, enduring bliss that arises from true spiritual awakening.

The Trap of Immediate Gratification

Immediate gratification has become the defining feature of modern life. Whether it's fast food, instant streaming services, or one-click shopping, our world is engineered to satisfy our desires at unprecedented speeds. While this convenience can make life easier, it also cultivates a mindset of impatience and impulsivity, where the pursuit of quick rewards often overshadows the benefits of delayed gratification. Over time, this constant craving for instant results leads to dissatisfaction, undermines personal growth, and stalls our spiritual progress.

A well-known psychological study, the **"Marshmallow Experiment"** conducted by Walter Mischel in the 1970s, sheds light on the power of delayed gratification. In the experiment, children were given a simple choice: they could have one marshmallow immediately or wait 15 minutes and receive two marshmallows. Years later, follow-up studies revealed that the children who had been able to resist the immediate temptation generally fared better in life. They demonstrated higher academic achievement, greater emotional stability, and better coping mechanisms in stressful situations. This study highlights a key principle: the ability to delay gratification is closely linked to long-term success and overall well-being.

In contrast, a society that prioritizes immediate gratification often fosters impulsive behavior and poor decision-making, diverting focus from higher, more meaningful goals. The instant nature of social media, online shopping, and other digital platforms offers temporary satisfaction but can prevent us from cultivating patience, discipline, and long-term vision.

The **World Health Organization (WHO)** has noted a growing prevalence of mental health issues, particularly anxiety and depression. One of the underlying causes is the overwhelming flood of stimuli from social media and digital platforms, which condition the brain to expect quick rewards. This constant reinforcement of immediate gratification makes it difficult for individuals to tolerate the discomfort that comes with delayed satisfaction. As a result, many struggle to focus on long-term goals or endure the necessary discipline required for spiritual growth and self-awareness.

From a spiritual perspective, the pursuit of immediate pleasures often keeps us anchored in the lower chakras.

In essence, when we prioritize instant gratification, we remain stuck in the material world, unable to transcend the lower impulses that bind us to suffering. It is only by learning to delay gratification, exercising patience, and embracing the discomfort of growth that we can ascend to higher levels of consciousness. This not only improves our mental and emotional well-being but also opens the door to greater spiritual fulfillment and lasting joy.

By becoming aware of the trap of immediate gratification, we can begin to break free from its hold, allowing our energies to flow beyond the lower chakras and into the realms of higher awareness. Developing the capacity to wait, reflect, and prioritize long-term gains over short-term pleasure is key to unlocking our full potential.

Modern Society's Obstruction to Awakening

Modern society, with its relentless focus on material success, sensory gratification, and constant connectivity, presents significant obstacles to spiritual awakening. We live in an age where distractions abound—advertisements, social media, and consumer-driven lifestyles constantly pull our attention outward, making it difficult to turn inward and connect with our true essence. This external focus not only keeps us engrossed in superficial pursuits but also distances us from the deeper, more meaningful path of spiritual growth.

One of the greatest challenges is the emphasis on material wealth as a measure of success. According to the **American Psychological Association**, 72% of Americans report feeling stressed about money, while 31% feel stressed about work. This constant stress drives individuals to seek refuge in temporary pleasures such as overeating, excessive drinking, or mindlessly scrolling through social media. These quick fixes may provide momentary relief but often exacerbate feelings of dissatisfaction, leading to a cycle of craving and indulgence that obstructs spiritual progress.

A prime example of this modern predicament is the phenomenon known as **FOMO** (Fear of Missing Out). The constant exposure to other people's seemingly perfect lives through social media cultivates feelings of inadequacy, comparison, and anxiety. People become trapped in the need for external validation, chasing experiences, possessions, or status symbols to feel worthy or fulfilled. This focus on external gratification distracts from the inner work required for spiritual awakening, pulling us further away from the higher states of consciousness we seek.

As I said earlier, the design of modern life keeps us anchored in the lower chakras, particularly the **Muladhara (Root Chakra), Svadhishthana (Sacral Chakra)**, and **Manipura (Solar Plexus Chakra)**. These chakras are concerned with security, pleasure, and personal power, and while they are essential to our survival and emotional well-being, an overemphasis on them can lead to an imbalanced energy system and trap us in a cycle of seeking short-term satisfaction. When we become overly focused on material success, physical pleasure, or the need for control, the energy in our body gets stuck, preventing us from accessing the higher chakras—such as the **Anahata (Heart Chakra)** and **Sahasrara (Crown Chakra)**—which are associated with love, wisdom, profound states of consciousness and spiritual awakening.

Modern society's pace and distractions make it incredibly difficult to move beyond these lower impulses. The culture of immediacy, driven by technology and consumerism, reinforces the need for quick results and instant gratification, making the slow, deliberate process of spiritual growth seem unappealing. The result is a disconnection from the true self, as we become more invested in the world of appearances than in the reality of the inner self.

Scriptural Insight

The ancient wisdom of the Upanishads offers a profound antidote to the distractions of modern life, emphasizing the importance of transcending material attachments to attain spiritual awakening. The *Katha Upanishad* (2.1.3) states:

"The **wise man** relinquishes both **joy** and **sorrow**, having realized that they are both born from **ignorance**. By attaining the higher knowledge, one **transcends** the **duality** of **pleasure** and **pain**, and becomes established in the self."

This teaching reminds us that both pleasure and pain are rooted in the external world and are fleeting in nature. To experience lasting peace and fulfillment, we must move beyond these dualities and connect with the deeper, unchanging truth within us. The wisdom of the Upanishads encourages us to let go of the material world's constant pulls and instead seek the higher knowledge that leads to inner freedom and true awakening.

By shifting our focus away from external distractions and toward cultivating inner awareness, we can begin to transcend the limitations imposed by modern society. Practices such as meditation, mindfulness, and self-inquiry offer powerful tools to help us access higher states of consciousness, break free from the grip of materialism, and reconnect with our true nature. Through consistent effort, we can rise above the external noise and find the stillness within, where spiritual awakening becomes possible.

Habits: The Foundation of Consciousness

Habits form the bedrock of our daily existence, influencing not only how we live but also how we perceive ourselves and the world around us. Over time, these repeated actions—whether conscious or unconscious—become the framework through which our consciousness is shaped. Every habit we nurture, whether positive or negative, leaves a subtle imprint on our mind, reinforcing specific neural pathways and creating patterns that dictate our responses to life's challenges.

Negative habits, such as overeating, substance abuse, or excessive screen time, act like anchors that tether the mind to lower vibrational states. These behaviours keep the mind preoccupied with material desires, which are often associated with the lower chakras. When the mind is stuck in this lower energetic field, it becomes difficult to transcend to higher levels of awareness and spiritual growth. The higher chakras, like **Ajna** (Third Eye) and **Sahasrara** (Crown), which are associated with intuition, wisdom, and divine connection, remain out of reach when we are entrenched in unproductive or harmful habits.

At the root of these habits lie *samskaras*, deeply ingrained patterns of behaviour that have been etched into our psyche over time. These samskaras are formed through repeated actions, thoughts, and emotional responses, often stretching back to early childhood or even past lives. They are like grooves in the mind, and the deeper they are, the more challenging they are to break. The more we indulge in negative habits, the stronger these samskaras become, locking us into cycles of behavior that limit our growth.

However, just as samskaras can bind us, they can also be transformed. The Bhagavad Gita (6.5) offers profound guidance in this regard:

"Let a man lift himself by his own self; let him not lower himself; for he alone is the **friend of himself,** and he alone is the **enemy of himself.**"

This verse highlights the dual role we play in our own lives. We can either elevate ourselves through conscious, mindful actions that foster spiritual growth or lower ourselves by succumbing to negative habits and thought patterns.

Conscious living involves recognizing the habits that are holding us back and taking steps to replace them with behaviours that support higher states of consciousness. Through consistent practice, mindfulness, and self-discipline, we can reshape our samskaras, creating new, positive patterns that enable us to rise beyond the limitations of the lower mind. In this way, habits not only reflect our current state of consciousness but also serve as the tools through which we can actively shape and elevate it.

Breaking Free: A Path to Awakening

To embark on the journey of awakening, we must first develop an awareness of the subtle yet powerful chains that bind us to the lower pleasures and distractions of life. These attachments—whether they be to material possessions, fleeting desires, or the constant pull of sensory experiences—create an illusion of fulfillment, but in truth, they keep us stuck in a cycle of craving and dissatisfaction. Recognizing this cycle is the first step toward liberation.

Awakening requires a conscious and deliberate shift from the external world, where distractions are abundant, to the inner world, where true peace and clarity reside. In the modern age, where overstimulation from technology, social media, and the pressures of daily life dominate our attention, this inner shift becomes even more essential. We must learn to quiet the noise, to step away from the constant allure of superficial pleasures, and to tune into the deeper, more profound experiences of the self.

This transition is not easy; it demands persistent effort, discipline, and most importantly, the cultivation of habits that promote self-awareness and inner peace. Meditation, breathwork, yoga, and mindful living serve as powerful tools in this process, helping to dissolve the layers of conditioning that obscure our true nature. By engaging in these practices, we begin to witness the habitual patterns that drive us toward lower desires, and with awareness, we can start to loosen their grip.

One of the key challenges on this path is breaking free from the cycle of desire. Desires, when left unchecked, are like fires—no matter how much they are fed, they continue to burn, consuming our energy and distracting us from the pursuit of higher consciousness. To transcend this cycle, we must practice *vairagya*, or detachment, which does not mean renouncing the world, but rather changing our relationship with it. Instead of being pulled by every desire, we learn to observe them from a place of non-attachment, choosing consciously what serves our higher purpose and letting go of what does not.

As we cultivate habits that foster inner stillness, our awareness begins to expand. We become more attuned to the subtler aspects of our being—our thoughts, emotions, and the deeper motivations behind our actions. This self-awareness acts as a gateway to higher consciousness, where we move beyond the ego and the limited perception of self, and begin to experience life from a place of unity, compassion, and wisdom.

In this state of heightened awareness, we can break free from the conditioned responses that keep us trapped in lower states of consciousness. The mind, once preoccupied with fleeting pleasures, becomes a tool for self-inquiry and spiritual growth. With each step on the path of awakening, the false layers of identity begin to dissolve, revealing the boundless, luminous nature of our true self. This is the essence of liberation—freedom from the cycles of desire, attachment, and suffering, and the awakening to a higher state of consciousness that transcends the ordinary and touches the divine.

As Swami Vivekananda said, "Meditation can **turn fools into sages**, but unfortunately **fools never meditate**."

Study the scriptures and teachings of realized masters to gain a deeper understanding of the self and the nature of reality. This knowledge will guide you on your path to awakening and help you navigate the distractions of the modern world.

Adi Shankaracharya's Vivekachudamani (Verse 21) advises, "By **discrimination** between the **real** and the **unreal**, one should **give up** the unreal and seek the real. Only through such **discrimination** does one reach the ultimate truth."

My Heartfelt Invitation to Inner Awakening

The journey to awakening is not an easy one. In a world that constantly pulls us towards fleeting pleasures, distractions, and the illusions of material success, it often feels like we are trapped in a cycle of desires and dissatisfaction. Yet, within each of us lies an eternal truth—a blissful state of being that remains untouched by the turbulence of the outer world.

Remember relying solely on any particular scripture can be limiting when pursuing spiritual truth. While scriptures provide valuable guidance, they are ultimately reflections of higher truths that need to be realized within. They act as signposts, pointing us in the right direction, but the journey of realization must be undertaken by each individual. Blind attachment to any text, even sacred ones, may hinder one from experiencing the depth of truth beyond words and intellectual understanding. True wisdom emerges when the seeker transcends the boundaries of scriptures and experiences direct knowledge through inner realization.

The Bhagavad Gita acknowledges that few people even strive for this level of spiritual realization. In the verse 7.3, it states: "Amongst thousands of persons, hardly one strives for perfection; and amongst those who have achieved perfection, hardly one knows Me in truth." This verse highlights the rarity of true understanding and realization, emphasizing that spiritual knowledge is not for the masses but for the dedicated few who seek to transcend worldly illusions.

Furthermore, the Gita encourages striving for a state beyond mere intellectual or ritualistic practice. In the verse 6.46, it says: "A yogi is superior to the tapasvi (ascetic), superior to the jnani (a person of learning), and even superior to the karmi (ritualistic performer). Therefore, O Arjun, strive to be a yogi." Here, the yogi is praised as one who surpasses both asceticism and intellectualism. The path of the yogi leads to direct, experiential knowledge and realization, which is far greater than simply reading or performing rituals. Therefore, instead of being bound to any single scripture, one should strive to cultivate inner awareness and realization, which ultimately leads to the highest truth.

Throughout history, countless people have chased money, fame, power, and even relationships—believing that these things would grant them fulfillment. Many have attained these ambitions, building empires, names etched in stone, fortunes amassed, influence that shaped nations earning admiration, and surrounding themselves with companions and admirers. Yet, when the final breath escaped their lungs, when death came for them, none of it mattered. They left behind everything they had so feverishly pursued. Not a single coin, title, or applause accompanied them into the unknown. Their empires crumbled, their names faded, and the world moved on. With this in mind, is it truly worth envying, praising, or idolizing those who seem to have it all when the truth is that everything we cling to is fleeting?

We often measure our worth by the relationships we have, the achievements we accumulate, or the status we acquire. It's easy to feel jealous of others—those who seem to have perfect families, a romantic partner, more friends, or professional success. It's easy to get caught up in the rat race—feeling like you're falling behind when you're not earning as much, not gaining followers, or not clearing a competitive exam. But all these pursuits—whether romantic, professional, or material—are fragile. They can be lost in a moment, or they may simply fade away.

What are these fleeting successes in comparison to the vast, unshakable peace that comes from realizing the truth of who you are? Your worth has nothing to do with external achievements. The fear of not being famous, not reaching a position of power, or not checking off society's boxes is a mirage. These pursuits are just distractions from the deeper truth that lies within each of us. It is not the accumulation of things or accolades that defines you—it is the awareness, the peace, the self-realization that transcends all worldly measures of success. Turn inward. In that stillness, in that knowing, you'll find something far more precious than anything the world could ever offer you.

I will conclude with a Hindu legend: Once, in the beginning of time, when the Earth was still young, humans walked freely across the lands in search of power and understanding. They sought to uncover the secrets of existence, and their thirst for knowledge became insatiable. They ventured into the depths of forests, climbed the highest peaks, and even sailed across uncharted oceans in their quest. Yet, the more they searched outside, the more distant and elusive the ultimate truth seemed.

Watching the humans grow more restless with each passing day, Brahma, the Creator, sensed the urgency to protect the divine essence that resided within the cosmos. He feared that in their pursuit, humans might misuse or misunderstand this sacred force, leading to chaos and further suffering.

Thus, Brahma summoned the council of gods, a gathering of the most powerful and wise deities from all corners of creation. Seated on celestial thrones that shimmered like the stars themselves, the gods discussed the great dilemma.

"Where shall we hide the essence of divinity so that humans cannot easily find it?" Brahma asked.

Varuna, the god of the oceans, spoke first. "Let us hide it in the depths of the sea. Humans may venture near the shores, but the vast, uncharted depths of my domain will remain unreachable to them."

Brahma shook his head, his expression thoughtful. "In time, humans will build great ships and submerge into the depths. They will explore the ocean and may eventually find it."

Then, Agni, the god of fire, spoke, his eyes glowing with intensity. "Hide it in the fiery heart of the Earth. They cannot reach the molten core, for it will burn them."

Again, Brahma shook his head. "They may one day find ways to delve beneath the Earth, to touch its core, and even harness its power. They will not stop."

Indra, the king of gods and ruler of the skies, stepped forward with a bold suggestion. "Hide it atop the highest mountain peaks, where the cold and storms will keep them at bay."

But Brahma remained unconvinced. "Humans are resilient. They will climb the tallest mountains, even if it takes generations. They will eventually reach the summit and uncover the secret."

The gods grew silent, pondering Brahma's words. Every suggestion they made seemed futile, for the Creator could foresee the ingenuity and determination of humans. Eventually, Saraswati, the goddess of wisdom, spoke, her voice soft yet resonant.

"What if we hide it within them?" she suggested. "The one place they would never think to search—within their own hearts. In their pursuit of external wonders, they will overlook the truth that has always been within."

Brahma's eyes brightened at this idea, and he smiled knowingly. "Yes. This is the perfect hiding place. The essence of divinity shall be concealed within the core of their own being, for they will search high and low, across land, sea, and sky, never realizing that what they seek is already inside them."

And so, with the agreement of the council, the gods placed the divine essence—the ultimate truth, the infinite potential—within the heart of every human. Hidden in plain sight, it was placed where humans would least expect to find it: within themselves.

Time passed, and as expected, humans continued their search. They looked to the stars, to the wonders of the natural world, to science, philosophy, and religion. Yet, no matter how far they ventured, they felt a persistent longing, an emptiness they could not fill. They wondered why the answers eluded them, despite all their efforts.

Only those few who turned inward, seeking the stillness within, discovered the treasure that lay hidden. In moments of deep meditation, through practices of self-reflection and spiritual realization, they found the divine essence glowing softly, like a flame in the center of their being. It was then they realized that the divinity they sought had never been far away. It was part of them, always present, awaiting discovery.

This ancient story, passed down through generations, serves as a reminder: the divine is not something to be found outside, in distant lands or unattainable realms. It exists within every soul, patiently waiting for those who dare to turn inward and realize the truth.

The gods smiled from their heavenly abodes, knowing that while few would discover this secret at first, many more would eventually follow.

And thus, the greatest journey of humanity continues—not in the outer world, but in the infinite depths of the soul.

This book is an invitation to rediscover that truth. It is time to awaken from the dream of material existence and reconnect with the boundless joy of our true nature. While the path may seem challenging, history bears no exception—every individual who has attained spiritual awakening, enlightenment, or self-realization has found only fulfillment, never disappointment.

May this journey inspire you to look within, shed the layers of misconception, and embrace the eternal light that resides in us all. True awakening leads to a peace and fulfillment that surpasses all worldly achievements, and it is within reach for anyone who dares to seek it.

Hari Om Tat Sat!

"That is Truth!"

"The manifest and the unmanifest are not separate but one in essence!"

"The creator and the creation are one; creation is the apparent manifestation of the creator through Maya!"